Introduction to Corrections

ASPEN COLLEGE SERIES

Introduction to Corrections

Richard Tewksbury
Professor
Department of Justice Administration
University of Louisville

Wolters Kluwer
Law & Business

Published by Wolters Kluwer Law & Business in New York.

Wolters Kluwer Law & Business serves customers worldwide with CCH, Aspen Publishers, and Kluwer Law International products. (www.wolterskluwerlb.com)

To contact Customer Service, e-mail customer.service@wolterskluwer.com,
call 1-800-234-1660, fax 1-800-901-9075, or mail correspondence to:

Wolters Kluwer Law & Business
Attn: Order Department
PO Box 990
Frederick, MD 21705

Printed in the United States of America.

1 2 3 4 5 6 7 8 9 0

ISBN 978-1-4548-4126-5

Library of Congress Cataloging-in-Publication Data

Tewksbury, Richard A.
Introduction to corrections / Richard Tewksbury, Professor, Department of Justice Administration, University of Louisville.
pages cm.—(Aspen college series)
ISBN 978-1-4548-4126-5
1. Corrections—United States. 2. Crime—United States. 3. Prisons—United States. 4. Criminal justice, Administration of—United States. I. Title.
HV9471.T45 2015
364.60973—dc23

2014020319

About Wolters Kluwer Law & Business

Wolters Kluwer Law & Business is a leading global provider of intelligent information and digital solutions for legal and business professionals in key specialty areas, and respected educational resources for professors and law students. Wolters Kluwer Law & Business connects legal and business professionals as well as those in the education market with timely, specialized authoritative content and information-enabled solutions to support success through productivity, accuracy and mobility.

Serving customers worldwide, Wolters Kluwer Law & Business products include those under the Aspen Publishers, CCH, Kluwer Law International, Loislaw, ftwilliam.com and MediRegs family of products.

CCH products have been a trusted resource since 1913, and are highly regarded resources for legal, securities, antitrust and trade regulation, government contracting, banking, pension, payroll, employment and labor, and healthcare reimbursement and compliance professionals.

Aspen Publishers products provide essential information to attorneys, business professionals and law students. Written by preeminent authorities, the product line offers analytical and practical information in a range of specialty practice areas from securities law and intellectual property to mergers and acquisitions and pension/benefits. Aspen's trusted legal education resources provide professors and students with high-quality, up-to-date and effective resources for successful instruction and study in all areas of the law.

Kluwer Law International products provide the global business community with reliable international legal information in English. Legal practitioners, corporate counsel and business executives around the world rely on Kluwer Law journals, looseleafs, books, and electronic products for comprehensive information in many areas of international legal practice.

Loislaw is a comprehensive online legal research product providing legal content to law firm practitioners of various specializations. Loislaw provides attorneys with the ability to quickly and efficiently find the necessary legal information they need, when and where they need it, by facilitating access to primary law as well as state-specific law, records, forms and treatises.

ftwilliam.com offers employee benefits professionals the highest quality plan documents (retirement, welfare and non-qualified) and government forms (5500/PBGC, 1099 and IRS) software at highly competitive prices.

MediRegs products provide integrated health care compliance content and software solutions for professionals in healthcare, higher education and life sciences, including professionals in accounting, law and consulting.

Wolters Kluwer Law & Business, a division of Wolters Kluwer, is headquartered in New York. Wolters Kluwer is a market-leading global information services company focused on professionals.

Summary of Contents

	Table of Contents	*ix*
	Preface	*xvii*
Chapter 1	Crime and Corrections	1
Chapter 2	Corrections and Criminal Justice: An Overview	13
Chapter 3	Punishment	29
Chapter 4	History of Corrections	45
Chapter 5	Administration of the Prison	67
Chapter 6	The Prisoner	81
Chapter 7	Prisoners' Rights	101
Chapter 8	Prison Violence	121
Chapter 9	Corrections for Women	147
Chapter 10	Jails and Local Corrections	161
Chapter 11	Community Corrections	185
Chapter 12	Correctional Programs	213
Chapter 13	Corrections Staff	241
Chapter 14	Contemporary Challenges in Corrections	257
	Index	*275*

Table of Contents

Preface xvii

1 Crime and Corrections 1

Corrections and Criminology 1
A Profile of Crime in the United States 3
  Uniform Crime Reports 4
  Victimization Studies 5
  Nonreporting and Underreporting of Crime 6
Society's Historical Reaction to Crime 8
  Retaliation 8
  Retribution 9
  Reformation 9
  Prevention 10
Goals of Corrections 11

Summary 12
Key Terms 12

2 Corrections and Criminal Justice: An Overview 13

Social Functions of Criminal Justice 13
Role of Law in Society 14
Substantive and Procedural Law 15
Sources of Law 16
  Legislatures 16
  Constitutions 17
  Case Law 18
  Administrative Law 19

Components of the Criminal Justice System 19
Law Enforcement 19
Judicial Process 20
Corrections 22
Criminal Justice as a System 24
Barriers to System Success and Achievement 24

Summary 26
Key Terms 27

3 Punishment 29

Justice: Equity or Equality? 29
Evolution of Punishment 30
The Primitive 30
Vengeance 31
The Classical-Positivist Dilemma 33
The Classical View of Crime 33
The Positivistic View of Crime 34
Radical Views 34
Ideologies of Corrections 35
Retribution or Vengeance 35
Deterrence 36
Contrasting Views 37
Rehabilitation 39
Reintegration 40
Incapacitation 40
Just Deserts 41

Summary 42
Key Terms 43

4 History of Corrections 45

The Historical Perspective 46
The "First" Penitentiary 47
Forerunners of the Penitentiary 47
The House of Corrections 48
The Hospice of San Michel 48
The Maison de Force 48
Galley Ships 48
The Penitentiary Emerges: The Walnut Street Jail 49
The Pennsylvania System 50
The Auburn System 50
After Auburn and Pennsylvania 51

The Reformatory Movement 52
Southern Prisons 53
Beginning of the Modern Era of Corrections 56
Development of Alternatives to Incarceration 58
Benefit of Clergy 58
Judicial Reprieve 59
Filing of Cases 59
Founding of Probation 59
Origins of Parole 61
Alexander Maconochie 62
Sir Walter Crofton 63
Parole in the United States 64

Summary 66
Key Terms 66

5 Administration of the Prison 67

Administrative Goals for Prisons 67
Security 68
Segregation 68
Discipline 68
Treatment 68
Working to Achieve Administrative Goals 69
The Prison Staff 70
Prison Administrative Management 72
Autocratic Wardens 73
Bureaucratic Wardens 74
Delegative Wardens 75
Participatory Management 76
The Prison's Influence on Staff 77
"The Other Prisoners" 77
Prison Staff Subculture 78

Summary 79
Key Terms 80

6 The Prisoner 81

Prison Populations 82
Experiences of Long-Term Imprisonment 85
Elderly Inmates 86
Gangs 88

Transgender Inmates ... 91
The Culture of Prison ... 92
Separating the Inmate from the Subculture ... 93
Penetrating the Subculture ... 95
Prison Economic Systems ... 96
The Ex-Prisoner ... 97

Summary ... 99
Key Terms ... 99

7 Prisoners' Rights 101

Prisoners' Rights in a Historical Context ... 101
Judicial Intervention ... 102
The Prisoners' Rights Movement ... 104
The Rights of Inmates ... 106
Freedom from Cruel and Unusual Punishment ... 107
Visitation ... 110
Use of the Mail ... 110
Religious Rights ... 111
Medical Care ... 113
Privacy and Searches of Inmates ... 114
Rights Related to Prison Disciplinary Procedures ... 115
Access to the Courts ... 116
Evolution of Inmates' Rights ... 117

Summary ... 119
Key Terms ... 120

8 Prison Violence 121

Forms of Prison Violence ... 122
Physical Violence by Inmates on Inmates ... 122
Physical Violence by Inmates on Staff ... 125
Physical Violence by Staff on Inmates ... 126
Sexual Violence ... 127
Self-Inflicted Physical Violence ... 130
Economic Violence ... 131
Psychological Violence ... 132
Explanations for Violence in Prison ... 133
Violent Inmates ... 133
Prison Gangs ... 134
Adaptations to Deprivation ... 136

Overcrowding 136
High Incidence of Mental Illness 138
Organized Disturbances and Riots 139
Explanations for Prison Riots 141
Environmental Conditions 141
Spontaneity Model 142
Conflict Model 143
Collective Behavior and Social Control Model 144
Rising Expectations and Relative Deprivation Model 145

Summary 145
Key Terms 146

9 Corrections for Women 147

Women Inside Prisons 147
Currently Incarcerated Female Offenders 148
Correctional Entities and Institutions 149
Women Inside Jails 150
Social Ties and Pseudo Families 152
Challenges with Women as Correctional Clients 155
Sexual Violence Inside Jails and Prisons 155
Institutional Programs 157
Medical Services 158
Maternal Bonds 158

Summary 159
Key Terms 160

10 Jails and Local Corrections 161

Contemporary Jails 161
Evolution of Local Correctional Efforts 162
Local Correctional Populations 167
Demographic Variations 167
Geographic Variations 168
Jail Administration and Management 168
City and County Government Administration 168
State Government Administration 169
Cooperative Administration 170
Private Corrections 171
Problematic Aspects of Jails 172
Substandard Physical Facilities 173

Minimal Programming Opportunities 175
Staffing Deficiencies 175
Recruitment and Retention 176
Training 177
Staff Turnover 177
Poor Inmate Health 178
Substance Abuse 179
Suicide 179
Mental Health 180
Additional Forms of Local Corrections 181
Day Reporting Centers 181
Diversion Centers 182
Home Incarceration 182

Summary 183
Key Terms 184

11 Community Corrections 185

Community Corrections versus Institutional Corrections 185
Arguments Against Community Corrections 186
Arguments for Community Corrections 187
Probation 189
Conditions of Probation 190
Special Types of Probation 191
Intensive Supervision Probation (ISP) 192
Nonreporting Probation 193
U.S. Probationers 193
Legal Rights of Probationers 194
Revocation of Probation 195
Due Process Rights 196
Parole and Other P-Words 197
Contemporary Parole 198
U.S. Parolees 200
The Parole Process 200
Granting Parole 201
Conditions of Parole 202
Parole Revocation 203
Shock Incarceration 205
Aftercare for Former Inmates 207
Problems Facing Former Inmates 207
Contemporary Aftercare Programs 208

Summary 210
Key Terms 211

Preface

The writing of any textbook is a process that undoubtedly is filled with both the thrill and enjoyment of an author exploring and explaining a topic that is close to his or her heart, as well as the challenges and frustrations of presenting material in a way that allows others to understand and come to love a topic. Both of these extremes have been present in the writing of this text. As a corrections scholar and teacher for more than 20 years, I find the field intriguing, exciting, and something about which I always want to know more. When teaching corrections courses, I strive to instill in my students the importance of the topic and, hopefully, a desire to know more. These are the goals behind my approach to the writing of this text.

This is a textbook that focuses on presenting information in a straightforward, easy-to-understand, and hopefully interesting way. This is not a textbook that contains every single fact, statistic, or issue that is present in American corrections. Undoubtedly, after reading the text, students will have more questions come to mind, and will be interested enough to seek answers to these emerging questions, whether on their own or through the assistance of the instructor. Any good textbook should both provide the basic information about a topic and instill a curiosity in students that leads them to want to learn more. I hope I have achieved that in this text.

One of the challenges of a corrections textbook is deciding the order in which to introduce and discuss topics. There are a number of ways of doing this, and the approach in this text represents just one. First, Chapters 1, 2, and 3 highlight what corrections is, and where it fits into our criminal justice system and larger society. Following this, Chapter 4 introduces a discussion of historical developments in corrections, both in the Western world and in the United States specifically. This background should help students better understand the how and why of the issues presented in each of the subsequent chapters of the book.

Chapters 5, 6, and 7 focus on structural aspects of the prison, which is our primary institution for the conduct of corrections. These chapters highlight the organizational structure and administration of prison, characteristics of inmates that are brought under the supervision of correctional administrations, and the legal rights of inmates, all of which serve to structure the organization and activities of day-to-day life and work in corrections.

Following these structurally focused chapters, the discussion moves to issues of two relatively unique and in some ways rare aspects of corrections: violence and corrections for women. Violence is given its own chapter, to examine the common assumption (largely thanks to media portrayals) that prisons are exceedingly violent and dangerous places. While violence is certainly present in prisons, Chapter 8 shows that this is not an overwhelming day-to-day or minute-to-minute concern for inmates or staff. Chapter 9 focuses on women, the "important minority" of prison inmates. In simple terms, women represent less than 10 percent of prison inmates, yet present as unique and different from men in a number of important ways. While it would be possible to integrate the issues of women's experiences into all of the other chapters, this would undoubtedly lead to discussions of men's experiences, followed by a "but on the other hand, with women . . ." approach. In my eyes, that is a marginalizing approach, and thus I consciously decided to discuss women as the important minority in a chapter devoted solely to them.

Following this are discussions of corrections outside of prisons: in jails (Chapter 10); community corrections (Chapter 11); in a programming focus, whether in prison, jail, or community corrections (Chapter 12); and from the experience and perspective of those who work in corrections (Chapter 13).

Finally, emerging operational and policy issues are addressed in Chapter 14, with a look to the future and the hope of encouraging readers to think about what could or should be the new issues to be tackled by corrections.

Writing this text has been an experience of exhilaration, frustration, excitement, stress, and accomplishment. Corrections is a topic to which I was first introduced as a young, budding scholar, and it grabbed my attention and interest from the outset. That was at least in part due to the excitement my first professor brought to the course and the way that the basic issues were explained by the first text I read. I hope I have done my part in this text to introduce a new generation of scholars, practitioners, and simply educated members of society to the special world of corrections.

I would like to thank *David Patrick Connor* for his contributions to Chapters 9, 10, and 11.

Richard Tewksbury
June 2014

Chapter One

Crime and Corrections

CORRECTIONS AND CRIMINOLOGY

Crime is one of the major social issues that concern people in our world. For some of us, crime seems to be everywhere and ever present. For others, crime is something we know about and recognize to be a problem, but it is something we think we can avoid. And for all of us, crime impacts our lives because it is an important political, economic, and social issue that shapes what we do as individuals and groups and how our society (most importantly, government) responds to its presence of crime.

Understanding crime — why it happens, who commits it, who is victimized by it, and how we can and should respond to it — is one of the most important areas of knowledge that citizens need to have in our society. Knowing where crime happens and how social control agents work to prevent and respond to crime allows us as citizens to plan and conduct our daily lives in ways that maximize our safety and comfort. As citizens we expect the police to respond to crimes and work to find and arrest the criminals. We expect the courts to weigh evidence against and in support of alleged criminals and determine both if criminal defendants are guilty of crime, and if so, what is an appropriate response or reaction. And, we expect our corrections system to carry out the sentences of the courts and work to achieve some combination of punishment and treatment of convicted criminals, with the ultimate goal of preventing future crimes from occurring.

Corrections: a set of interrelated organizations, agencies, and programs in the American criminal justice system that hold, treat, and sometimes punish those persons convicted of crimes, and hold those charged with crimes as they are processed by the courts.

Corrections in the American criminal justice system is a set of interrelated organizations, agencies, and programs that hold, treat, and sometimes punish those persons convicted of crimes, and hold those charged with crimes as they are processed by the courts. One-third of a three-part criminal justice system, corrections is almost entirely dependent on the law enforcement and judiciary components of the criminal justice system and process in terms of receiving "clients," the conditions under which offenders are sent to corrections, and the length of time for which offenders remain under the authority of corrections. While being very dependent on law enforcement and the judiciary, corrections does not have much authority over or influence on the first two segments of the criminal justice system. Rather, the activities, policies, and decisions of law enforcement and the courts essentially control the scope of activities that are required and expected from corrections.

Correctional efforts in the United States have undergone significant changes in recent decades. For many years, corrections appeared to exist solely for the purpose of punishing criminal offenders. During the twentieth century, these changes first emphasized helping (rehabilitating) offenders to change into law-abiding people. Here the idea of "corrections" of behavior was viewed as primary, and hence led to the naming of the efforts and structures as corrections. However, when such efforts were not seen as fully effective, political forces worked to change the focus of attention, and the focus of corrections then shifted to working with criminals to help them to better cope with their life situations and social environments, and hopefully to learn how to avoid "falling into" criminal ways. Finally, and most recently, the focus appears to be moving toward simply separating criminals from the rest of society and warehousing law-breakers. These changes in focus mean not only that the actual workings of the correctional system have changed, but also that how we view and devote resources to corrections has changed. In the long run, the issue is how effective and efficient our attempts to correct criminals can be. Recent history suggests that we have not been very effective or very efficient.

Criminology: the study of crime.

While corrections is obviously directly connected to studying the criminal justice system functions, we also know that studying corrections is related (but not as obviously) to the study of criminology. **Criminology** is the study of crime. More specifically, as defined by Bartollas and Dinitz, "the objective of criminology is the development of a body of general and verified principles regarding the process of law, crime, and treatment."[1] Through a focus on how laws are made and lawbreakers are processed and treated, we enter into the overlap with corrections. After all, if one of the main goals of corrections is to work with criminal offenders so as to produce persons who do not commit crimes any longer, it is important to understand how and why crimes happen in the first place. Only if we know the reason that crimes occur can we effectively and efficiently design programs and efforts to intervene and change such behaviors.

In many ways, criminology gives us the basic knowledge and understandings of criminal behavior that are used to design and evaluate the workings of the correctional systems. Without understanding how criminal events occur and

1. Clemens Bartollas and Simon Dinitz. 1989. *Introduction to Criminology: Order and Disorder.* New York: Harper & Row.

why offenders commit crimes, our efforts in corrections would be without guidance. This would mean we would be even less able to make informed decisions about how to treat offenders and to protect society against criminals who repeat their crimes. **Recidivism**, when criminals repeat their crimes after being convicted and processed through some correctional process, is the primary issue to which most observers point as a way of assessing whether corrections is successful or not. If convicted offenders leave corrections and do not commit additional crimes, we can argue that corrections has been successful. However, if offenders leave prison, probation, or parole and do commit more crimes, then we can easily point to corrections and say that it has failed. The criminologist is ultimately interested in reducing crime by understanding the who, what, where, when, and especially the why of crime in general. On the other hand, the correctional professional is concerned with preventing or reducing the likelihood of a known criminal recommitting crime. In these ways, the criminologist and the correctionalist are very similar, and each has important influences on the other.

Recidivism: a term used to identify criminals who repeat their crimes after being convicted and processed through some correctional process.

Before embarking on a serious and in-depth examination of how the work of corrections is accomplished, we must first review what we know about crime in our society. The remaining portion of this chapter will discuss the size of the crime problem and will review how modern societies have traditionally reacted to crime and attempted to prevent it. We will conclude this chapter by returning to the question,what is the goal of corrections? Finally, we will briefly examine how the structure of our correctional organizations, agencies, and programs works to hold, treat, and sometimes punish lawbreakers, while pursuing these goals.

A PROFILE OF CRIME IN THE UNITED STATES

One common political issue in the twenty-first century, and one that has been a political "hot button" for decades, is the "crime problem." No doubt, crime is a major problem in our society. However, a close examination of the statistics on crime suggests that not everything that we are led to believe is necessarily true. For instance, a common belief in our society is that crime is rampant and that crime rates are higher than ever before. Most people seem to believe that crime is increasing, and society is less safe than ever before. However, this is in fact not the case. For the last decade, crime has actually been decreasing in the United States. In 1992, the National Crime Victimization Survey reported that there was a total of 33,649,340 incidents of criminal victimization in the United States. These incidents affected 23 percent of all U.S. households.[2] But, in 2011 there

2. Patsy Klaus. 1994. *The Cost of Crime to Victims*. Washington, D.C.: U.S. Department of Justice, Bureau of Justice Statistics.

were "only" a total of 22.9 million instances of criminal victimization in the United States.[3]

Household crimes: offenses against one's property or one's place of residence.

Personal thefts: the act of stealing money or belongings directly from a person.

Violent crimes: offenses that directly bring or directly threaten physical harm to a person.

The level for all crimes has decreased, as has the number of **household crimes** (offenses against property or one's place of residence) and **personal thefts** (stealing of money or belongings directly from a person). The only type of crime that has increased in the past decade has been domestic violence,[4] a form of **violent crime** (offenses that directly bring or directly threaten physical harm to a person).

Crime is also one of the most costly social problems in our society. In 2007, it was estimated that crime cost victims more than $15 billion.[5] Additionally, more than $179 billion was spent by all levels of government to respond to crime. These are huge amounts of money, equating to more than $500 for every man, woman, and child in the nation, on average. Criminal justice is among the most expensive government activities, ranking among national defense, education, and health care.

What this suggests is that we must exercise care when discussing the scope of the "crime problem." We must also be careful when we use crime statistics. Not all crime statistics are the same, and you can easily find a statistic to support almost any point of view. This is not to say that crime statistics are not useful or important, for they provide information that guides our planning and working in corrections. Without crime statistics we would not know what to expect today, tomorrow, or next year in our organizations, agencies, and programs. Therefore, we need to examine carefully our sources of statistics and how these statistics are gathered.

Uniform Crime Reports

Uniform Crime Reports (UCR): a collective report compiled from information sent by nearly all U.S. law enforcement agencies, allowing the FBI to draw together information from throughout the nation to construct a clear picture of where, when, to whom, and by whom reported incidents of crime occurred.

The rapid development and population growth in the past several decades has made it clear that all segments of the U.S. criminal justice system need reliable and consistent data on the occurrences of crime. Whereas at one time local and state law enforcement agencies kept most crime statistics, there was no organized effort to compile national crime figures until 1930. That is when the Federal Bureau of Investigation (FBI) began collecting and dispensing the **Uniform Crime Reports (UCR)**. Representing the reporting of crime by nearly all U.S. law enforcement agencies, the UCR allows the FBI to draw together information from throughout the nation and put together a clear picture of where, when, to whom, and by whom reported incidents of crime occurred. Those crimes reported to a law enforcement agency (by victims, witnesses, or complainants) or discovered by law enforcement officers are included in the UCR.

---

3. Jennifer L. Truman and Michael Planty. 2012. *Criminal Victimization, 2011.* Washington, D.C.: Bureau of Justice Statistics.
4. *Ibid.*
5. Federal Bureau of Investigation.2008. *Crime in the United States: Uniform Crime Reports, 2007.* Washington, D.C.: Federal Bureau of Investigation.

The most commonly used and referenced portion of the UCR is Part I. This is reporting on what the FBI has identified as the eight most serious crimes in our nation: murder, rape, robbery, assault, burglary, larceny-theft, motor vehicle theft, and arson. The reported incidence of these crimes is combined to create the **crime index**. Therefore, each of these offences (except arson, due to problems with accurate reporting), because it is part of the crime index and because each is believed to be an important crime to track, is also referred to as an **index offense**.

Crime index: collection of statistics throughout the nation on the total numbers of the following reported crimes: murder, rape, robbery, assault, burglary, larceny-theft, motor vehicle theft, and arson.

Index offense: a term applied to the crimes of murder, rape, robbery, assault, burglary, larceny-theft, and motor vehicle theft because they are a part of the **crime index** and are believed to be important crimes to track.

In 2011, more than 10.2 million serious crimes were reported to law enforcement agencies.[6] The majority of these crimes are property crimes, not violent crimes. Because the numbers for the entire nation are large, and so as to provide a context within which to understand these numbers, the FBI also reports on crimes in terms of a standardized rate. For each of the index offenses, we can easily calculate an index rate that shows the number of each type of crime for every 100,000 people.

These statistics inform us about the patterns and trends of crime in society. By examining several years' worth of statistics, we can determine whether particular forms of crime are increasing, decreasing, or remaining stable in frequency. We can also use these statistics to learn about the distribution of crime in society.

Victimization Studies

Officially reported crime, such as that reported in the UCR, is important and provides one way of understanding the scope and distribution of crime in society. However, not all crime is reported to the police, and therefore not all crime is included in the official statistics. In order to get a more complete picture of the amount and types of crime in society, it is necessary to supplement official statistics with information collected directly from crime victims. There are a number of reasons and types of situations that might lead some crime victims to not report what happened to them to the police, and we will look at these issues in more detail shortly. But, for now it is important to focus on identifying ways that we can measure the amount of crime in society in addition to simply counting offenses known to the police.

The primary alternative form of crime statistics comes from surveys conducted with the general population to identify and count criminal victimizations. The largest and most important source for this information is the **National Crime Victimization Survey (NCVS)**. The Bureau of the Census conducts this national study every year, and the Bureau of Justice Statistics analyzes and distributes the results. Begun in 1972, the NCVS is designed to gather data from a representative sample of almost 100,000 people throughout the United States.

National Crime Victimization Survey (NCVS): annual representative study of 100,000 people in the United States conducted by the Bureau of the Census and distributed by the Bureau of Justice Statistics for the purpose of calculating the extent of criminal victimizations across society.

6. Federal Bureau of Investigation. 2012. *Crime in the United States, 2011*. Washington, D.C.: Federal Bureau of Investigation, table 1.

This information is used to calculate the extent of criminal victimizations across society.[7] The focus of the NCVS is on identifying the total number of criminal events, not the number of people out of 100,000 who were victimized, as is reported in the UCR. So, in this way, the NCVS has a slightly different focus than the UCR.

Almost without exception, the NCVS reports crime rates higher than those that are reported in the UCR. This makes sense as the NCVS gathers data directly from victims of crime. There is no "middleman" to act as a filter, and people do not have the same motivations for keeping quiet about the crimes that happen to them when they are telling it to a researcher in an anonymous survey. This is important because in the eyes of many criminologists, the NCVS provides a more accurate and clearer picture of the scope and distribution of crime in the United States than do the official numbers included in the UCR.

However, while the numbers in the NCVS report crime rates higher than those reported in the UCR, the general patterns between and within crime categories remain essentially the same across the sources. While more crimes are reported in the NCVS, it is simply more of the same proportions of crimes; there is not a major shift in evidence about which types of crimes are more or less common. So, the NCVS may be more accurate regarding how many crimes occur, but for understanding which crimes are more or less common, there is little difference between the UCR and the NCVS.

Nonreporting and Underreporting of Crime

Even with the higher numbers of crimes reported by victims in the National Crime Victimization Survey, it is still highly unlikely that every single crime that happens gets reported and counted. The NCVS makes it clear that many persons who are crime victims, for some reason, do not report the crime to law enforcement agencies. Victims report many of these incidences to NCVS surveyors, but we would be very naïve to believe that victims share all such "hidden crime" with researchers. Therefore, the logical questions that arise are (1) just how much crime in our society is actually reported to the police?, and (2) what are the reasons someone would not report being a victim?

The NCVS statistics suggest that victims actually report relatively small percentages of criminal incidents (approximately 35 percent of all crimes) to law enforcement officials.[8] The severity of the offense and the amount of loss suffered may be victims' primary determining factors for reporting crimes to the police. For instance, 50 percent of violent crime victims report the incident to law enforcement authorities, but only 33 percent of household crimes and 25 percent of personal thefts are reported. Among theft offences, the most likely to

---

7. U.S. Department of Justice. 1991. *Criminal Victimization in the United States,1990.* Washington D.C.: Bureau of Justice Statistics.
8. *Ibid.*

be reported are automobile thefts (93 percent reported).[9] Think about why this would be the case. If your car is stolen, in all likelihood you have insurance on it, and in order to collect the insurance you need to "prove" that it was stolen — so you report the theft to the police. But, if you have something like a pen, a book, or $20 stolen out of your backpack, are you going to pick up the phone and call the police? You have just been a victim of a crime, so it would be easy to argue that you should report the offense. But, what is going to happen? Do you really expect the police to conduct an investigation and track down the thief and be able to return your $20 to you? Probably not. So, many of us would not bother to make a police report and would instead think about how we might better protect our pens, books, and money so that we do not get victimized again.

The reporting of crime also appears to be determined, at least in part, by victims' personal characteristics. Very simply, how likely someone is to report a criminal victimization is influenced by sex and race. Women are more likely to report being victims of crime, and African Americans and Hispanics are more likely to report instances when they are victims of violent crimes. But, even here comparisons of UCR and NCVS statistics show that less than one-half of even violent crimes are reported to the police.

We can probably think of many reasons why some people might not call the police to report a crime. For example, they may be involved in crime themselves or may fear "authorities" such as police officers. Consider the case of Mike, who is selling marijuana to his friends. If Paul, who also sells marijuana, hears about Mike's business, comes to Mike's apartment, beats him up, and steals his drugs, how likely is Mike to call the police to report the assault or theft?

However, some of the reasons that actual crime victims give for not reporting may not be quite so obvious. The most common reason that victims say they do not report their crimes is that the offender's attempt to harm them or to take something from them was unsuccessful. Consider that $20 you had stolen from your backpack. If instead of the thief actually getting your money you saw him start to go into your backpack and stopped him, are you going to report it to the police? Some of us might, but most of us would not; after all, you did not lose anything, and is it really worth the time and effort to make an official report? Other commonly cited reasons for not reporting crimes include the following: The victim reported the incident to some other (non-law enforcement) authority; the victim believed there was no evidence of proof; the victim believed the police would not invest enough time or energy to make the reporting worthwhile; the victim believed that recovering his losses was highly unlikely; and the victim believed the incident was either not important enough to report or simply a private or personal matter.

---

9. U.S. Department of Justice. 1995. *Highlights from 20 Years of Surveying Crime Victims.* Washington, D.C.: Bureau of Justice Statistics.

This lack of reporting suggests that, even with a criminal justice system that processes literally thousands of persons/cases on a daily basis, and where it can easily take a year or longer for a criminal case to come to court, only a small portion of all "criminals" ever enter the system. However, this is not the only time that a filtering process works in the system. As we will see throughout the text, we need to study crime statistics at several points throughout the system to get a complete picture of how the system works and what persons are actually processed through the police and courts to the correctional system.

SOCIETY'S HISTORICAL REACTION TO CRIME

The way our society reacts and responds to crime, as is the case with the way most things in society operate, has changed dramatically and in numerous ways over the course of history. The way we view crime in today's world is not the way civilized societies have always viewed and handled crime. In fact, our views today — that crime is a major social problem and criminals need to be either controlled or treated — is historically a relatively recent way of thinking and acting. As we review the historical evolution of views on crime, we quickly realize that societies have chosen four primary ways to respond to crime. In this section, we will briefly discuss each way of responding to crime and how some aspects of these ways of responding are actually still in use today.

Retaliation

Retaliation: a crime-control philosophy aimed at striking back at people who deserve to have done to them what they did to others.

The primary way that early societies responded to and tried to control crime focused on the idea of exacting revenge on those who harmed others. **Retaliation**, the idea at striking back at people who deserve to have done to them what they did to others, was originally used as a way to please the gods. Early civilizations believed that it was necessary to retaliate against wrongdoers so as to avenge the wrongs done against the gods. Here the idea is that crime is not something done against a particular other (the person we would call the "victim"), but rather is an offense against a higher power. Remnants of this idea remain today in that in American courts it is the state that is seen as the affronted party, and it is the state, not the direct victim, that brings charges against an alleged criminal. Retaliation, then, was seen as a responsibility, not simply as a desired response to crime. Over time, the idea of retaliation also evolved into a view that victims themselves should be allowed to get revenge against an offender, and in some societies in some points in history the individual that was directly harmed was provided with the opportunity to do to the offender what he had done to that individual. "An eye for an eye" has, at least at some points historically, been taken in a very literal sense.

Retaliation in early societies typically took the form of some type of physical punishment, but not always. Instead, retaliation has also been interpreted to mean that offenders should be removed from society. **Banishment**, the act of being permanently removed or thrown out of a group or place, is a way of striking back at those who harm others. To banish an offender also meant that the society no longer needed to worry about that individual committing more crimes — if the offender was no longer physically present in a community, he did not have any opportunities to recidivate. In early societies, banishment was essentially the same as the death penalty. Being removed from a group meant that one was left to fend alone against nature, roving bands of thieves, murderers, and wild animals. Membership in a group provided security in early societies; removal from the group left one defenseless. But, because an individual had shown himself to be unable, or unwilling, to live peacefully in the group, he "deserved" to be removed from the group.

Banishment: an early crime-control model designed to permanently remove or throw out of a group/place an individual who has done harm to others.

Retribution

As societies progressed in complexity and grew in size, the emphasis shifted from retaliation to **retribution**. That is, a wrongdoing should be punished because the act deserves punishment. When an individual does wrong, it is society's responsibility to show the wrongdoer that her actions will not be tolerated and will result in negative reaction (a punishment).

Retribution: a crime-control philosophy designed to punish an individual for an act because the act simply deserves punishment.

Retribution replaced retaliation as society judged that individual criminals were responsible for their actions and that their actions were against other individuals, not against some higher power (gods). Because individuals were held responsible for their actions, society needed to direct a response (or punishment) to the individual. In one way, this was a change to thinking that people could be trained and their behavior adjusted or guided into proper forms. Just as when our ancestors trained animals — by physically punishing them when they misbehaved — so too it was believed that people could be trained. That is, when people misbehaved, they deserved to be punished. In this way, society hoped that people could learn from their misbehavior.

Reformation

Perhaps one of the most significant shifts in how communities thought about crime and chose to respond to it happened in the mid-1800s, when the idea of training/guiding people's behavior came center stage and replaced the heavy focus on simply punishing offenders. Recognizing that behavior is something that can be guided and instilled in persons, the idea of using punishment not only for the purpose of making offenders suffer, but also as a way to have them learn from their punishment, led to attempts to change or reform criminals. Through a combination of punishment and treatment designed to elicit change, these efforts focused on transforming offenders into law-abiding citizens. This movement toward **reformation** emphasized change in the individual, which would benefit all of society. We usually think of reforming something as making

Reformation: a crime-control philosophy designed to change the individual's ways to benefit all of society.

it better. In order to try to make criminals "better," we needed to be able to understand why they engaged in criminal behavior. With the emergence of criminology as a science, communities began to try to find ways to remove or overcome the negative influences that lead people to crime, and to replace those influences with positive things that would lead the criminal to "better" behavior. Reform is treating criminals and making them better (or more law-abiding) people.

In this era, the term *corrections* began to be used to refer to the activities officials did with convicted criminals. To talk about corrections earlier than this would have been meaningless, as nobody was attempting to "correct" anything, but instead simply punishing criminals. In the mid-1800s, the focus shifted to working with offenders so as to correct their behavior. Corrections, in the modern sense, then, was born in the nineteenth century, out of a recognition that we could identify reasons that individuals were criminal. Once we could point to a cause of crime, we could then work to try to identify ways to correct, or overcome, the influence of such factors. As such, the change in philosophy was to focus on the individual and how changes in the individual could bring about a safer society.

Prevention

Toward the end of the twentieth century, societies again modified their thinking and efforts, this time with an emphasis on trying to do all they could to protect the community, maximize safety, and prevent crime. Crime can be prevented in several ways. First, we can protect society by removing those persons who threaten our safety. Just as early societies banished wrongdoers in a way that ensured they could not harm members of that community any more, we developed policies and practices in the latter half of the twentieth century that functioned in very similar ways. The thinking that has come to dominate corrections in the latter half of the twentieth century and into the first decades of the twenty-first century is that if we can find a way to remove dangerous people from our midst, then we can protect the community from them. While banishment is no longer a possibility, we have worked to find ways of achieving similar outcomes, usually though close supervision and/or locking offenders away. Incarcerating criminal offenders for long periods of time means they are unable to victimize others. This is the idea behind public policies that call for long prison terms for repeat offenders.

But, contemporary efforts to prevent crime are not only centered on removing criminals from the community. We can also work to prevent crime by trying to change offenders into law-abiding persons. Treatment programs — such as substance abuse and psychological counseling — are designed to erase or overcome the causes of individuals' criminal behavior. If we can remove the reason people commit crimes, then it logically follows that they are less likely to commit crimes and society becomes safer.

The prevention of crime is a concern of numerous social institutions and efforts, not just the criminal justice system and corrections. However, corrections and the idea of removing offenders from opportunities to commit crimes are the major ways that our society works to prevent crime.

GOALS OF CORRECTIONS

Corrections exists for the purpose of both carrying out the sentences given to convicted criminal offenders by the courts and holding until trial those alleged criminal offenders that the courts deem necessary to incarcerate so as to ensure their appearance at court proceedings. It is the primary goal of corrections to supervise and monitor offenders in ways that are safe, secure, and humane, and to advance the protection of society from continued criminal activities by known criminal offenders. Individual correctional workers have as their primary goal to carry out the specific duties of their job effectively and efficiently in ways that advance the institution or agency toward its goal of controlling crime.

However, the goal of controlling crime can be realized only when several more specific objectives are also achieved. First, as corrections strives to control the amount of crime in society, there needs to be a reduction in the number of criminals in society. To be effective in making society safer, the programs and opportunities presented to offenders also need to achieve a reduction in the likelihood of individual offenders continuing their criminal actions. All of the efforts of corrections, however, also need to be done in ways that are cost-effective. This does not mean that corrections attempts to operate in an inexpensive way, because that is probably simply not possible. But, what is done needs to be less expensive than the alternative — continued crime by offenders. Efficiency concerns include not only the financial costs of programs, but also the efficient use of resources (people, physical facilities, time). Finally, efficiency concerns look not only at what resources corrections uses, but also from where these resources are diverted. To be efficient, a program or opportunity for criminals must make good use of resources. A program should also avoid diverting resources from some other social program, which may use those resources better.

Overall, we can say that the goals of corrections are of two general types. First is the outcome of the activities of corrections. The goal here is to stop or lower crime among individuals and across society as a whole. Second, the process by which this outcome is pursued must be done in as efficient a manner as possible. The combination of these two goals — effectiveness and efficiency — is the key to any assessment of how well corrections works. With this in mind, we will now turn to the how, why, where, and with whom corrections operates. First, though, we have to consider how corrections fits in with and functions dependently on the activities of the other two components of the American criminal justice system — law enforcement and the courts. As we will see in Chapter 2, the most important thing to remember about the place of corrections and its relationship with law enforcement and courts is that everything that happens in corrections is directly dependent on what happens in law enforcement and the judicial components of the system.

Summary

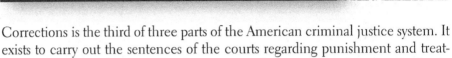

Corrections is the third of three parts of the American criminal justice system. It exists to carry out the sentences of the courts regarding punishment and treatment of convicted criminals. As a piece of the process that is completely dependent on what the police and courts do in regard to how many persons are to be processed and how they are to be processed, corrections has a huge task.

Crime is a common occurrence in the United States. Contrary to popular belief, crime rates have actually been decreasing in the past two decades, yet the population of prisons, jails, and all correctional programs remains exceptionally high. The most common types of crimes in our society are nonviolent offenses, including property and drug crime. Therefore, the typical offender that is a client of corrections is not the stereotypical violent offender.

The ways that societies respond to criminals have changed over time, with a movement away from revenge and simple punishment, toward efforts to change offenders, and finally toward a heavy emphasis on protecting society by keeping offenders physically removed from opportunities to continue criminal behaviors. Achieving a safer society is primary among the goals of corrections, but this is a very large and difficult task given the number of offenders that corrections is responsible for and the political and social contexts (as will be described in Chapter 2) in which corrections operates.

Key Terms

- Banishment
- Corrections
- Crime index
- Criminology
- Household crimes
- Index offense
- National Crime Victimization Survey (NCVS)
- Personal thefts
- Recidivism
- Reformation
- Retaliation
- Retribution
- Uniform Crime Reports (UCR)
- Violent crimes

Chapter Two
Corrections and Criminal Justice: An Overview

SOCIAL FUNCTIONS OF CRIMINAL JUSTICE

The criminal justice system exists for the purpose of providing society with a way to both enforce the law on lawbreakers and to maintain stability in society. In order to do this, it is necessary both for the law to exist and be known to members of the public (as possible criminals and victims), and for community members to respect, trust, and value the criminal justice system and all of its tasks. An important part of the effort to control the behaviors of known offenders is that a majority of the members of a community believe that what the criminal justice system does is fair, appropriate, and deserved. Only in this situation will society become more stable and predictable as a result of criminal justice actions. Only if community members trust the system are they likely to report most crimes to the police and thereby put the system in motion.

However, as we saw in Chapter 1, it is very common for victims to not report a large portion of crime to police. This means that the criminal justice system is often not even involved with crimes. When this is the situation, it is impossible for the criminal justice system to enforce the law and work toward the goal of a stable, safe, and predictable community. However, when victims do report crimes, the criminal justice system is put into motion and begins working toward this goal. And, when the criminal justice system does identify and apprehend criminals, and process and subject them to corrections, the system is likely to be seen by members of the community as more trustworthy and effective. In this instance, we would then expect community members' respect, trust, and value for the system to increase, and subsequently lead to yet more reporting of crime. In this way, when the system does function well (or at least is perceived to function well), there is motivation and impetus for ongoing activities and a move toward a safer community.

The criminal justice system is not only an active collection of agencies, processes, and people that works to address known instances of crime, but also an important symbol of the government's power. Society maintains order through a combination of force and authority. **Force** is the actual use of power to gain physical control over others, whereas **authority** is gaining control over others by implying that force can or may be used. Our system of criminal justice uses both force and authority to ensure that order is maintained in society. For example, force is used when individual offenders are arrested, tried, and committed to prison. These actions are not wanted by the offender, and they show what the government actually can do to lawbreakers. Authority, on the other hand, is less concrete: It is how individuals view the criminal justice system as a potential user of force to enforce laws. That is, the presence of a criminal justice system gives law-abiding people good reason to stay law-abiding and stands as a message to would-be criminals that if they break the law, they will be subject to force.

Force: the actual use of power to gain physical control over others.

Authority: the act of gaining control over others by implying that force can or may be used.

ROLE OF LAW IN SOCIETY

All societies have rules that regulate people's behaviors and that work to establish and maintain order. There are a variety of types of rules that regulate social behavior, which vary in their degree of complexity and importance. **Folkways**, those "usual ways" of a group of people, are the most informal. These are expectations for behavior that when broken lead to usually small-scale types of negative reactions from others. Folkways are important for keeping things running smoothly, but if people violate them, there are not major disruptions to social order or social activities; instead, those who do break folkways are seen as "unusual" or "different" or simply mildly deviant. For example, one unwritten rule in college classrooms is that we dress "appropriately." We assume that we all know what *appropriately* means. However, what if the person sitting next to you came to class one early fall day dressed in a parka, snow boots, gloves, and a big furry hat? That person would likely get a few stares; perhaps some classmates would laugh, and many would undoubtedly think, "What's wrong with him?" These are negative reactions that other classmates use to control that student's future behavior.

Folkways: "usual ways" of a group of people that serve as an informal way of regulating social behavior within a society.

A second type of social rule, **mores** (pronounced "mor-ays") are more serious than folkways and carry moral overtones. What if the person sitting next to you comes to class totally nude? In this case, it is likely that others in the class would not only wonder what's wrong with him, but would also be very likely to think that this person has loose morals or is a "bad person."

Mores: generally more serious than *folkways* and usually has moral overtones.

Finally, the most formal and strict rules of our society are our laws. Laws serve as the backbone of a civilized society. In simple terms, a law is a rule about what behavior is and is not appropriate for an identifiable group of people. Laws are not necessarily rules that govern more serious or more important things, but they are the "official" rules, and when broken those who break them can (and often will) be officially sanctioned.

More formally, a **law** is a rule of conduct that a governmental authority creates, recognizes, and enforces. In rather direct terms, laws tell people what actions are expected of them and what people may expect from others in society. Our **rights** are what actions we may legitimately expect from others, whereas our **obligations** are the actions that society may legitimately expect from us, based on our specific roles and statuses. Both our rights and our obligations are not only expectations, they can also be compelled by the law's use of force. For any rule to be considered law, it must meet several criteria:

Law: a rule of conduct that a governmental authority creates, recognizes, and enforces.

Rights: actions we may legitimately expect from others.

Obligations: the actions that society may legitimately expect from us, based on our specific roles and statuses.

1. The rule must have *conformity pressures* from an *external source* in the form of *threats* of action.
2. The external pressures for conformity must be *coercive.*
3. Enforcers of the rule need to be *socially authorized* to carry out enforcement activities.
4. Enforcers of the rule need to have *legitimate authority* to use coercive tactics.

Laws exist to structure the daily organization and flow of activities in a society. We assume that the law exists to provide citizens with a sense of safety and to promote a greater good. That is, we feel safe when we believe we can live our lives knowing that we can expect certain things from others and that we must do (or not do) certain things. Feeling safe also means that if and when anyone fails to honor his or her obligations, someone in authority will take official action to correct that failure. This is where the criminal justice system enters the picture.

SUBSTANTIVE AND PROCEDURAL LAW

Law exists not only for the purpose of outlining what activities must or must not and may or may not be done. Laws also provide the basic building blocks of the systems that make, interpret, and enforce the laws of behavior. This is the distinction between substantive and procedural law. **Substantive law** is the set of rules about what behaviors are allowed and required from people. That is what we usually think of when we discuss "law." The substance of the law — the identification of acceptable and unacceptable forms of behavior — comprises the major focus of the law for most people. However, perhaps even more important for a legal system's continued functioning are **procedural laws**. These are the rules about how laws are made, interpreted, and enforced. Procedural laws are

Substantive law: the set of rules about what behaviors are allowed and required from people.

Procedural laws: the rules about how laws are made, interpreted, and enforced.

similar to the written rules of a board game. Procedural laws tell us what people do to create a new rule, how rules are determined to be "fair," and how people whose job it is to catch rulebreakers may go about their work. Procedural law establishes the structure and ways that substantive laws are made and enforced.

When we think about procedural law, in addition to substantive law, we realize that our legal system is more complex than most people initially think it is. Procedural laws can often have more influence on maintaining peace and order than can the actual substantive laws of behavior. When we learn that a criminal has not been convicted, or perhaps not even arrested, for crimes that we know were committed, we may complain about the "loopholes" or "technicalities" in the law. What we are actually saying is that substantive law has not been enforced, because the "rules of the game" — the procedural law — is set up in such a way that police, the courts, or corrections are not allowed to do what we believe "should" be done. That is, someone violated the spirit of the rules of the game, but in technical ways it is not possible to sanction them. Therefore, loopholes found in the law do not mean that there is a gap in the law. Instead, loopholes mean that procedural law is set up in such a way as to not allow certain things that we may believe to be right to actually be done.

SOURCES OF LAW

One of the common misconceptions held by many Americans is that we have one way to make laws in our society: through elected representatives in state and federal legislatures who write, discuss, and vote on bills that become laws. Considering ourselves a representative democracy, we believe that the individuals whom we elect to office make and modify all our laws. While legislatures most certainly make laws, the fact is that they are responsible for less than one-half of all laws in our society.

Yes, legislators make laws and then governors or the President approve, sign, and put them into place. This type of law, called **statutory law**, is typically substantive laws (rules about what we can and cannot, and must and must not, actually do). Statutory laws are those that have the most public input, and are those with which people are most likely to be familiar.

Statutory law: typically substantive laws that generally have the most public input, and with which people are most likely to be familiar.

Laws in the United States come from four different sources. In addition to statutory laws created by legislatures, we also have law created by constitutions, courts (e.g., case law), and administrative agencies. Each type of law tends to focus more or less on either procedural or substantive issues, and each type also has a different degree of involvement in the criminal justice process. Before studying the ways that the criminal justice system (especially corrections) operates, we need first to examine these sources of law.

Legislatures

Legislative bodies at all levels, from Congress at the federal level down to city councils at the local level, are the groups of elected individuals that are given authority to make (pass) laws. (These bodies are "given" this power by constitutions, as will be discussed below.) Legislative laws are called **statutes** and are organized and maintained in **statutory codes**, which are the cumulative collection of all statutes that govern a particular jurisdiction.

Statutes: laws made by the legislatures and organized and maintained in *statutory codes.*

Statutory codes: an organizational structure used to effectively maintain statutes made by legislatures.

Substantive criminal law is primarily found in the national, state, and local statutes. The majority of laws that define crimes and outline the possible punishments for them are found at the state and local levels. Federal law is actually only rarely involved in criminal cases. Generally speaking, federal law becomes involved in criminal matters only when crimes cross state lines, when our national defense is threatened, or when the offenders or victims are representatives of the national government and are involved in crimes as a matter of their jobs.

Legislatures are also involved in the creation and modification of procedural laws, although this is less common than their involvement in substantive law. Our nation is based on the political philosophy of representative government. This means that we believe in the power of the people, through their elected representatives, to govern themselves. Therefore, the legislative process is central to the principle of government by the people. This is one reason that most Americans believe that the creation of laws is centralized in legislatures.

Because substantive law is created legislatively at the state and local level, this means that there are usually differences across jurisdictions in how particular crimes are defined. Whereas a specific action in one state may be considered a crime, in a neighboring state the exact same action may be perfectly legal. One of the best examples of this today is in how some types of drug laws are written in different jurisdictions. Consider the laws about marijuana possession and use. In a handful of states, possession of small quantities of marijuana is completely legal, but if someone in a neighboring state were to be found with the same amount of marijuana, she might be subject to a fine or in some states even incarceration. The variation in the actual content of the law from one jurisdiction to another can be a problem for some people, and at times it can be very important to know the law in your community specifically, not just to have a general sense of what the law "usually" says.

Constitutions

Constitutions are the formal documents creating the structural and procedural parameters of government. Constitutions are the foundation for all laws within a given jurisdiction and serve as the basis for the how and what of procedural and substantive laws that can be enacted within a jurisdiction. They create the structure of governments and outline how and what powers are given to particular people and governmental agencies. Constitutions, therefore, are primarily concerned with procedural law, not substantive law.

Constitutions: formal documents creating the structural and procedural parameters of government.

Each state, as well as the federal government, has a constitution. However, the federal Constitution explicitly establishes that any state constitution shall be subordinate to, or less influential than, the federal Constitution. Article VI states that the Constitution of the United States is supreme law of the nation and that all state laws must follow with federal law. The earlier example of marijuana laws varying from jurisdiction to jurisdiction highlights the possible challenges that may arise due to conflicts between federal and state law. For while some states have decriminalized marijuana, the cultivation, possession, sale, and use of marijuana is a violation of federal law. So, in states where state laws have been changed to make possession legal, there is a direct conflict with federal law. The way this conflict will be settled is through the courts, in the form of case law.

Case Law

Case law refers to the decisions of appeals courts; the decisions of such courts carry the weight of law. What an appeals court does is to hear arguments about procedural laws, and whether or not particular actions constitute violations of procedural laws. When a court of appeals decides whether a particular action is or is not within the scope of a particular procedural law, this decision is considered the law for all future instances of such behaviors or actions. In this way, the interpretations of the law that are made by appellate courts are also laws in themselves.

The courts in our judicial system interpret the law in two basic ways. First, the courts apply the law. When people are suspected of having violated the law, they are brought to court for an official determination of whether the law actually applies to their actions. This is the function of trial courts. Second, courts are responsible for interpreting the legality of our laws. This means that when the passage of a statutory (or administrative) law or the enforcement of such a law is suspected to violate the more powerful constitutional law, the judiciary decides the issue. These decisions are the focus of appellate courts.

Together with the principle of government by the people, our founding fathers tried to ensure that our legal system would have a built-in system of checks and balances on power. In part, this is accomplished by separating the three branches of government and giving each branch — executive, legislative, and judicial — a different function. Each branch of government is given a method to question and to override the other branches' actions. Executive officers of a state or of the federal government may veto a piece of legislation; the legislature may, in turn, override the veto. The judiciary can decide that a particular piece of legislation or an executive order violates the Constitution and can thereby overturn either action. If the legislature or executive officers wish, they may initiate a movement to amend the Constitution, thereby overriding the judicial decision. Obviously, none of these efforts are easy to accomplish, but this is how our founding fathers structured the checks-and-balances process.

Judicial review: the process whereby an appellate court hears an appeal of a trial court decision and determines whether the action and law behind the trial court's decision is based on, or is within, legal boundaries established by the Constitution.

When an appeals court interprets a statute or administrative action, it engages in the process known as **judicial review**, whereby an appellate court hears an appeal of a trial court decision and determines whether the action and the law behind the trial court's decision is based on, or is within, legal boundaries established by the Constitution.

Because they are made by legal system representatives and are about the content of the law, these decisions are actually laws themselves. We call this **case law** because it is law made in particular cases. This means that the appellate court's decision is carried forward as the law; this is the legal principle known as ***stare decisis***. *The Law Dictionary* defines *stare decisis* as follows:

Case law: the decisions of appeals courts that dictate how future court cases involving the interpretation of a law are decided.

> [t]o follow a precedent. A flexible doctrine of Anglo-American law that when a court expressly decides an issue of law . . . that decision shall constitute a precedent which should be followed by that court and courts inferior to it, when deciding future disputes, except when the precedent's application . . . is unsuitable to the character or spirit of the people of the state or nation, and their current social, political and economic conditions.[1]

Stare decisis: a term used to describe the process of an appellate court's decision being carried forward as the law.

Administrative Law

Administrative law refers to the rules and regulations that government agencies create. State and federal legislatures give these agencies the power to make "laws." Here, we are talking about laws made by government agencies such as the Internal Revenue Service, the federal Aviation Administration, the Environmental Protection Agency, or the Federal Communications Commission.

Administrative law: the rules and regulations that government agencies create.

Contrary to the popular assumption that most laws in our nation are made by legislatures, in fact most of the "laws" in our society are administrative. When we consider the various types of government agencies and the vast range of responsibilities each agency may have, it quickly becomes clear that we can easily be dealing with hundreds of thousands of individual laws. For this reason, administrative law is a very complex, often very difficult form of law to comprehend.

COMPONENTS OF THE CRIMINAL JUSTICE SYSTEM

The U.S. system of criminal justice has three separate, but overlapping, components. Criminal justice is carried out through the operations of law enforcement, the judiciary, and finally, the corrections components. Within each component are rules, regulations, and specific roles and functions that must be filled. In the following sections, we will briefly discuss each component and then review how all three components work together to form a system of criminal justice.

Law Enforcement

Law enforcement is the most visible part of our nation's criminal justice system. The persons and agencies charged with the responsibilities of keeping order in

---

1. Wesley Gilmer. 1986. *The Law Dictionary.* Cincinnati: Anderson Publishing, p. 308.

society and making certain that lawbreakers enter the system are found in various types of organizations, but all carry the same basic responsibilities. When we think of law enforcement, we usually think of our local police. We also need to include in this category law enforcement agencies from other governmental jurisdictions, such as counties, states, and special organizations. Sheriffs represent the law enforcement efforts of county governments, and state police or highway patrols exist in 49 of our 50 states.[2] While the federal government also has a number of law enforcement agencies, there is no national equivalent to the city or state police. Law enforcement is also conducted by other special police forces with limited jurisdictions, and other agencies. For instance, fish and wildlife agency officers are law enforcement officers and have special sets of laws that they enforce, as well as in many states having the same arrest powers as "regular" police. Many large airports have their own police departments, which focus on enforcement of laws at airports. Similarly, there is a police agency in Washington, D.C. that is specific to the United States Capital, and the museums of the Smithsonian Institution have their own special police force.

Federal law enforcement agencies enforce only certain areas of the law. For instance, the Secret Service is the law enforcement arm of the treasury department; the Bureau of Alcohol, Tobacco and Firearms devotes itself to enforcing laws about alcohol, tobacco, and firearms; and the Drug Enforcement Administration enforces our drug laws. There are numerous law enforcement agencies in the federal government; however, none of these agencies have broad, overreaching powers.

The major focus of most law enforcement agencies and officers is to ensure the public's basic security needs. Additionally, law enforcement officers are commonly recognized as one of, if not the only, "24-hour emergency social service agency." When citizens need assistance and no one else is available, they commonly call the police.

Holding a position equivalent to the front lines in battle against crime, the law enforcement officer makes the crucial decision whether an offender enters the criminal justice system. Without the actions of law enforcement, the judiciary and the corrections components are simply not put into motion.

Judicial Process

We saw earlier in this chapter that American courts are charged with two primary responsibilities: applying the law and interpreting the law. We have already read about the interpretation process — judicial review — in making case law. More important to the daily functions of the criminal justice system is the task to which our courts actually devote most of their time: applying the law.

---

2 Hawaii is the only state without a state-level law enforcement agency.

Criminal courts are where our criminal justice system formally decides disagreements about whether an individual's actions are within his or her legal rights and obligations. The criminal court's purpose is to hear evidence the government brings against a person who is believed to have violated the substantive criminal law. In making this decision, the court applies the law to the specific incidents of a person's behavior. There are specific arrangements of steps or processes involved in a criminal trial that must be followed (e.g., procedural law) as a court considers evidence against and in defense of a person charged with a crime. If, following the legally required process and rules of evidence, either the individual's actions are found to be within her legal rights, or the evidence against a person does not establish her guilt beyond a reasonable doubt, that individual will be declared not guilty of the crimes charged against her. This is known as an **acquittal**. If, however, as is the outcome of the majority of criminal actions, the individual charged with a crime pleads guilty or is found to be guilty of the charges, the trial ends in a **conviction**.

When acquitted, a person is finished with the criminal justice system. That is, once acquitted, the person is free and has no further processing by the criminal justice system (at least in regard to the charges for which he or she was acquitted). Also, once acquitted on a particular charge, the person may not be tried again for that specific action. This is the protection against **double jeopardy** guaranteed by the Fifth Amendment to the Constitution. As stated in the Constitution, "Nor shall any person be subject for the same offence to be twice put in jeopardy of life or limb."

For offenders who are convicted, the next step is for the court to determine the appropriate **sentence**. A sentence is "the court judgment specifying the penalty imposed upon a person convicted of a crime."[3] The procedural law of the court's jurisdiction (either state or federal government) outlines the sentencing process and possible sanctions that can be applied to the convicted individual. In this process, a number of issues, along with the crime's actual facts, are taken into consideration. Of course, statutory law established the possible sentence that may be imposed on the convicted offender. However, in most jurisdictions, there is some variance in what exact sentence an individual offender will receive.

The judge decides and actually imposes the appropriate sentence on a convicted offender. In most jurisdictions, judges are provided information in a **presentence investigation (PSI)** about offenders, their backgrounds, ties to the community, details of the offense in question, and information about other important life circumstances for the offender. Usually prepared by probation departments, PSIs make recommendations to judges about appropriate sentences for individual offenders. Originally developed to provide important information to judges, PSIs also provide some uniformity to the sentencing process.

Acquittal: the process whereby, following the legally required process and rules of evidence, the individual's actions are found to either be within his or her legal rights, or that the evidence against a person does not establish their guilt beyond a reasonable doubt, that individual will be declared not guilty of the crimes charged against him or her.

Conviction: refers to when an individual charged with a crime either pleads guilty to or is found to be guilty of the charges through a criminal trial.

Double jeopardy: a protection guaranteed by the Fifth Amendment of the Constitution whereby an individual is protected from being subject to punishment for the same offense more than one time.

Sentence: the penalty of law that is imposed on an individual for being found guilty of a crime in a court of law.

Presentence investigation (PSI): a report typically prepared by probation departments whereby a judge is informed about an offender's background, ties to the community, details of the offense in question, and information about other important life circumstances for the offender that can impact sentencing.

3. George E. Rush. 1986. *The Dictionary of Criminal Justice*, 2d ed. Guilford, CT: Dushkin Publishing Group, p. 217.

Corrections

Corrections, as we saw in Chapter 1, is the collection of organizations, agencies, and programs that hold, treat, and sometimes punish those people known or strongly believed to have committed a crime. Contrary to the assumptions of many people, however, corrections is more than just jails and prisons. In fact, jails and prisons, while the most obvious and frequently thought of part of corrections, actually account for less than one-half of all people who are processed through the corrections system. Where most people under correctional supervision are found is in community corrections — typically probation and parole.

Corrections brings together the act of subjecting criminal offenders to the authority and force of the government in regard to the punishment of those members of society who commit wrongdoings, with efforts to work with wrongdoers in ways that are believed to lead to a safer community. Accompanying the punishment of either being incarcerated or supervised and regularly reporting to an official in the community are processes designed to lead to changes in offenders' behaviors. Corrections also is responsible for persons who have been charged with crimes, but are awaiting processing by the courts.

It is important to remember that a wide range of types of correctional programs and institutions exists in the United States. Not only is there a wide range of types of sentences and punishments, but there is also a wide range of differences within each type of sentence. For instance, the idea of "going to prison" is not the same for all persons. Not all prisons are alike. If we randomly select two prisons from the more than three thousand U.S. prisons in operation today, in all probability we will find two facilities that vary in size, physical structure, age, security level, type of housing, and characteristics of inmates. Most important, these differences mean that the experiences of both staff and inmates of these institutions are also likely to differ. But, most Americans do not realize these differences exist, and instead think of prison as a very harsh, dark, dangerous, and intimidating place — essentially the image they have seen on television or in the movies. Our society tends to think that "prison is prison." But, this is far from reality. Yes, some prisons are just like the frightening images we see in entertainment media, but most prisons are not like this. Prisons are like people: Although we may have a lot in common, the specifics about each of us make us unique and easily distinguished from one another.

Legal requirements (laws, including constitutional, statutory, case, and administrative) strictly guide the structure and operations of corrections institutions and programs. This is the same for law enforcement and the judiciary. However, the major differences between corrections and the other two components of the criminal justice system are the amount of control over and the disposition of cases or people that corrections has compared with law enforcement and the courts. Both law enforcement and the judiciary have many opportunities to exercise discretion in how they handle individual cases, and have the power and opportunity to remove people from the criminal justice system — police and the courts can "drop" a case and the person involved is removed from the criminal justice system. Although corrections can use some discretion in individual cases (such as to which prison an offender is sent and the conditions imposed on a probationer), it has much more limited opportunities to determine exactly what it does, and with whom it does things. People are ordered into the correctional system. This means that not only must people go to corrections, but also that corrections officials must accept them. Whereas the police can decide to no longer pursue an investigation of an individual, no one in corrections can decide to "drop" an individual or case. The judiciary and the law enforcement agencies can dismiss a case whenever they believe it is necessary or proper. Corrections officials cannot simply decide to release someone from jail or probation because they feel think the person has served long enough or does not deserve to be incarcerated. The position that corrections occupies in the criminal justice system is one with minimal self-control opportunities. Thus, corrections as a component of the U.S. criminal justice system depends on the actions of law enforcement and the judiciary.

While ostensibly "equal" with law enforcement and the courts in the structure and conduct of criminal justice, corrections has limited opportunities to control the flow of offenders through its doors. Corrections has little opportunity to expand or increase its resources, and little control over how many of its resources it is required to spend. All of these issues are controlled by both law and the number and types of offenders passed to corrections by the police and courts. Corrections, then, is a dependent component of the criminal justice system; we might say that corrections is at the mercy of its peers in policing and prosecution. It is completely the actions and decisions of these antecedent systems that determine the resources, tasks, and clients of corrections.

Across the United States, one of the most pressing problems affecting the criminal justice system is the exceptionally large number of people in our jails and prisons. Overcrowding is a major problem in terms of physical space, finances, and demands on corrections staff. During the 1990s, a political movement to "get tough on crime" dominated both the media coverage of criminal justice issues and the actions of legislatures. As politicians continued to take a harsher and harsher stance toward crime and criminals, more and more offenders were sentenced to prison and jail, and for longer and longer periods of time. As a result, most state prison systems and many (especially large, urban) local jails reached the point that they simply could not accommodate any more offenders. As a result, and as we will discuss later in this text, the courts had to intervene either to loosen up the requirements, such as those regarding space and programming, for incarcerated offenders, or to order the release of offenders, so as to avoid dangerous and unconstitutional (according to the Eighth Amendment prohibition against cruel and unusual punishment) conditions in prisons and jails. Note that it was not corrections that did these curative actions. In the way our government and criminal justice system is structured, it was the courts that had to provide relief for the increasingly bad conditions created in prisons and jails.

CRIMINAL JUSTICE AS A SYSTEM

We say that our society has a "criminal justice system." What we mean by this is that the three main components — law enforcement, courts, and corrections — all work together (although not always cooperatively) in pursuit of a common goal. The goal of the criminal justice system is to control and reduce the amount of crime in society.

A systemic approach to criminal justice is based on the idea that each component of the system — and, in fact, each individual job within the criminal justice system — can be best done when one person or one set of people is responsible for one or only a few tasks. This is very similar to the concept of the assembly line. Rather than having one person responsible for finding, apprehending, holding, trying, sentencing, and punishing an offender, each of these tasks is delegated to someone or some agency. This process becomes a system when clear rules and procedures are established to regulate how the system's goals are pursued.

When we analyze the criminal justice system as a "system," we must remember that we deal not only with a system of institutions and agencies, but also with *people*. The way that each part of the system operates affects not only the other agencies in the system, but also the people who work and live in those agencies, and those who are served by each agency. One issue running through this study of corrections is that corrections changes people, including the people who live and work in corrections.

Criminal justice, as a system, sometimes works very well and sometimes not so well. One of the primary goals of scholars of criminal justice is to identify where the system works less well than it could, and to try to identify how to improve the functioning of the system. In order to improve the system and its operations, however, we need to understand why it is being held back. There are a number of things that can lead to ineffective and/or inefficient operations. Some of these are conscious and intentional on the part of some group or organization that has a reason to want to see the system not work well, and some of these things are unintentional, perhaps occurring without any recognition of the reason.

BARRIERS TO SYSTEM SUCCESS AND ACHIEVEMENT

The idea that criminal justice operates as a system in our society suggests that there are ways the system may or may not work as well as desired or intended. As with any activity in life, there are potential barriers to criminal justice operating at full efficiency and effectiveness. While the specific reasons that some part or action in the system may not work well can vary quite widely, it is possible to conceptualize the barriers to successful operation in several categories of reasons. As you read about prisons, jails, community corrections, and other types of programs and efforts of the American correctional system, keep in mind these five primary types of barriers that can hold us back from working as smoothly and effectively as possible and prevent systems from achieving their goals:

1. *Flaws in the design of the system.* When the basic plan for how parts work together has errors, the system is doomed to failure or, at least, to poor working conditions.
2. *Failure of the system to keep up with changing social conditions.* Because social systems work with and are staffed by human beings, systems have to consistently modify themselves to meet the needs that society expects them to meet. If the world changes and we do not change to meet new needs or we do not stop pursuing unnecessary goals, we will eventually not be needed. Thus, we will fail to meet our goals.
3. *Attacks from outside sources.* Social systems compete with other social systems for resources. Other systems, seeking to strengthen themselves, may make political organizational attacks to defer another system's resources. The attacking system may win; the attacked system may collapse.
4. *Attacks from internal sources.* Not only do different systems compete for resources, but so do the parts of an individual system. These attacks, just like attacks from outside forces, can weaken a part of a system and can lead to the breakdown in the system's functions. Eventually, the entire system will collapse.
5. *Poor leadership.* Any system, just like an organization or company, needs a strong, intelligent, forward-looking set of leaders. If the system's leaders do not have these qualities, the system can be expected to fall victim to the preceding reasons for failure. Also, without leadership to direct its activities, the system could break down on its own.

In the corrections area, we know that workers perform their jobs as guided by official procedures and by their personal values and perceptions. This means we must know about the people we assign to different jobs. This way we can predict how and how well they will perform their jobs, and we can develop policies and practices that will guide them in performing their jobs properly. In simple terms, some people are better suited for some jobs than they are for other jobs. As an example, research tells us that correctional officers have a more punitive view of offenders (especially sex offenders) than do case workers and psychologists who work in the system.[4] This is not necessarily a bad thing; it is simply something we need to consider as we develop policies and practices for correctional officers. Knowing that particular types of persons, in particular types of jobs, may or may not work especially well with particular types of offenders,

---

4. Wagdy Loza. 1993. Attributions of Blame Toward Incarcerated Rapists Among Correctional Workers: Implications for Staffing. *Canadian Journal of Criminology,* 35, 59-60.

in particular types of situations, can be very important for making personnel decisions and assigning staff to particular jobs.

If we understand that different persons have different approaches to working (and living) in corrections, we are one step closer to understanding that corrections — and, in fact, all of the criminal justice system — operates in the much larger context of society. The operations of the criminal justice system have wide-ranging effects. Both the actions of offenders and our institutionalized means of responding to them have a ripple effect, eventually reaching all parts of society.

Collateral costs: negative impacts, such as financial, psychological, and/or social costs, felt by an offender's family and/or friends once the offender is sanctioned by the criminal justice system.

Placing offenders in jail or in prison affects people beyond those who are themselves locked up. Those persons' families and friends also are impacted by how an offender is sanctioned by the criminal justice system. We call these effects **collateral costs** of corrections. Collateral costs are the disruptions to the personal lives of offenders, as well as to their family members, that come from an offender being sanctioned. Consider, for example, the losses a wife experiences when her husband goes to prison, and the financial problems that involvement in the criminal justice system may cause. (For example, an offender may lose his job if that person has to wait several weeks or months in jail before a trial.) Or, consider the millions of American children who have a parent in jail or prison — certainly there are psychological, emotional, and social costs that are borne by these children. Collateral costs also include more abstract consequences such as psychological disturbances for offenders and their friends and family members, disruptions to the family unit, and losses that an employer may encounter when an important worker is lost due to criminal involvement. Here, think about whether there would be any costs or consequences for you as a student if during the next weekend your professor were to be arrested and put in jail where she would stay for the remainder of the semester. What "costs" would be experienced by you, her student? How would this affect you? How would your college be affected? Who else might suffer collateral costs in this instance?

Summary

Laws within a society are what establish the realm in which the criminal justice system operates. There are two primary types of laws within the United States: substantive law and procedural law. Substantive law is a set of rules for what is allowed and required of people; whereas procedural law dictates how laws are made, interpreted, and enforced. Procedural laws are generally considered to be the most important for a legal system to function. There are four sources of laws within the United States: legislatures, constitutions, courts, and administrative agencies.

The U.S. criminal justice system consists of three connected, yet different, components. These are the components of law enforcement, judicial process (i.e., courts), and corrections.Corrections is responsible for holding, treating, and sometimes even punishing those found guilty of committing a crime. Corrections is highly dependent on the actions and operations of the first two components.

The primary goal of the criminal justice system is to control and reduce the amount of crime within the confines of the law. But, there are obstacles to operating a successful criminal justice system. The five main barriers to the success of the criminal justice system are flaws in the design, failure of the system to keep up with changing societal conditions, attacks from outside sources, attacks from internal sources, and poor leadership.

Key Terms

- Acquittal
- Administrative law
- Authority
- Case
- Collateral costs
- Constitutions
- Conviction
- Double jeopardy
- Folkways
- Force
- Judicial review
- Law
- Mores
- Obligations
- Presentence investigation (PSI)
- Procedural
- Rights
- Sentence
- *Stare decisis*
- Statutes
- Statutory codes
- Statutory law
- Substantive law

Chapter Three
Punishment

JUSTICE: EQUITY OR EQUALITY?

Crime and deviance are difficult enough to understand. However, what may seem even more difficult to understand are the following questions: What constitutes fair and valuable punishment in the context of the criminal justice system? How should we decide what makes an appropriate punishment for crime? Should punishment be based on what society as a whole thinks is "enough" to convince a criminal to not do such crimes again? Should we rely on the advice of experts to tell us what is enough, too much, or too little? Should punishment be given simply to make the criminal suffer in some way, or should punishment serve a purpose? Should all instances of a particular crime, such as burglary or assault, receive the same punishment? Should punishment be designed to fit the crime or fit the criminal?

To understand these questions, we must first make an important distinction between easily confused concepts. As Karl Menninger has stated, a difference exists between **punishment**, "pain inflicted over the years for the sake of inflicting pain," and **penalty**, "a predetermined price levied automatically."[1] In the minds of most experts, and criminal justice practitioners, penalty should be the goal of the criminal justice system. While causing individuals pain is sadistic and against human nature, it is not inappropriate to impose a penalty to change their behavior. However, knowing what punishment, and how much, in what form, and the

Punishment: pain that is administered at various time points for the sole purpose of causing pain.

Penalty: a price decided on prior to committing a certain act that will be applied once that certain act is actually committed.

1. Karl Menninger. 1968. *The Crime of Punishment.* New York: The Viking Press, Inc., p.202.

timing of its application so as to achieve a positive outcome is an inexact science. And, decisions about what constitutes an appropriate method and application of punishment or penalty are influenced by many social factors, including how much crime occurs and how the public perceives crime. Whenever crime rates significantly increase, the public calls for increased and strong punishments (pain). Little effort is made to determine if increased penalties actually achieve the desired goal of reducing criminal activity. As a result, as we will see in Chapter 4, this typically means a growing and overcrowded correctional system and increased expenses to taxpayers.

Society imposes punishments on criminals for the purpose of achieving justice. However, what does "justice" mean? Although most people assume they know what it is, *justice* has several definitions. The simplest definition is that of the Greek philosopher Aristotle, who said that justice means "equality for equals." In contemporary society, most people believe that justice means a system that is "fair."

Equality: the concept that all similar people and acts receive the same punishments or rewards.

Equity: the concept that all individuals are rewarded or punished according to their contributions to a particular outcome.

Determinate sentences: legal sanctions that offer narrow sentencing options and where all instances of a particular crime receive essentially the same penalty.

Indeterminate sentences: sentences that prescribe a minimum and maximum period of time to serve in a correctional program.

Justice can be seen as a system of beliefs centered on either equality or equity. As foundations for the pursuit of justice, **equality** means that all similar people and acts receive the same punishments or rewards, whereas **equity** means that all individuals are rewarded or punished accordingly to their contributions to a particular outcome. Therefore, equality-based systems are likely to use legal sanctions such as **determinate sentences** that offer narrow sentencing options and in which all instances of a particular crime receive essentially the same penalty.

A determinate sentence is a fixed period of time that a convicted offender must serve in prison or on some other form of punishment. On the other hand, equity-based systems rely heavily on discretion and offer **indeterminate sentences**. These are sentences that name a minimum and maximum period of time to serve in a correctional program. Individual variations are possible (and common) depending on the offender's individual circumstances and progress toward change.

These two competing views of justice become important when we consider how a society determines punishments and the goals behind specific punishments. When a society seeks to rehabilitate or change individual offenders, it must have laws and legal procedures based on equity. Similarly, when a society emphasizes protecting citizens from dangerous offenders, equity must guide its decisions. Equality-based systems are usually found in societies that place greater emphasis on ensuring that members know what punishments to expect in response to their criminal acts and therefore hope that such knowledge deters people from criminal behavior.

EVOLUTION OF PUNISHMENT

The Primitive

In many primitive societies, life was largely regulated by fear and the unknown. When social norms and rules were broken, primitive societies feared that their gods would be displeased. Therefore, taking actions to soothe the gods, primitive people punished offenders so that their gods would not make everyone suffer. This was not punishment in a modern sense, though. Individuals settled their arguments, and others were not involved unless serious violence or a blood feud developed. If **taboos**, the acts considered so bad that they are essentially unthinkable, were committed, primitive societies could impose death or could banish the offender. **Banishment**, forcing somebody to leave a particular society, had the effect of a death sentence, however. Outside their communities, individuals were usually unable to protect, feed, and care for themselves. The goal of banishment, however, was for the security of the society, not to punish the member who had done wrong.

Taboos: acts considered to be so bad that they are essentially unthinkable in a given society.

Banishment: the act of forcing someone to leave a particular society.

As they advanced culturally, people settled into permanent communities. In time we learned to control the waterways, to build great ships, and to make trips across the oceans from continent to continent. Our means of transportation, our architecture, our weapons, and our tools illustrated our progressive discoveries and increasing mastery of the earth's natural resources. One area in which we failed to progress, however, was in the treatment of criminals. Comforted by a consistent tradition, advancing civilizations found no other remedy than severe physical punishment for criminals.

Vengeance

As late as the nineteenth century in England, more than 200 different offenses carried a potential death penalty. Execution methods displayed incredible imagination, and offenders were put to death in a wide variety of ways. The methods by which executions were conducted were symbolic, with some methods considered "worse" than others; the end results, however, were all the same. For instance, in some cases people were fed to starving animals, torn apart, burned, crushed, mutilated, and crucified. In the eleventh-century reign of King Canute in England, preference was shown for execution by skinning offenders alive and then impaling them on stakes. At various points in history, criminals were stoned to death, drowned, beheaded by axe or guillotine, poisoned, hanged, suffocated, and boiled in oil. The retributive philosophy dominated European correctional efforts until the mid-nineteenth century. In the society of titled landowners who prevailed in the early Middle Ages, violation of property rights was not an important concept. The main concern was to prevent vengeance from developing into a blood feud. Crime was considered an act of war, and peace was maintained almost exclusively by the imposition of fines. The so-called criminal justice system was based on class distinctions, and the lower classes (as has seemingly always been the case) received harsher treatment than did the upper classes. The inability of the poorer classes to pay the fines gradually led to the introduction of corporal (physical) punishment. The economic inferiority of large numbers of people, the feudal lords' increasing domination of judicial rights, and the uncontrollable impulse to increase the revenue from fines were major factors that ultimately caused the end of the fines system.

After the fifteenth century, the number of poor people increased. This of course meant that the number of people that did not own property increased. In turn, the city populations increased and jobs of skilled workers were threatened by the increase in population. The usual problems that accompany sudden population growth developed. When wandering bands of workers increased, landowners quickly hired this cheap labor. It could well be said that the exploitation of the masses caused the rise of capitalism.

The poorer the masses and the larger the visible mass of poor people became, the harsher were the punishments imposed on crimes. Physical punishments, originally substitutes for fines, became the rule. Once exceptions, execution and mutilation became common forms of punishment. During the entire reign of Henry VIII, an estimated average of five hangings occurred per day.[2] That is, approximately 72,000 major and minor thieves were hanged in 38 years.[3] Not only were many physical punishments imposed, but they also became increasingly harsh and physically extreme.

There were occasional, if somewhat isolated, reactions to the severities of punishment. Trial by ordeal, common in the thirteenth century, was outlawed. As early as the seventeenth century, the Quakers opposed inhumane treatment in the North American colonies. Their efforts, perhaps more than any other factor, caused Pennsylvania to become the cradle of prison reform in the United States. Houses of correction began operating in Britain, Europe, and North America. These institutions were, at least in part, concerned with the welfare of the young. The first European house of correction, established in Amsterdam, was one of the few that offered some hope of correction. Most, however, were miserable places.

In the eighteenth century, the thrust for reform was advanced by men like John Howard (1726-1790), perhaps the greatest of all prison reformers. Though his celebrated and widely read book, *The State of Prisons*, Howard brought to the world's attention the critical need for prison reform. Sir Samuel Romilly (1757-1818), a British lawyer, was an untiring opponent of the English criminal code with its excessive capital punishments. Through his efforts, England's first modern prison, the Millbank Prison, was built. Four years after Romilly's death, as a result of the continuing reform of the criminal code, the death penalty was removed as the prescribed punishment for 100 petty offenses. Not until the 1700s and 1800s did punishment shift from imposing pain on the physical body to the more modern, and humane, approaches of restricting the offender's liberties and social life.[4]

The need for punishment remains today, but the time for excessive cruelty in punishment has long since passed. The Eighth Amendment to the United States

---

2. Harry Elmer Barnes and Negley K. Teeters. 1950. *New Horizons in Criminology.* Englewood Cliffs, NJ: Prentice-Hall, p. 417.

3. George Rusche and Otto Kirchheimer. 1939. *Punishment and Social Structure.* New York: Columbia University Press, p. 19.

4. Michel Foucault. 1977. *Discipline and Punish: The Birth of the Prison.* New York: Random House.

Constitution explicitly forbids "cruel and unusual punishments." However, according to many critics of American death penalty laws, we do impose cruel and unusual punishments. Robert Johnson's examinations of life on death row and working on death row[5] show the chilling emotional impacts that our most extreme form of punishment have on the individual involved and on society as a whole. However, is this "cruel and unusual"? Legally, no; morally and ethically, this is still being debated and is subject to individual interpretation.

Whether explicitly stated or simply unconsciously felt, there are several competing philosophical bases for punishment. We will examine the broader meanings of these bases in the next section. But first we will review a central and important dilemma that punishment theorists face.

The Classical-Positivist Dilemma

Do human beings have and exercise free will? That is, do people actually have complete control over what they do, when they do it, how, where, and with whom? Similarly, are criminals to blame for their acts? A great deal of scholarly inquiry and research has attempted to resolve these questions and to place punishment in its proper perspective. It is difficult to imagine a society entirely without punishment. Whether punishment prevents crime is one issue that has not been settled. Criminologists, politicians, philosophers, and just about everyone else has a view about why we should punish criminals, how we should carry out punishment, and what results of punishment we should expect. The debate boils down to the issues of why do we punish?, and what is, and how do we determine, appropriate punishment?

The Classical View of Crime

In the **classical view** of crime, people are considered free to determine their own behavior and commit crime as a matter of choice. It logically flows, then, that because people have free will, punishment is proper so as to influence people's future decisions about whether or not to do such actions again and to serve as a symbol or message to all members of society about what is and is not acceptable behavior. Because people choose to break the law, society has a moral responsibility to remind them that their actions are unacceptable. If people can freely choose whether to commit crime, then they can be freely condemned for wrong choices and be appropriately punished. The classical view strongly influences our criminal justice system. The use of determinate sentences implies that criminals are responsible for their actions and must suffer to an extent equal to or greater than the amount of suffering they have brought to others. When we

Classical view: the viewpoint of crime that people are free to determine their own behavior and commit crime as a matter of choice.

5. Robert Johnson. 1981. *Condemned to Die: Life Under Sentence of Death.* Prospect Heights, IL: Waveland Press. Robert Johnson. 1990. *Death Work: A Study of the Modern Execution Process.* Pacific Grove, CA: Brooks/Cole Publishing.

believe that punishment is the goal of sentencing, we want potential criminals to know exactly what punishment they will suffer if they commit a particular crime.

However, freedom of choice is not necessarily absolute. Behavioral choices are influenced by a variety of conditions, including immaturity, organic brain damage, epilepsy, alcoholism, drug addiction, compulsiveness, and strong social forces. The recognition in the seventeenth and eighteenth centuries that criminals often displayed these (and other) problems led to Cesare Lombroso's work, the beginning of positivism in criminology.

The Positivistic View of Crime

Positivistic view: the viewpoint of crime where physical, mental, and social characteristics are believed to heavily influence one's tendency for crime, also referred to as *utilitarian view.*

Most social scientist take a **positivistic view** (sometimes referred to as *utilitarian view*) of human behavior. Beginning with Lombroso's attempts to identify criminals by their less evolved physical, mental, and social characteristics, positivistic views of crime have always emphasized factors that cause or push people into crime. This view endorses a "value-free approach"[6] to uncover factors in the environment that explain why people engage in criminal behavior. The idea here is that there is some identifiable characteristic of a person that can be pinpointed as the cause of the individual's behavior, including criminal behavior. It is not the fault of individuals that they have a particular characteristic, but instead offenders are destined and guided into their behavior by something — most probably something biological about their bodies or brains — that is wrong or different about them.

Just as with their bodies determining their behaviors, for some criminals it is their social environment that is believed to track them into particular behaviors. So, once again, the individual is not (fully) responsible for his or her behaviors. And, if our behaviors are beyond our control, the question that logically arises is, "Is it just to punish someone for something he has done, but which he cannot control?" The view that it is not appropriate to punish such persons because of their lack of control over their behavior is what philosophers would call *deterministic*. This is contrary to the notion of free will in classical school explanations of crime. Rather, when individuals are "pushed" into crime, for whatever reason, they clearly need some type of help. With indeterminate sentences, where offenders can be sentenced to a range of time, individuals can get "help" and have an incentive (getting out earlier) to work through their problems.

Radical Views

An interesting phenomenon occurred during the 1960s and continued through the 1980s: the return of the Marxist point of view to explain criminal and delinquent behavior. Following a perspective the Dutch criminologist

---

6. Max Weber. 1949. *Methodology of the Social Sciences.* Glencoe, IL: The Free Press.

William A. Bonger made popular in the early part of the twentieth century,[7] some scholars reemphasized the economy when explaining crime. The distribution of wealth, coupled with significant corruption in the business world and in government, led to varying theories that saw the criminal justice system as one mechanism for those in power to maintain such power. In simple terms, the radical theorists blamed the capitalist system for the creation of crime and injustice, and saw the criminal justice system as a tool of a powerful elite segment of society for controlling the behaviors of those below them.

This view, while for some easily understood and recognized, never gained significant hold on academics, practitioners, or many regular members of society. However, it is important to recognize and understand that aspects of society taken for granted — such as the existence, value, and importance of a criminal justice system — are not necessarily seen with universally shared views. And, just because minority views, such as the radical view of criminal justice and corrections that arose in the late twentieth century, never gained widespread popularity, such views still can and do have at least some influence on systems like criminal justice.

IDEOLOGIES OF CORRECTIONS

If we examine the historical record, we see that different ideologies at different times have motivated how societies deemed it appropriate to respond to criminals. The ways that are believed to be proper and most beneficial for responding and reacting to crime are determined by a number of factors, including the political philosophy of a society, religious influences, economics, the size of a society, and perceptions of the severity of the "crime problem" in a society.

Altogether, there are six major theoretical approaches for how a society responds to and handles criminals (or, how they perform "corrections"). These six approaches — retribution, deterrence, rehabilitation, reintegration, incapacitation, and just deserts — each offer a guiding set of beliefs about why punishment is applied, whether punishments should fit the crime or fit the criminal, and how severe punishment should be, or needs to be. The remaining part of this chapter will be devoted to explaining each of these approaches, showing what each idea means and how it is translated into practice.

Retribution or Vengeance

Some people believe that lawbreakers simply *deserve* to be *punished.* This is known as **retribution**. When punishment is justified on the basis of retribution

Retribution: a punishment philosophy where lawbreakers simply deserve to be punished.

7. W.A. Bonger. 1916. *Criminality and Economic Conditions,* translated by Henry P. Horton. Boston: Little, Brown and Company.

or vengeance, two major concepts are involved: 1. Punishment is an end in itself; and 2. The act committed *deserves* punishment.

The first concept means that punishment is not designed to achieve any change or reform in the criminal. If the primary justification for punishment is that the act deserves punishment (the second concept), then we restrict the results that we seek to achieve. Retribution does *not* include two important factors that other ideologies emphasize: any gain for society and any gain for the individual. Retribution simply means punishment for punishment's sake. There is no intention that whatever is done as punishment will achieve anything beyond imposing something bad, some type of suffering, for the criminal. Punishment can be seen as a way of "getting back" at a criminal, or a form of vengeance.

The actual practice of retribution (vengeance) is perhaps the oldest of our modern approaches to punishment. But, it was not until the mid-eighteenth century that Immanuel Kant (1724-1804) and Georg Hegel (1770-1831) first spelled out the underlying philosophy behind punishment for the sake of punishment. Kant held that punishment was a "categorical imperative" (an incontestable, self-evident truth), and Hegel insisted that punishment was the criminal's "right." Their ideas gave support to the classical school of criminology, and one of their major premises was that people's behaviors are a result of choice or of free will. Therefore, because criminals chose to do something bad, it is only right that they receive something bad in return.

A final, important aspect of retribution is that it is always a reaction to an earlier event. Punishment is not, and cannot be, proactive. By definition and as intended, any and all actions that arise from retribution are focused on the past. Thus, retribution as an ideology is not concerned with future events, but rather with past events. Criminals are punished for what they did, with no concern about whether or how punishment may relate to what they may do in the future.

Deterrence

Deterrence: the punishment philosophy that emphasizes the notion that punishing past behavior has an influence on one's future behavior.

Vengeance and retribution, the first ideology guiding how societies respond to criminals, eventually was replaced with an idea that brought in a focus on attempting to change future behaviors. This idea, **deterrence**, emphasizes that punishing past behavior can and should influence future behavior. The desired effects of punishment are to influence the future behavior both of the individual who receives the punishment and of others who know of ("see") punishment applied to criminals.

A fairly common belief in our society is that punishing someone now, for what they did in the past, will have an effect on what they do in the future. Typically, people believe that the more (or more harshly) someone is punished the more likely punishment is to effectively guide future behavior. However, the severity of punishment is actually less important than two other aspects of punishment: certainty and swiftness. In short, when a punishment is certain, and when potential criminal offenders know with certainty that they will be punished if they do a particular act, they are more strongly influenced than if they believe that there is just some chance of being punished, even if the punishment is very severe. Likewise, in order for punishment to have a deterrent effect it needs to be applied swiftly after the crime is committed (or becomes known about). In making a decision about whether or not to do some criminal behavior, a possible punishment that would come months or years later is not very influential on decision making. Here, think of the classic threat of punishment from a mother to her child, "Just wait until your father comes home!" For many children, this is not a realistic threat, as their father may not be home for hours, their mother may forget about their bad behavior, or it just does not seem very realistic that the punishment will actually happen.

The ideas of severity, certainty, and swiftness are all clearly seen in the debate about whether the death penalty is a deterrent to crime. Yes, to be put to death is a severe punishment. But, is it a punishment that will come about with certainty for any crime? No, even for premeditated, first-degree murder the death penalty is far from a certain punishment. And, is the punishment swift? No, it is not at all uncommon for offenders sentenced to death to wait a decade or longer for their punishment to be carried out, if it is carried out at all. With this information, and the understanding that deterrence is most likely when a punishment is certain, swift, and maybe severe, it is not surprising that there is very little evidence to support the argument that the death penalty deters crime.

Contrasting Views

An interesting minority viewpoint states that the primary purpose of punishment is not to change the criminal's behavior, but to reward law-abiding citizens. This "reward" comes in the form of visible evidence (the imprisonment of criminals) that those citizens' way of life is valued. The "reward" is the absence of punishment, and the knowledge that staying within the parameters of the law keeps one away from punishment.

What we have, then, are actually two different purposes or focuses for deterrence. **Specific deterrence** is the preventive effect that a punishment will have on a specific person. When Johnny is imprisoned for three years for assaulting Jimmy, we like to believe that the punishment of prison will "teach Johnny a lesson." That is, he will learn not to assault people again. **General deterrence** is the preventive effect that a punishment will have on all others who observe or have knowledge of the punishment given to a specific offender. So, in our example, general deterrence will be achieved if Johnny's friends and family members realize that they should not assault others if they wish to avoid the punishment that Johnny received.

Specific deterrence: the preventive effect that a punishment will have on a specific person.

General deterrence: the preventive effect that a punishment will have on all others who observe or have knowledge of the punishment given to a specific offender.

Although the majority of people in the field of corrections and in related disciplines in the behavioral sciences do not agree with the theory, deterrence does have some current support. Those who favor deterrence believe that people can learn from punishments both personally experienced and witnessed. In order to believe in deterrence, it is necessary to also believe that all people, both criminals who receive punishment and others who witness punishments being applied, mentally process information in a way that connects the present (punishment being applied), the past (the reason one is being punished), and the future (remembering the punishments given for particular acts and weighing this in any future decisions about committing the acts that are punished). This also means that deterrence can only be achieved if and when crime is the result of free will and individual choices about behavior. If the "true" cause of crime is some biological, psychological, or social setting characteristic of a criminal, punishing that person cannot and will not influence his future behavior. Deterrence can only work if and when there is a decision being actively made by a (potential) criminal. Without free will, deterrence simply cannot be achieved.

Though scientific evidence may never conclusively tell us whether punishment truly prevents crime, the majority of studies and data that are available indicate that punishment is *not* an effective or efficient deterrent.

A major argument against the effectiveness of deterrence focuses on scientific evidence that most criminals simply do not consider the penalties for their crimes. Do robbers, traveling through several states, consult the laws of those states to determine the penalties that might be imposed for their robberies? Do burglars determine in advance the difference between first-degree and second-degree acts of burglary (and their penalties), and do they plan burglaries on that basis? Do rapists choose one victim rather than another because they know the difference between statutory and forcible rape? And, in crimes of passion, which make up the vast majority of homicides, how often do murderers stop to think about whether their state enforces the death penalty?

This is not to say that people never weigh the potential consequences of their actions when deciding what to do. But, for serious, and especially spur-of-the-moment, types of behaviors, active consideration of the likelihood, swiftness, and potential severity of punishment does not appear to be taken into account. And, keep in mind also that many of us simply do not know the likely punishments for many actions. Do you really know the type of punishment you are likely to receive if you steal another student's backpack? What about if you beat them up? The point is, without the information necessary to make informed decisions, how can we expect people to do so? While there may be some importance in the severity of punishment in deterring particular crimes, if people do not know what the punishment is likely to be, they are not likely to be influenced by the threat of such punishment.

In addition to the practical question of whether punishment prevents crime, there may be a more important issue: the ethics of deterrence. This, though, is rarely discussed. If the sanctions (punishments) threatened for breaking laws are to be believed, they must actually be enforced. This issue is not new. Even the "father of deterrence," Jeremy Bentham, recognized the need to actually carry out threatened punishments. Because individuals weigh the cost and benefits of actions, Bentham believed that the severity of the punishment needed is just enough to exceed the severity of the crime. To deter people from criminal acts, the costs of those acts must outweigh the benefits gained, but only somewhat. If punishments are "overly severe," it is likely that such punishments will not be perceived as realistic — we simply would not believe they would be carried out. For instance, consider again the crime of stealing another student's backpack. If you knew that the punishment for such a crime was 50 years in prison, would this seem to you to be realistic and at all likely to be imposed? Most probably not. Hence, you are not that likely to be deterred. Think about how parents punish children. If as a teenager your parents told you that if you came home late (after your curfew), you would be kicked out of the house, they would not help with paying for college, and they would never speak to you again, would this seem realistic to you and ensure that you were home on time? What if instead their threatened punishment was not being able to go to a concert that coming weekend? Which seems realistic and more likely to actually be imposed?

Rehabilitation

The large-scale shift to a rehabilitative or (reformative) attitude toward criminals that came about in the 1960s did not occur because of any one specific event or idea. Perhaps the most influential factor in this change was the large-scale emergence of scientific investigations of crime and punishments.

Today, **rehabilitation** focuses on the efforts to return individuals to their original (supposedly noncriminal) state. In recent American history, the ideology of rehabilitation has relied heavily on the medical model. Just as in early classical views of crime it was believed that there was something "wrong" with an individual that accounted for his criminal behavior, in the medical model approach to criminology it is argued that there is something wrong or different about criminals' bodies, minds, or social contexts that can be identified and then changed (or "cured"). In this way, it is possible to fix, or rehabilitate, persons and thereby remove or reduce the likelihood of that person committing crimes again.Rehabilitation rests on the positivistic explanations of crime; that is, the purpose of corrections is to identify and treat the causes of crime. The rehabilitation movement, then, focuses correctional efforts on medical and psychological treatments and on social skills training, all designed to "correct" the problems that led the individual to crime.

Rehabilitation: the effort to return individuals to their original, supposedly noncriminal, state.

During the 1970s, rehabilitation came under harsh criticism. As the widely known Martinson report[8] most clearly exemplified, nothing really seemed to achieve rehabilitative success. However, because rehabilitation programs had been expensive to develop and implement and because many still believed in rehabilitation, this guiding ideology remained important throughout the 1970s. Even today, neither correctional officials nor the general public[9] has completely discarded a belief in rehabilitation. In fact, governments and private

8. Robert Martinson. 1974. What Works? Questions and Answers About Prison Reform. *The Public Interest,* 42, (22), 22-54.
9. Frank Cullen and K.E. Gilbert. 1982. *Reaffirming Rehabilitation.* Cincinnati: Anderson Publishing Co.

organizations are today returning to a belief in rehabilitation, emphasizing education. The belief today is that a "do nothing" attitude is highly inefficient and perhaps very dangerous (for inmates, correctional employees, and society as a whole). One of the motivations behind this change has included Robert Martinson's claims that his earlier work was flawed and seriously misinterpreted. His retraction and attempts to clarify his earlier work, however, have not been discussed as widely as his original claims.

As the late 1980s and early 1990s, critiques proclaim, the "nothing works" claims were overstated and neglected possible successes given improved inmate classification systems, better refined treatment programs, and more careful matching of offender needs and risks with programs. Today, there are calls for a resurgence of rehabilitative efforts and claims that such a philosophy has not died, but rather was only temporarily displaced during the 1990s and early years of the twenty-first century.

Reintegration

Reintegration: the effort to return individuals to society by reshaping them to better mesh with the structure and expectations of society, with the belief that there is something about the individual that precludes him from fitting into society in a noncriminal way.

The ideology of reintegration is very similar in focus to and often confused with the ideals of rehabilitation. Whereas rehabilitation tries to "fix" individuals so they do not commit future crime, **reintegration** tries to "change" individuals so they can better fit into their communities. The difference here is that there is not something about the individual that is "wrong" and needs to be cured (as is the basis for rehabilitation), but instead the guiding belief is that there is something about the individual that precludes him from fitting into society neatly, cleanly, and in a noncriminal way. So, instead of fixing the person, we need to reshape them so that they better mesh with the structure, flow,and expectations of society. As a result, many correctional efforts geared toward reintegrating offenders in communities rely on community-based corrections, not incarceration. Included here are programs such as home incarceration, intensive supervision probation, and work release programs. (These will be discussed in detail in later chapters.)

Reintegration programs seek to provide offenders with social skills, to teach them positive behaviors, and to assist them in understanding and utilizing community resources. With their focus on preventing recidivism, these programs shape offenders in ways that do not make it necessary (or even attractive) to commit additional crimes. Reintegration programs can also be found in prisons, most likely in the form of pre-release programs. Some prison systems provide soon-to-be-released inmates with special training at pre-release centers for up to 90 days preceding their release. The goals of these programs are to teach inmates the skills they need to successfully adjust to life outside of prison.

Incapacitation

Rehabilitation of criminals and protection of the public go hand in hand. If offenders can be successfully rehabilitated, then the public is that much safer.

However, the philosophy has shifted from a focus on rehabilitating or assisting in reintegrating criminals to efforts designed to ensure the prevention of crime. Rehabilitation and reintegration seek to prevent crime by making changes in and for criminals, but many times our efforts to fix or help such offenders better fit into society are not successful. Therefore, in order to keep society safe, a new philosophy has developed, that of separating criminals from noncriminals, and erecting walls (both literal and figurative) between criminals and those that they could victimize.

The dominant philosophy of the 1980s through the present time has focused on **incapacitation**, or public protection and prevention. We incarcerate offenders for a period of time to protect society from this particular threat for that time period.[10] To incapacitate people is to remove their ability to commit further undesirable acts. This may mean sentencing criminals to prison to prevent their access to those in free society. There, criminals' only potential victims (theoretically) are other criminals. However, because of their status as criminals, these individuals are not defined as real (or, worthy of protection) potential victims. When our society shifted to a goal of separating criminals from free society, prison populations increased rapidly. This trend continues today as more offenders are segregated from society for longer and longer periods of time.

Incapacitation: the primary philosophy of corrections where individuals are incapacitated in order to remove their ability to commit further undesirable acts.

Another way of seeing incapacitation in action, yet outside of the obvious approach of locking individuals up, is in the area of modern sex offender laws. One of the most popular responses to sex offenders in recent years has been the use of sex offender registries, community notification, and residency restrictions laws. The idea here is that by informing the public of the identities and locations of known sex offenders, people can better protect themselves by knowing who to avoid. And, when we add on the additional issue of restricting sex offenders from living in close proximity to schools, day care centers, playgrounds, and other "child congregation locations," the idea is that we are preventing (or at least inhibiting) such offenders from being able to access potential victims. While this may seem logical and beneficial to many people, in fact research suggests that this is not an effective means of achieving public safety.[11]

Just Deserts

A final guiding ideology for corrections is an outgrowth of the perceived failure of the rehabilitation models and increasing rates of crime and violence. This approach is known as the **just deserts model**. The belief here is that criminals should receive punishments equal to the negative experiences they caused society. In some ways, the just deserts model is very similar to the idea of retribution.

Just deserts model: the belief that criminals should receive punishments equal to the negative experiences caused to society by their criminal actions.

10. Gordon Hawkins. 1976. *The Prison: Policy and Practice.* Chicago: University of Chicago Press.

11. Grant Duwe, William Donnay, and Richard Tewksbury. 2008. Does Residential Proximity Matter? A Geographic Analysis of Sex Offense Recidivism. *Criminal Justice and Behavior*, 35, 484-504. Richard Tewksbury and Wesley G. Jennings. 2010. Assessing the Impact of Sex Offender Registration and Community Notification on Sex Offending Trajectories. *Criminal Justice and Behavior*, 37, 570-582.

But, remember that retribution centers on the idea of punishing criminals simply for the sake of imposing punishment. The just deserts model refines this idea and says we need to punish criminals in ways that are proportionate to the harm they have caused to society and other individuals. So, just deserts is more specific than retribution and offers an additional way to justify punishment. Whereas earlier we saw that retribution promotes punishment solely for punishment's sake, just deserts adds an element of general deterrence. That is, not only do criminals deserve to be punished, but also the punishments criminals receive should discourage others from committing similar crimes. Thus, just deserts is a combination of the retribution and deterrence ideologies.

The basic premises of just deserts may be summarized as follows:

1. The mission of the criminal justice system is to reduce crime and delinquency.
2. The best way to achieve this objective is to increase the risk for criminal behavior. This can be best accomplished by enhancing techniques for crime detection, certitude of apprehension, and sentencing.
3. Discretionary devices, such as good-time credits and parole, should be eliminated from the criminal justice system because they are inequitable.
4. Punishment is a valid object of the criminal justice system; people should go to prison *as* punishment.
5. Certitude should prevail over severity, and confinement should be imposed only for offences above a legislatively prescribed degree of serious behavior.
6. Sentences should be for specific and definite periods of time; recidivists should receive increased penalties; the employment of a weapon in an offence should result in an increased, mandatory penalty.
7. Plea bargaining should be eliminated.

Although just deserts may sound harsh, its principles reveal a strong belief in matching punishments to the size and severity of the crime to achieve justice.

Summary

Over the course of history, there have been very large changes in thinking about what types of actions deserve punishment, why punishment is used, and what types of actions are appropriate punishments. For the last three hundred years or more, there have been six basic ideas about the goal of punishment, and each of these ideas has had influences on how governments respond to criminals. These correctional ideologies are retribution, deterrence, rehabilitation, reintegration, incapacitation, and just deserts. Retribution refers to the belief that individuals should be punished because they simply deserve to be punished for the criminal behavior. Deterrence is the use of punishment to keep people from committing more crimes in the future. Rehabilitation is the idea that we should "treat" or try to fix what is wrong with people so that they do not commit more crimes. Reintegration is about working with criminals to help them better fit into society. Incapacitation is the idea of removing someone from society, or making them unable to reach potential victims, thereby eliminating opportunities for crimes to be committed. And, just deserts is the idea that offenders need to receive a punishment equal to the negative impact of their criminal behavior on society.

Key Terms

- Banishment
- Classical view
- Determinate sentences
- Deterrence
- Equality
- Equity
- General deterrence
- Incapacitation
- Indeterminate sentences
- Just deserts model
- Penalty
- Positivistic view
- Punishment
- Rehabilitation
- Reintegration
- Retribution
- Specific deterrence
- Taboos

Chapter Four
History of Corrections

Understanding the history of corrections provides us with not only an understanding of "how things used to be" but also a rationale for why things are structured and done as they are today, and perhaps most importantly, insights into what we want to be sure to avoid doing again. Any study of history is important because, as explained by the American Historical Association,

> [t]he past causes the present, and so the future. Any time we try to know why something happened . . . we have to look for factors that took shape earlier. Sometimes fairly recent history will suffice to explain a major development, but often we need to look further back to identify the causes of change. Only through studying history can we grasp how things change; only through history can we begin to comprehend the factors that cause change; and only through history can we understand what elements of an institution or a society persist despite change.[1]

In the study and practice of corrections, we find that there have been many different approaches to responding to and sanctioning criminals in society. What we do today — primarily incarcerating offenders or monitoring them while they live in the community — are actually fairly recent developments. But, knowing why we do these things, and how the ideas for such practices came to be, is something that requires looking at our previous practices. This includes both those ways of sanctioning criminals that were and those that were not considered

1. American Historical Association. Why Study History? Available at http://www.historians.org/pubs/free/WhyStudyHistory.htm.

to be effective, efficient, or humane. Looking at the history and development of modern corrections also means looking at changes in society at large, developments in social science, evolving ways of thinking about the role of government and religion in society, and technological advances. All of these parts of life are important for understanding how we practice corrections today and why we do what we do.

THE HISTORICAL PERSPECTIVE

As with every social activity, corrections has been influenced by customs, changes, and major social upheavals. We could trace correctional practices all the way back to the very beginning of known history. However, to do so is beyond the scope of this book, and actually doing so would show us little more than the fact that from the beginning of known history up until the 1500s, communities did little more than physically punish (and often simply kill) members who harmed others or who broke the rules of the community. When we first start to see a change in thinking and practice is during the major shift in social systems that arose with the breakdown of the feudal system. Under this community model, a few wealthy landowners lived well and benefitted from the labor and production of serfs, individuals who lived on the wealthy lords' land, worked the land, and lived in a manner only slightly better than slaves. We have already referred to the tight social system of feudal lords and serfs and to the changes that gradually destroyed this system.The breakdown and dissolution of the feudal system in the fifteenth and sixteenth centuries brought about major changes in how people lived and worked, and in who made the rules and laws of a community, as well as how those rules and laws were enforced.In order to understand how criminals were viewed and sanctioned, it is important to recognize that criminals were considered another example of the poor (in many ways not unlike common views today). In 1563, the English Parliament passed a law requiring churches to collect alms. These were to be used for the relief of the poor, the diseased, and the helpless. The mayors of towns were also obliged to collect money for the poor. This legislative act is considered the beginning of the shift in responsibility for the indigent from church to state. At the same time, however, the laws were very repressive. Beggars who were arrested once for loitering could have an ear cut off, and a second arrest for loitering subjected the beggar to hanging and burial in a pauper's grave. In addition, the charitable person who dared to give alms directly to a beggar was subjected to a fine ten times the equivalent of the gift to the beggar.

Corporal punishment: use of physical punishment for those believed to have broken a law.

The widespread use of capital and **corporal punishment**, such as whipping, stoning, or burning, continued from earlier times in the later Middle Ages. Corporal punishment continued in many cultures for centuries, and even today is still common in some countries. In simple terms, physical punishments have been the most common type of punishment administered to lawbreakers throughout all of history. The idea of simply punishing lawbreakers became dominant because it was easily done, was inexpensive, and provided for a quick, supposedly effective, means of attempting to control the behavior of lawbreakers. Punishment was delivered quickly, and there was little need to hold criminals so as to ensure that they would be available to receive their punishment. The first generally used holding facility was a variation of what we call today a jail. At the Assize of Clarendon in 1166, Henry II ordered the construction of a "gaol" in each English county that did not already have one. However, several centuries would pass before anything like a modern prison arrived.

The "First" Penitentiary

English criminal justice officials consider the English house of corrections established at Bridewell in 1557 as the origin of the prison. American correctional officials, in contrast, give that credit to the Walnut Street Jail, which was built in Philadelphia in 1773 and remodeled as a state prison in 1790 by the Pennsylvania Assembly. The first prisons were referred to as **penitentiaries**. Which facility — Bridewell or Walnut Street Jail — was the first penitentiary is less important than the fact that both were developed. The Walnut Street Jail, in any event, was the birthplace of the penitentiary in the United States. Despite its name ("jail"), Walnut Street operated as a prison.

Penitentiaries: the first form of prisons used in the United States, which began in the 1700s and were intended for individuals to do their "penitence."

Forerunners of the Penitentiary

Many historical influences, including religion, architecture, philosophy, and social custom, combined to produce the penitentiary. The penitentiary is basically an American contribution to corrections, not something we inherited from England and Europe. In this regard, we can easily see that American innovation and thinking influenced the rest of the (developed, Western) world.

Before the nineteenth century, to be sent to a penal institution was done not as a punishment, but instead as a way to keep track of criminals' whereabouts and to ensure that they would be available when the time for their actual punishment arrived. Political prisoners were imprisoned, of course, and people were put in jail for failure to pay debts or for religious deviance, but even in these situations being imprisoned was primarily for purposes of awaiting trial, making individuals available for torture, or to keep individuals until their "real" punishment was to be imposed. There is some evidence that suggests imprisonment was occasionally imposed as a punishment during the fourteenth century in Italy[2] and even earlier in England,[3] but not until the nineteenth century were the penitentiary system and conventional sentencing widely used.

---

2. Barnes and Teeters credit Professor Marvin Wolfgang with contributing the information that this occurred in the fourteenth century Florentine prison, Della Stinche. Harry Elmer Barnes and Negley K. Teeters. 1963. *New Horizons in Criminology*, 3d ed. Englewood Cliffs, NJ: Prentice-Hall, Inc., p. 329, footnote 2.

3. Taft and England point out that sentences of imprisonment actually began in the reign of Edward I (1272-1307). Donald R. Taft and Ralph W. England, Jr. 1964. *Criminology*. New York: The Macmillan Company.

The House of Corrections

To deal with the increasing numbers of both adult and child vagrants, houses of corrections were developed. The philosophy and purpose of these institutions were not to punish criminals, but rather to correct people who were not contributing, productive members of society. Therefore, the purpose of the house of corrections was to compel those confined there to perform hard, unpleasant labor, which it was believed would deter crime and convert "lazy," idle, and noncontributing individuals into disciplined, hard workers. Houses of correction were seen in a positive way by wealthier people (those who made the laws and established such institutions) and rapidly spread throughout Europe. Notable houses of corrections were established in Amsterdam in 1596 and at Ghent, Belgium, in 1773. Founded by Jean Jacques Vilain (1717-1777), the Ghent house of correction, known as a **Maison de Force**, is often considered, along with the Hospice of San Michel, as the first institution that evolved to embody the penitentiary idea. In the next sections, we will examine these historical institutions in depth to show how these very first institutions were both similar to and different from our modern prisons.

Maison de Force: located in Ghent, Belgium; institution seen as more progressive that separated felons and misdemeanants in addition to women and children.

The Hospice of San Michel

Hospice of San Michel: located in Rome, Italy; used as the first home for delinquent boys in 1704, where the value of work was central to "correcting" noncontributing members of society into contributing members.

Pope Clement XI established the **Hospice of San Michel** in Rome as the first home for delinquent boys in 1704. This institution was guided by the motto inscribed over its door: "It is insufficient to restrain the wicked by punishment, unless you render them virtuous by corrective discipline." The value of work was central in the Hospice of San Michel and in other houses of correction — remember that the purpose of such places was to "correct" noncontributing members of society and produce contributing members. At the Hospice of San Michel, the guiding belief was that what was needed to reform noncontributing members of society was hard labor and silence.

The Maison de Force

In 1773, 69 years after the opening of the Hospice of San Michel, Vilain opened his house of corrections in Ghent, Belgium. The most significant differences that Vilain introduced in this new, more progressive and innovative institution were: 1. Felons and misdemeanants were separated; and 2. Women and children had separate quarters.

Vilain was both a strict disciplinarian and a kind man. He believed all prisoners should serve at least a year to learn a trade and, thus, be reformed. Believing in individual cells, medical care, productive labor, and consistent discipline, Vilain was strongly opposed to life imprisonment. After all, the idea was that houses of correction changed people, so it was important for them to return to society.

Galley Ships

One innovation in sanctioning both criminal offenders and other undesirable community members that was used in England (and in a few other European nations) was the holding of such individuals on former military and merchant ships, what were called **galley ships**. Such ships would be positioned off shore and offenders placed on them, allowing for easily imposed security (escape would require swimming to shore or having a boat come and pick you up, something easily observed and stopped). Relatively few staff were required to supervise and manage the galley ship, and criminals and their facility were kept largely out of sight.

Galley ships: former military or merchant ships that were used in England to house criminal offenders and other undesirable community members of society that often confined offenders in unsanitary conditions.

While there were clear advantages to incarcerating in this way, there were also some significant problems associated with the practice. Perhaps the most notable problem was that hygiene and health conditions on galley ships were very poor (a not uncommon state on all ships of the time) and when combined with often overcrowded conditions, many of the persons forced to be there died. Horrible living conditions, difficulties maintaining the physical structure of the ships, frequent violence, and high rates of disease and death directly contributed to what we would today call a "public relations problem" and as a result galley ships were eased out of widespread use.

What should be seen here is that some of these ideas that were considered normative and standard for the very first corrections institutions are things that remain in our philosophy and practice today. As you read the later chapters of this text, keep in mind these basic ideas of the world's first corrections institutions and note how some of our modern and "innovative" ideas in corrections today reflect these original, founding ideas.

The Penitentiary Emerges: The Walnut Street Jail

Additional reform and innovation was introduced to corrections institutions by John Howard in the years following the American Revolution. Based on the idea of helping people become better members of society found in earlier efforts, Howard advocated for improved treatment of the poor and criminal. Howard's ideas were first put into practice in the **Walnut Street Jail** in Philadelphia. Here was instituted John Howard's philosophy of separate and silent conditions. Also introduced was a simple classification system that included segregation of the sexes and separation of debtors and witnesses from criminals. In addition, Walnut Street Jail had a simplified form of inmate self-government, productive labor, and a provision for separate housing of hard-core offenders in a block of cells that became known as the "penitentiary house." This model would become one of the two dominant, early models of correctional institution in the United States.

Walnut Street Jail: located in Philadelphia; focused on isolating inmates and placing them in silent conditions based on the direction of reformist John Howard.

The Walnut Street Jail's use of new ideas and techniques attracted observers and scholars from around the world, promoting its foundational ideas for use throughout numerous parts of the world. However, some major problems with the system soon became apparent, including poor architecture, overcrowding, public apathy, and lack of productive work opportunities for inmates. The Philadelphia reformers went back to the state legislature seeking funds to this time erect a penitentiary in which the correctional philosophy of solitary confinement and hard labor could be implemented.

The Pennsylvania System

Pennsylvania system: consisted of the Western and Eastern Penitentiaries in Pennsylvania in the 1800s, where segregation was a central tenet of their organization for inmates being "separate" or "isolate."

Auburn system: developed in 1817 in Auburn, New York; emphasized using inmates for profit-producing labor (also known as "congregate" system).

In response to the funding request, the Pennsylvania legislature authorized funding for the construction of two penitentiaries: one in Philadelphia for the eastern part of the state and the other in Pittsburgh for the western part. Together the two penitentiaries are referred to as the **Pennsylvania system**. The Western Penitentiary (opened in 1826) and Eastern Penitentiary (opened in 1829) both featured rigorously enforced complete segregation of inmates. Hence, the Pennsylvania system is often referred to as the "separate" or "isolate" system. This is in contrast to the so-called **Auburn system** discussed below, which was known as the "congregate" system.

Eastern Penitentiary consisted of seven blocks of outside cells, radiating outward from a central hub like spokes on a wheel, and featured segregation and silence. Each cell had a private exercise yard in which the prisoner had two brief exercise periods daily. Prisoners worked, ate, and slept in their cells; and their only visitors were prison personnel or officials from outside the prison, such as the members of the prison reform society of Philadelphia. Prisoners were blindfolded when first brought to the institution, and their blindfolds were not removed until they were placed in their cells. Inmates were thus prevented from observing other prisoners or the prison's basic architecture. Quickly recognized as a problem, complete isolation was believed to have caused many prisoners to become "incurably insane." As a result, officials soon realized that total isolation was impractical because of both overcrowding and the effects on the prisoners.

The Auburn System

Congregate work: a labor system associated with the "Auburn system." Refers to multiple prisoners in the same room performing work while remaining silent.

In Auburn, New York, in 1817 a penitentiary was opened that differed in several important ways from the Pennsylvania system. By accident, the inside cells were too small for inmates to use spinning wheels and other vocational equipment, such as was common in Pennsylvania. **Congregate work** (work performed by several prisoners in the same room) was therefore necessary in order for the prison to have any financial income. However, while inmates were brought together to work, silence was still enforced on inmates at all times. Here the infamous lockstep was instituted to make supervision of inmates easier. By requiring inmates to walk — actually march — in unison, while holding the shoulder of the inmate in front of them, staff could easily detect troublemakers and those who might require discipline.

The idea of bringing inmates together to work and produce products to be sold on the market was clearly very successful at Auburn. By 1828, the administrators at Auburn informed the state legislature that they would not need financial appropriations from the state, as inmates were producing sufficiently to be able to pay for the prison's expenses.[4]

---

4. Samuel Walker. 1998. *Popular Justice: A History of American Criminal Justice.* New York: Oxford University Press.

The Auburn model was seen as advantageous for other reasons as well. First, the system was seen as more efficient in that the physical construction of the prison could have more than one floor of cells. Whereas in the Pennsylvania system all cells had to have their own outdoor area for inmates to access, in the Auburn system inmates left their cells, so they could be taken outside in groups. Therefore cells could be stacked on top of one another, as floors in a building. Auburn was also considered superior to Pennsylvania because prisoners were less likely to become sick or deteriorate physically. This was largely due to getting exercise outside of their cells, and to the mental stimulation that accompanied interaction (such as it was) with facility staff and other inmates. Finally, cells in the Auburn style institution could be smaller, as they did not have to accommodate tools and materials for the inmates to do work and produce goods to sell.

Modern U.S. prisons are more closely modeled on the Auburn system than the Pennsylvania system. However, the idea of a correctional institution in which all inmates are completely segregated from one another and communications between inmates are prohibited — as was the case with the Pennsylvania prison system — has made a return to American corrections in the last two decades. Today, prisons where inmates are always kept completely apart, never communicate with one another, and only have a very small fenced-in outdoor area to access on occasion are referred to as supermax prisons. Here we see that one of our "new" and innovative ideas is actually a resurrection of a very old concept.

After Auburn and Pennsylvania

A number of changes have occurred in the design and operation of American prisons since the early development of the Pennsylvania and Auburn systems. While the Auburn model has been most influential, we have moved away from many of the central ideas of such a model. While American prisons generally still rely on congregate work and programming arrangements, the idea of silence and individual housing is only used in a few prison units in the United States.

The idea of imposing silence on inmates — so that they could not communicate and therefore teach one another criminal ways — was simply too difficult to enforce. While silence was sometimes maintained, prisoners developed ways to communicate by gestures and tapping out messages in code, and at other times they simply openly ignored the rule against speaking, especially when in work areas. Auburn officials tried their best to enforce silence though, and even went so far as to effectively lobby the state legislature in 1819 to authorize whipping of inmates as a form of punishment (used primarily to enforce silence).[5]

One of the major changes that became common starting during the era of emphasis on rehabilitation has been the development and proliferation of specialized institutions. Today, prisons are designed for the different security needs of inmates, as well as their different programming needs (mental health,

---

5. *Ibid.*

substance abuse, sex offender treatment). Though this has defined prisons for several decades, other important developments include an evolving degree of emphasis on either treatment or punishment; introduction of educational and recreational activities; community interaction on a much larger scale than the early Pennsylvania prison reformers could have imagined; and physically larger living spaces with more ventilation and light.

The Reformatory Movement

Reformatory: designed as a modification of the penitentiary, where inmates would take an active role to be "reformed" instead of the passive role emphasized by previous ideologies.

In addition to the early models of the Pennsylvania and Auburn systems of penitentiaries, a third model developed in the late 1800s, also in New York. This model, the **reformatory**, instituted one of the most important changes in U.S. corrections. No longer would prisons be based on the idea of trying to change offenders' behaviors by isolating them from one another and hoping that through penitence they would realize the errors of their ways and make changes in their thinking and behavior. Representing an ideological change regarding corrections, the reformatory was designed as a modification of the penitentiary. As such, the ideology shifted from believing that inmates should be passive and contemplate their wrongdoings to believing that inmates should be active and be "reformed." With the reformatory came the first real organized effort of state officials to actually intervene with offenders and "correct" them.

Opened in 1877, Elmira Reformatory was designed to house first-time offenders between the ages of 16 and 30. These were the criminals who were thought to be the most likely to be able to be "changed." However, the original plans for Elmira were never completely fulfilled. Because of overcrowding and the large numbers of sentenced offenders who were recidivists, about one-third of Elmira's inmates were repeat offenders. Unfortunately, as seen with many plans and ideas throughout American correctional history, the realities of crime, budgets, and politics interfered with plans and required modifications to the original idea.

The idea behind the reformatory was that for inmates to change, they needed to be educated, to know the value of hard work, and to learn to work to achieve personal goals. In pursuit of these objectives, the Elmira Reformatory operated on principles very different from those of the Pennsylvania or Auburn systems. First, the idea of isolation was removed and inmates were grouped according to their progress in educational and work programs. This led to the second major difference in Elmira: the earning of "marks" (or points) for achievements. Inmates earned marks in order to gain more privileges and to eventually earn their release from prison. In this way, inmates were provided with an incentive to work at their programs and jobs and to achieve progress and change. However, earning their release was not a possibility if sentences were for fixed periods of time, so the reformatory concept required the use of indeterminate sentences instead. It was (and still is) believed that only with the incentive of earning release could inmates be motivated to truly improve themselves.

The reformatory idea was generally judged a success, at least in its early years. By 1913, 37 years after Elmira opened, 18 other states had opened reformatories, based on their observation and belief that such a model was preferable to that of the Pennsylvania or Auburn system. Additionally, the reformatory model was seen as advantageous because it placed an emphasis on education and work for the individual inmate, rather than on industry that would benefit the prison. Whereas the Pennsylvania and Auburn systems focused on inmates producing goods for sale (to offset expenses), Elmira's officials focused on activities that would improve the inmates, making them less likely to return to prison. In this way, the reformatory idea focused on reducing expenses in the long term, although the short-term costs were higher than for the other systems.

At the same time as the founding of the reformatory in Elmira, there also came to be prisons designed specifically for women. The first woman to enter a prison designed and operated exclusively for women was Sally Hubbard, who entered the Indiana Woman's Prison on October 8, 1873.[6] Prior to the opening of prisons specifically for women, the few women who were convicted and sentenced to incarceration were held in men's prisons, but in separate quarters or buildings. Even though correctional officials worked to keep the male and female inmates separate, this did not always happen. Perhaps the most obvious example of the fact that the sexes intermixed is seen in the fact that in the Georgia prison for women at least 25 illegitimate children were found to be living with their mothers following birth in prison resulting from sex between inmates.[7]

Basically, incarceration of women inmates occurred in four distinct phases. First, there was the period during which women were held in the general population along with men. Then, they were removed to a separate room or wing in a men's prison. The third era saw separate buildings constructed for the housing of women, and finally, starting with the opening of the Indiana Woman's Prison, separate institutions were constructed.[8] The specific development of correctional institutions and programs for women will be discussed in more detail in Chapter 9.

Southern Prisons

In addition to the penitentiaries of the Pennsylvania system and the reformatory movement developing out of the Auburn system, there was also a different model of prison development that was common in the Southern states. Prior to the American Civil War, Southern states relied on penitentiaries for sanctioning criminal offenders, just as was the norm in the Northern states. During the

6. *Ibid.*
7. Edward L. Ayers. 1984. *Vengeance and Justice: Crime and Punishment in the Nineteenth-Century American South.* New York: Oxford University Press.
8. Nicole Rafter Hahn. 1985. *Partial Justice: Women in State Prisons, 1800-1935.* Boston: Northeastern University Press.

Civil War (1861-1865), there was a sharp change in how corrections operated. During the war, concerns about crime and punishing criminals were secondary thoughts. One of the most common sentences for criminals during this period was conscription in the army. But, whereas following the end of the Civil War the Northern prison systems remained much as they had been previously, being largely designed to facilitate work in an industrial setting, in Southern prisons there was a distinctively different development. In the South, the Civil War meant the end of slavery, and hence there was a large need for laborers to complete the work that previously had been done by slaves. Corrections was identified as a way to fill this void. This meant that Southern states largely abandoned penitentiaries (in some places because they were essentially destroyed during the war) and instead established and followed a system of corrections referred to as the **leasing system**.

Leasing system: a work system of inmates that emerged in the mid-1800s, where convicts were rented out to nearby businesses to engage in profit-making labor for the respective state.

Following the Civil War, there was a huge increase in crime in the Southern states. Not surprisingly, the vast majority of these reported crimes were committed by former slaves (who were quickly apprehended and convicted). Although it can easily be argued that there really was not a crime wave occurring, but the criminal justice system was just used as an alternative way to commit former slaves to the same labor they had previously done, our concern here is with the effects of this "crime wave" on corrections. Corrections, with as high as a 95 percent former slave population, did not have many prisons or other facilities in which to house criminals, and therefore needed an alternative way to manage such offenders.

Here the convict leasing system came into being. Under this approach, corrections provided a pool of workers that private industrialists or landowners were able to lease from the state. Just as today you can lease a car, furniture, or a piece of electronics, in the final four decades of the nineteenth century people who needed cheap labor could lease bodies from the state. This idea had been used in some Northern states, but in those cases employers (private contractors) leased the labor of convicts, and did not necessarily take the inmates away from the physical confines of the prison. However, leasing as it developed in the South following the Civil War operated such that when an employer leased convicts, it took responsibility for feeding, housing, caring for, and securing them. The inmates were literally picked up and taken from the state and put to work, typically on plantations or in projects rebuilding the infrastructure of the South. For many former slaves, they were returned to if not the exact same type of work they previously did, to at least very similar conditions and work. Here we see the origin of the phrase that following the Civil War in the American South, prison became a "functional replacement for slavery."

The leasing system was justified on five major reasons and contributions. First, it provided an effective way to handle a large and quickly growing correctional population. Second, it filled a need for cheap labor for Southerners. Third, the state was essentially freed from the obligation of providing for inmates and therefore did not have to be concerned with the conditions or treatment of such offenders. This was important as a way to save money. Fourth, the leasing system was advocated as a way to teach offenders job skills. As they were taken and put to work by employers or landowners, they would learn the skills of the trades they were compelled to do. And, fifth, the leasing system facilitated profits for Southern businesses, which in turn sped up the recovery of the Southern states following the Civil War.

The convict leasing system, however, was an exceptionally brutal system. Contractors leasing convicts were largely unmonitored for how they housed, fed, worked, and generally treated leased convicts. And, as leasing was done so as to secure a cheap labor force, few contractors were interested in spending more than the absolute minimum on caring for leased convicts. Housing was typically overcrowded, with poor hygiene and health conditions; food was minimal; and conditions often were described as significantly worse than what had been known by slaves. In some states, the officially reported mortality rates for leased convicts reached 25 percent,[9] and this is likely an underreported figure.

The work for which convicts were leased included mining, building railroads, and of course agricultural work (doing the work that slaves had previously done). Work was forced, and leased convicts who did not work hard enough, fast enough, or with the "right attitude" were subject to harsh punishments. Often the punishments given to leased convicts were worse than those that had been used with slaves. With slaves, to punish in such a way as to injure meant that one was decreasing the value of one's property. With leased convicts, if injury meant they were unable to work, the contractor would just return the convict to the state, essentially losing nothing in the process. Housing was in the mines, or in railroad cars, or in the housing formerly used by slaves (but now neglected for many years).

The convict leasing system obviously had a number of problems and by the 1920s had largely been ended. In its place, Southern states developed large, agriculturally based prisons, modeled on the well-known plantation system that had characterized the South during the slavery era. In this model, states operated large farming operations, as a way to make prisons largely economically self-sufficient and to hopefully produce at least some income. At the extreme, such prison farms were massive endeavors, such as the more than 20,000-acre Parchman Farm in Mississippi or the Louisiana State Penitentiary at Angola, both of which are in the sweltering Mississippi River Delta. In these prisons, there were actually multiple "camps" or prisons, each operating largely independently. As economic considerations were driving the development of such institutions, states were anxious to do all they could to limit their costs. One of the best ways found to control costs was to limit the number of employees at the institutions. In order to do this, however, some convicts had to be trusted to do the work of staff, and this gave birth to the inmate trustee system. Such inmates were given responsibility to oversee work crews of inmates and housing areas, and they were rewarded (in many different ways, some of which were

---

9. Joseph F. Spillane and David B. Wolcott. 2013. *A History of Modern American Criminal Justice*. Los Angeles: Sage.

undoubtedly illegal) for keeping production up and problems down. Over time trustees were even entrusted with firearms so as to ensure their authority and ability to control other inmates. As you might suspect, this system spawned numerous abuses, and the brutality that had characterized the leasing system was transferred to the plantation prisons.

One alternative to the large-scale plantation prisons in the South that built on the basic ideas of the leasing system was the development of the chain gang. Here prisoners did not work on the massive farms, but instead on smaller road camps scattered throughout the state. These groups of convicts were moved throughout the state, largely rebuilding the infrastructure (including roads, one of the most common types of projects for chain gangs) that had been destroyed in the Civil War. Chain gangs were groups ("gangs") of inmates that were kept chained together at all times. This was done to prevent escapes. If a group of men were all chained together by leg irons, it would be all but impossible for them to run away. Here the notorious use of prison striped uniforms became most famous. Chain gangs provided a means for states (and often cities and counties) to get public works completed at a very low cost.

What we see very clearly in the development and evolution of Southern prisons is that economics, not correctional ideologies or political concerns, were the driving force behind decisions. This is not uncommon in American corrections. As we know, corrections can be hugely expensive, and politicians and correctional administrators have always been charged with attempting to limit expenses. The Southern experience is simply one, albeit very obvious, example of this practice.

BEGINNING OF THE MODERN ERA OF CORRECTIONS

The beginning of the modern era of American corrections is generally identified as the 1870 meeting in Cincinnati of the National Prison Congress. Here prison administrators, legislators, and others involved in prisons met to discuss best practices and how to set up prisons. The first president of this group was Rutherford B. Hayes, the Ohio Governor and later the nineteenth President of the United States. The National Prison Congress is influential through two legacies. First, this organization is the original incarnation of what today is the American Correctional Association, the nation's leading professional organization for and of corrections officials. Second, at the 1870 meeting the National Prison Congress put together a list of 37 guiding principles and values that would serve to guide the development of corrections.

Among the "new" ideas introduced in the Declaration of Principles from the 1870 National Prison Congress were:

> . . . 2. The treatment of criminals by society is for the protection of society. But since such treatment is directed to the criminal rather than to the crime, its great object should be his moral regeneration. Hence the supreme aim of prison discipline is the reformation of criminals, not the infliction of vindictive suffering.

> 3. The progressive classification of prisoners, based on character and worked on some well-adjusted mark system, should be established in all prisons above the common jail.
>
> 4. Since hope is a more potent agent than fear, it should be made an ever-present force in the minds of prisoners, by a well-devised and skillfully-applied system of rewards for good conduct, industry and attention to learning. Rewards, more than punishments, are essential to every good prison system. . . .
>
> 7. Special training, as well as high qualities of head and heart, is required to make a good prison or reformatory officer. Then only will the administration of public punishment become scientific, uniform and successful, when it is raised to the dignity of a profession, and men are specially trained for it, as they are for other pursuits. . . .
>
> 9. Of all reformatory agencies, religion is first in importance, because most potent in its action upon the human heart and life.
>
> 10. Education is a vital force in the reformation of fallen men and women. Its tendency is to quicken the intellect, inspire self-respect, excite to higher aims, and afford a healthful substitute for low and vicious amusements. Education is, therefore, a matter of primary importance in prisons, and should be carried to the utmost extent consistent with the other purposes of such institutions. . . .
>
> 14. The prisoner's self-respect should be cultivated to the utmost, and every effort made to give back to him his manhood. There is no greater mistake in the whole compass of penal discipline, than its studied imposition of degradation as a part of punishment. Such imposition destroys every better impulse and aspiration. It crushes the weak, irritates the strong, and indisposes all to submission and reform. It is trampling where we ought to raise, and is therefore as unchristian in principle as it is unwise in policy. . . .
>
> 19. Prisons, as well as prisoners, should be classified or graded so that there shall be prisons for the untried, for the incorrigible and for other degrees of depraved character, as well as separate establishments for women, and for criminals of the younger class. . . .
>
> 28. The proper duration of imprisonment for a violation of the laws of society is one of the most perplexing questions in criminal jurisprudence. The present extraordinary inequality of sentences for the same or similar crimes is a source of constant irritation among prisoners, and the discipline of our prisons suffers in consequence. The evil is one for which some remedy should be devised. . . .
>
> 37. This congress is of the opinion that, both in the official administration of such a system, and in the voluntary co-operation of citizens therein, the agency of women may be employed with excellent effect.

Note how each of these ideas that were considered innovative and progressive nearly 150 years ago remain with us today. Each of the ideas continues to guide what corrections is and how we believe we should conduct correctional practices. History is important, for showing us how we both can and should conduct ourselves.

DEVELOPMENT OF ALTERNATIVES TO INCARCERATION

Probation: alternative to incarceration where offenders are kept in the community under the close watch and supervision of an agency and are provided access to programs and services with the intended purpose of bringing change in their behavior.

While imprisonment became a more popular mode of punishment for lawbreakers in the nineteenth and twentieth centuries, during this period there was also a growing recognition that such punishment might not be the most appropriate or most beneficial sanction for all offenders. However, rather than to revert to earlier ways of more physical or barbaric punishments, progressive thinkers sought ways both to more closely monitor the behavior of offenders and also to try to bring about change in their thinking and behavior. This gave rise to the idea of **probation** — keeping criminal offenders in the community, but closely watching them and helping them to access programs and services that are believed to help bring about change in behavior. The formal development of probation, including creating it as an actual sentence to be given by a court, was developed in the middle of the nineteenth century.

Prior to the development of "real" probation, there were some efforts by various courts that served as forerunners of probation. Each of these alternative ways of responding to criminals has some of the ideas of probation as we know it today, but also some important differences. There are three important predecessors of probation: benefit of clergy, judicial reprieve, and filing of cases. Each procedure will be discussed briefly to illustrate the developmental process that led to what today we call probation.

Benefit of Clergy

Although its origin is unknown, benefit of clergy began in the thirteenth century, when clergymen who were found guilty of crimes could have their cases transferred to church tribunals for sentencing. In essence, clergy received the benefit of having the church handle their sanction rather than the community or government. This is in large part a reflection of the larger role that the church played in society in earlier times. Whereas today church law mainly governs its members' religious affairs and pertains to a particular denomination, in medieval Europe canon or ecclesiastical law was as important as civil law.

Benefit of clergy indirectly resulted from the monarchy's increasing power and a struggle between the civil government and church for who would be responsible for controlling the behavior of church representatives. Henry II insisted that clerics who violated the secular laws be tried in the civil courts, but the church argued that its representatives should be subject to church law and processing. Benefit of clergy was a compromise and, of course, actually a benefit to the offender. Though the church could impose severe penance, whatever the sanction was that was given to the offender was undoubtedly more tolerable than the most common civil penalty of the time — hanging. Benefit of clergy remained a common practice for several centuries, and even followed the colonists to the American colonies. However, shortly after the American Revolution, the emerging American government took control of sanctions of all offenders, including clergy.

Judicial Reprieve

At the foundation of a modern sentence of probation is the suspension of a sentence. This means that a court actually levies a sentence of imprisonment on an offender, but holds off on imposing the sentence and instead provides the convicted offender an opportunity to remain in the community. If the offender does not refrain from crime or abide by all conditions and restrictions placed upon him, the offender can have his probation revoked and instead have to serve the sentence of imprisonment originally given by the court. Historians have traced suspension of sentence to the judicial reprieve that English courts used. A **suspended sentence** is simply withholding imposition of a sentence for a period of time. Judicial reprieve was a temporary suspension that permitted the defendant to petition the Crown for full or partial pardon. In simple terms, this was the way of appealing one's conviction and allowing the offender not to suffer the pains of punishment while pursuing this option. Judicial reprieve first involved only a postponement of a sentence, but over time developed to the point where many suspended sentences were not re-imposed. Basically, judicial reprieve was a reliance on the court's discretionary power. In a way, judicial reprieve was similar to probation in that the offender was still convicted, but did not have to serve time in prison.

Suspended sentence: the act of withholding the imposition of a sentence for a certain period of time if the offender meets specific conditions set forth by a judge.

Filing of Cases

Massachusetts developed an unusual form of reprieve: A sentence could be suspended and a case "filed." Filing a case required both the defendant's and prosecutor's consent, and the judge could set conditions to which the defendant was subject. The primary objective of this practice was to lessen the penalty, which reflected the courts' willingness to recognize extenuating circumstances. The suspension of a sentence, conditional release, and the imposition of conditions are also characteristic of today's versions of probation. However, unlike probation, no court-appointed official supervised the offender.

FOUNDING OF PROBATION

The American founder of probation, **John Augustus**, was 57 and a very successful Boston boot maker when he became interested in court activities in 1841. In his spare time, Augustus enjoyed spending time in court, watching the proceedings. Since major changes were also taking place in the British courts at the same time, evolution was occurring simultaneously on both sides of the Atlantic. Seeing a bedraggled man appear for sentencing on a common drunk charge, Augustus was drawn to the unfortunate man. Augustus talked with the offender for a few moments and was so impressed that he asked the court to release the man to his care rather than sentencing him to the house of correction. As Augustus saw the situation, to put the man in jail would do no good. Instead Augustus believed that he could work with the man, help him out, and in the

John Augustus: the "American founder of probation," who asked a Boston judge to release a man suffering from alcoholism into his care rather than sentencing him to the house of correction, thus giving birth to the concept of probation.

end have a better shot at getting him sober and out of crime than the state could by simply locking him up for a period of time. In describing this experience, Augustus first used the word "probation."[10] Therefore, Augustus is known as the "father of probation."

After Augustus's first effort at working with individual offenders in place of seeing the court send such men to jail or prison when they did not need to be there, he sought to work with more petty offenders, and eventually drew other volunteers into such work. Extending his labors, Augustus became almost a fixture in the Boston lower courts. By 1858, he had bailed out 1,152 men and boys, and 794 women and girls, and he had also helped 3,000 neglected women.[11] Of the first 1,100 on whom Augustus kept records, only one individual forfeited bond. His work was remarkable, and his compassion was desperately needed, for the times were heavily oriented toward punishment. Among the people Augustus helped were a 10-year-old who had been charged with highway robbery for keeping 6 cents that belonged to a friend and a 7-year-old child who had been charged with rape. However, even though today we regard John Augustus favorably, this was not necessarily the way he was viewed during his lifetime. The press's initial coverage of his actions and the public's reaction were not favorable. Augustus was criticized for being too easy on criminals and for preventing them from being properly punished.

John Augustus died in 1859, leaving a legacy that would have a lasting impact on the course of U.S corrections. However, he did not live to see his work become a permanent part of the U.S. criminal justice system. Not until 1878 did Massachusetts pass the first state probation law, which began the slow spread of probation.

In fact, it was not until the development of the juvenile court system in 1899 that probation became popular in the United States. The new juvenile court system emphasized reforming delinquents. Many people recognized the importance of keeping juvenile offenders with their families; and the way to accomplish this, while also providing an active role for the courts and criminal justice system, was to use probation. After probation became relatively common for juveniles, the process slowly spread to adult corrections. Not until 1956 did all the states have adult probation programs in place.

Today, probation is the most common sentence for criminal convictions in the United States. This figure includes all criminal convictions; when we look just at felony convictions we see that "only" 19 percent of felony convictions result in a sentence of probation.[12] Probation is a sentencing option for essentially all criminal offenses, even, in some states and in some circumstances, homicide. Whereas probation began in the United States with the assistance

---

10. John Augustus. 1852. *A Report of the Labors of John Augustus, for the Last Ten Years, In Aid of the Unfortunate.* Boston: Wright & Hasty.

11. Walker, supra n.4.

12. Sean Rosenmerkel, Matthew Durose, and Donald Farole, Jr. 2009. *Felon Sentences in State Courts, 2006.* Washington, D.C.: Bureau of Justice Statistics.

of volunteers, today probation is among the largest employers in corrections. And, there are more persons on probation than in prison and jail combined.

Origins of Parole

Parole has been part of the U.S. criminal justice system since the late 1870s. **Parole** is the practice of releasing an offender from incarceration prior to the expiration of his sentence and supervising the offender in the community. Once the offender is released from prison, he is treated very similarly to the ways that offenders on probation are supervised. And, parole, also just like probation, can be revoked and the offender returned to prison for the remaining portion of his sentence if he commits a new crime or violates any of the conditions of release. As originally conceived and practiced in the United States, parole was determined by a panel of reviewers (a parole board) who reviewed the details of an offender's offense and how he spent his time in prison, and attempted to determine whether the offender was sufficiently rehabilitated to merit return to the community. This was a discretionary decision that was made once the offender had completed the minimum length of time on an indeterminate sentence. Today, some states continue to use this model of parole and decision making while others have transitioned to a model whereby parole is more or less automatic after a certain percentage of one's sentence is served, and unless the offender does something while incarcerated to demonstrate that he is not appropriate for return to the community, he will be paroled.

Parole: the practice of releasing an offender from incarceration prior to the expiration of his sentence and supervising the offender in the community.

What we know as parole in today's world, though, is not what its founders originally envisioned or what they first developed. In all likelihood, what we know as parole today will not be the same in another decade or two. However, the practice for modifying or lessening the sentences given to criminals has a long history in Western civilization. Parole in the United States originated out of adherence to the ideology of rehabilitation, and was established as a way to encourage inmates to actively work on changing and improving themselves and their behaviors. In this regard, parole was an incentive for inmates to work toward. However, in the years following the demise of the dominance of the rehabilitation ideology, when prison populations soared and overcrowding became a major administrative problem in corrections, parole evolved into a tool for administrators to use in attempting to control institutional populations. Here parole became more or less a safety valve that could be opened and closed to limit the number of inmates in a particular institution.

Interestingly, the concern with controlling overcrowded institutions was at the core of the issues behind the original development of parole. In sixteenth- and seventeenth-century England, there were significant concerns about overcrowded conditions in the jails and prisons of the era. The galley ships that had been used for centuries had lost their popularity, largely because of the terrible conditions on the ships. After the American colonies declared their independence in 1776, the British could no longer banish criminals to the colonies and had to seek other solutions to their problem. Shortly after the American Revolution, the British started to transport convicts to Australia, which had been discovered by Captain Cook in 1770. Although this was not a form or predecessor of parole, the transition to banishment to Australia set the stage for the development of parole.

Alexander Maconochie

Ticket of leave: the practice originating in the Norfolk Island penal colony near modern-day Australia where convicts were excused from their work assignments by the governor to live relatively independent lives as an incentive toward which convicts could work.

Marks system: the practice of inmates accumulating points for earning or losing privileges with the goal of easing convicts' transition from closely supervised custody to freedom.

The conditions in the Australian penal colonies, like any correctional setting of the era, were never considered very good. Because of the awful conditions, the penal colony residents were often very brutal and very difficult to control and discipline. One innovative method was developed to control these convicts: The **ticket of leave**, originally used at the Norfolk Island penal colony, allowed the governor to excuse convicts from work assignments and to live relatively independent lives. It is interesting that the Norfolk Island penal colony was actually located about a thousand miles off the eastern coast of Australia and was the place for the "worst of the worst." As a means to try to rehabilitate such offenders, the ticket of leave was created to serve as an incentive toward which convicts could work. The thought was that holding out the goal of basically earning their freedom would make convicts more willing to cooperate and follow orders. However, even if they were able to earn such freedom of movement and were allowed to establish their own homes, they continued to be restricted to particular geographic areas for their residence and movements. Alexander Maconochie, who became governor of the Norfolk Island penal colony in 1840, modified how tickets of leave were used, though he did not actually first develop the idea.[13]

Maconochie is best known for developing and putting into practice a five-stage program that included the ticket of leave and **marks system**. The use of marks is similar to the accumulation of points for earning (or losing) privileges. The goal of the marks system was to ease convicts' transition from closely supervised custody to freedom. Prisoners earned their marks by fulfilling their work assignments or doing good deeds, and the marks could be used to cut time off the end of their sentences. Previously, the issuance of a ticket of leave was wholly discretionary, where the governor of the penal colony had total control and could basically make any decision he saw fit.

A ticket of leave was not a complete release from supervision and restrictions, however. When offenders were released on tickets of leave, they did have to abide by three general conditions. First, the ticket of leave was a conditional privilege. This meant that if offenders were found to have engaged in any form of misconduct, their tickets of leave could either be revoked or the specific conditions of the ticket could be made stricter. Second, not only did offenders have

[13] David Dressler. 1969. *Practice and Theory of Probation and Parole*, 2d ed. New York: Columbia University Press, p. 61.

the constant threat of losing their privileges, but they also had to prove, throughout the period of their leaves, that they were deserving of keeping them. This condition reminded offenders that their tickets of leave were never to be considered permanent. Rather, convicts had to continually strive to remain in the good graces of authorities and to constantly demonstrate that they deserved to be allowed the ticket of leave. Third and finally, revocation of their tickets of leave did not require convictions for new crimes. All the authorities had to do was to show that individuals were leading lives likely to lead to crime. Such discretionary revocation powers meant that if the supervising authorities believed the offenders were not supporting themselves or were associating with "bad characters," they could simply pull the offenders back into custody.

As we can see, the ticket of leave operated much like parole in the United States does today. Both a ticket of leave and parole are privileges, both are earned through one's behavior and programming while incarcerated, and both are readily revocable. The ticket of leave, while obviously a forerunner to our contemporary system of parole, was not the only predecessor practice to influence American corrections, however.

Sir Walter Crofton

The head of the Irish prison system, Sir Walter Crofton, was perhaps even more influential in the development of parole than Maconochie was with his ticket of leave process. Crofton's system, which became known as the "Irish system," had a very strong, and direct, influence on American correctional authorities and was the actual foundation on which parole was developed in the United States.

Crofton's system was a modification of the Maconochie ticket of leave. The development of the Irish system was possible because of two related developments. Australian citizens, like the American colonists, became increasingly resentful of the English for dumping unwanted criminals in their country. By threatening to revolt against England, the Australians finally brought an end in 1857 to the British practice of **transportation**. When England no longer had a place to send its criminal convicts, it needed to develop a new way to handle the large number of convicts whom the courts sentenced.

Transportation: the British practice that ended in 1857 of sending convicts to Australia and other colonies as punishment.

Crofton's "intermediate system" helped with this problem. A notable innovation, the intermediate system involved the community and used an official parole officer to supervise offenders released to the community. Under the Irish system, any inmate released early had to conform to six conditions:

1. Report immediately to local law enforcement officials when arriving in their destination, and continue to do so weekly.
2. Refrain from any and all violations of the law.
3. Refrain from regular association with "bad characters" in the community.
4. Work and be able to provide for oneself and one's dependents.

5. Produce the "ticket of leave" (e.g., paperwork) when requested by any court or law enforcement officer.
6. Not change residences without reporting such a move to law enforcement.

PAROLE IN THE UNITED STATES

Some historians believe that indenture, putting a person in the service of a master for a specified period of time (similar to contracting with someone to be a slave for a particular period of time), was the American version of a forerunner of parole. Usually, indentured servants entered into such agreements to learn trades or sets of skills. Some believe indenture was a predecessor of parole because the activities of indentured individuals were very restricted, and their social and recreational activities as well as their work habits were regulated.

Good-time laws: the shortening of an inmate's sentence in exchange for good behavior; a forerunner of parole in the United States.

An important and necessary legal development that also served as a forerunner of parole in the United States was **good-time laws**. First used in 1817 in the state of New York, good-time laws were legislatively created laws that gave prison officials the power to shorten an individual inmate's sentence in exchange for good behavior. All that this did was shorten the time until release from prison; when an inmate had his sentence shortened he left at the expiration of the new (e.g., shorter) time and was a completely free individual. This meant that when inmates were released and left prisons, they were not supervised in any way. Lack of continuing supervision and full discretionary power of wardens and other officials (with no rules or limits on their power) are what distinguishes good-time release from the modern practice of parole.

The contemporary U.S. version of parole is based on three concepts:

1. Reducing the length of incarceration as a reward for good conduct.
2. Supervising offenders' release from custody.
3. Using indeterminate sentences.

Indeterminate sentences: sentences that prescribe a minimum and maximum period of time to serve in a correctional program.

A second legal development, the move away from fixed periods of time as sentences to a range of a minimum and maximum period of incarceration, what we call an **indeterminate sentence**, was also a development necessary for parole to come into being. An indeterminate sentence is one that has a minimum and maximum length, and the court transfers authority to the correctional system to determine exactly how much of the maximum sentence length each individual offender needs to serve. Therefore, the United States had to enact statutory laws that allowed indeterminate sentencing before parole could become a reality. In 1869, the first indeterminate sentence statutes were enacted in Michigan and New York. However, the Michigan statute was challenged in court and found to be a violation of the state constitution. This considerably slowed the development and spread of parole.

The New York statute allowed Zebulon Brockway, the warden at the new Elmira Reformatory, to discontinue the use of good-time laws and instead to give inmates specific criteria that he would use in determining when they would be released during the span of their sentences. Under Brockway's system, inmates were graded on their overall conduct, performance at work assignments, progress in mandatory education programs, and personal adjustment. In this way, Brockway borrowed the earliest idea of marks, which placed the responsibility of earning release directly on the individual offenders.

Specific legal and institutional developments preceded parole, but the actual origin of parole in the United States is found in two basic prison reform movements. First was the belief that good conduct in prison should be rewarded by the reduction of the length of a sentence. That release could be revoked if offenders did not continue their good behavior once they were returned to the community. The second major influential movement was the development of volunteer prisoner aid societies. Prisoner aid societies were originally developed to provide food, fuel, and clothing ("aid") to colonial jail inmates who had no family or friends to provide them with supplies. When jails and prisons began providing the basic necessities to inmates, prisoner aid societies slowly turned their attentions to assisting released inmates. Courts assigned volunteers to supervise and assist offenders released from prison. For several decades, supervision of offenders in the community relied exclusively on volunteers. Not until 1845 was the first publicly paid employee hired in Massachusetts to assist released offenders in readjusting to the community.

Supposedly, the guiding ideology for using parole is rehabilitation. Under indeterminate sentencing, inmates are presumed to want to work to achieve release. The way to achieve this privilege is to actively participate in treatment programs and to change one's ways. This may be the ideal. In reality, parole (in fact, all forms of early release) today has become a way to control overcrowding and financial problems in prisons. (Recall the discussion above about economics influencing correctional decisions.) While the rehabilitation focus has not been abandoned, it is no longer the driving force behind parole. However, even though the reasons for using such forms of release may have changed, parole has remained a common practice in the United States, although it is now typically not based on discretionary decisions.

Parole is not the only way that inmates are released from prison before the end of their sentences. Today, more common than parole are **mandatory early release programs**. Such programs are much more focused on meeting the needs of prisons, not inmates and their rehabilitation. Early release programs are methods by which prisons and prison systems control the size of their inmate population to keep these populations within legally defined acceptable limits. One model of this form of release is that inmates are released when an institution's population reaches the facility's maximum capacity. The decision about who gets released is based on which inmates have served the greatest percentage of their sentences and which have had the least number of disciplinary problems. This does not mean that only those inmates with no disciplinary problems or

Mandatory early release programs: methods by which prisons and prison systems control the size of their inmate population by releasing inmates who meet certain terms from their sentences early in order to keep these populations within legally defined acceptable limits.

those close to the end of their sentences are released. Instead, this simply means releasing the least dangerous of an often dangerous lot. A second model of mandatory early release calls for inmates to be released when they have served a specified percentage of their court-imposed sentence. This practice is often criticized as violating the spirit (if not the law) of what a court sentence represents. This is because under this model, an offender may be sentenced to ten years in prison, but if the state's law provides for mandatory early release upon serving of 80 percent of a sentence, then the sentence is "really" only eight years. In some states,this practice has been stopped, through what are known as "truth in sentencing laws." However, under both models, early release is a mandatory practice, not a privilege.

Summary

The history of corrections is not very clear until about the sixteenth century. The use of physical punishments was the norm well into the nineteenth century. But, starting in 1773, Americans began to experiment with the idea of incarceration as a part, if not the entirety, of punishment for crime with the opening of Walnut Street Jail in Philadelphia. During the 1800s, there were two competing forms of prisons in the United States, the Pennsylvania system (based on the ideas of Walnut Street Jail) and the Auburn system. For several reasons, the Auburn system became dominant, and was the primary model of prisons in the United States for well over a hundred years. Both prior to and after the Civil War, corrections in the American South developed on a different path. Here the idea of leasing inmates became popular, but was eventually ended due to abuses of inmates.

Community corrections, specifically probation, came into being in the late 1800s, originating as a way to manage offenders who committed lesser offenses, and for whom incarceration did not seem appropriate. After a slow development and spread, probation has grown to be the most common criminal sentence in the United States.

Key Terms

Auburn system
Congregate work
Corporal
Galley ships
Good-time laws
Hospice of San Michel
Indeterminate sentences
John Augustus
Leasing system
Maison de Force
Mandatory early release programs
Marks system
Parole
Penitentiaries
Pennsylvania system
Probation
Reformatory
Suspended sentence
Ticket of leave
Transportation
Walnut Street Jail

Chapter Five

Administration of the Prison

Prisons are in many ways small communities. Inside prisons are residents (inmates), businesses (the services and programs), workplaces (inmate and staff job assignments), infrastructure (the plumbing, heating, and cooling systems, etc.), laws (the rules of behavior for inmates and staff), law enforcement (staff who enforce rules), and government (the administrators). As we will see throughout the rest of the text, each of these parts of a community works in different ways, and yet works together with the other parts to ensure a smoothly running community. In this chapter, we will begin by looking at the people and tasks that are involved in the running of a prison — administrators and administration.

We begin this examination with a look at the overall goals for prison operations.

ADMINISTRATIVE GOALS FOR PRISONS

The operation and function of prisons exists to achieve several goals simultaneously. The easiest way to think about this is to think of prisons as having four primary administrative goals. While these goals may initially appear to be quite divergent, and at times their pursuit does cause conflict, in practice these can be pursued and achieved at the same time, and by a unified team of staff. But, it is also important to keep in mind that in the daily world of prison administration, each goal must be weighed whenever any activity or policy is considered. The four primary administrative goals for prisons are security, segregation, discipline, and treatment.

Security

Security: the primary goal of corrections, mostly referring to the prevention of the escape of inmates and intrusions from outsiders while keeping order among inmates.

Prison administrators' primary and most important goal is maintaining custody and **security** of all inmates. Above all else, prisons are expected to be secure facilities where the public can be assured that inmates will remain. Maintaining security means, among other things, preventing escapes of inmates and intrusions from outsiders and keeping order among inmates. The ultimate goal of prison is to keep people locked up, and to do so in a safe, secure, and humane way.

Segregation

Segregation: one of the main ways administrators maintain custody and security by classifying various types of offenders within the institution.

Prison administrators are responsible not only for maintaining custody and ensuring the security of the *outside* community, but also for maintaining security *inside* the prison. One primary way this is achieved is by **segregation**; that is, by classifying various types of offenders. Classification procedures (which are discussed later) protect inmates from other inmates and also reduce the potential for problems that could threaten the prison's internal and perhaps external security. The goal of segregation is to divide the inmate population in ways that minimize opportunities for disruptive, criminal, or otherwise harmful behavior and the likelihood of inmates being disruptive among themselves.

Discipline

Discipline: the reaction to inmates or staff when institutional rules are broken with the ultimate goal of maintaining an orderly and safe community.

Prison administrators are also responsible for enforcing the prison's rules on both inmates and staff. To have a safe and secure prison, rules are needed, just as with any society. When inmates or staff break these rules, they need **discipline**, or punishment. The goal of discipline is to keep the community orderly and safe for everybody. In some ways, the goal of maintaining discipline is especially challenging as the population of the prison (e.g., the inmates) are in prison precisely because they are known to not abide by the rules of society. Therefore, in prison, administrators have the challenge of monitoring and enforcing rules on a population of persons who are known to be at least somewhat predisposed to not follow rules. And, just as the inmates are in prison as discipline for breaking society's rules on the outside of prison, inside of prison there need to be sanctions and punishments for breaking the rules of this community.

Treatment

Treatment: various types of programming available in some institutions that often include psychological, substance abuse, basic/advanced education, behavioral modification, and job-training programs.

One of the goals of prisons that some people believe is often overlooked and not achieved is to actually "correct" the behavior and thinking of inmates. **Treatment**, in a multitude of forms (as will be discussed in Chapter 12), is provided for the purpose of changing, correcting, or rehabilitating inmates. One thing that we know about treatment programs is that they are much more likely to be successful when they are provided within an environment that is safe, secure, and orderly. In simple terms, if a prison does not achieve the goals of security, segregation, and discipline, it is all but impossible for it to be conducive to treatment. Only when inmates (and staff) are able to go about their daily lives without major concerns about their safety can they effectively participate in treatment programs such as psychological and substance abuse counseling, basic and advanced education, and behavioral modification and job-training programs.

WORKING TO ACHIEVE ADMINISTRATIVE GOALS

While suggested as the ideals for all prisons, the above listed four administrative goals are met in varying degrees and by various methods. The keys to individual prisons meeting these goals are numerous, and include not just the obvious issues of having dedicated and qualified staff and a solid physical plant, but also having both the financial and political support that encourages and sustains the efforts of administrators.

With skyrocketing costs and accompanying budgetary problems in essentially all jurisdictions, many prisons and correctional systems have been forced to reduce their programs, services, staff, and physical maintenance and improvement projects. In doing so, prison administrators have had to make difficult decisions about prioritizing their goals and correspondingly have had to cut resources from lower priorities. When political decisions are made to reduce allocated funding to corrections, yet criminal statutes and public sentiments call for increasingly strict criminal sanctions, correctional administrators are caught in the middle. Such a situation usually means something must be cut. After a short time, it simply is not possible to continue to do more, but with less.

In all circumstances, custody and security goals are held as top priorities. Services to inmates that are not primarily focused on maintaining custody and control are typically lower priorities. Therefore, these "other" (e.g., treatment) services are more likely to suffer in times of financial hardship. However, for those priorities that are not highly valued, middle-range political decisions are also very important. Correctional administrators (system directors and wardens) in the United States are typically politically appointed officials and, therefore, subjected to rapid and sometimes unanticipated turnover. When top correctional administrators, who may hold their positions for relatively short time periods, decide to pursue particular forms of programs and organization, correctional personnel who are most directly affected by these changes may oppose them.

Correctional staff who have daily contact with inmates — in fact, nearly all staff in prisons — may feel safely removed from the political workings of corrections and may believe that directives from top administrators are unrealistic and unworkable. It is not uncommon for corrections staff, as with staff in many types of organizations, to believe that those at the top making decisions are "out of touch" with what "really happens" in prison. Consequently, when staff believe administrators are not informed about daily life in prison and instead are concerned primarily with politics, they may resist implementing changes. When combined with their belief that top-level administrators will rapidly turn over, middle management and other institutional workers commonly resist changes and maintain the status quo.

Consequently, prison administration is a field in which change happens both relatively frequently, but also very slowly. Change in staff — both at the top administrative levels and among institutional staff — tends to happen fairly quickly. Yet, change in actual routines, activities, and structural aspects of institutions happens very slowly, if at all. Due to the political nature of corrections management, the sheer size of the population with which most corrections systems work, and the restrictions of architectural designs, change in activities and philosophies guiding activities is difficult to implement.

THE PRISON STAFF

Every prison has staff hierarchy. The director of the correctional system is supported by the **warden** or superintendent, who acts as the primary manager of an individual institution. Within each prison, the warden is assisted by between one and four **deputies** or assistant wardens, who are commonly responsible for one of the major areas of operations or goals for the prison: security and custody, operations, treatment and programming, and possibly health care services. Comparable in rank and authority to the counterpart in a military police organization, the **captain of the guard** is the commanding officer of the security staff who directly supervises the inmates. The security staff consists of a number of watch lieutenants and sergeants and a larger number of correctional officers (sometimes called **line officers**). In essentially all correctional institutions, the security staff is easily recognized by the fact that they wear uniforms.

Warden: the primary manager of an individual institution that is in charge of overseeing all operations and maintaining safety and security in a particular institution.

Deputies: individuals who are primarily responsible for one of the following operations and/or goals: security/custody, operations, treatment/programming, and possible health care services.

Captain of the guard: the commanding officer overall other security staff who directly supervise the inmates.

Line officers: members of the security staff that are in charge of maintaining general security matters within the institution.

Paramilitary model: organizational structure, similar to that of the military, with clear and easily identifiable ranks along with explicit and obvious delegation of tasks across ranks/levels.

One of the most obvious differences between the staff of a prison (or jail) and most other organizations is that correctional staff are organized along a **paramilitary model**. This means that the organizational structure is similar to that of the military, with very clear and easily identifiable different ranks, and explicit and obvious delegation of tasks across ranks and levels. The staff is organized using terms that are also borrowed from the military, such as Captain, Lieutenant, Sergeant, etc. Military-style insignia and uniforms are the norm. Promotions are based on well-established criteria and overt signs of respect and deference are expected to be shown across rank. To most observers, the appearance and interactions of correctional staff are very much like those seen in any branch of the military.

At the lowest rank in the paramilitary structure are the individuals who hold the rank of correctional officer. It is these front-line staff who hold the primary day-to-day and moment-to-moment responsibility for maintaining security and custody in the prison. This does not mean that an officer's main job is preventing escapes. The physical structure of the prison and perhaps a few armed officers in towers around the prison's periphery ordinarily ensure that inmates do not escape. Instead, the correctional officer has the most frequent and intense forms of interaction with inmates. Therefore, the correctional officer also has the greatest impact on the behaviors of individual inmates. While primarily concerned with maintaining security (both internal and external) and discipline, the correctional officer is, perhaps, in a position where the most significant degree of treatment may occur.

Depending on the institution, the region of the country, the state, the budget for the particular department, and the prevailing philosophy and prioritized goals, the prison's treatment staff may consist of a wide range of professionals. What is found most often in prison is that the treatment staff includes persons such as psychiatrists, psychologists, medical personnel, chaplains, substance abuse counselors, social workers, lawyers, academic teachers, and vocational teachers. Support staff in prisons includes a variety of persons who oversee the business affairs, maintenance, public relations, and clerical functions as well as coordinate contacts between inmates and both institutional personnel and outside services and agencies. Support staff in prison have the same types of jobs as people found in support roles in any large organization or company.

In addition to these groups of staff, prisons also include service and maintenance staff (plumbers, carpenters, kitchen staff, etc.) and in most institutions volunteers. Volunteers do a variety of tasks, almost always centered on some type of programming for inmates. The most common type of volunteer in prison is a person who comes in, often in a group, to meet with inmates in some type of religious service.[1] These individuals typically report that they feel "called" to their work, and report fairly high levels of satisfaction with their volunteer work. Of course, all persons who volunteer in a correctional facility, regardless of the reason or task that they do, are carefully screened by administrators to ensure that they are not family members, friends, enemies, or in any other way associated with individual inmates or in any way a potential threat to security and custody. This also means that only in rare cases are individuals with a criminal history allowed to do volunteer work in prison.

Relations between correctional personnel and inmates are unpredictable and volatile yet usually rather impersonal and mild. The idea perpetuated by some movies and television shows that staff and inmates are openly hostile and combative to one another is an exaggeration. Yes, there is a natural gap that exists between staff and inmates, and the gap is aggravated by a range of sociocultural factors. In some ways, this difference is not unlike the difference between students and professors — we have different roles and there is an aspect of authority and control that defines our different roles. But, in prisons there are some additional differences that play important roles in how staff and inmates interact. First, most inmates come from urban areas, while most prisons are in rural settings. The inmate population is largely from lower socioeconomic classes,

---

1. Richard Tewksbury and Dean Dabney. 2005. Prison Volunteers: Profiles, Motivations, Satisfaction. *Journal of Offender Rehabilitation*, 40: 173-183.

whereas most staff members' social classes are more economically and culturally privileged. Disproportionately large percentages of inmates are minorities; disproportionately small percentages of correctional personnel are minorities.

One important development in the prison staff that has only occurred in the last generation or two is that since the late 1970s there have been increasing numbers of women who work in corrections. This includes in both treatment and security positions, as well as in top administrative positions. This means that the male inmates are under the direct supervision of women, a situation many working class, urban, minority men may find offensive and unacceptable. These facts obviously bring to the prison two different, often conflicting value systems and natural barriers to communication and the establishment of personal relationships.

Women in corrections face some serious barriers and challenges arising from what has historically been a very sexist set of ideas and structures. Even today, many inmates, and certainly at least some staff persons, hold sexist attitudes and do not believe that it is proper for women to be in positions of authority over men. Many advocates of having women in corrections, including in administrative positions, however, argue that having women in these types of positions exposes sexist men to the fact that women can do such jobs, and often do them very well. Through modeling of behavior and success, the presence of women may lead to a greater acceptance of women in corrections.

PRISON ADMINISTRATIVE MANAGEMENT

As the primary manager of a prison, the warden has responsibility for overseeing the prison's daily functions as well as supervising staff, making budget decisions, and implementing programs and policies for pursuing the prison's administrative goals. In terms of demographic characteristics and work styles, wardens of the twenty-first century are very different from their predecessors. These changes are in large part a response to the evolving needs of inmates, staff, and the public.

Today, wardens are usually highly educated (at a minimum holding a bachelor's degree) individuals for whom corrections is a career. In the past — until the 1980s — wardens were often appointed by governors not for their skills and expertise that applied to running a correctional institution, but instead because of their success in business. Other times, warden jobs were seen as primarily rewards for political supporters. Until the late twentieth century, prison wardens often had little or no experience in prison operations. As you might expect, this often times created conflict with prison staff and introduced problems through how these inexperienced persons decided to govern their institutions. However, today wardens typically have risen through the ranks, having served in a number of security, treatment, and/or administrative positions inside various prisons.

Wardens of today also are quite varied demographically. Whereas such jobs were once the exclusive province of white men, today women and persons of all races are found in warden's offices. The warden of today is expected to be knowledgeable about a wide range of issues and is responsible for many different tasks. As a result, the demographic characteristics of wardens are not that important, but what is important is the skill set that they bring to the institution.

When looking at the expectations for what a warden does, it is instructive to examine the stated job qualifications for a warden. According to the Michigan Civil Service Commission, the job duties of a prison warden include:

- Coordinating activities of scheduling work assignments, setting priorities, and directing the work of subordinates.
- Evaluating employee performance.
- Identifying staff development and training needs and ensuring training is obtained.
- Establishing and maintaining custody, security, and control measures of a facility.
- Supervising and controlling the inside movement of inmates, including initial assignment to housing units.
- Implementing policies and developing procedures in the areas of housing, treatment, custody, and security.
- Supervising the classification and orientation of new inmates.
- Developing and implementing procedures for educational and treatment programs based on department policies.
- Ensuring proper labor relations and conditions of employment are maintained.
- Representing the facility to the Department of Corrections' central office, other state departments, local agencies, and the public.

These are just a few of the responsibilities of a prison warden. As you can see, these are the issues involved in overseeing the overall operation of a prison, and in most cases are rather broad in scope.

While the expectations and responsibilities of wardens are generally consistent across institutions and systems, the ways that these responsibilities can be carried out can be quite varied. Individual wardens carry out their tasks based on their set of beliefs (in part based on how they see the purpose of corrections, as discussed in Chapter 3) about the goals of corrections and basic management. We turn next to these different approaches in carrying out the job of warden.

Autocratic Wardens

In the earliest decades of American corrections, prison wardens had total control and discretion in how they ran their prisons. From the birth of the penitentiary movement until after World War II, politically appointed wardens were viewed as totalitarian leaders whose only concern was staying in the good graces of the governor. These individuals were appointed to their positions and basically told that the best thing they could do was to prevent escapes, scandals, and anything else that could politically embarrass the governor. Only the governor oversaw the warden, and the warden was almost always given very, very broad leeway in what

Autocratic warden: the pre-WWII warden position where an individual was politically appointed and had total control over his institution with the only oversight coming from the respective state's governor.

he chose to do in the prison and how he chose to supervise both inmates and staff. This is the idea of the **autocratic warden**. Such individuals held responsibility for every aspect of the prison, from building facilities, to hiring, supervising, and firing staff, to what inmates were fed, how they were fed, and when they were fed. When this very broad sense of authority and power was coupled with a limited (if any) degree of knowledge about inmates and their behavior, it should not be surprising that most autocratic wardens compelled compliance with their orders through a mix of terror, incentives, and favoritism. These management tools were used with both inmates and staff.

The idea of the autocratic warden is not only a historical relic. Although for at least the last half-century wardens (and in fact all prison operations and activities) have been much more closely watched and supervised, the basic principles of governing via autocratic means still remain with some persons and in some places. Autocratic wardens of today strive to establish an administrative culture in which only a few individuals have much influence ("power") in making decisions and directives, and orders are issued without input or consideration of responses from those to whom such orders pertain. The autocratic warden is one who sees himself as the ultimate power, and he acts in ways that tell others that he believes he is in charge, completely. Sometimes such an approach is seen as tyranny, or attempts to function as a dictator. In many ways, autocratic means of governing are similar to the actions of a dictator. Fear is used to control inmates and staff, discipline is swift and harsh, and favoritism is believed to be common and obvious in the decisions of such leaders.

Autocratic wardens, as with autocratic leaders of any type of organization, are usually seen as ineffective, short-lived, and inherently unstable. Subordinates typically do not respect the actions and views of an autocratic leader, and will frequently work to subvert the decisions and actions of such leaders. Consequently, an autocratic approach to governing a prison is typically seen as a poor management style.

Bureaucratic Wardens

Bureaucratic model: the post-WWII model whereby additional layers of supervision were added above the level of warden with the idea of tempering the total control of prison wardens that existed in decades prior.

Following the end of World War II, most U.S. social institutions, especially those associated with government, moved toward an increasingly **bureaucratic model**. For corrections, this meant the development of statewide correctional systems and additional layers of supervision added above the level of warden. The idea was to temper the total control of prison wardens and to institute a statewide system of organization ("bureaucracy") that would promote consistency across institutions within a given jurisdiction. When individual prisons were tied more closely together in a state system, the new layer(s) of supervision created above the level of wardens took over issues of policy development and priority setting. Whereas wardens had previously made and enforced policies as they pleased, these functions were now given to or supervised by a coordinating system office.

In the bureaucratic system, wardens' powers were eroded, and such persons became more focused on implementing policies and procedures as identified by jurisdiction-wide administrators. This also lead to relations between facility administrators and both staff and inmates changing significantly. No longer did the warden have as much opportunity to do as he pleased, reward and punish on a whim, and more or less completely control the lives of those who lived and worked in the prison.

For staff, part of the bureaucratization of government included the implementation of a **civil service system**. Correctional staff had job security, and wardens could not dole out jobs as political favors quite so easily. With personnel policies established and procedures for hiring, firing, disciplining, and promoting in place, staff no longer needed to play politics as overtly and strongly as they had previously. With civil service came the idea of rewarding staff based on how they did their jobs, not necessarily on who they knew and who liked them.

Civil service system: the practice of having clear rules in place to hire, fire, discipline, and promote government workers that emerged with the bureaucratic model after WWII.

It was with the emergence of bureaucratic wardens and a coordinated system of corrections within a jurisdiction that organizational issues were introduced for jurisdictions. This move brought with it protections for staff and inmates, and a large degree of predictability in how day-to-day life would be led in prison. Although for many people the idea of a "bureaucracy" is unwelcome and seen in a negative light, in actuality this simply meant the creation of a predictable, known, system of division of labor and assignment of responsibilities based on criteria other than the whims and personal preferences of an autocratic leader.

Delegative Wardens

In the late twentieth century, a third style of management became popular across the United States, including in correctional facilities. The **delegative model** of management and leadership is the idea that the warden of a prison is the person who coordinates the work of others, including coordinating decision making. Rather than making decisions and informing others of what to do, the delegative leader distributes responsibilities to subordinates, and empowers them to make decisions and implement policies and procedures within a particular area or scope of responsibility. By delegating tasks and responsibilities, the delegative warden is seen as a team-builder instead of a tyrant or someone who simply carries out the orders of someone above him.

Delegative model: the management and leadership organization where the warden of a prison is the person who coordinates the work of others, including coordinating decision-making.

The key to success for a delegative leader is to have qualified, capable, and trustworthy staff around him or her whom can be counted on to carry out their jobs. This style of leadership assumes that others are competent and do not need to be instructed on everything to do and do not need to have all of their activities and decisions closely monitored. A successful delegative warden is able to motivate others to want to succeed and to achieve whatever the vision is for "success" in that particular organization. Delegative leaders do, however, have to be alert for subordinates who may see such actions as a sign of weakness or an opportunity to try to make the warden look bad and therefore get themselves promoted. In this way, it is critical that delegative wardens do promote and maintain a true sense of team among their staff.

Participatory Management

Participatory management: the idea of structuring the management tasks of an institution around the central issue of input from others and even group-based decision making.

Another major change to occur after the implementation of a bureaucratic management model was the inclusion of correctional staff and inmates in actually making management decisions. **Participatory management** has been accompanied by a shift from considering wardens as specialists to viewing them as generalists in management. The participatory management approach is more than simply delegating tasks and responsibilities to specific subordinates, however. Rather, this is the idea of structuring the management tasks of an institution around the central issue of input from others and even group-based decision making. In a participatory management scheme, wardens see themselves as the individuals responsible for conceptualizing an overall plan for the prison and then developing a framework for implementing that scheme. However, this is done with the active solicitation and serious consideration of input and reactions from other staff, and perhaps even inmates.

The participatory portion of the management approach enters when planning and implementing specific goals of the general plan. Groups of staff and inmates are involved, in one of several ways, in developing specific ways to implement the general ideas. There are two basic benefits to such an approach. First, the warden has the burden of developing and implementing all policies. Second, when people whom these policies and procedures will affect are involved in the planning process, they will less likely oppose them when implemented. In this way, a participatory management approach helps to pursue all four primary administrative goals: security and custody, segregation, discipline, and treatment.

Texas control model: the management model made popular in Texas where strong and powerful inmates were recruited to maintain order in their units in exchange for special privileges.

Consensus model: the management model made popular in California where administrators meet and discuss with inmate groups changes to institutional policies and programs.

Responsibility model: the management model where a sense of community was encouraged among inmates by imposing minimum restraints on daily life with the intention to build inmates' individual responsibility to ease reintegration to the community.

The path to success of participatory management in corrections has not necessarily been smooth, however. In various states and individual prisons, problems have arisen when different groups, often correctional officers, have used their input to advance their own interests over those of the institution. In these instances, the participatory nature of the management plan has had to be reduced to avoid deep resentments and large-scale problems between inmates and correctional officers.

Various forms of participatory management have been attempted in prisons, but failed. The **Texas control model**, where strong and powerful inmates were recruited to maintain order in their units in exchange for special privileges, was ruled unconstitutional by the U.S. Supreme Court in the 1982 case of *Ruiz v. Estelle*. California's **consensus model** attempted to have administrators meet and discuss with inmate groups changes to institutional policies and programs. This model was designed to have inmate leaders endorse and convince other inmates to accept changes. However, when inmate gangs fought for dominance in the program, the model failed. Finally, Michigan's **responsibility model** attempted to encourage a sense of community among inmates by imposing minimum restraints on daily life. The intention was to build inmates' individual responsibility to ease reintegration to the community. The model failed when rather than building a community sense, inmates maneuvered and fought to gain power over other inmates. In essence, this model failed because inmates acted just like people in the free world.

One development that has survived in many prisons is the **inmate council**. These are groups of inmates, selected either by the administration or preferably by the inmate population, who are provided opportunities to lobby administrative representatives for the "inmate perspective." Such groups also commonly organize activities and plan initiatives, including public service projects and social and recreational activities for inmates. Think here of the idea of student council in high school; the idea, structure, and functions are very comparable.

Inmate council: a group of inmates, selected either by the administration or preferably by the inmate population, who are provided opportunities to lobby administrative representatives for the "inmate perspective."

THE PRISON'S INFLUENCE ON STAFF

While the destructive effects of imprisonment on prisoners have been well documented, the prison's influence on the staff has received significantly less consideration. However, this has been changing in recent years. Working within a prison means being subjected to essentially all of the same conditions, and many of the same restrictions, that apply to inmates.

Physical conditions in many prisons are less than ideal. Prisons are often quite hot and humid in warm weather, and cold and drafty in winter. Furnishings are sparse, and made to be indestructible, so they are less than comfortable. Restrictions on personal property, to maintain security and custody, apply to staff as well as inmates. Contacts with persons outside of the prison are difficult if not impossible to make while staff are at work. Hours can be long, and either very tedious or on rare occasions dangerous (and "exciting"). Social interactions with others can be tense and stressful. Because of the fact that the environment is experienced in much the same way by staff as it is by inmates, many prison staff refer to their jobs as "simply doing time, but eight hours at a time."

"The Other Prisoners"

Prison staffs are commonly referred to as "the other prisoners" because of the pressures they experience being locked into institutions and having to live and work according to the strict rules, regulations, and restrictions. One observer, focusing on the impact of a correctional career on an individual's mental health, has concluded:

> Prison conditions place a significant degree of strain on the workforce, strain which can actually be damaging to the personality of the employee, and thus . . . his effectiveness as a prison officer.[2]

2. Paul Schlacter. 1980. *Concept of Self and Perceived Stress: A Study of Correctional Officers.* Unpublished doctoral dissertation, The Ohio State University, Columbus, OH, p. 81.

This is what is sometimes called the "dehumanizing" effect of corrections. Not only are inmates reduced to numbers, but correctional officers may also find that they are performing simply rote tasks, being something more similar to a robot than to a rational, responsive, and responsible person. A correctional officer may well spend an entire shift watching one door, opening and closing it a couple of hundred times a day, with little or no other responsibilities or tasks. Many particular jobs (or "**posts**") within a prison are tedious and require few if any skills or thought.

Post: a job within the institution that often is tedious and requires few, if any, skills or thought.

Many correctional officers initially enter their jobs with idealistic goals of helping to change or rehabilitate inmates. However, many such staff persons quickly realize these ideals are unrealistic and naïve. Because of the high rates and frequency of contacts with abnormal behavior, brutality, racial conflicts, and general states of tension and anxiety, young correctional officers soon lose their enthusiasm.[3] Also, pressures to conform to peers' ideals and views lead many correctional officers to view inmates similarly to how their superior officers view them. Also leading to a loss of idealism is the high rate of recidivism. When the officers (and other staff) see inmates whom they believed had in fact "rehabilitated" return to the prison, often in very short order, their hopes for rehabilitation are dampened. As a consequence, correctional staff's generally negative attitudes toward inmates and correctional efforts minimize the chances of such efforts being successful.

Prison Staff Subculture

Just as inmates develop a culture of their own, so too do staff — especially correctional officers — develop a sense of community and shared values, views, and expectations. This subculture is typically quite different from that portrayed in many entertainment media depictions of prison. Whereas in movies and television shows prison staff are often portrayed as brutal, uncaring, and opposed to all inmates for all purposes, this is far from the truth. As mentioned earlier, many correctional officers come to their job very idealistic about trying to help and rehabilitate inmates. While this idealism often wanes in a relatively short period of time, this does not mean that prison staff go to the opposite extreme.

What does typically happen is that prison staff come to see inmates as a set of unified groups, and they then look to other staff for purposes of developing their own group or "team" that can support one another and resist attempts by inmates to manipulate them, intimidate them, or in any other way oppose them. The "prison guard subculture" has been well outlined by Kauffman, who showed that the development of an "us versus them" perspective arises out of values officers bring with them to the job, socialization to the ways of prison life, and changes in culture that are witnessed and experienced as one works in prison.[4] As outlined

---

3. A. Guenther and M. Guenther. 1974. Screws and Thugs. *Society*, 11, 42-50.
4. Kelsey Kauffman. 1988. *Prison Officers and Their World.* Cambridge, MA: Harvard University Press.

by Kauffman, the prison guard subculture is comprised of seven primary beliefs and guiding principles:

1. Always go the aid of an officer in distress.
2. Do not traffic drugs.
3. Do not be a snitch.
4. Never disrespect another officer in front of inmates.
5. Always support an officer who is in a dispute with another inmate.
6. Do not be friends with inmates.
7. Maintain cohesion against outside groups.

What you may recognize about this list of beliefs and principles is that it is not really unique or specially focused on prison but instead is really about maintaining a sense of group and standing in opposition to inmates. The ideas here are to unite prison guards together in ways that provide them with strength and some degree of safety and protection against an "enemy" such as inmates. This is really just the way that many groups function throughout society.

When we talk about a staff subculture, it is important to keep in mind that this refers primarily to lower-rank staff and not administrators. In this way, we can see three distinct groups of persons in prison: inmates, staff, and administrators. And, although all three groups need to be able to co-exist peacefully and work together at least to the point of providing for a somewhat smoothly operating daily routine in the prison, each group tends to have at least some notable differences with both of the other two groups. Each group has its own somewhat unique set of values and beliefs, a subculture that guides what they do and with whom, how, and when, and their own goals and priorities for both day-to-day and long-term events. The prison, then, can be seen from an administrative point of view as very complex and populated by divergent groups that both get along with and oppose one another on multiple issues and in multiple ways.

Summary

The idea of a prison is centered on four primary goals that administrators use to guide their operations. These are the goals of security, segregation, discipline, and treatment. Security is the idea of keeping the offenders in and others out, or keeping the institution secure. Segregation is the idea of separating different types of inmates from one another, for purposes of safety needs and maintaining a smoother day-to-day operation. Discipline is the idea of enforcement of rules for all aspects of life inside the prison. Treatment is providing services to address the social, psychological, physical, and other needs of inmates, with a goal of returning them to a crime-free way of living.

The two primary jobs that pertain to the overall management and operations of a prison are the positions of warden and deputy warden(s). Underneath these positions, the majority of the staff of a prison, and especially the correctional officers (security), are organized in a paramilitary model.

Within a prison, the management team, or warden specifically, has four basic models of management that they can implement. Autocratic wardens rule as a monarch would, making decisions themselves and giving orders. A bureaucratic warden is focused on enforcing the rules and ensuring that there is a smooth-running institution, with rule enforcement as the primary goal. Wardens who adopt a delegative style of leadership build teams and assign responsibility (with minimal oversight usually) to others for key functions of the prison. And, participatory wardens seek input and ideas and participation from throughout the ranks of staff, and sometimes from the inmate population as well.

Work in a prison has very definite effects on staff persons, some of which can be very negative. Jobs in corrections can be physically challenging, tedious, boring, very repetitive, unrewarding, and overwhelming. Such experiences lead some people to view prison staff as "other prisoners."

Key Terms

Autocratic warden
Bureaucratic model
Captain of the guard
Civil service system
Consensus model
Delegative model
Discipline
Inmate council
Line officers
Paramilitary model
Participatory management
Post
Responsibility model
Segregation
Texas control model
Treatment
Warden

Chapter Six The Prisoner

This chapter focuses on the "client" of corrections (specifically of prisons), prisoners. While it may be easy to get caught up in thinking about a prison as a unique physical structure, a place where administrators make decisions and enact policies for achieving particular purposes and goals, and as a historically evolving concept and set of practices, what prisons are really about at the core is housing convicted criminal offenders. This chapter looks at who these individuals are, what their characteristics are, and how living in prison can have effects on such persons' actions and identities.

The approach from which we will be examining prisoners is one that emphasizes that they are living in a setting that is, at least in most meaningful ways, completely controlled by others. This is the idea of a **total institution**. This idea, originally put forth by sociologist Erving Goffman[1], emphasizes that the residents of such places are controlled in who they are, whom they have opportunities to interact with, how both their long-term and day-to-day lives are structured, and what physical, tangible material goods are available for consumption. In a total institution, essentially all aspects of life are provided for, controlled, and under the authority of someone other than the person(s) living in such a situation.

Total institution: emphasizes that the residents in institutions are controlled in who they are, whom they have opportunities to interact with, how both their long-term and day-to-day lives are structured, and what physical, tangible material goods are available for consumption.

Before we discuss the characteristics and experiences of prisoners living in the total institution of the prison, we must first examine the number of persons who are in prison. As we will see throughout both this and later chapters, the raw number of persons who are in prison is important in many ways, including how life is structured and experienced.

1. Erving Goffman. 1961. *Asylums.* Garden City, NY: Anchor Books.

PRISON POPULATIONS

With 1.6 million adults incarcerated in state and federal prisons at the end of 2011,[2] the United States has one of the largest prison populations in the world today. This total population is more than 14 percent larger than it was in 2000, and 106 percent larger than it was in 1990. During the 1990s alone, the total number of imprisoned adults increased by nearly 7.5 percent every year.[3] However, during the first decade of the twenty-first century, the rate of growth among prison populations slowed, and starting in 2009 actually began to decrease. Between 2000 and 2010, the total number of persons in prison in the United States increased an average of 1.3 percent, but between 2009 and 2010, and again between 2010 and 2011, prison populations decreased by approximately 1 percent annually.

Prison populations vary quite considerably across states, as we might expect. In very simple terms, of course, states like California, Texas, and Florida would be expected to have the most prison inmates — they have the largest populations of residents. However, it is interesting to note that the size of the state's inmate population is not necessarily correlated with the state's total population. Table 6-1 presents the 50 states' rankings of total prison population. What we can rather quickly see here is that while there is a general correlation between larger population states having larger prison populations, there are some notable exceptions to this. For instance, Louisiana ranks as the eleventh largest state in terms of prison population, but is certainly not one of the nation's largest population states. Similarly, on the smaller prison population end of the continuum, we see that fairly large population states rank low in terms of prison population, including Iowa, Minnesota, and Massachusetts.

Another way of looking at the number of persons in prison is to standardize this number based on the total number of persons in society. Looking at the issue this way, we see that in 2011 there were 492 persons in prison for every 100,000 adult Americans. This number has grown significantly in recent years. In 2000, there were "only" 470 prisoners for every 100,000 Americans. This number, known as the **incarceration rate**, peaked in 2007 and 2008 when the rate of prisoners was 506 for every 100,000 persons.

Incarceration rate: the number of individuals incarcerated in a jail or prison in America per 100,000 persons.

Looking beyond the simple total number of inmates in prison, we can also see some important patterns and trends in the demographics of prisoners. Most notable about U.S. prison inmates is the sex distribution — only 10 percent of all U.S inmates are female. This represents a significantly larger portion of prison inmates than in the past. As recently as 2004, women comprised only 6.4 percent of prison inmates. In terms of a rate, we see that in 2011 women were incarcerated at a rate of 65/100,000, compared to their 2000 rate of 59/100,000.[4]

---

2. E. Ann Carson and William J. Sabol. 2012. *Prisoners in 2011*. Washington, D.C.: Bureau of Justice Statistics.
3. U.S. Department of Justice. 1995. *Prisoners in 1994*. Washington D.C.: Bureau of Justice Statistics.
4. Carson and Sabol, supra n.2.

TABLE 6.1 STATE PRISON POPULATIONS, 2011

Jurisdiction	Population counts	Jurisdiction	Population counts
U.S. total	1,598,780	Mississippi	21,386
Federal	216,362	Connecticut	18,324
Texas	172,224	Washington	17,847
California	149,569	Arkansas	16,108
Florida	103,055	Oregon	14,510
Georgia	55,944	Nevada	12,778
New York	55,436	Massachusetts	11,623
Pennsylvania	51,578	Minnesota	9,800
Ohio	50,964	Kansas	9,327
Illinois	48,427	Iowa	9,116
Michigan	42,940	Idaho	7,739
Arizona	40,020	New Mexico	6,998
Louisiana	39,710	Utah	6,879
North Carolina	39,440	West Virginia	6,826
Virginia	38,130	Delaware	6,739
Alabama	32,270	Hawaii	6,037
Missouri	30,833	Alaska	5,412
Indiana	28,906	Nebraska	4,616
Tennessee	28,479	Montana	3,678
Oklahoma	25,977	South Dakota	3,535
New Jersey	23,834	Rhode Island	3,337
South Carolina	22,914	New Hampshire	2,614
Wisconsin	22,654	Wyoming	2,183
Maryland	22,558	Maine	2,145
Colorado	21,978	Vermont	2,053
Kentucky	21,545	North Dakota	1,423

**Source:* E. Ann Carson and William J. Sabol. 2012. *Prisoners in 2011*. Washington, D.C.: Bureau of Justice Statistics.

TABLE 6.2 INCARCERATION RATES BY RACE AND SEX

Incarceration Rate per 100,000	African-American Men	Hispanic Men	White Men	African-American Women	Hispanic Women	White Women
	3,023	1,238	478	129	71	51

Evidence of yet more clearly seen patterns in who is in prison is apparent when we add the issue of race to the mix. When looking at race and sex together, we find widely disparate rates of incarceration across demographic groups. Table 6.2 shows that in 2011, African-American and Hispanic men far outdistanced white men and all women in regard to their likelihood of being in prison. African-American men have an incarceration rate nearly 2.5 times higher than Hispanic men and nearly 6.5 times higher than white men. Although the discrepancy is not nearly as large among women (African-American women have 1.8 times the incarceration rate of Hispanic women and 2.5 times that of white women), there is still a clear, easily seen difference.

One final important way to look at who is in prison is to examine the types of criminal offenses for which persons are in prison. Table 6.3 shows that inmates in state prisons in 2011 were primarily violent offenders. Nearly one in five offenders was incarcerated for a property or drug offense respectively.

TABLE 6.3 MOST SERIOUS OFFENSES OF INMATES IN STATE PRISONS, 2011

	All Inmates	Males	Females
Violent	53%	54%	37%
Property	18%	17%	29%
Drugs	17%	17%	25%
Public Order	10%	10%	8%
Other Offenses	2%	2%	1%

When looking at sex differences, it is quickly seen that women are less likely than men to be in prison for a violent offense, although more likely than men to be incarcerated for a property or drug offense.

EXPERIENCES OF LONG-TERM IMPRISONMENT

Now that we have looked at who is in prison, it is important to move on to examine what life is like for these more than one and a half million prisoners. One thing that characterizes corrections in the twenty-first century that is different than in earlier decades is that when persons go to prison, they stay significantly longer today than in the past. As sentence length has grown (due to changes in criminal statutes allowing or explicitly requiring longer sentences), this has meant that more prisoners stay in prison for longer periods of time. As such, correctional officials today face challenges from two new kinds of prisoners. These are prisoners who are experiencing **long-term incarceration**, and those who are elderly (due to growing old while in prison). Here we will examine some of the dynamics and consequences of long-term incarceration (elderly inmates will be discussed next in this chapter).

Long-term incarceration: individuals who serve a minimum sentence ranging from 7 or 8 years, according to some researchers, to a minimum of 20 years, according to others, with most being unmarried white men who are in their late 20s or early 30s when imprisoned and remain until they are elderly.

Most researchers determine the cutoff for being defined as a long-term incarceration inmate to be serving either 7 or 8 years, although others apply such terminology only to those inmates serving a minimum of 20 years.[5] Most long-term inmates are unmarried white men who are in their late 20s or early 30s when first imprisoned and who remain incarcerated until they are elderly.

All prison inmates experience a number of problems beyond the simple disruption of their lives. However, long-term inmates face difficulties that may be more intense and have a greater impact than what short-term inmates face. Most notable, the problems that impact inmates most severely are social: disruption of relationships with outsiders and problematic relationships with fellow inmates.[6] Many long-term prisoners have an almost obsessive fear they will deteriorate (physically and mentally) before their release. However, psychological studies have systematically failed to demonstrate significant deteriorations.[7]

What most characterizes long-term inmates is their common development of alternative modes of adjustment, which are often exaggerated. Some of these adjustments may have negative consequences for both individuals and the institution. Those who serve lengthy sentences present more cases of prison

5. Barry Richards. 1978. The Experience of Long Term Imprisonment: An Exploratory Investigation. *British Journal of Criminology*, 18, (2), 162-169. Cindie A. Unger and Robert A. Buchanon. 1985. *Managing Long Term Inmates*. Washington, D.C.: National Institute of Corrections. Deborah G. Wilson and Gennaro F. Vito. 1988. Long Term Inmates: Special Needs and Management Conditions. *Federal Probation*, 52: 21-26. Edith Flynn. 1992. The Graying of America's Prison Population. *The Prison Journal*, 72, (1-2), 77-98.

6. Richards, supra n.5.

7. R.J. Sapsford. 1978. Life-Sentence Prisoners: Psychological Changes During Sentence. *British Journal of Criminology*, 18, (2), 128-145.

suicides,[8] psychological disorders,[9] and detachment from significant others outside the correctional institutions.[10] Long-term inmates also suffer a lower sense of self-efficacy (individuals' assessment of their effectiveness, competence, and ability to influence events).[11] These issues pose additional programming, classification, and supervision difficulties for correctional officials. Consequently, it becomes obvious that not only do inmates experience long-term imprisonment differently, but correctional personnel as well have different experiences with long-term inmates.[12]

ELDERLY INMATES

Similar to the general U.S. population, the population of prison inmates is growing older. In the year 2011, fully 38.9 percent of prison inmates were age 40 or older, 15.6 percent were over the age of 50, and 3.8, or one of every 27 prisoners, was age 60 or older.[13] The first major influx of elderly inmates occurred during the 1980s, when prison populations increased dramatically. During this time period, not only did more people start coming to prison, but so too did prison sentences begin to lengthen as the belief in rehabilitation waned and a get-tough movement took hold in society, courts, and corrections. During the 1980s, the number of inmates over age 55 increased by more than 50 percent. This trend continues today, not due to more older people committing crimes, getting caught, and being sentenced to prison, but instead due to persons who are experiencing long-term incarceration growing older while in prison. Those inmates who were sent to prison in the early to mid-1980s are now roughly 30 years older than when they went to prison. This means they are easily in their 50s or 60s, if they are still alive.

One of the biggest challenges for correctional administrators who house large numbers of older inmates is that the actual facilities and services of our prisons and jails need to be modified so as to accommodate the needs of **geriatric inmates**. Whereas inmates who are age 55 (or sometimes even just 50) are considered "older" or "elderly" inmates in corrections, those who are both older and have significant impairments due to their age are labeled as geriatric — older and in need of special accommodations. This is just one example of what we refer to as **special needs inmates**. Keep in mind that most prison inmates

Geriatric inmates: inmates age 55 (sometimes 50) and above that generally have significant impairments due to age, thus requiring special accommodations.

Special needs inmates: those who have significant impairments due to age or mental/physical disability and require special accommodations by prison administrators.

8. Deborah G. Wilson. 1986. *Inmates' Suicides in the Kentucky Corrections System:* 1973-April, 1986. Frankfort, KY: Kentucky Corrections Cabinet.

9. Hans Toch. 1975. *Men in Crisis, Breakdowns in Prisons.* Chicago: Aldine.

10. Wilson and Vito, supra n.5.

11. Edward A. Parker. 1990. The Social Psychological Impact of a College Education on the Prison Inmate. *Journal of Correctional Education,* 41: 140-146.

12. However, other researchers dispute these findings and, in fact, claim that most inmate suicides are in the earliest days of a sentence (if not prior to sentencing) and that long-term inmates actually display more positive functioning on psychological tests than do shorter-term inmates. J. Stephen Wormith. 1984. The Controversy over the Effects of Long Term Incarceration. *Canadian Journal of Criminology,* 26, (4), 423-437.

13. Carson and Sabol, supra n.2.

come from economically disadvantaged backgrounds, which means that they are more likely to have poor health, to have not had regular health care, and to suffer from a number of physical and mental health problems. This is especially true for incarcerated elderly inmates, who have higher rates of health problems than do nonincarcerated elderly people.[14]

However, it would be a mistake to think of all elderly inmates as a homogeneous lot. Just as all elderly people in the community are not completely alike, so too are there a wide range of differences — in physical ability, in mental acuity, in personality, values, etc. — among elderly prison inmates. For simplicity's sake, though, we can think of elderly inmates as comprising three types of individuals. First, and numerically the smallest of the three groups, are those offenders of advanced age who are arrested for the first time and subsequently sentenced to prison. Often these individuals are incarcerated for killings. Second are those offenders who have been in and out of the criminal justice system for many years and who are returned to prison at an advanced age. In popular discourse, these are referred to as **career criminals**. Third, and the group with the most significant impact on contemporary corrections, are individuals who have aged in prison. Convicted and sentenced for especially severe offenses or for a large number of serious offenses, these offenders have lengthy sentences and spend many years in prison.

Career criminals: offenders who have been in and out of the criminal justice system for many years and who are returned to prison at an advanced age.

Elderly inmates, similar to long-term inmates (as there is considerable overlap between these categories), experience some special problems and present some special needs to correctional officials. Vito and Wilson have identified the following major categories of problems and special needs of these offenders:[15]

1. *Adjustment to imprisonment.* Elderly first-time offenders may have greater difficulties adjusting to the conditions of imprisonment. These adjustments are primarily concerned with social environments (being supervised by younger, culturally diverse people and coping with loss of one's well-established daily routines) and loss of one's culture and material possessions.
2. *Vulnerability to victimization.* Elderly inmates are often viewed by predatory inmates as easy targets for exploitation, especially economic and sexual exploitation.
3. *Adaptation to physical conditions.* Elderly inmates must live in physical facilities that may aggravate or cause physical problems. Things such as concrete floors and walls, stairs, long corridors separating housing, food services, and program offices make incarceration more difficult for many elderly inmates.

---

14. E. O. Moore. 1989. Prison Environments and Their Impact on Older Citizens. *Journal of Offender Counseling, Services and Rehabilitation,* 13, (2), 175-191.
15. Gennaro F. Vito and Deborah G. Wilson. 1985. Forgotten People: Elderly Inmates. *Federal Probation,* 49: 18-24.

4. *Lack of suitable programs.* Most prison recreational programs (primarily sports-related) are geared to younger inmates, as are most educational, vocational, and counseling programs. Because of the cultural isolation most elderly inmates perceive in prisons, they often feel unwelcome, uncomfortable, or vulnerable if they attempt to participate in available programs.
5. *Diversity of the elderly inmate population.* When institutions attempt to serve the needs of the elderly community, they must realize that such efforts need to be culturally diverse. Elderly inmates are not a homogeneous group; the only thing they share universally is age. They have cultural, educational, economic, and social and political differences. This diversity must be addressed in any programming efforts; failure to acknowledge such differences will most likely mean the failure of such efforts.

GANGS

A prison gang is one type of dangerous inmate organization that is also identified as a group of special needs inmates. Whereas elderly inmates are considered special needs because they often require accommodations in the physical plant of a prison or its services in order to be able to go about daily life, inmates in a prison gang require special attention and monitoring in order to maintain the security and custody in the prison. A prison gang can be defined as "any group of three (3) or more persons with recurring threatening or disruptive behavior (i.e., violations of the disciplinary rules where said violations were openly known or conferred benefit upon the group would suffice for a prison environment), including but not limited to gang crime or gang violence."[16] According to the American Correctional Association, a prison gang is defined as "two or more inmates, acting together, who pose a threat to the security or safety of staff/inmates, and/or are disruptive to programs and/or to the orderly management of the facility/system."[17]

Prison gangs are important to understand for several reasons. First, these gangs can be very violent. Both non–gang-affiliated inmates and inmates in rival gangs may be targets of assault, sexual assault, and murder by a prison gang. So too are prison staff frequent targets for the actions of prison gang members. Prison gangs are also important to understand because they pose a strong and direct challenge to the authority and ability of prison officials and staff to control the daily life of inmates. When prison gangs engage in not only violence, but also drug smuggling and the sales, making, and selling of homemade alcohol,

16. George Knox. 2005. *The Problem of Gangs and Security Threat Groups in American Prisons Today: Recent Research Findings from the 2004 Prison Gang Survey.* Peotone, IL: National Gang Crime Research Center, p. 2.
17. Knox, *ibid.*, p. 3.

weapons, and sex, it is clear that prison gangs are dangerous. However, when a prison gang gains power in a prison (largely through violence and instilling fear in other inmates), the members not only control the major forms of deviance in a prison, but so too do they control the small issues of daily life. This may include what is watched on the televisions in dayrooms or dormitories, how much food inmates receive at meals, who can use the telephones and when, what personal possessions inmates keep, and where inmates spend their recreational time inside the prison. Clearly, prison gangs are powerful and important for the daily life of both other prison inmates and prison staff.

Prison gangs are not necessarily referred to as "gangs" in correctional facilities.[18] In some jurisdictions and facilities, such groups and their members are known as **security threat groups** because they are groups that actively threaten the security of the institution. Or, in other locations, they may be referred to with the more innocuous label of a "disruptive group." Regardless of the specific terminology used, however, such groups operate on and with the same principles, goals, and behaviors that are central to the definition of a "gang." One interesting and important aspect of all of the definitions of a prison gang is that the number of inmates involved is not that important; by definition, so long as there are two or three individuals working together in pursuit of illicit or disruptive behaviors, the group meets the definition of a "prison gang." Typically, though, we think of prison gangs as comprised of larger numbers of inmates.

Security threat groups: groups of individuals or "gangs" in correctional facilities that are characterized as a security threat due to their disruptive, often violent, behavior.

Gangs in prison are sometimes directly affiliated with street gangs where members have simply moved to prison when sentenced to prison, and at other times prison gangs are groups that develop and emerge inside the prison (referred to as indigenous to prison). When looking at prison gangs as branches or chapters of gangs that exist on the outside, we see the prison gang having the same organizational structure as the gang on the street, and frequently being under the direction and control of the gang leaders on the outside of prison. Most members of gangs in prison were members on the streets.[19] According to reports by prison wardens, only about 11 percent of male prison gang members and 3 to 4 percent of female prison gang members are recruited to membership while incarcerated.[20] When an individual who was in a leadership position in the gang on the streets enters prison, he is most likely to also occupy a leadership position in the gang in prison.[21]

Indigenous prison gangs are developed by inmates coming together inside of prison for purposes of both enhancing their lifestyle and seeking a sense of belonging and protection from other inmates. Most scholars suggest that the idea of protection is the key issue in gangs developing inside of prisons.

---

18. Knox, *ibid.*
19. Knox, *ibid.*
20. Knox, *ibid.*
21. Randall Shelden. 2005. Gangs, in Mary Bosworth (ed.), *Encyclopedia of Prisons and Correctional Facilities.* (Vol. 1.) Thousand Oaks, CA: Sage, pp. 359-362.

Identifying the exact number of members of prison gangs is a very difficult, probably impossible task. While some members of prison gangs are open and proudly proclaim their status as a gang member, for many others there is reluctance to publicly claim the label, since gang members may have increased risks of being victims of attacks (as discussed below) or having their movements, privileges, and activities closely monitored and controlled by prison officials. Prison gangs are believed to be present in one form or another, and to varying degrees, in all prison systems in the United States. Gangs are most likely in the prisons of states that are more urban and have a greater presence of gangs on the streets. States like California, Florida, Texas, and Arizona — all of which are states with urban areas — tend to have a greater proportion of gang members among their prison populations. Smaller population states, and those without any large cities — such as North Dakota, Wyoming, Delaware, Vermont, New Hampshire, Montana, and Arkansas — do not have as serious of a gang problem as larger states, although some individual gang members are in prisons in these states. A few smaller states that one might expect to be relatively gang free, however, do have a significant gang presence in prison. For instance, Idaho has a sizable number of white supremacist gang members in prison, largely because many of the Aryan movement groups and members live in Idaho.

Not surprisingly, corrections officials in higher-security prisons are more likely to perceive gang members to be present in their population of inmates, and to believe that there is a greater concentration of gang members in the prison.

Inside of prisons, gangs and their members occupy and fulfill a number of roles and tasks that are important to both the day-to-day and long-term culture of the prison. In some prisons, gangs control the market for contraband, including drugs, alcohol, weapons, cellphones, cigarettes, and anything else that inmates are prohibited to have. As reported by a national sample of prison wardens, gangs do (or try to) control the black market for contraband in most prisons. Across prisons, the percent of institutions where gangs control various forms of contraband are 88 percent for drugs, 45 percent for illicit sex, 56 percent for contraband food, 40 percent for contraband and extra clothing, 60 percent for loans among inmates, and 73 percent for gambling.[22] Gangs are also believed to control the extortion activities in 70 percent of prisons and are the primary inmates involved in offering "protection" to inmates in exchange for goods, services, or payment in 76 percent of American prisons.

Prison gangs also commonly control decisions about individual inmates' activities, including such innocuous things as where inmates may spend their time in a housing unit, what commissary items they are allowed to purchase (and keep), what is shown on communal televisions, etc. In many respects, what this suggests is that prison gangs can be very powerful inside the culture of prison.

---

22. Knox, supra n.17.

Although gangs do not have official or legitimate authority to control anything in prison, they use their size, threats and actual use of violence, and the fear that they instill in others to assume power and control.

TRANSGENDER INMATES

One group of inmates that has come to be recognized as a special needs group in the last decade or so is **transgender inmates**. These are individuals who are biologically and (usually) physically either male or female, but psychologically, emotionally, and socially the "other" sex. As in free society, transgender individuals have a number of challenges, mostly centered on issues of acceptance or rejection from others who do not understand and/or accept their status. But, in prison these issues are made even more prominent and important in that transgender inmates may be singled out and targeted for violence, especially sexual violence.[23]

Transgender inmates: individuals who are biologically and (usually) physically either male or female, but are psychologically, emotionally, and socially the "other" sex.

In the first decade of the twenty-first century, a great deal of policy attention was devoted to the issue of sexual violence in prisons, as well as to attempts to identify ways to control and eliminate sexual violence. Through the research that accompanied this policy work, it became clear that one of the most frequently targeted types of inmates is transgender inmates — especially those biologically male inmates who believe themselves to be, and who socially present themselves as, female. As a result, this group of inmates presents special challenges for correctional administrators who have a legal responsibility to protect all, including transgender, inmates from victimization while incarcerated. As a result, many transgender inmates are found in special security housing, often restricted to their cells or dormitories as a way to limit their interactions with and exposure to other inmates.

Transgender inmates are also special needs inmates in that they present some unique, and often times very challenging, health care needs. An inmate who on the streets had begun sex reassignment, perhaps being on hormones to minimize his male secondary sex characteristics and to bring out female characteristics (including the development of breasts), may need to continue on a course of hormone therapy so as to not jeopardize her health. While actually completing sex reassignment via surgery is not done by correctional health providers, in many jurisdictions hormone therapy is maintained, and the costs of such are borne by the state. Health care costs are also higher for transgender inmates due to the fact that they are often singled out (due to their "difference") for violent physical and sexual assault.

---

23. Valerie Jenness, Cheryl L. Maxson, Kristy M. Matsuda, and Jennifer Macy Sumner. 2007. *Violence in California Correctional Facilities: An Empirical Examination of Sexual Assault.* Irvine, CA: University of California at Irvine, Center for Evidence Based Corrections.

THE CULTURE OF PRISON

In 1940, Donald Clemmer, a sociologist at the Menard Prison in Chester, Illinois, began his classic study of the prison as a separate culture or community. His perceptive observations and description of the formal organizational structure of the prison counterculture were the first of numerous systematic efforts.[24] Since the publication of Clemmer's work, many other studies have been made. Nearly all of these studies have agreed on the power, influence, organization, and pathology of the prison culture. It has a code, a normative order, a status hierarchy, and a language of its own, typically referred to as **prison argot**.

Prison argot: the code, normative order, status hierarchy, and/or language that is unique to a prison.

Similar to someone moving to a different country and needing to speak and understand that culture's language to survive, the correctional professional must know the language spoken in prison. However, prison language can differ among institutions. For this reason, staff must carefully listen to the words used (and their specific meanings) when entering a new prison or jail. The influence of language on behavior is clearly evident in the work of those who adhere to **labeling theory**. This school of thought believes that the labels, or names, attached to people and actions significantly influence their self-concept and subsequent behavior. For example, people who are repeatedly told that they are stupid or worthless will eventually believe these statements. As a result, they will have very low self-esteem and expectations for themselves.

Labeling theory: the school of thought that believes that the labels, or names, attached to people and actions significantly influence their self-concept and subsequent behavior.

While incarcerated, inmates are effectively removed from free society and are subjected to life within a controlled, restrictive, and punitive structure. As a consequence, inmates experience suffering or, as Sykes says, "pains of imprisonment."[25] First is the deprivation of liberty. As its most basic function, prison serves to segregate offenders from society, thereby depriving inmates of their freedom. Second, inmates are deprived of or have limited access to material goods (food, clothing, entertainment devices, personal care products, etc.) and to professional and care services. Third, inmates suffer deprivation of heterosexual relationships. Although opposite sex staff are fairly common in prisons, strict rules govern sexual relationships between staff and inmates. Only a few states (most notably California and Mississippi) allow inmates **conjugal visits**, where spouses can spend time together in private (and have sex), but these are relatively rare. Fourth and perhaps surprising to some, inmates suffer a deprivation of security. Prison is filled with people who are often violent, predatory, and threatening. As we will discuss in more depth in Chapter 8, prison can be a very violent place, and many inmates have a sense of vulnerability. Finally, inmates suffer a loss of autonomy. The highly structured nature of many prisons means that inmates do not make many decisions about their daily or long-term activities. In many ways, inmates are treated as if they were children, unable or too

Conjugal visits: visitation privileges allowed in a select number of states where an inmate and spouse can spend time together in private, usually to have sex.

---

24. Donald Clemmer. 1966. *The Prison Community.* New York: Holt, Rinehart & Winston.
25. Gresham Sykes. 1956. *The Society of Captives.* Princeton, NJ: Princeton University Press.

irresponsible to make intelligent decisions. As a result, inmates are not taught to make intelligent decisions.

However, the experience of incarceration not only creates "pains" for individuals, but, because it is stressful, imprisonment also magnifies problems people bring to jail or prison. Many people who are incarcerated are dependent on alcohol or other drugs. They may be mentally ill, may have chronic medical conditions, and may be responsible for the welfare (or survival) of significant others and children. Many find that the support networks on which they have long relied are stretched beyond their useful points. Thus, when initially incarcerated, many people have a myriad of problems with which to cope. As a result, they may not be able to handle any specific problem particularly well.

Separating the Inmate from the Subculture

Can treatment efforts effectively prevent prisoners from identifying with the prison subculture? Much evidence reveals that treatment is ineffective in this way, but some evidence suggests that it is effective. Daniel Glaser, in studying how the prison experience affects various types of offenders, found that a majority of ex-prisoners, when asked if they have identified with the convict population while in prison, had tried actively to remain apart from the other prisoners. Three-quarters of the 250 "successful" releases (those not rearrested) studied replied as such. Glaser discovered that their identification with other prisoners and the prison culture was higher during the middle period of imprisonment than it was at the beginning or just before release.[26]

Clemmer's original work focused on the process of **prisonization**, whereby inmates internalize the institution's norms, values, and activity patterns. This is the process of learning, internalizing, and adhering to the cultural milieu of the correctional institution. However, for decades correctionalists debated the presence and form of the prisonization process. This debate culminated in the 1960s, when Stanton Wheeler found that the prisonization process does not simply take place in greater degrees with increasing length of incarceration. Rather, during both the first and last six months of incarceration, inmates have low levels of adherence to prison culture. During the remaining, middle period, prisonization increases to a peak and then decreases as inmates approach release.[27]

Prisonization: when inmates internalize the institution's norms, values, and activity patterns.

More recently, other researchers have argued that new inmates, especially those with relatively short sentences, may pursue adaptation strategies whereby they "suspend" their pre-prison identities and adopt a new, temporary identity that serves their needs as inmates.[28] However, such strategies are not completely

26. Daniel Glaser. 1964. *The Effectiveness of a Prison and Parole System.* New York: The Bobbs-Merrill Company, Inc., pp. 89-117.

27. Stanton Wheeler. 1959. Social Organization and Inmate Values in Correctional Communities. Proceedings of the Eighty-Ninth Annual American Correctional Association, Miami Beach, Florida.

28. Thomas Schmid and Richard Jones. 1991. Suspended Identity: Identity Transformation in a Maximum Security Prison. *Symbolic Interaction*, 14, (4) 415-432.

successful. Unable to totally leave behind their pre-prison selves, inmates are unable to completely recapture their original sense of identity after leaving prison. In contrast, Sykes claimed that some inmates do not conform to the convict culture. Rather, these inmates seek to maintain a sense of personal dignity, to keep strong ties to the outside, and to display an ability to tolerate imprisonment.[29] Generally defined as "easy to manage," these inmates have an easier time readjusting to life on the outside.

Wheeler had earlier pointed out that inmates differ in their responses to the prison community. His general conclusion was that the degree of identification depended on how much contact inmates had with other prisoners and how long they had been in prison.[30] Thus, thrown into contact with each other in reception centers, new inmates share the cultural values formed before entering prison. However, before integrating into institutional culture, new inmates must work through a grief process similar to what terminally ill patients experience.[31] Beginning with the stage of denial and working through the stages of anger, bargaining, depression, and finally acceptance,[32] new inmates experience a range of stresses and emotions. The stresses can cause emotional and psychological damage and can potentially place inmates in positions of physical vulnerability.

As new inmates involve themselves in the prison's daily activities and structure, they are increasingly exposed to the prison culture and its code of conduct. Eventually, they give their loyalty to the prison society, rather than to the administration. Then, as release approaches, many inmates shift their identification to those reference groups with whom they identified before prison. Mabli and his colleagues found that as inmates of one federal correctional institution approached their release dates, they experienced increased levels of stress, exhibited in both their mood and behaviors.[33] Taking a step further, inmates who adopted behaviors conforming to the institutional culture were more likely to experience difficulties readjusting to free society upon release than were those inmates who actively resisted conformity pressures while incarcerated.[34]

These generalizations, however, are not true of all prisoners. Thoroughly institutionalized criminals, for example, do not identify with the free culture *regardless of whether they are in or out of prison.* In addition, most institutions by their very nature are not treatment oriented. Treatment, therefore, cannot overcome the negative influences of the prison subculture. Some observers have

---

29. Sykes, supra n.25.
30. Wheeler, supra n.27.
31. Carolyn Brastow Pledger. 1985. Do Incarcerated Offenders Experience the Five Stages of Grief as Do Terminally Ill Patients? *Journal of Offender Counseling,* 6, (1), 9-17.
32. This stage model of grief for the terminally ill was originally proposed by Elisabeth Kubler-Ross. Elisabeth Kubler-Ross. 1969. *On Death and Dying.* New York: Macmillan Publishing, Inc.
33. Jerome Mabli, Steven M. Glick, Marilyn Hilborn, Jerry Kastler, David Pillow, Kevin Karlson, and Scot Barber. 1985. Prerelease Stress in Prison Inmates. *Journal of Offender Counseling, Services and Rehabilitation,* 9, (3), 43-56.
34. Lynne Goodstein. 1979. Inmate Adjustment to Prison and Transition to Community Life. *Journal of Research in Crime and Delinquency,* 16, (2), 246-272.

identified one major dilemma that subcultural participation helps inmates overcome: the lack of personal control. When people are restricted in controlling the outcomes of their actions, have no choices of actions, and cannot predict their future actions, they will cease taking responsibility for their actions.[35] This is one contribution that the inmate subculture can make to participating individuals. Similarly, participation in prison programs has helped inmates adjust to life while in prison, but not to life after release.[36] This suggests that programs provide inmates with opportunities to control some aspects of their lives while in prison.

Nor can one assume that prisoners are part of a unified, loyalty-based subsystem. Inmates' greatest enemies are often other prisoners, who may be psychotic, exploitative, or simply violent.

Penetrating the Subculture

To keep from becoming hard-core "convicts," inmates must overcome the negative aspects of the prison culture. Some inmates have been successful in their efforts. The closer an institution is to minimum security, the more progress inmates can make in overcoming or avoiding the negative aspect of incarceration. In minimum-security institutions, inmates have fewer negative psychological and social impacts of tight custody and fear. In contrast, if placed in institutions where custody is the main goal, prisoners will be segregated into a convict-ruled subculture and controlled by fear. Under such circumstances, treatments or rehabilitation efforts will be less successful. Security, of course, cannot be abandoned, but it can be kept at a reasonable level. This is where the need for classification schemes becomes clear.

Using minimum-security prisons and correctional institution camps are ways that correctional professionals attempt to overcome the high social costs of incarceration. Although many Americans express great disappointment and outrage when white-collar offenders (and others considered little or no immediate danger to society) are incarcerated at fenceless camps, the reason for such actions should now be quite clear. Incarcerated in highly restrictive, inmate-dominated prisons, these offenders could easily become "worse" rather than "better." In minimum-security facilities, the effects of prisonization can be held in check.

The **inmate code** has been clearly understood. Considering the evolving nature of prison norms, correctional officials can now make serious attempts to control or neutralize its impacts. Sykes has made the clearest statements regarding the inmate code's components. According to Sykes, the basic tenets of the normative system are to "do your own time" and "don't inform on another convict."

Inmate code: the universally understood code of conduct for most inmates that includes the following: don't interfere with inmate interests, don't fight with other inmates, don't exploit other inmates, be strong, and don't trust the staff.

35. Lynne Goodstein, Doris Layton MacKenzie, and T. Lance Shotland. 1984. Personal Control and Inmate Adjustment to Prison. *Criminology*, 22, (3), 343-369.

36. Harjit S. Sandhu. 1986. Recidivists and Non-Recidivists Perceptions of Prison Experience and Post-Prison Problems. *Free Inquiry in Creative Sociology*, 14, (2), 193-196.

More specifically, the universal aspects of the inmate code include the following:

1. *Don't interfere with inmate interests.* This is the idea that one should mind his or her own business and not become involved in other prisoners' activities, whether legal or not.
2. *Don't fight with other inmates.* Devote your attention to your own affairs, and do not make things more difficult on yourself or on others by fighting.
3. *Don't exploit other inmates.* If you do become involved in dealing with others, be true to your word and do not try to manipulate others.
4. *Be strong.* Accept the conditions of your imprisonment. Excessive complaining or showing signs of physical, psychological, or emotional weaknesses are dangerous to one's status in the prison community.
5. *Don't trust the staff.* This also includes not adhering to staff's or officials' values and desires. At the base, this norm says that an inmate is to value other inmates, and what they believe and stand for, over staff at all times and in all situations.[37]

Obviously, these norms are not always maintained in the prison community. However, similar to the basic norms and laws of society in general, they provide the foundation upon which the prison community's normative structure is based. When inmates violate norms of the inmate code, other inmates may sanction them. Or, just as in society in general, if those violating the norms hold enough social power, they may escape social sanctioning.[38]

PRISON ECONOMIC SYSTEMS

As in free society, one of the major aspects that structure the inmate community is an economic system. Two economic systems exist inside prison: legitimate and illegitimate systems of exchange. The legitimate system centers on the wages inmates earn at prison jobs and other funds that people outside the prison deposit in institutional accounts. Inmates are permitted to withdraw and spend a predetermined amount from their accounts to make purchases at the prison store (sometimes called the "canteen"). This allows inmates to obtain name-brand toiletries, rather than prison-issued generic brands, snack foods, and small amenities for their cells and personal activities (stationery, pens, stamps, etc.). In some states, inmates are allowed to carry a small amount of cash as well.

Contraband: any unauthorized material that is possessed by inmates that fuels the illegitimate economy in prison.

The prison's illegitimate economy centers on the distribution of **contraband**, or any unauthorized material possessed by inmates. Contraband goods and

37. Sykes, supra n.25, pp. 63-108.
38. James W. Marquart and Julian B. Roebuck. 1985. Prison Guards and "Snitches": Deviance Within a Total Institution. *British Journal of Criminology*, 25, (3), 217-233.

services can be summarized in nine general categories: drugs, alcoholic beverages (usually homemade), gambling, appliances, clothing, institutional privileges, weapons (both homemade and smuggled), food, and prostitution. Inmates may obtain contraband goods and services by either barter or purchase. Purchases can be made with cash (which may be contraband itself), vouchers used to draw on one's institutional account, or most commonly, packs and cartons of cigarettes or certain food items. Barter systems work most efficiently for those inmates who have special skills that others desire (legal skills, tattoo paraphernalia, or handicraft work) or who are willing to trade sex for goods.

The two economic systems overlap and influence each other. Goods and services obtained on the legitimate market may be introduced to the illegal market in exchange for contraband. Also, the legitimate system, by its very structure and operation, makes possible the existence and profitability of the illegitimate market. As Kalinich concluded from his study of the institutional economy at State Prison of Southern Michigan,

> the legitimate economic system supports and facilitates the sub-rosa system in two ways. Many of the institutional assignments place residents in positions of trust and allow them freedom of movement, which permits them to deal rather freely in the sub-rosa system. Residents may buy and sell contraband by having funds placed in the supplier's personal bank account or resident fund from the buyer's bank account or outside contacts. This system can be and often is used to transfer money from one resident's fund to another.[39]

Prisons typically have very active economies, and inmates expend much time and energy to maintain the system and to work to accumulate the things they desire. Inmates benefit from their underground economy in that working within it allows them some degree of easing the pains of imprisonment. However, institutional authorities may also benefit from the existence of an underground economy. By devoting time and energy to maintaining their economic system, many inmates' time and minds are occupied, meaning that they are not focusing on other activities, which might be detrimental to the security and custody of the institution. Also, the underground economic system serves many inmates' varied needs, which would be too costly for the institution to meet. Finally, at least in the minds of some observers, the introduction of some contraband items, specifically alcohol, drugs, and prostitution, may actively work to prevent stress, frustrations, and potential violence.

THE EX-PRISONER

No matter what constructive activities occur in the prison, when all is said and done, it will be an unproductive investment if the free community outside of

39. David Kalinich. 1980. *Power, Stability and Contraband: The Inmate Economy.* Prospect Heights, IL: Waveland Press.

prison will not accept and provide opportunities for the former inmate once the inmate is released. However, the fact is that many men and women discharged from our "correctional" systems find themselves in a hostile and rejecting community upon release from prison. When this occurs — and it commonly does — how can we expect them not to readopt criminal ways because their community exercised discrimination and rejection and proved inflexible?

Returning ex-inmates have many built-in psychological barriers between themselves and their communities. Former inmates have lived in an artificial community, some for many years. They have had little contact with the opposite sex, at least very little "normal" types of interactions. Although they are rational people with decision-making abilities, almost all of their decisions about day-to-day and moment-to-moment life have been made for them. Also, if someone has been incarcerated for more than just a few years, many things have changed on the outside; and the longer they have been away, the more difficult it is for them to readapt. Consider for a moment if you had been in prison for the past ten years and were just today coming to your life as you know it. What things — technologies, words, ways of shopping, etc. — would be completely new to you? In all probability, most things that the rest of us take for granted. But, this is not all. So too must most individuals returning from prison relearn and reestablish relations with loved ones and friends. Those people have had their lives continue on the outside, and they have changed, they have learned to go about life without the offender, and now when the offender returns, he or she must be incorporated into the routines of life.

Another type of barrier is related to ex-inmates' vocational plans. In simple terms, it can be extremely difficult for former inmates to find and maintain work. Some offenders will have completed at least one job training program while incarcerated, and come back to the community expecting to be able to find steady work that will support them. However, especially in recent years with widespread recession in American society, there are not that many jobs, and many employers prefer to hire employees without, rather than with, a criminal record. Combined with the usually low-level skills and education that most inmates (and, therefore, ex-inmates) possess and their interrupted or absent employment record, it is no surprise that the vast majority of released offenders are confined to the secondary labor market. This is the world of unskilled, poorly paid, and nonsecure work, temporary employment, jobs without benefits, and part-time or seasonal work. Essentially, as undesirable employees, ex-inmates are relegated to jobs that most people take only when they have no other options.

When released from prison, inmates are typically provided very little material, treatment, or vocational assistance. This means that inmates must plan for their releases and gather their own resources. Many inmates save portions of their institutional incomes, but these rarely amount to significant totals. Therefore, released inmates rely very heavily on their families and friends for support.

However, many inmates find this support to be either partially or completely absent. A criminal conviction, especially when accompanied by a prison sentence, is highly stigmatizing. The public's misunderstandings of and the myths about life in prison make most people fear being with "ex-cons." Many people also fear that their own characters may be tarnished if others know they associate with ex-inmates. Such negative repercussions not only affect ex-inmates, but they also directly impact offender's families and close friends. **Courtesy stigmas** are those negative labels others apply to people whom they perceive as associated with known or suspected offenders. Because of other's negative perceptions, as well as the shame, embarrassment, and anger they feel, many family members and friends do not continue relationships with released offenders. This means that ex-prisoners have yet more obstacles to overcome in their quest to remain free in the community.

Courtesy stigmas: negative labels others apply to people whom they perceive as associated with known or suspected offenders.

Summary

There are over one and a half million adults incarcerated in the United States. More than 429 out of every 100,000 adults are in prison. This rate of incarceration is among the highest in the world, and has been increasing for several decades. Minorities are incarcerated at higher rates than whites, and more than 90 percent of inmates are males.

Among the fastest growing segments of the incarcerated population are the elderly, gang members, and transgender inmates. Each of these groups presents unique challenges for corrections, including issues of security and safety, treatment, special needs, and threats to smooth day-to-day operations of an institution.

Life in prison is distinctively different than life in free society. Inmates establish their own unique culture within a prison. This institutional culture both socializes new inmates to the rules and expectations of this society, as well as creates a unique language (argot), expectations, types of relationships, and rules for with whom and how individuals are expected to interact. Perhaps most pronounced among these rules are the expectation to avoid anything approaching a positive form of relationship with staff members.

Key Terms

Career criminals
Conjugal visits
Contraband
Courtesy stigmas
Geriatric inmates
Incarceration rate
Inmate code
Labeling theory
Long-term incarceration
Prison argot
Prisonization
Security threat groups
Special needs inmates
Total institution
Transgender inmates

Chapter Seven
Prisoners' Rights

The idea of talking about "prisoners' rights" may strike some as an odd thing to talk about, or to even consider as existing. Some people believe that criminal offenders should have no legal rights, that when a person commits a crime he forfeits all of his rights. For others, the idea of convicted criminal offenders having legal rights is at the core of American values, and is one of the issues that distinguishes our social and legal systems from those of "less developed" cultures. Regardless of whether we believe that criminal offenders, and prison inmates in particular, should have any legal rights, the fact is that there are a range of legal rights that are guaranteed to such persons. As we will see throughout this chapter, these rights are largely the result of court decisions, often cases that interpret the United States Constitution.

PRISONERS' RIGHTS IN A HISTORICAL CONTEXT

When we look at the history of prisoners' rights, we quickly see that the legal status and rights of inmates today are completely different than where we started out as a nation. In the earliest days, Americans convicted of crimes had essentially no legal rights, and in fact were stripped of nearly every right and privilege of citizenship. This was largely the case in other nations of the eighteenth century and earlier. However, over time and accompanying changes in how society has viewed the legal rights for all citizens, the reasons for individuals to commit crimes, and the purpose of corrections, social change has brought about legal change that has led to the "discovery" or creation of legal rights for prisoners.

The movement from convicted criminals having absolutely no legal rights to today's status of inmates as citizens who have legal disabilities has been a long, sometimes slow development that has seen most of the change happen in the last 50 or so years. The changes that have occurred in the last five decades have been immense, and prisoners' rights have been an outgrowth of larger, society-wide legal developments. In fact, the "prisoners' rights movement" has followed on the development of large-scale (some might say "radical") changes in citizens' — especially minority citizens' — rights. As will be discussed in more detail later in this chapter, the development and recognition of prisoners' rights follows on the developments of the much larger civil rights movement in the United States that peaked in the 1960s.

JUDICIAL INTERVENTION

In simple terms, all of our legal rights as American citizens stem from the United States Constitution and the ways that courts have interpreted the Constitution. As a basic tool and process for our legal system, the judicial branch of government holds the power to review and interpret the meaning of the Constitution, legislatively created laws (statutes), and administrative law (rules made by agencies of the executive branch of government that carry the power of law). This ability of the courts to review and interpret the meaning and application of laws is known as **judicial intervention**.

Judicial intervention: the ability of the courts to review and interpret the meaning and application of laws.

Hands-off policy: the approach by many judges toward corrections where they explicitly avoid involvement in correctional issues.

The history of judicial intervention in corrections most often centers on courts deciding whether certain practices violate the Constitution. In practice, judicial intervention has a relatively short history in America. Throughout most of U.S. history, judges have approached corrections with a **hands-off policy**. Not really a specific policy, hands-off is an approach judges use to explicitly avoid involvement in correctional issues. Instead of ruling on cases that contest the policies, procedures, and conditions of correctional institutions, judges stated that their limited expertise leaves them incapable of deciding how prisons should operate. Rather, judges have (both explicitly and implicitly) deferred to correctional "experts" and have relied on their decisions about how best to administer corrections. These experts, of course, have typically been administrators of correctional systems and institutions. So, in terms of judicial intervention in corrections, for most of American history the courts avoided hearing and ruling on issues related to prisons and jails, and instead deferred to the judgment of corrections officials. Therefore, for most of our nation's history, the courts have rendered few decisions about changes in prison operations.

Civil death: the legal equivalent under English common law to physical death for certain felonies such as treason or outlawry.

Under English common law, the forerunner to our U.S. system, conviction for certain felonies such as treason or outlawry carried with it **civil death**, which was the legal equivalent of physical death. Convicted felons were deprived of all their normal legal capacities, such as owning or inheriting property, voting, and being able to participate in government. Before the various U.S. states modified the principle by statutes and constitutions, civil death was commonly applied to all people who received life sentences. Over time, the idea of civil death has been eased, and some of the rights that citizens hold have been retained by convicted offenders. Today, in almost all cases, the rights that offenders lose at the time of conviction can be restored, although in a number of states there are procedures that must be enacted in order for offenders to regain (many of) their citizenship rights.

In the twenty-first century, some states continue to permanently remove some rights from convicted felons. However, which rights and in what states varies considerably. For instance, in some states convicted felons experience **disenfranchisement** — or the loss of the right to vote, permanently. Imprisoned felons may have their parental rights terminated in some states. The right to hold elected office or other government job is withdrawn in other states, and in many states there are legal prohibitions on convicted felons holding a wide range of jobs (typically those involving a position of trust or contact with the public). And, of course, some offenders (such as convicted sex offenders) lose the right to live in particular places. Convicted offenders in many jurisdictions also lose the right to sit on juries, and in some states one's spouse can file for divorce on the grounds of the other spouse being incarcerated. In some states, people may also lose their parental rights. However, while such laws are still in force in numerous places around the country, the permanent nature of such laws has been eased in recent decades.

Disenfranchisement: the permanent loss of the right to vote once convicted of a felony offense, loss of the right to hold public office, and housing restrictions for certain offenses.

Convicted criminals have been historically considered as individuals undeserving of legal rights. Having shown their inability or unwillingness to live within the law, criminals were considered unworthy of any protections of the law. In other words, convicted criminals have been commonly viewed as deserving removal from society, in all ways, shapes, and forms. Thus, for most of our nation's history, convicted felons were stripped of essentially all legal rights, except those explicitly provided by the United States Constitution. The primary basis of these rights, of course, is the Eighth Amendment to the Constitution, which contains the well-known protection from "cruel and unusual punishment," as well as restrictions against *excessive* bail and fines. This one sentence, while at least on the surface being very clear-cut, has been the focus of some very long, complex legal battles. As we will see in the following section, nothing in the law is really "clear-cut."

Today, we consider inmates as legally disadvantaged citizens. This is in sharp contrast to the situation that existed for many decades in the United States. The government's relationship with convicted criminals is similar to an authority figure's relationship with a younger, perhaps disabled, and immature individual. Put more simply, our government's relationship with convicted criminals is essentially the same as a relationship between a parent and child. Here we see that the legal principle of ***parens patriae*** has guided how the legal system conceives of convicted criminals. That is, the government (in this case correctional officials) should take responsibility for supervising children (inmates) and all others who cannot properly care for themselves. *Parens patriae* is also the basis of the judicial hands-off policy regarding involvement in the actions of the "parental" correctional system.

***Parens patriae*:** the legal principle that has guided how the legal system conceives of convicted criminals by viewing the relationship between the government and convicted criminals as a parent-child relationship.

The fact that for most of our nation's history courts have explicitly avoided becoming involved in issues related to corrections can also be attributed to the explicit legal devaluing of convicts. For most of our nation's history, convicts and inmates were considered as having less legal value than "good" citizens. This status was explicit and guided both our popular and legal beliefs about criminal convicts. Although best known for abolishing slavery, the Thirteenth Amendment to the Constitution, ratified in 1865, explicitly stated that criminal convicts forfeit all their legal rights. While it eliminated slavery, the Thirteenth Amendment left open the door for slavery-like treatment of convicts. The Amendment reads:

> Neither slavery nor involuntary servitude, except as punishment for crime whereof the party shall have been duly convicted, shall exist within the United States.

This position held sway in the United States for the better part of a century. Following on the heels of the Thirteenth Amendment, a Virginia court clearly reinforced the idea that convicted offenders were without legal rights. As the court stated in the 1871 case *Ruffin v. Commonwealth*:

> As a consequence of his crime [he] not only forfeited his liberty, but all his personal rights except those which the law in its humanity accords to him. He is for the time being the slave of the state.[1]

The idea of criminals as a "slave of the state" meant that government could do what it wished with convicted offenders, and that offenders had no legal recourse. Although convicts held no rights, the Supreme Court in the 1892 case of *Logan v. United States* did place on the federal government the responsibility of protecting convicted offenders from "lawless violence all persons in their service or custody in the course of administering justice." This important phrase would later give inmates a foundation upon which to build their cases for other rights, most notably the rights to be free from cruel and unusual punishment, for access to the courts, and for receiving medical care. However, during the nineteenth century, convicts' status as "slaves of the state" permitted the perpetuation of the courts' hands-off policy.

THE PRISONERS' RIGHTS MOVEMENT

Only in the past half century have the courts increasingly moved toward recognizing prisoners' rights. As Burton, Cullen, and Travis conclude, "with few exceptions . . . and despite a broader swing recently toward 'get tough' criminal

1. Ruffin v. Commonwealth, 62 Va. (21 Gratt.) 790 (1871).

justice policies, states generally are becoming less restrictive in depriving the civil rights of offenders."[2]

The 1961 Supreme Court ruling in *Monroe v. Pape*,[3] which made the Civil Rights Act of 1871 applicable to prison inmates, initiated and laid the foundation upon which the modern prisoners' rights movement developed. The Civil Rights Act of 1871 provided newly freed slaves the opportunity to sue state officials in federal court, and the 1961 Supreme Court decision extended this opportunity to state prison inmates. Under Section 1983 of the 1871 Civil Rights Act, prison inmates could sue public officials for monetary damages in response to violations of "clearly established constitutional rights" and the courts could then validate those rights.

Accompanying these legal changes, some important social changes within prisons facilitated the development of the prisoners' rights movement. First, during the 1960s and 1970s, the American prison population increased dramatically. Second, the longer sentences given to convicted felons added to the problem of overcrowding in our prisons. Third, the inmate population became increasingly diverse, less educated, more likely to be substance abusers, and increasingly violent. All these factors added to the stressful nature of most prisons and created a context in which the need for change was obvious.

The social change inside U.S. prisons (and throughout U.S. society) created a tense situation that demanded legal changes. The societal changes that spurred the prisoners' rights movement were the growing diversity of our nation's population and the advances of the civil rights movement. Not only were prisons becoming more diverse racially, economically, and culturally, but so was society. Additionally, minority groups became increasingly politically active in the 1960s and 1970s. This resulted in changing legal statuses for minorities in society and for those inside our prisons.

As with the civil rights movement in general, the prisoners' rights movement was actually conducted through a fast growing number of lawsuits against government officials filed by citizens/inmates. Because of the possibility of bringing lawsuits against government and corrections officials allowed by *Monroe v. Pape* (1961), there were a wide range of prison conditions and restrictions on inmates that were brought to public attention, and for which the courts found it increasingly difficult to maintain a hands-off policy. The flood of court cases did, in fact, lead to a number of legal victories for many inmate claims. Just as was happening with the civil rights movement, the prisoners' rights movement established an ever-widening range of constitutional rights for prison inmates. Although we have never seen a direct overturning of the statements in *Ruffin* and the Thirteenth Amendment, the words of the landmark 1974 case *Wolff v. McDonnell*

---

2. Velmer S. Burton Jr., Frances T. Cullen, and Lawrence F. Travis, III. 1987. The Collateral Consequences of a Felony Conviction: A National Study of State Statutes. *Federal Probation*, 51, 52-60.

3. Monroe v. Pape, 365 U.S. 267 (1961).

clearly show how a new view of prison inmates had taken hold: "Though his rights may be diminished . . . a prisoner is not wholly stripped of constitutional protections."[4]

This leads us, then, to the question, which rights are stripped from prisoners? The primary achievement of the prisoners' rights movement has been striking down previously common restrictions on what prisoners could do and possess, and the movement created procedural practices for reviewing and determining the constitutionality of correctional policies and practices. Another way of viewing this is to see that the prisoners' rights movement more or less forced the judicial system to abandon its hands-off policy and to become actively involved in the structured, daily operations of correctional facilities. Important outgrowths of these precedents have been the substantive rulings of appeals courts that have required changes to prison operations. In these changes of prison operations, the courts have established and specified prisoners' legal rights.

THE RIGHTS OF INMATES

Inmates — in fact, all convicted criminals — do not have all their legal rights removed. Instead, inmates in the twenty-first century take many of their basic citizenship rights with them to prison. However, this does not mean that they maintain all of the legal rights of citizenship — individuals forfeit some not-so-obvious rights when they are convicted of felonies.

Two rights that individuals forfeit when convicted of felonies are holding public office and voting in elections. Disenfranchisement is the loss of the right to vote, which is commonly paired with the loss of the right to hold public office. The legal basis for placing these restrictions on convicted felons is found either in statutory law or in the state's constitution. Although laws vary somewhat from state to state, they are ordinarily stated in precise language. Even so, some confusion exists in interpreting them. Individuals can regain the rights lost, including disenfranchisement, in one of four ways: (1) by executive clemency, (2) by discharge, (3) by pardon, or (4) by special legislative act.

Executive clemency: a special power granted to certain elected officials (typically a governor or the President) that permits them to overrule particular types of court decisions.

Executive clemency is a special power granted to certain elected officials (typically a governor or the President) that permits them to overrule particular types of court decisions. The constitutions of most states (and the United States Constitution) allow governors (or the President) to dismiss criminal courts' convictions and sentences of offenders. Granted very rarely, clemencies are used only in cases when the official considers a conviction inappropriate or a sentence much too extreme. Since clemencies can also be politically dangerous, governors usually grant them only in the last few days or weeks of their terms of office.[5]

---

4. Wolff v. McDonnell, 418 U.S. 539 (1974).

5. Patricia Gagne. 1993. *The Battered Women's Movement in the "Post-Feminist" Era: New Social Movement Strategies and the Celeste Clemencies.* Unpublished doctoral dissertation, The Ohio State University, Columbus, OH.

However, when discussing prisoners' rights, it is not so much a matter of examining what rights they forfeit, but what legal rights they retain. In keeping with our historical foundations, we assume that people convicted of felonies give up all their rights, *except those specifically enumerated by law*. Case law, or occasionally statutory law, covers the area of prisoners' rights. This tells us that the majority of legal rights inmates retain are a result of changes in the judicial system's hands-off policy.

Today, inmates have a number of specific rights guaranteed to them by the Constitution. Included are the rights to be free from cruel and unusual punishment (the Eighth Amendment), to receive visitors, to send and receive mail, to practice their chosen religion, to receive necessary medical care, and to have access to the courts.

Freedom from Cruel and Unusual Punishment

The Eighth Amendment to the United States Constitution expressly forbids "cruel and unusual punishments." The courts have interpreted this prohibition to apply to the sentences imposed, to the conditions in which convicts are imprisoned, and to an institution's internal disciplinary procedures.

Our founding fathers may have known exactly what they considered cruel and unusual punishment. For us, however, this concept is neither a clear nor a precise legal principle. The U.S. Supreme Court has repeatedly offered differing interpretations of that concept. Furthermore, the Supreme Court has argued that "cruel and unusual," being linked to contemporary cultural standards, can be interpreted differently at different points in history. Specifically, in 1910, the Supreme Court stated that the Eighth Amendment "is not fastened to the absolute but may acquire meaning as public opinion becomes enlightened by humane justice."[6] As an Amendment to the United States Constitution, the Eighth Amendment for years was considered to apply only to federal inmates held in federal prisons. However, the fact that the prohibition applies to all prisoners, even those held in prisons operated by states, was clarified by the 1962 case of *Robinson v. California*.

But, the question still remains: What is cruel and unusual punishment? Perhaps the best answer to the question is: There is no one answer but several related answers. First, the courts have commonly used a three-prong test to determine whether a particular form of punishment is cruel and unusual. In order to be considered an acceptable form of punishment, each of three questions must be answered in the negative. These issues were laid out in the landmark Supreme Court case of *Furman v. Georgia* (1972), which is best

6. Weems v. United States, 217 U.S. 349 (1910).

known for having struck down as unconstitutional the death penalty as it was known. These three questions are:

1. Whether the punishment shocks the conscience of a civilized society;
2. Whether the punishment goes beyond legitimate penal aims; and
3. Whether the punishment is unnecessarily cruel and unusual.

Another way to look at what constitutes cruel and unusual punishment is to refer to the 1991 decision by the U.S. Supreme Court in the case of *Wilson v. Seiter*. This case established that the Eighth Amendment contains both an objective and a subjective component. For any particular correctional action or sentence to be declared in violation of the Eighth Amendment, it must violate both components of the Amendment's prohibitions. To be in violation of the objective component of the Eighth Amendment, the practice in question must be shown to violate "contemporary standards of decency."[7] Usually, a correctional practice will be declared to violate this standard if it results in a serious physical or psychological injury to an inmate(s). However, a practice may also violate this standard if it has an imminent threat of actual injury, and this threat could be (but is not) prevented.[8] Whether a practice or action violates the subjective component depends on whether it was performed *as a punishment*. If something is done that harms or injures an inmate, but is not done with the intent to punish, then it cannot be in violation of the Eighth Amendment.[9] Remember: The Constitution provides protection only from cruel and unusual *punishment*.

Conditions of confinement: the prisons' actual physical conditions and the positive/negative impacts they have on inmates.

Conditions of confinement are the prisons' actual physical conditions and the positive and negative impacts they have on inmates. The Constitution guarantees that inmates will be held in physical facilities that do not impose undue hardships or dangers to their safety and health. *Holt v. Sarver*, a 1969 federal District Court ruling, is one significant court case in this area of law. In this case, the inmates of two prison farms in Arkansas claimed that the combined, overall conditions in these institutions were cruel and unusual punishment. The court agreed with the inmates, declaring the Arkansas correctional system to be in violation of the Eighth Amendment because of its **totality of conditions**. As the court stated:

Totality of conditions: when conditions and practices of an entire institution are so bad as to be shocking to the conscience of a reasonable civilized people and are prohibited by the Eighth Amendment.

> Confinement itself within a given institution may amount to cruel and unusual punishment prohibited by the Constitution where confinement is characterized by conditions and practices so bad as to be shocking to the conscience of a reasonable civilized people. . . . [10]

---

7. Hudson v. McMillian, 503 U.S. 1 (1992).
8. Helling v. McKinney, 509 U.S. 25 (1993).
9. *Hudson*, supra n.7, at 998; Whitley v. Albers, 475 U.S. 312, 320 (1986).
10. Holt v. Sarver, 309 F. Supp. 362, 372-373 (E.D. Ark. 1970).

Holt v. Sarver opened the doors, and courts found entire institutions or even whole correctional systems to be in violation of the Eighth Amendment. When this is done, courts typically specify either detailed and specific changes or establish broad guidelines for changes that prisons must make to improve conditions that are *not* cruel and unusual punishment.

One area in which the totality of conditions argument has been used to challenge prison conditions is in regard to overcrowding of correctional institutions. One way that correctional officials have tried to cope with the rapidly growing prison populations of the past five decades has been to house more people in spaces than the spaces were originally intended to hold. In 1981, Ohio inmates challenged the practice of housing two inmates in prison cells originally intended for only single occupancy. Here the Supreme Court in the case of *Rhodes v. Chapman* ruled that double-celling does not constitute cruel and unusual punishment, because doing so is not intended as a means to inflict harm and did not contribute to loss of any issue other than privacy and physical space.

The Eighth Amendment also impacts the specific treatment and disciplinary procedures that prisons use with inmates who violate institutional rules and regulations. Most significant here is that correctional employees no longer have complete and open access to use corporal punishment or physical force on inmates. In fact, legally there are only five situations in which correctional personnel may use physical force with an inmate:

1. As an act of self-defense against inmate aggression.
2. As an act of defense to protect a third party under attack by an inmate.
3. As an act to enforce prison rules and regulations (but only when all other, less severe methods to bring about compliance have been exhausted).
4. As a means to prevent an escape.
5. As a means to prevent the commission of a crime.

This represents a huge change in how correctional staff maintains discipline and order among inmates. Until the late 1960s, corporal punishment was the norm for how inmates who violated prison rules and regulations were handled. In the 1968 case of *Jackson v. Bishop*, the U.S. Court of Appeals for the Eighth Circuit ruled that whipping inmates who violated institutional rules violated their Eighth Amendment protection from cruel and unusual punishment.[11] This case was a major precedent for later cases, and today any form of corporal punishment a correctional institution uses is interpreted as illegal behavior.

---

11. Jackson v. Bishop, 404 F.2d 571 (8th Cir. 1968).

Visitation

Receiving visitors while incarcerated is not a fundamental right. Rather, it is a right that must be balanced against the needs of institutional security.[12] Legally, however, any restrictions on visitation procedures and on who is determined to be a permissible visitor must be precise.[13] Examples of policies that have been determined to be unconstitutional include an Ohio restriction on visits from individuals whose conduct is "objectionable,"[14] and a California ban on visitation between persons of different races.[15] Additionally, based on legal rulings, a prison must provide some degree of privacy for visits (although what constitutes "privacy" may well be seating an inmate and his visitor a prescribed distance from other inmates or visitors), and visitors and inmates must be able to simultaneously see each other and converse. Consequently, visits must be conducted in either an open, unrestricted area (such as a cafeteria or outside) or in visitation booths. If the latter, then only clear partitions can separate inmates and their visitors, and communication must be facilitated through open screens or over effective, modern voice communication apparatus.[16] However, contact visits, while allowed in many prisons, have not been declared a right of inmates.

But, there are limits to visits that inmates can receive. Most recently, the case of *Overton v. Bazzetta* in 2003 saw the Supreme Court uphold a Michigan Department of Corrections policy that denied most visits to prisoners who had committed two substance abuse violations while incarcerated. The reasoning is that such a policy is in the interest of maintaining order and custody, and inmates who lose the right to receive visits under this rule do not suffer any loss of relationships or association (they can still communicate via the mail and telephone), and to continue to allow such inmates to receive visits would impose additional hardships and unnecessary costs on the institution in monitoring such visits.

Use of the Mail

Prisoners' ability to send and receive mail is another legal right that is the result of judicial interpretations, this time of the First Amendment to the Constitution. Specifically, the right to use the mail is guaranteed by the language of the First Amendment: "Congress shall make no law . . . abridging the freedom of speech, or of the press." The right of free speech is widely considered to be one of the most fundamental rights of all Americans, and today that includes prison inmates. This is a legal right of prisoners that is widely supported by most correctional officials who would not want to restrict or eliminate inmates' use of the mail, as this is perhaps the most common form of contact inmates have with the

---

12. McMurray v. Phelps, 533 F. Supp. 742 (W.D. La. 1982).
13. Feazell v. Augusta County Jail, 401 F. Supp. 405 (W.D. Va. 1975).
14. Taylor v. Perini, 413 F. Supp. 194 (N.D. Ohio 1976).
15. Martin v. Wainwright, 525 F.2d 983 (5th Cir. 1976).
16. *McMurray*, supra n.12.

outside world. Without maintaining outside contacts, inmates typically display weakened morale, increased tensions (and, consequently, more rule violations and violence), and difficulties readjusting to society upon release. So, being able to send and receive mail is considered a good thing, and something that is (in most cases) widely supported by correctional officials.

But, it is not just the ability to place a letter in the mail or to have a letter arrive at the prison and be delivered to the inmate that is legally protected. So as to ensure that communications are maintained with people outside the prison, inmates are guaranteed the right to be provided with stationery and stamps if they cannot afford these themselves.[17] This does not mean that prison officials are not allowed to restrict inmates from receiving stamps from outsiders, as there may be a security concern about incoming materials. And, while corrections officials must allow for mail to be sent and received, the courts have drawn the line at requiring prison officials to provide inmates with typewriters/computers for writing letters, nor are officials required to provide inmates funds for certified mail.

Where restrictions are placed on mail, the focus is on maintaining institutional security. Specifically, officials are concerned with controlling contraband. Prior to 1974, prison officials routinely censored inmates' mail to monitor for contraband and escape plans. However, in 1974, the U.S. Supreme Court ruled in *Procunier v. Martinez* that officials' censoring of mail could be done within the confines of known standards.[18] Included in the category of mail subject to special conditions are allowable prohibitions on correspondences with inmates in other institutions and mail to or from former inmates now outside of the prison.[19] Also in a special category, in this instance requiring mail to not be reviewed/censored, is mail with one's attorney and the courts, and with outgoing mail addressed to news media (officials may not simply prohibit contact with the media).

To balance inmates' First Amendment rights and prison officials' security concerns, a "correspondence list" (individuals approved for mail exchanges) may be required for all inmates. Prison officials may open all incoming mail, but only to determine whether it is actually from an approved person. Censorship of mail, unless containing contraband or information dangerous to institutional functioning (such as escape plans), is prohibited. Incoming mail from attorneys may be opened and shaken out in the inmate's presence (to check for contraband), but prison personnel cannot read it.

Religious Rights

In addition to freedom of speech, the First Amendment also prohibits government establishment of religion and guarantees protection of religious freedom. The protection of religious freedom has also been extended to prisoners.

---

17. Morgan v. LaVallee, 526 F.2d 221 (2d Cir. 1975).
18. Procunier v. Martinez, 416 U.S. 396 (1974).
19. Farmer v. Loving, 392 F. Supp. 27 (W.D. Va. 1975).

Religious teachings and worship have been core components of U.S. corrections since the founding of the Walnut Street Jail. The practice of religion has always been a critical aspect of American correctional efforts. However, not until the Black Muslims brought legal challenges in the 1960s were inmates' constitutionally guaranteed religious rights recognized. Previously, while religion was seen as valuable and important, what religions were allowed to be practiced was restricted. However, today, as the result of several important court cases, essentially all religions are allowed to be practiced, although certain types of worship activities may be restricted (in the name of security).

The prohibition of government establishment of religion centers on the separation of church and state. This clause in the First Amendment has consistently been interpreted to mean that states cannot use public resources to create and to impose on people religious organizations and practices. Consequently, correctional officials cannot force any inmates to attend any form of religious activity. Since inmates would not have access to religious services and counseling if these were not provided, the courts have broadened the range of permissible (and, in fact, required) governmental actions to require equal provision of services across religious faiths. The Supreme Court uses the guiding principle that state governments neither favor nor hinder particular religions or religious practices.

This right becomes problematic for correctional authorities when inmates demand that clergy be provided to them for the practice of their religion. Yes, prisons are required to provide access to clergy to tend to the spiritual needs of inmates.[20] However, this does not mean that prisons must provide full-time employed staff clergy for any and all religious groups. Clergy may be provided who serve the needs of all inmates, not only those of particular faiths.[21] Similarly, institutions need not provide special, individual facilities for worship. One facility that different faiths share meets the constitutional requirement.[22] And allowing access to the prison for volunteer clergy from outside fulfills the legal requirements of the First Amendment.

Furthermore, while the state cannot establish and impose religion, it must provide opportunities for inmates to freely practice their religions. However, there are permissible restrictions here, almost always tied to the top priority of all correctional facilities — security. Therefore, any religious practice that can reasonably be determined to potentially pose a threat to institutional security may be restricted in how it is carried out, or it can simply be prohibited. For instance, several practices of various Native American–based religions, as well as Satanists, have been determined to be possible threats to security, order, and custody. Correctional officials may not prohibit belief and practice of such religions, but they may prohibit any specific activities that would be a threat

---

20. Theriault v. Carlson, 339 F. Supp. 375 (N.D. Ga. 1972).
21. Gittlemacker v. Prasse, 428 F.2d 1 (3d Cir. 1970).
22. Cruz v. Beto, 405 U.S. 319 (1972).

to security, order, and custody. Also, in order for a set of beliefs and practices to receive First Amendment protections of freedom of religion, there must be a convincing argument that the set of beliefs and practices in question are in fact a "religion." Several widely known federal court decisions have examined what practices qualify as a "real religion."[23] In order for a set of beliefs and practices to be determined to be a religion, inmates must show the presence of a set of comprehensive beliefs that address fundamental and ultimate questions concerning imponderable matters and formal and externally recognizable symbols must identify the religion. And, perhaps most important, the "practicing" followers must show sincerity in their beliefs.

Although belief in and practice of any religion is protected by the First Amendment, actual practices in religious services can be restricted when necessary to ensure institutional order and security. To legally prevent a religious group gathering or specific activity, correctional officials must show that the teachings and/or practices present a "clear and present danger" to the prison's functions. Also, correctional officials can prohibit attendance of individual inmates who can reasonably be expected to cause disruptions or other security problems. This is a valid security measure, especially when alternative forms of religious services (visits from clergy in housing units, provision of religious reading materials, etc.) are provided.[24] Clearly, despite the growth in recognizing legal rights of inmates, the courts have continued to recognize and maintain the prominence of institutional security above issues of individual rights.

Medical Care

When the government incarcerates an individual and removes the possibility of the individual tending to his or her own medical care, the government (e.g., correctional authorities) becomes responsible for providing the prisoner with necessary medical care. Prisoners have a constitutionally guaranteed right to receive necessary medical care while incarcerated, and if and when corrections officials either fail to provide it or deny it, the courts have determined that the prisoner's rights have been violated. In such a situation, the courts have determined that the state is guilty of cruel and unusual punishment. And, this right pertains not only to an inmate's physical health and needs, but to psychological/mental health care as well.[25] However, as with all areas of prisoners' rights, this has not always been the situation.

The major turning point in establishing inmates' rights to medical care came in the 1976 Supreme Court ruling in the landmark case of *Estelle v. Gamble*.[26]

---

23. Africa v. Pennsylvania, 662 F.2d 1025 (3d Cir. 1981); Fulwood v. Clemmer, 206 F. Supp. 370 (D.D.C. 1962); *Theriault*, supra n.20; Remmers v. Brewer, 361 F. Supp. 537 (S.D. Iowa 1973).

24. Belk v. Mitchell, 294 F. Supp. 800 (W.D.N.C. 1968); Cooper v. Pate, 382 F.2d 518 (7th Cir. 1967).

25. Bowring v. Godwin, 551 F. Supp. 44 (2d Cir. 1977).

26. Estelle v. Gamble, 429 U.S. 97 (1976).

Here the Supreme Court introduced a new standard for determining whether and when provided medical care fulfilled constitutional requirements for adequacy. From this point forward, inmates who claimed they did not receive proper medical care would need to show "deliberate indifference to serious medical needs" on the part of the corrections officials in order to establish that their constitutional rights had been violated. This does not mean that inmates must be cured of any and all medical problems (whether real or imagined).[27] Neither does "deliberate indifference" mean that all medical care must be provided. Instead, there remains the factor of determining what rises to the level of "necessary" medical care so as to maintain prisoners at "reasonable" levels of health. As established by the Court in the 1992 case of *Rufo v. Inmates of Suffolk County Jail*, *Estelle v. Gamble* applies to instances of "serious medical needs of prisoners," and a serious medical condition is defined as one that "causes pain, discomfort, or threat to good health."

However, the provision of medical care can also be (to some degree) balanced against the costs of particular forms of care and services. Correctional officials are expected to balance the costs of medical care for one inmate against the necessity, value, and costs of providing other, necessary services for the inmate population as a whole.

Privacy and Searches of Inmates

Due to the importance of maintaining a safe and secure environment inside of correctional institutions, prisoners have no Fourth Amendment right to freedom from unreasonable search and seizure. For the same reasons, the courts have determined that prison officials can monitor prisoners' movements throughout prisons and watch prisoners in their cells and essentially all other areas inside the boundaries of a correctional facility. Whereas for most Americans the right to privacy is considered one of our most sacred and important personal and legal rights, for prisoners there is no such expectation. Stated simply, the right to privacy is one legal right that is plainly and simply forfeited upon incarceration. In *Hudson v. Palmer* (1984), the Supreme Court ruled that prisoners have no reasonable expectation of privacy in their prison cells entitling them to Fourth Amendment protection.

In addition, it is not just the possessions and surroundings of prisoners that are subject to searches by correctional officials. So too are prisoners themselves subject to search, including both on and inside their bodies, at almost any time. Because one of the primary ways that inmates smuggle or transport some forms of contraband (especially drugs) is by holding the contraband inside of a body cavity (mouth, vagina, anus), it is legally permissible for correctional officials to conduct body cavity searches of inmates. Such searches can be conducted via visual

---

27. Priest v. Cupp, 545 P.2d 917 (Or. Ct. App. 1976).

inspection, probing the body cavity, and with technology such as x-rays. The legal foundation for this is found in the 1979 *Bell v. Wolfish* Supreme Court case, in which the Court held that correctional officials could conduct a body cavity search on anyone, including those persons being held prior to trial, in a jail. The Court has denied prisoners any rights to privacy because of the need for prison authorities to have access to cells and prisoners' personal belongings for security reasons. Recall that maintaining security is always considered the top priority for correctional officials.

Relatedly, it is interesting to note that the courts have not only upheld the right of correctional officials to conduct searches on and of inmates at virtually any time, but so too have the courts upheld the use of searches of both correctional employees and visitors. For staff persons, it is standard practice in most facilities for employees arriving at work to have their belongings (purses, pockets, lunchboxes, etc.) searched, and to also be subject to a pat down search and metal detector. Searches of a more intrusive nature are permitted only when officials have a reasonable belief that an employee may be smuggling contraband. For visitors, it is standard practice for institutions to condition admission to the institution upon consent to a search. Just as with staff persons, such searches are typically of one's possessions, a pat down, and use of a metal detector. More intrusive searches are only legally permissible with reasonable suspicion of a visitor attempting to violate the law.

Rights Related to Prison Disciplinary Procedures

The Fifth and Fourteenth Amendments to the United States Constitution guarantee that all citizens will receive due process when being prosecuted for crimes by the government. While this clearly applies to the investigation and trial of offenders prior to their incarceration, due process has also been extended to prisoners in instances in which they are investigated and "charged" with disciplinary violations while incarcerated. The idea here is that when an individual has a "liberty interest" or stands to lose something of value (most notably his freedom), it is imperative that officials seeking to take that something of value follow explicit procedures so as to not be abusive toward the citizen. The question then arises of how much process are inmates due in disciplinary proceedings. In *Wolff v. McDonnell* (1974), the Supreme Court held that when inmates may lose good time (a form of freedom), due process demands that certain procedures be in place so inmates are not arbitrarily deprived of their freedom. These rights include:

- The right to be notified of charges against them before their disciplinary hearings.
- The right to call witnesses to testify at their hearings.
- The right to assistance in presenting a defense (which doesn't, however, include the right to an attorney).

- The right to a written statement explaining the evidence used in reaching a disposition.
- The right to an impartial decision maker.

In subsequent cases, the courts have sided with correctional officials and have limited some of the due process rights that inmates have in disciplinary proceedings. In 1976, three important cases limited inmates' due process rights. First, in *Baxter v. Palmigiano*, it was held that inmates do not have a right to have the assistance of legal counsel in disciplinary proceedings, even when there is a serious or substantial potential consequence for the inmate. Second, *Meacham v. Fano* held that inmates do not have their due process rights violated by being transferred between institutions, even with no hearing or notice. Correctional officials have the leeway and discretion to house inmates in institutions that they believe are most appropriate.

Access to the Courts

All of the legal rights we have discussed so far concern actual activities in which prisoners engage or ways in which correctional officials interact with inmates. Each of these rights has been created (or "discovered") through legal processes whereby prisoners have challenged the rights of correctional officials to prohibit or restrict prisoners' activities. But, each of these rights would not exist if it were not for one very important, foundational right that was not recognized for inmates until the launch of the prisoner's rights movement in the early 1960s. This foundational right for inmates is their ability to air grievances and seek judicial solutions to what they perceive as violations of their legal rights. Without the ability to challenge the legality of correctional officials' actions, no changes would have come about in how prisoners are housed and treated, and in how they are allowed to communicate with others. The origin of the right of prisoners to access the courts was originally stated in the 1961 Supreme Court case of *Ex parte Hull*. In this case, it was held that prison officials may not impair a prison inmate's right to apply to a (federal) court for redress of grievances.[28] Additionally, not only are inmates guaranteed the right to file lawsuits against correctional officials, but in the process of doing so inmates' mail to and from courts and legal officials generally may not be censored or read by constitutional officials.[29]

Not only must inmates be allowed access to courts, but they must also be allowed assistance in preparing their cases for court submission. One way that this can occur and that is not permitted to be prohibited by correctional officials is through the work of self-taught **jailhouse lawyers** to assist inmates.[30] The right

Jailhouse lawyers: inmates who are self-taught in legal matters, who cannot be prohibited by correctional officials to assist fellow inmates with legal issues.

---

28. *Ex parte* Hull, 316 U.S. 546 (1961).
29. However, there are a few states that have had regulations upheld for restricting the mailing of legal papers for inmates. See, e.g., Kirby v. Thomas, 336 F.2d 462 (6th Cir. 1964), and In re Green, 669 F.2d 770 (8th Cir. 1981).
30. Johnson v. Avery, 393 U.S. 483 (1969).

to have another inmate assist one with legal proceedings is not absolute, but if a correctional system chooses to prohibit such assistance, then it must make available attorneys or other forms of "professional legal assistance." One problem with this, however, is that the courts have not been very consistent in ruling on what constitutes acceptable forms and amounts of provided professional legal assistance. Some states allow law school students to come to prisons; some provide paralegals to work with inmates; and some provide attorneys for a varying number of hours per week.

But, providing legal assistance alone does not satisfy the requirement of providing access to the courts. The Supreme Court ruled in the 1977 case of *Bounds v. Smith* that in order to be able to properly prepare their cases and materials to be submitted to the court, inmates must also be provided with access to legal materials, including law books and materials (forms, etc.) for the actual petitions to the courts. In practice, this means that prison officials must provide access to a law library, whether on site at the institution or through services that will gather and deliver requested materials to inmates. Because of the costs (financial and personnel) of gathering materials, most states stock law libraries in each institution.

EVOLUTION OF INMATES' RIGHTS

Although it has not been the case for more than about a half-century, today prison inmates are recognized as people with legal rights, although some rights are restricted or limited in scope. The creation of these legal rights began with the flood of litigation filed by and on behalf of prison inmates in the 1960s and continues today, although it appears that the courts have slowed the momentum of change. In 1995, there were over 40,000 lawsuits filed in federal court, accounting for approximately 15 percent of all cases filed in the federal courts,[31] and in 2000 over 50,000 cases were filed.[32] However, more recently, in 2012, the U.S. District Courts reported a total of "only" 12,993 cases filed by prisoners.[33] Clearly, this shows a decrease in the number of cases filed by inmates, in all probability due to the restrictions and conditions placed on inmate lawsuits as a result of the **Prison Litigation Reform Act (PLRA)** of 1996. However, this still means that there are nearly 13,000 cases annually, or an average of more than 35 for every day of the year, or one every 40 minutes.

Prison Litigation Reform Act (PLRA): federal legislation that was directly aimed at limiting the filing of frivolous lawsuits by inmates and attempted to loosen the backlog of cases in federal courts due to the large number of cases awaiting processing.

The prisoners' rights movement had a great deal of influence for several decades, but by the mid-1980s the courts began to back away from their positions of establishing and discovering inmates' rights. From the mid-1980s until today,

31. Margo Schlanger. 2003. Inmate Litigation. *Harvard Law Review*, 116, 1555.

32. John Scalia, *Prisoner Petitions Filed in U.S. District Courts, 2000, With Trends, 1980-2000.* Washington, D.C.: Bureau of Justice Statistics.

33. U.S. District Courts. *U.S. District Courts — Civil Cases Commenced, by Nature of Suit and District, During the 12-Month Period Ending September 30, 2012.* Washington, D.C.: United States Administrative Office of the Courts.

Frivolous lawsuits: cases that have no founding in fact and are generally brought by inmates for publicity, political reasons, or simply as a way to keep correctional officials distracted and overly busy.

there have been a number of issues and court cases that have drawn the line of where inmates' rights end, and even some movement to limit prisoners' rights. Accompanying this change (and some would say causing this change) was the recognition that inmate-filed lawsuits were not only much more frequent and numerous than citizen-filed lawsuits, but many were also considered **frivolous lawsuits**. These are cases that have no founding in fact and are generally brought by inmates for publicity, political reasons, or simply as a way to keep correctional officials distracted and overly busy. Efforts have been put forth to limit such cases. One important way in which the government has sought to limit frivolous lawsuits is in the passage of the PLRA. This piece of federal legislation was directly aimed at limiting the filing of frivolous lawsuits by inmates and attempting to loosen the backlog of cases in federal courts due to the large number of cases awaiting processing. The PLRA has eight major provisions:

1. Inmates filing lawsuits must pay the required filing fees unless they can claim indigence, and once an inmate has three lawsuits declared to be frivolous, he may not claim indigence and avoid the filing fee on subsequent lawsuits.
2. Limits are placed on the amount of attorneys' fees that the state can be made to pay if an inmate wins her case; this means that inmate lawsuits are not very attractive to attorneys.
3. Judges are required to screen all inmate lawsuits and immediately dismiss those deemed frivolous.
4. Inmates determined to be filing malicious lawsuits may have any earned good time revoked.
5. Inmates may not sue based on claims of mental or emotional injury if there is not an accompanying physical injury.
6. Courts are limited in the amount and degree of changes in correctional practice they may order and can only order changes that are directly related to the particular inmate's civil rights violations or problems in the case at hand.
7. The duration of various court orders is limited to two years, at which time such order must be either renewed or allowed to expire.
8. A single judge may not order the release of federal inmates due to overcrowding.

The PLRA was further extended in 2001 and 2003, when the Supreme Court ruled in the cases of *Booth v. Churner* and *Porter v. Nussle* that prior to filing a lawsuit against correctional officials, inmates must exhaust all administrative processes in the prison that could provide relief from their problematic situation. The PLRA has largely been seen (at least by correctional and court officials) as successful, as the number of inmate lawsuits, and especially the number of frivolous lawsuits, has declined dramatically following implementation of this law.

The end of the era of expanding prisoners' rights and of unfettered access to the courts for airing any and all grievances that may be held by inmates means that in some ways the courts of the 1990s through twenty-first century are moving back toward the hands-off doctrine that characterized most of American correctional history. This is clearly seen in the language of the Supreme Court in the 2003 case of *Overton v. Bazzetta*:

> The Court accords substantial deference to the professional judgment of prison administrators, who bear a significant responsibility for defining a corrections system's legitimate goals and determining the most appropriate means to accomplish them.

Prison inmates do have legal rights. The foundation of these rights is found in the basic rights of citizenship in the United States, and in the (few) enumerated rights of the United States Constitution. It has been through legal challenges filed by and on behalf of prison inmates that these rights have been carved out, and the status of civil death for convicted criminal offenders has been whittled away. The basis of the idea of prisoners having and being able to exercise legal rights is found in two basic concepts: first, the Eighth Amendment to the United States Constitution and its prohibition on cruel and unusual punishment, and second, the common correctional philosophy that correctional officials have a responsibility to carry out their functions in ways that are safe, secure, and humane.

Summary

The United States Constitution serves as the core whereby all prisoners obtain their rights. It is through the judicial system that inmates bring challenges to correctional administrators when they believe certain rights have been violated. Although certain rights are guaranteed through the United States Constitution, which rights and how they were specially applied to inmates remained unclear until a series of court cases in the 1960s and 1970s. As a result, specific rights afforded to inmates through the United States Constitution were defined and explicitly outlined during this time period.

Through the process of judicial review, the judicial branch reviews and interprets the meaning of the Constitution for specific issues in cases, and dictates how it applies to prisoners. Prior to the 1950s and 1960s, judges traditionally took a hands-off approach, citing their "limited expertise" in correctional matters as reasons to not accept suits brought by prisoners. However, societal changes from the civil rights movement in the 1950s and 1960s brought about a new approach for the judicial branch whereby a series of court cases clarified and outlined procedures for determining when a prisoner's right has been violated.

Throughout the 1960s and 1970s, many prisoners' rights were specifically defined and procedures were developed to ensure that inmates could exercise these rights. Such guaranteed rights included the prohibition of cruel and unusual punishment, the right to receive visitors, the right to receive mail, freedom to practice religion, access to medical care, and access to the courts. Although these rights were guaranteed to some extent, certain limits were placed upon each to keep them within reason. The prisoner's rights movement has continued to develop, although the federal Prison Litigation Reform Act of 1996 instituted a number of curbs and controls on the types of lawsuits inmates could file, as well as procedural requirements and sanctions for "frivolous" lawsuits.

Key Terms

Civil death
Conditions of confinement
Disenfranchisement
Executive clemency
Frivolous lawsuits
Hands-off policy
Jailhouse lawyers
Judicial intervention
Parens patriae
Prison Litigation Reform Act (PLRA)
Totality of conditions

Chapter Eight
Prison Violence

One of the commonly "known" facts about prisons in the twenty-first century is that they are violent places, full of violent men, who threaten, assault, rape, riot, and spend their days both actively seeking opportunities to attack other inmates and staff and trying to protect themselves from being attacked. Such ideas and images come from multiple sources, including movies and numerous reality television series. While such things do happen, they are much, much less common than most people believe. In fact, although violence does happen in prison, prisons for the most part are places where boredom and routine and monotony are the norm. The popular images of prisons and prisoners as violent, predatory, and continuously dangerous are extreme exaggerations, not reality.

Violence does happen in prison, though, just as it does in free society. All of the types of violence that happen in the community also happen in prison, although their form, frequency, and context may be different in prison than outside. In a world where resources are restricted, activities are limited, and all of one's interactions are with the same group of others for days, months, or years on end, it should not be surprising that tensions can be high and violence can erupt. Couple these structural issues with the fact that the people in prison have a history of violence and aggression, extremely high rates of mental illness, sexual deprivation, and a sense of disempowerment and emasculation for male inmates, and it may actually be surprising that there is not more violence among prison inmates.

In this chapter, we will examine the types of violence that are most common in prison, looking at both individual and collective forms of violence and theorized explanations for how and why violence occurs. First, we will examine seven common forms of violence, highlighting individual forms of violence. Second, we will focus on the organized, collective forms of violence — including riots — as these are the form of violence that is of greatest concern to the public and policy makers. Here we will focus on not only how riots tend to occur and play out, but also on examining the potential causes that have been suggested for explaining riots.

FORMS OF PRISON VIOLENCE

The types of violence that occur in prison are the same types of violence that happen in the free community. As we will see when discussing each of the major forms of violence that influence daily life and administrative practices in prisons (and jails), the specific ways that some of these types of violence are carried out may differ from that on the outside, and specific forms of violence may occur in greater or lesser frequency than in free society, but in the end, violence is violence. For our purposes, we will consider violence in prisons as existing in eight forms, including seven individual forms of violence and one that is collective:

1. Physical violence by inmates on inmates.
2. Physical violence by inmates on staff.
3. Physical violence by staff on inmates.
4. Sexual violence (usually confined to inmate on inmate).
5. Self-inflicted physical violence.
6. Economic violence.
7. Psychological violence (among both staff and inmates).
8. Organized disturbances and riots.

We will examine each form of violence in detail, focusing on the prevalence and dynamics of each of these specific forms of violence.

Physical Violence by Inmates on Inmates

Physical violence among inmates is perhaps the most common form of violence in correctional facilities. However, accurate statistics on inter-inmate violence are difficult to find. Inmates simply do not report many incidents, and institutional personnel do not enter some incidents into any official reporting mechanism. However, both those who work and those who live in prisons (as well as in jails) know that violence among inmates is more than a rare event.

Due to institutions' cultural and population differences, profiles of inmate perpetrators and victims of physical violence can be difficult to generalize. Additionally, "common knowledge" has long told us that inmates convicted of certain types of crimes (those even prison inmates see as "wrong") are more likely than others to be victimized. These include sex offenders and those who victimize children. These characteristics support a **routine activities theory** of crime, suggesting that inmates' usual, daily activities place them in contact with others who have opportunities to victimize them.

Routine activities theory: a theoretical explanation that suggests for a crime to occur there must be a convergence of a motivated offender, a suitable target, and the lack of capable guardianship. When applied to corrections, it suggests that inmates' usual, daily activities place them in contact with others who have opportunities to victimize them.

Who commits physical acts of violence in prison? The strongest predictor seems to be that the individual who commits violent acts in the community is the individual most likely to commit violent acts while in prison. Basically, someone who is known to be violent in one aspect of life is the most likely to be violent in other aspects of life.

The most obvious, easily measured, and most significant concern for inmates and administrators related to violence is seen in the murder of inmates. While it is true that murder among inmates does happen, it is far from a common occurrence, and in fact is less common today than in the past. According to the Bureau of Justice Statistics,[1] between the years 2001 and 2010, a total of 515 prison inmates were victims of homicide in American prisons, an average of 51 per year. Considering that the population of American prisons during that time period is well over one million, this rate is substantially less than that for American cities of similar population sizes. Viewed in a different way, homicide accounted for only between 1.4 percent and 2.1 percent of all inmate deaths during these years. In comparison, suicide (as will be discussed more below) accounts for about three times as many inmate deaths every year. In jails, homicide is less common than in prison, with an average of 16 inmate deaths due to homicide for the decade of 2001 to 2010.[2]

Just as in free society, there are some very clear trends and patterns in the characteristics of inmates who are homicide victims in prisons.[3] Inmates who die due to homicide in prison are nearly all males. Between 2001 and 2010, fully 99.2 percent of inmate homicide victims were men. Whites account for 45 percent and African Americans 34 percent of inmate homicide victims. And, inmate homicide victims tend to be slightly older than homicide victims in the community. Whereas in the free community homicide is most common with young adult victims, in prison only 12 percent of homicide victims are under the age of 25. However, fully 30 percent of inmate homicide victims are over the age of 45.

Homicide is not the only form of physical violence among inmates, however. In fact, violence in the form of physical assault is much, much more common than homicide. And, here this form of violence is more likely to affect the entire inmate community. One recent study reports that fully one-third of male prison inmates and a quarter of female inmates reported at least one physical victimization during the preceding six-month period.[4] This is not

---

1. Christopher J. Mumola. 2005. *Suicide and Homicide in State Prisons and Local Jails.* Washington, D.C.: Bureau of Justice Statistics. Margaret E. Noonan. 2012. *Mortality in Local Jails and State Prisons, 2000-2010—Statistical Tables.* Washington, D.C.: Bureau of Justice Statistics.
2. Noonan, supra n.1.
3. *Ibid.*
4. Nancy Wolff and Jiang Shi. 2009. Type, Source, and Patterns of Physical Victimization: A Comparison of Male and Female Inmates. *The Prison Journal,* 89, 172-191.

to say that all inmates are physically victimized, but the very real threat of such is common and does extend to all inmates. When they fear being victimized, inmates commonly exhibit high levels of tension, anxiety, or depression; have little energy; and cannot concentrate on tasks.[5] Also, when fearful some inmates may interpret innocuous actions of others as threatening and may strike out in self-defense. What this suggests is that the simple recognition of the possibility and threat of physical violence may actually be an instigator of such forms of violence.

However, not all inmates respond in this manner. Rather, inmates adopt two other patterns of behavior as personal precautions against victimization.[6] Older inmates and inmates who are not as tightly integrated to the institutionalized culture tend to use passive, avoidance techniques. However, other inmates could interpret this approach as signs of weakness and vulnerability. Victimization in prison is largely a result of being perceived as weak. In some instances, being perceived as mentally ill is to be perceived as weak; inmates with a history of diagnosed mental illness are 1.6 times more likely than other inmates to be victims of physical assault by other inmates.[7] Also reflecting the role of perceived weakness, younger inmates and white inmates are therefore more likely to be physically assaulted by other inmates.[8] For younger inmates, the situation may be more complicated, however, as they more commonly adopt more aggressive, proactive techniques of self-protection, which may lead to altercations and situations in which they become victims. As a result of both types of situations, prisons with a greater concentration of younger inmates are the prisons that have higher rates of inmate-on-inmate assaults.[9]

One of the best known correlates for female inmates' physical (and sexual) victimization while incarcerated is a history of victimization, especially during childhood. This relationship, however, holds true for both male and female inmates.[10]

Other research[11] shows that when inmates either witness violence among other inmates or are victims of physical violence themselves, they are more likely both to engage in their own violent acts and to use drugs and/or alcohol while incarcerated. This too supports the idea that the violence that occurs in prison leads to yet more violence, either as a way that inmates act to protect themselves

---

5. Richard C. McCorkle. 1993. Fear of Victimization and Symptoms of Psychopathology Among Prison Inmates. *Journal of Offender Rehabilitation*, 19, 27-41.
6. Richard C. McCorkle. 1992. Personal Precautions to Violence in Prison. *Criminal Justice and Behavior*, 19, 160-173.
7. Cynthia L. Blitz, Nancy Wolff, and Jing Shi. 2008. Physical Victimization in Prison: The Role of Mental Illness. *International Journal of Law and Psychiatry*, 31, 385-393.
8. Nancy Wolff, Jing Shi, and Jane Siegel. 2009a. Understanding Physical Victimization Inside Prisons: Factors That Predict Risk. *Justice Quarterly*, 26, 445-475.
9. Karen F. Lahm. 2008. Inmate-on-Inmate Assault: A Multilevel Examination of Prison Violence. *Criminal Justice and Behavior*, 35 (1), 120-137.
10. Nancy Wolff, Jing Shi, and Jane Siegel. 2009b. Patterns of Victimization Among Male and Female Inmates: Evidence of an Enduring Legacy. *Violence and Victims*, 24, 469-484.
11. Shelly A. McGrath, Catherine D. Marcum, and Heith Copes. 2012. The Effects of Experienced, Vicarious, and Anticipated Strain on Violence and Drug Use Among Inmates. *American Journal of Criminal Justice*, 37, 60-75.

from (continued) victimization or through the use of the well-known violence-related activities of using drugs and/or alcohol.

All of these approaches — striking out in fear, avoidance, and aggressive displays of strength — highlight the potential for increasingly self-destructive cycles of violence. Therefore, when many new correctional staff ask, "How do I protect myself?" the answer may be that there is no completely effective method of ensuring one's self-protection. However, one of the oldest laws regarding prison staff's responsibility is to minimize violence and to protect both staff and inmates from "lawless violence."[12]

Physical Violence by Inmates on Staff

Of greater personal concern to most correctional personnel are acts of violence that inmates direct toward staff. Again, while reliable and valid statistics are very difficult to find, anecdotal evidence consistently warns correctional staff of the dangers of working in prison. Violent acts that inmates commit against staff run the range from simple blows to throwing objects (chairs, cans of food, feces, etc.), to beatings by individual or groups of inmates, to stabbings, biting, and occasionally homicide. For this reason, most correctional systems require all personnel who work inside prisons to complete extensive personal defense training.

However, while danger is inherent in correctional officers' work, the frequency of injuries among correctional staff is relatively low. Also, correctional officers are not the only targets for inmates' violence. Treatment staff, office workers, maintenance workers, and management personnel have all been recipients of inmates' violence. Correctional staff are one of the seven occupational groups that report the most work-related injuries every year.[13] Among correctional officers, the Bureau of Labor Statistics reports a rate of 629 injuries requiring time off of work for every 100,000 individuals. And, the median length of time off of work due to injury is 24 days.

There is not much research to identify characteristics of inmates most likely to be involved in physical violence on staff. What little bit there is suggests that such assaults are more likely to be committed by younger inmates (especially those under the age of 25), inmates who are more aggressive to begin with, inmates with fewer or no maintained relationships with individuals outside of prison, and inmates that are involved in fewer or no institutional programs.[14] Additionally, when looking at correctional institutions and inmate on staff

12. Logan v. United States, 144 U.S. 263 (1982).

13. Bureau of Labor Statistics. 2012. *Nonfatal Occupational Injuries and Illnesses Requiring Days Away from Work, 2011.* Washington, D.C.: United States Department of Labor.

14. M. Harer and J. Steffensmeier. 1996. Race and Prison Violence. *Criminology,* 34, 323-357. Peter Kratcoski. 1988. The Implications of Research Explaining Prison Violence and Disruption. *Federal Probation,* 52, 27-32. Karen Lahm. 2009. Inmate Assaults on Prison Staff: A Multilevel Examination of an Overlooked Form of Prison Violence. *The Prison Journal,* 89, 131-150. Richard McCorkle, Terrence Miethe, and Kriss A. Drass. 1995. The Roots of Prison Violence: A Test of the Deprivation, Management, and Not-So-Total Institutions Models. *Crime and Delinquency,* 41, 317-331.

assaults, the research has shown that such assaults are more likely to occur in institutions with a higher ratio of staff to inmates and institutions with higher levels of crowding.[15]

Physical Violence by Staff on Inmates

In addition to violence committed by inmates on correctional staff, so too are there instances of staff being violent against inmates. Such behaviors may be well known in popular media, and in the minds of at least some prison observers such behaviors are often overlooked (or supported) as necessary, appropriate, or acceptable means for controlling inmates. As discussed in Chapter 7, physical assaults by staff on inmates are generally considered violations of the Eighth Amendment, unless such actions qualify as self-defense, defense of a third person, a last resort to enforce institutional rules, prevention of escape, or prevention of criminal acts.

Physical coercion: the use of force to make someone follow directions; used as an easily accessible and an immediately effective way to secure compliance with orders.

However, security staffs often use **physical coercion** — the use of force to make someone follow directions — as an easily accessible and immediately effective way to secure compliance with orders. In analyzing methods of Massachusetts's correctional officers for controlling inmates, Kelsey Kauffman reported that officers use six primary approaches to secure power: authority, persuasion, inducement, manipulation, force, and coercion.[16] Inexperienced correctional officers may frequently use force, an act to remove an inmate's element of choice to follow an order. However, force has serious, negative consequences in the long term. As Kauffman says:

> Force is a form of power within a prison. Legal limits exist on the length of time an inmate can be forced to spend in lockup. . . . More fundamental, force is not effective in compelling performance of complex tasks. Nor can it be realistically relied upon for the routine accomplishment of even very simple tasks.[17]

Staff may then become frustrated with their ineffective use of force and may escalate the violence, thereby pushing inmates to respond violently themselves. The real danger in staff's use of violence, whether for legitimate goals or not, is that inmates' violent responses may be triggered. While using force to get an inmate to do something may be effective in the immediate instance, in the long run force is likely to be counterproductive and give rise to animosities and even resistance.

Rather than using violence, staff will have more effective results if they respond to threats and attacks by using well-developed communication skills. Being able to rationally and calmly talk *with* (as opposed to *to*) inmates is a widely

---

15. Gerald Gaes and William McGuire. 1985. Prison Violence: The Contribution of Crowding versus Other Determinants of Prison Assault Rates. *Journal of Research in Crime and Delinquency*, 22, 41-65. Lahm, supra n.14.
16. Kelsey Kauffman. 1988. *Prison Officers and Their World.* Cambridge, MA: Harvard University Press.
17. *Ibid.*, p. 61.

recognized way to achieve smooth prison operations. Also, many correctional systems today train their staffs in conflict management skills. These skills and approaches are essentially the same as those commonly used by police officers in encounters with citizens, suspects, and others on the streets. These same methods of communication and persuasion are just as likely to be useful in prison as they are on the streets.

Interestingly, inmates who are most likely to be physically assaulted by staff are those who are non-white, convicted of violent offenses, and those with higher levels of education.[18] Also, inmates with a history of mental health treatment are significantly more likely than other inmates to be physically assaulted by staff.[19]

Sexual Violence

Sexual violence and assaults in prisons are of three basic forms: forcible rape, coerced sex, and coerced prostitution. Sex in prison is more about power than it is about sex. Being able to control another man and "make him into a woman" is the most common goal of sexual assaults. Most media and academic attention regarding sexual violence in prisons has been devoted to forcible rape, although this is probably the least common form of sexual violence. Coerced sex refers to inmates who are pressured or persuaded to perform sexual acts to avoid physical attacks or who are "trapped" into sexual acts when they cannot repay accumulated debts. Inmates who prostitute themselves usually do so because of pressure from physically intimidating inmates.

Sexual violence: the act of coercing someone into sexual acts against his or her will with the actual use of or threat of physical and sexual violence, falling into three forms: forcible rape, coerced sex, and coerced prostitution.

The issue of sexual violence in correctional facilities, or "prison rape," has been the focus of major policy debates and developments in the last decade. The 2003 federal legislation known as the **Prison Rape Elimination Act (PREA)** brought about major policy and practice changes in corrections, more research on the issue than had ever been completed previously, and more attention to the issue than most correctional administrators could have ever imagined.

Prison Rape Elimination Act (PREA): federal legislation passed in 2003 that brought about major policy and practice changes in corrections, leading to more research being conducted and more attention brought to the issue.

As one of the major outgrowths of PREA, the Bureau of Justice Statistics has undertaken the National Inmate Survey, a nationally representative survey study of prison and jail inmates across the nation, focused on identifying the incidence and prevalence of sexual victimization among inmates, and identifying characteristics of those most at risk of victimization. As identified in the National Inmate Survey, in 2011-2012, 4.0 percent of prison inmates and 3.21 percent of jail inmates reported at least one incident of sexual victimization by another inmate or a facility staff person in the previous 12 months.[20] This would suggest that approximately 96,000 inmates were victims of some form of sexual violence. Interestingly, the numbers of inmates who are sexually victimized by a

18. Wolff, Shi, and Siegel, supra n.8.

19. Blitz, Wolff, and Shi, supra n.7.

20. Allen J. Beck, Marcus Berzofsky, Rachel Caspar, and Christopher Krebs. 2013. *Sexual Victimization in Prisons and Jails Reported by Inmates, 2011-2012.* Washington, D.C.: Bureau of Justice Statistics.

correctional staff person are higher than are the numbers of inmates victimized by another inmate. Fully 2.4 percent of prison inmates and 1.8 percent of jail inmates reported at least one sexual contact with a staff person but "only" 2.0 percent of prison and 1.6 percent of jail inmates were sexually victimized by another inmate. These statistics have not changed in a statistically significant way since they were first collected in 2007; the numbers are very stable. One of the major developments of PREA has been to bring attention and recognition to the fact that any sexual contact between an inmate and a correctional staff person is considered sexual assault. In all 50 states, it is illegal for a correctional staff person to have any sexual contact with an inmate (and in most states this extends to community corrections as well).

There are important variations in the rates of victimization across categories of inmates.[21] Female prison and jail inmates report higher levels of victimization by other inmates (6.9%/3.6%) than do male inmates (1.7%/1.4%). This contradicts many popular assumptions and stereotypes about prison rape, where the common belief is that in men's facilities rape is "rampant" and "many" of the inmates present are likely to be victims. However, other findings of the National Inmate Survey do confirm common beliefs and stereotypes. For instance, victimization rates are higher for white and interracial inmates than for African Americans. Gay, bisexual, and transgender inmates have higher rates of victimization than do heterosexually identified inmates. Inmates who have previously been sexually victimized (whether in prison or jail or in the community) have higher rates of victimization. More highly educated inmates (especially those with a college education) are more likely to be sexually victimized. Inmates who are convicted and incarcerated for serious sexual offenses themselves are more likely to be victimized than inmates incarcerated for other offenses. And, inmates with serious mental health problems report rates of sexual victimization nine times higher than other inmates.

While many researchers have attributed prison rapes to racially motivated hostilities,[22] others have argued that the significant difference between victims and perpetrators is gender presentations and displays of physical strength. The patterns reported above would support this idea. Basically, the strong dominate and victimize the weak. Inmates who are targeted for sexual assault are commonly young, nonviolent, first-time offenders who have slim builds, are white, and may have a history of mental illness.

However, the potential of prison rape impacts inmates' fears of victimization and guides their interactions. Inmates who report the greatest level of fear of sexual assault are those who are shorter of stature and are heavier.[23] These

---

21. *Ibid.*
22. Leo Carroll. 1977. Humanitarian Reform and Biracial Sexual Assault in a Maximum Security Prison. *Urban Life*, 5, 417-437. Anthony Scacco. 1975. *Rape in Prison*. Springfield, IL: Charles C. Thomas.
23. Richard Tewksbury. 1989. Fear of Sexual Assaults in Prison Inmates. *Prison Journal*, 69, 62-71.

characteristics are associated with their perceived inability to physically defend themselves.

The role that fear plays in likelihood of victimization may also be behind the fact that a significant minority of inmates who are sexually victimized are targeted for victimization within their first 24 hours in the facility. Fully 13 percent of male prison inmates and 19 percent of male jail inmates who are sexually assaulted by another inmate report that they were victimized within the first 24 hours they were in their facility.[24] Early in one's time incarcerated is when sexual victimization is most likely to occur. Although an inmate may be able to navigate his way through the first day in prison or jail, risk of victimization has been shown to be highest in the first six months of an inmate's time spent at a particular facility.[25]

Another fact about sexual victimization that contradicts many popular beliefs is that instances of staff sexually victimizing inmates most often involves female staff and male inmates.[26] Here it is important to keep in mind that any sexual contact between a staff person and an inmate is considered victimization of the inmate (because they are not legally able to consent to sexual activities due to their status as inmates). While considered "victimization," many of these instances may actually be incidents initiated by inmates. As one team of researchers has suggested, such "victimizations" of inmates are actually the outcome of actions by inmates who actively seek to "violate boundaries" with correctional staff and who groom, manipulate, and maneuver into sexual situations female staff, much like pedophiles work to victimize children.[27]

Not all sexual victimization, however, is forcible or manipulated sex with staff. Inmates may also be coerced into sex or prostitution. When they are, they are victimized largely as a result of feelings of vulnerability to physical violence. Some men may be forced to prostitute themselves to benefit a gang, or some men may be intimidated into a one-on-one relationship with another who promises to protect him from rape and physical violence (referred to as "**protective pairing**"). Even so, while an inmate may "voluntarily" enter into such a relationship, he is victimized by the "protector" and sometimes by the protector's friends and associates. Sexual violence does not exist by itself. Rather, inmates who are sexually victimized while incarcerated are also highly likely to be physically (and not sexually) victimized.[28] In simple terms, inmates who are perceived as weak in prison are likely to be targeted for many types of victimization.

Protective pairing: a one-on-one relationship between one inmate who promises to protect another inmate from rape and physical force.

---

24. Allen J. Beck, Paige M. Harrison, Marcus Berzofsky, Rachel Caspar, and Christopher Krebs. 2010. *Sexual Victimization in Prisons and Jails Reported by Inmates, 2008-2009.* Washington, D.C.: Bureau of Justice Statistics.

25. Christopher Hensley, Tammy Castle, and Richard Tewksbury. 2003. Inmate-to-Inmate Sexual Coercion in a Prison for Women. *Journal of Offender Rehabilitation,* 37, 77-87. Christopher Hensley, Mary Koscheski, and Richard Tewksbury. 2005. Examining the Characteristics of Male Sexual Assault Targets in a Southern Maximum-Security Prison. *Journal of Interpersonal Violence,* 20, 667-679.

26. Beck, Berzofsky, Caspar, and Krebs, supra n.20.

27. Kelly Cheeseman Dial and Robert M. Worley. 2008. Crossing the Line: A Quantitative Analysis of Inmate Boundary Violators in a Southern Prison System. *American Journal of Criminal Justice,* 33, 69-84.

28. Wolff, Shi, and Siegel, supra n.10.

While common belief and most research and policy development is centered on the idea that sexual violence in prison and jail is primarily about displays of power and domination of weaker individuals (much like our common beliefs about sexual violence in the community), there is a slowly developing body of thought that at least some sexual violence in prison and jail may be about sex. Here we see support in the work of one team of researchers who in looking at state level reports of sexual violence show that in states where conjugal visitation is allowed there are lower reported rates of sexual victimization among inmates.[29] This would support the contention that sexual violence in prison is about a need for sexual release and gratification for inmates. However, even in these instances, the fact remains that inmates are being victimized, and correctional administrators have a responsibility (and typically a desire) to control or eliminate such behaviors.

Self-Inflicted Physical Violence

A fifth form of violence that is common in prison is violence that inmates do to themselves — whether self-mutilating behavior or suicide. While suicides may be more publicly known, self-destructive behaviors may be more common and perhaps more difficult for correctional officials to manage.

Self-injury is commonly believed to be associated with poor adjustment to incarceration and with mental illness. Although data are rare about such behaviors and inmates, one recent national study drawing on data from 473 prisons reports that 2.4 percent of inmates engaged in some form of self-injurious behavior and 0.7 percent of inmates have committed at least one serious act of self-injury while incarcerated.[30] The most common way that inmates seek to hurt themselves is via cutting. One study of all self-injuring inmates in South Carolina for a one-year period showed that such inmates use a disproportionately large portion of institutional mental health services, and that such inmates are likely to be the inmates most involved in disciplinary infractions in the prison.[31]

Suicide among prison inmates is also a not completely uncommon event. As was mentioned earlier in the discussion of homicide among inmates, deaths attributed to suicide are more common than homicide. In the decade from 2001 to 2010, a total of 1,994 inmates committed suicide in American prisons.[32] In jails, suicide is more common than in prisons. In the same decade of 2001 to 2010, 2,906 jail inmates died as a result of suicide, a number that is 45 percent greater than the number of suicides in prisons. When looking at all deaths

29. Stewart J. D'Alescio, Jamie Flexon, and Lisa Stolzenberg. 2013. The Effect of Conjugal Visitation on Sexual Violence in Prison. *American Journal of Criminal Justice*, 38, 13-26.

30. Hayden P. Smith and Robert J. Kaminski. 2011. Self Injurious Behavior in State Prisons: Findings from a National Survey. *Criminal Justice and Behavior*, 38, 26-41.

31. Hayden P. Smith and Robert J. Kaminski. 2010. Inmate Self-Injurious Behaviors: Distinguishing Characteristics Within a Retrospective Study. *Criminal Justice and Behavior*, 37, 81-96.

32. Noonan, supra n.1.

among prison inmates, suicide accounts for between 5.9 percent and 6.8 percent of inmate deaths annually.

The most common method of suicide among prison inmates is cutting (also the most common means of any type of self-injury), followed by hanging. However, inmates may commit suicide in many ways that are not always officially accounted as such, including overdosing on drugs, jumping from upper tiers, or deliberately instigating situations where other inmates will kill them.

In addition, between 2001 and 2010, an average of 21 inmates died in prisons due to "accidental self-injuries" and an average of 39 inmates died due to "other/unknown" causes.[33] In the eyes of some observers, these two reported causes of death are believed to include at least some inmates whose cause of death is actually either suicide or homicide, but is not reported as such for political reasons. (A prison or jail where inmates either kill themselves or kill one another is likely to be seen as a more problematic institution than one where inmates die for unknown reasons or due to an "accident.")

Self-mutilating behavior, often considered a sign of mental illness, most often involves such acts as inmates cutting themselves, starving themselves, or injuring themselves by beating their heads on walls, floors, and furnishings. Attempting to control such acts can be extremely difficult. However, correctional staff have responsibilities (1) to protect both other inmates and staff from injuries that result from such behavior and (2) to protect inmates' right to be held in a safe place while under the government's care. Also, numerous problems, including lowered morale, interpersonal physical violence, and other health concerns, may arise when inmates injure themselves and bleed in the presence of others. However, inmates determined to pursue self-mutilating behaviors may be nearly impossible to stop. Numerous creative ways exist to inflict self-injury, even without any potential "weapons" available.

Economic Violence

Economic violence, which involves both property and personal crimes against inmates and provides direct material benefits to perpetrators, is the sixth form of violence found in prisons. Common forms of economic violence are extortion, blackmail, robbery, burglary, and larceny. As discussed in Chapter 6, prison inmates are deprived of most material goods. However, all inmates do have valuables, whether these are simply the basic grooming and hygiene goods supplied by the institution or accumulated personal property (both legitimate and illegitimate) such as radios, televisions, books, art, etc.

Some inmates, especially those who are physically and socially stronger than others, may coerce others into forfeiting their goods or may simply steal from other inmates. After all, as most corrections personnel will remind you, all of the

33. *Ibid.*

residents in prison have committed crimes on the outside, and now that they are in prison, why would we not expect them to continue such behaviors?

Inmates who are likely victims of economic violence are largely those who are targets for physical and sexual violence as well. Here we see that the routine activities theory explains economic violence victimization. Both the characteristics of inmates and inmates' daily activities put them at risk for physical and economic violence. Theft is most likely for those inmates who have collected and are away from their possessions. So, inmates with material possessions who have work assignments, school, or other regular activities away from their cells or dorm areas are most likely to have things stolen.

Of course, economic violence is directly tied to other forms of violence. As discussed earlier, some inmates may be coerced into prostitution because they have no possessions or they desire additional possessions. Or, some inmates may be coerced (or physically forced) into sexual relations as a result of their indebtedness to others. Or, some inmates may use physical violence to rob others. Or, some inmates may display physical violence to protect themselves from economic victimization. Whenever economic violence is found in prison, other forms of violence are extremely likely to be involved as well.

Psychological Violence

Psychological violence, or continued threats of physical or sexual attacks, is perhaps the most difficult form of violence to identify. The most common form of psychological violence is intimidation. Such acts are usually for the perpetrator's material benefit, again highlighting the interrelated nature of forms of violence in prison.

Where psychological violence is distinguished from physical, sexual, self-directed, and economic forms of violence is that the impact of psychological violence is commonly believed to be more damaging and more constant in prison inmates' lives than any other form of violence. Because psychological intimidation and fear last long after perpetrators leave the targeted inmates' immediate presence, psychological violence impacts more than just the victims' immediate activities. Psychological victimization's effects may extend well after first being experienced, and in more extreme cases can even have effects on individuals well into the period following release from prison.

Psychological violence may then appear to have no obvious benefits for anyone, although those who perpetrate it through intimidation and domination of others do gain social status in the prison community and a sense of power. These gains can then, in turn, be materially beneficial to perpetrators. So, in the end, psychological violence *is* a self-benefiting behavior, although the benefits might be realized only indirectly.

When the various forms of individual-level violence that are common among prison inmates are viewed as a whole, it is obvious that there are myriad ways that violence can be and is practiced by inmates, and that many inmates are involved, as both perpetrators and victims. Whereas prisons stand on the idea of providing a safe, secure, and humane environment in which to house the dangerous members of society, this discussion of violence in prisons suggests that this mission is not being fulfilled completely or very well. Here the words of one prominent team of prison violence researchers are instructive:

> [V]ictimization inside prison warrants an increase in research, clinical, and administrative attention. Prison is a breeding ground for traumatization *and* retraumatization. Most people come to prison with a legacy of victimization. . . . The prison experience itself is likely to activate and exacerbate past trauma. The culture and climate of the prison environment may itself trigger unwelcome memories of prior victimization and provoke symptoms and create opportunities for (re)victimization (Wortley, 2002). More specifically, the ecology of prison environments may produce conditions that support or encourage victimization. . . . Overall, the potential number of individuals liable to suffer harmful consequences as a result of victimization inside prisons can be expected to be large.[34]

EXPLANATIONS FOR VIOLENCE IN PRISON

Explanations for why violence occurs in prison are often complex and frequently contradict one another. But, understanding why and how violence happens in prisons is critical for any attempt to curb or eliminate such acts. It is only with an understanding of the causes of a behavior that correctional administrators can have any hope of successfully addressing violence, and thus be able to effectively and efficiently work to eliminate violence (and its accompanying consequences). In the following sections, we will examine five commonly proposed explanations for prison violence: Prison inmates are simply violent by nature; violence is a necessary adaptation to conditions of deprivation; gangs are a major cause of violence; overcrowding leads to violence; and the high incidence of mental illness among inmates explains the high incidence of violence.

Violent Inmates

One common, and at least on the surface apparently logical, explanation for violence in prisons focuses on the violent natures of the inmates themselves. According to this view, because many prison inmates have histories of violent behavior, this behavior is expected to continue when individuals are confined with other, also violent people. This is a simple application of the importation model for understanding inmate behavior. Very simply, people who are violent to begin with bring (e.g., import) this behavior with them to prison.

This explanation is apparently logical when these facts are considered: Over the last five decades, the frequency and severity of violent acts in prisons have

34. Wolff, Shi, and Siegel, supra n.10, pp. 478-479.

increased, and this has accompanied increases in the number of violent inmates incarcerated. Violence is not, of course, characteristic of all prison inmates. Those with histories of violence on the streets and who possess certain social statuses are the most likely to be violent. Examinations of which prison inmates are good candidates for violence show that common characteristics include younger age, non-white status, divorce of parents before the inmate reached the age of 16, no father figure, low educational achievement, prior incarceration (either adult or juvenile), first arrest by age 12, and a history of disciplinary problems while incarcerated. In other words, the violent inmate usually has an unstable background and a long history of violence. As at least one study has clearly shown, physical assaults are more likely to occur in prisons with larger proportions of younger inmates.[35] We know that younger persons are most likely to be in physical fights in the community, so it should only be expected that as more of these violence-prone persons are in a particular prison, the more likely it is for there to be violence in that prison.

In a test of whether removal of the most dangerous and most violent inmates in a prison would be associated with a decrease in the level of violence, Briggs, Sundt, and Castellano[36] compared the overall violence levels in prisons in states that operated a supermax security prison with states that do not. Their results suggest that housing the most dangerous and violent inmates in the extremely restrictive setting of a supermax prison has no effect on the likelihood and frequency of inmate-on-inmate assaults in the other prisons of such states. This, therefore, calls into question the utility of an explanation for prison violence based primarily on the idea that violence is simply due to the nature of the inmates that are in prisons.

Prison Gangs

Prison gangs: groups of three or more individuals that demonstrate a recurring pattern of threatening or disruptive behavior and are often an extension of gangs in the free community.

A variation on the "violence is due to violent people" explanation focuses more specifically on the presence of a particular type of violent inmate: gang members. Many people believe that **prison gangs** are based on racial and ethnic divisions. While this is frequently the case, it is not always true. Prison gangs are often extensions of gangs in the free community. When incarcerated in the same prison, several members of a street gang reinitiate gang activities and recruit new members.

A prison gang is one type of dangerous inmate organization that is commonly referred to today by corrections officials as a "security threat group." The term *security threat group* (also known as STGs) refers to "an inmate group, gang, organization, or association that has a name or identifying signs, colors, or symbols, and whose members or associates engage in a pattern of activity or departmental rule violation so as to pose a threat to the staff, to public safety, to the

---

35. Lahm, supra n.9.

36. Chad S. Briggs, Jody L. Sundt, and Thomas C. Castellano. 2003. The effect of Supermax Security Prisons on Aggregate Levels of Institutional Violence. *Criminology*, 41, 1341-1376.

secure and orderly operation of a correctional institution, or to other inmates."[37] A prison gang can also be defined as "any group of three (3) or more persons with recurring threatening or disruptive behavior (i.e., violations of the disciplinary rules where said violations were openly known or conferred benefit upon the group would suffice for a prison environment), including but not limited to gang crime or gang violence."[38] According to the American Correctional Association, a prison gang is defined as "two or more inmates, acting together, who pose a threat to the security or safety of staff/inmates, and/or are disruptive to programs and/or to the orderly management of the facility/system."[39]

Prison gangs exist in almost all U.S. correctional systems. The exceptions are the least populated and least urban states (Montana, North and South Dakota, Vermont, and Wyoming). Gangs are also in federal prisons. Based on the intelligence gathered by corrections officials, it is estimated that approximately one in 4 male inmates and one in 17 female inmates come to prison as members of gangs.[40]

The most notable fact about members of prison gangs is that they are largely the same as non-gang members, at least in terms of personal and social characteristics. In comparison to non-members, members are more likely to abuse drugs and alcohol, are slightly more likely (40% to 58%) not to have held a legitimate job, and have, on average, a greater number of juvenile court referrals. In addition, gang members have significantly more arrests as adults and are more likely to have used weapons during the crimes for which they are incarcerated.[41] Gang members also have more disciplinary infractions, especially for fighting or abusing drugs (but not other forms of contraband), and are less likely than non-members to participate in prison programs.

Prison gangs present management difficulties for prison administrators. Gang members are more likely than non-gang members to be involved in misconduct, including violent offenses, in prisons.[42] Gang members' presence in a prison is directly linked to higher levels of violence in the institution. However, others[43] have shown that while measures of gang presence and members are important for understanding the amount of violence in prisons, such measures are actually less important than measures of individuals' histories of violence, prior incarcerations, and demographics. So, while gang membership is important, it cannot and should not be viewed as the sole factor for explaining violence in prisons.

---

37. Frank Schmalleger and John Smykla. 2007. *Corrections in the 21st Century*, 3d ed. New York: McGraw-Hill, p. 526.
38. George Knox. 2005. *The Problems of Gangs and Security Threat Groups (STGs) in American Prisons Today: Recent Research Findings from the 2004 Prison Gang Survey.* Peotone, IL: National Gang Crime Research Center, p. 2.
39. Knox, supra n.38, p. 3.
40. Knox. 2005. *The Problems of Gangs and Security Threat Groups (STGs) in American Prisons Today: Recent Research Findings from the 2004 Prison Gang Survey.* Peotone, IL: National Gang Crime Research Center.
41. Randall G. Sheldon. 1991. A Comparison of Gang Members and Non-gang Members in a Prison Setting. *The Prison Journal*, 71, 50-60.
42. Gerald G. Gaes, Susan Wallace, Evan Gilman, Jody Klein-Saffran, and Sharon Suppa. 2002. The Influence of Prison Gang Affiliation on Violence and Other Prison Misconduct. *The Prison Journal*, 82, 359-385.
43. Matt DeLisi, Mark T. Berg, and Andy Hochstetler. 2004. Gang Members, Career Criminals and Prison Violence: Further Specification of the Importation Model of Inmate Behavior. *Criminal Justice Studies*, 17, 369-383.

Institutions with higher security levels are more likely to house gang members and to have associated problems. A full one-quarter of prisons indicate that gang members present problems by threatening prison staff. However, only one-tenth of prisons report any assaults by gang members on staff.

Adaptations to Deprivation

Whereas some explanations for prison violence center on the ideas that people who go to prison are naturally violent, and that the incarceration of gang members means that violence is a behavior that is imported to prison, other suggested explanations for prison violence reflect the belief that violence is a product of how inmates adapt to life in prison. So, rather than explaining violence in prison with an importation explanation, others rely on an adaptation-based explanation. In this view, inmates' violent actions are simply attempts to cope with the new, stressful environment of prison. Many inmates, especially those who once had luxurious possessions and significant power, endure great hardships when imprisoned. When incarcerated, these inmates may find deprivation of so many important aspects of their lives too difficult. They may reestablish some semblance of their pre-prison lifestyles by exerting power over others. Having power allows them to regain some of their social clout. Also, with power inmates can accumulate personal possessions that, while not nearly what they possessed on the outside, are more and better than those of other inmates.

Absolute deprivation: the state in which people simply do not have adequate resources for survival.

Relative deprivation: the condition of having less than others in the same environment, regardless of the actual amount of possessions and resources owned.

Inmates may turn to violence to resolve feelings of both absolute and relative deprivation. **Absolute deprivation** is that state when people simply do not have adequate resources for survival. In this view, inmates' violence would be explained as a consequence of them trying to modify a feeling of having absolutely nothing, not even enough food, clothing, etc., to meet their basic needs. More commonly, and more easy to argue, inmates use violence to avoid feelings of **relative deprivation**. This is the condition of having less than others in the same environment, regardless of the actual amount of possessions and resources owned. Remember: Survival in prison depends on one's image of power and strength. To have less than others may be interpreted as a sign of weakness, which in turn is associated with victimization in many forms. This also means that to be perceived by others in prison as having more "stuff" is likely to be interpreted as a sign of strength. Violence is both easily accessible and important in constructing an image of strength. Therefore, many inmates will turn to violence to overcome their sense of deprivation.

Overcrowding

Overcrowding: when the number of inmates in a correctional institution significantly exceeds that facility's housing capacity.

One controversial explanation for prison violence centers on the issue of **overcrowding**. When the number of inmates in a correctional institution significantly exceeds that facility's housing capacity, a facility is considered to be "overcrowded." When this happens, common belief among correctional administrators and researchers is that violence is one of the many likely consequences.

The reasons that overcrowding may lead to violence centers on the idea that as inmates have even less privacy and opportunity to escape interactions with large numbers of other inmates they feel higher levels of stress, they are more likely to become engaged in disagreements with other inmates, and they may feel a need to exert themselves so as to establish their own "space" and sense of privacy. Considering the fact that those with whom one is forced to interact are probably violent people, and they are people who seek to overcome experienced deprivations, and then couple this with the fact that many others are likely to be mentally ill, and the increased potential for violence in an overcrowded institution becomes clear. In fact, Karen Lahm's research[44] has demonstrated that prisons with higher concentrations of population (e.g., more crowding) have higher numbers of physical assaults among inmates. Similarly, the commission (appointed by Congress and the President) charged with investigating prison rape that came out of PREA also found that crowded conditions in prison were a significant contributing factor to sexual assaults among inmates.[45]

That most U.S. prisons are overcrowded is simply a fact of life in contemporary corrections. However, our courts have also found some prisons to be so overcrowded that their conditions violate the Eighth Amendment protection against cruel and unusual punishment.[46] One of the most influential court rulings concerning overcrowding in prisons came in the 2011 Supreme Court case of *Brown v. Plata*, in which the Court found that the prisons in the California Department of Rehabilitation and Corrections were so overcrowded that they could be (and in fact were) ordered to reduce their population by 30,000 inmates. As this case makes very clear, when overcrowding is so severe as to make violence likely, correctional officials can be held in violation of constitutional standards. The courts have ruled that for correctional officials to maintain prisons with populations larger than they are designed to hold is evidence of them exhibiting deliberate indifference to their obligation to protect inmates from attacks.[47]

American courts have also interpreted the Eighth Amendment as including a guarantee of a "healthy habilitative environment."[48] One central component of such an environment is adequate living space. In early court cases about overcrowding, the courts adopted the standards of the American Public Health Association. These standards require a minimum of 60 square feet per inmate in cells and a minimum of 75 square feet per inmate in a dormitory arrangement.[49] However, in later challenges to prison conditions, these standards were abandoned in favor of those requiring less space.

---

44. Lahm, supra n.9.
45. National Prison Rape Elimination Commission. 2009. *Report.* Washington, D.C.: National Prison Rape Elimination Commission.
46. Kim Ellis. 1991. Prison Overcrowding, Inmate Violence and Cruel and Unusual Punishment. *Criminal Justice Journal*, 13, 81-99.
47. Riley v. Jeffes, 777 F.2d 143, 146 (3d Cir. 1985).
48. Battle v. Anderson, 564 F.2d 388, 395 (10th Cir. 1977).
49. *Ibid.*

It may be more than just the actual nature of crowding, however, that is important for understanding violence. Crowding is well known to be associated with other negative environmental aspects of prisons, such as noise, cleanliness, and opportunities for privacy for inmates. Using these issues in an aggregate fashion, research has shown, that at least in the federal prisons, institutions with a less desirable physical condition also have higher rates of violence. So, while the experience of feeling crowded and stressed is related to violent actions, so too does it appear that the other consequences of crowding, those that are seen in the wear and tear on the physical plant of the prison, are also connected to a likelihood of violence.[50]

High Incidence of Mental Illness

One of the unfortunate facts about prison inmates in the United States is that a large proportion of them have at least some form of mental illness. Treatment for mental illnesses is common in prisons and jails (as will be discussed in more detail in Chapter 12), but even with treatment and medication, the fact remains that mental illness is one of the most common characteristics of prison inmates. Accurate estimates of the prevalence of mental illness among inmates are difficult to make, and the numbers may vary (sometimes rather widely) depending on the sources that are used. Research literature has reported that anywhere from 1 percent to 77 percent of prison inmates have a "mental illness."[51] According to statistics compiled by the Bureau of Justice Statistics, among state prison inmates an estimated 56 percent of inmates have a diagnosed (or diagnosable) mental illness, compared with 45 percent of federal prison inmates and 64 percent of inmates in jails.[52] This compares with estimates that consistently show approximately 10 percent of the overall population of the United States having a mental illness.

Mental illness is clearly associated with a number of problems for incarcerated persons. Inmates with mental illnesses are more likely to have been in prison at least three times, are more likely to have received a disciplinary infraction write-up for violating institutional rules, and inmates with mental illness are twice as likely to have been involved in a physical fight while incarcerated. Not only are inmates with mental illness more likely to be involved in prohibited activities (e.g., to have received a disciplinary write-up) and to be involved in a fight, but so too are they more likely to have been victims of physical violence.[53] Mentally ill inmates are more likely to be victimized physically by both other

---

50. David M. Bierie. 2012. Is Tougher Better? The Impact of Physical Prison Conditions on Inmate Violence. *International Journal of Offender Therapy and Comparative Criminology*, 56, 338-355.

51. Anthony Swetz, Marcel E. Salive, Thomas Stough, and T. Fordham Brewer. 1989. The Prevalence of Mental Illness in a State Correctional Institution for Men. *Journal of Prison and Jail Health*, 8, 3-13.

52. Doris J. James and Lauren Glaze. 2006. *Mental Health Problems of Prison and Jail Inmates.* Washington, D.C.: Bureau of Justice Statistics.

53. Blitz, Wolff, and Shi, supra n.7.

inmates and staff. Rather obviously, mental illness for prison inmates is associated with both the perpetration of violence and victimization.

Perhaps one of the most telling pieces of research related to attempting to explain why violence happens in prisons is the work of Jiang and Fisher-Giorlando,[54] who examined instances of violence in a Southern prison. In their work, they tested for the possible influence of deprivation, importation, and situational and contextual influences on the occurrence of violence and misconduct by inmates. In the end, their research suggested that all three types of explanations are important. Or, in other words, there very likely is not one explanation for violence in prisons, but rather there are a multitude of reasons why it occurs. To try to identify the one (or even just a very few) reasons for violence in prison may be a frustrating and unproductive pursuit. Rather, the entire context of situation, inmates, staff, and physical aspects of prisons must be taken into account in order to understand both how and why violence occurs in American prisons.

ORGANIZED DISTURBANCES AND RIOTS

In addition to the seven types of individual-level violence that were discussed earlier in this chapter, the eighth form of prison violence is collective violence, or what are called organized disturbances and riot. **Organized disturbances**, or planned and coordinated uprisings, are minimally disruptive and damaging and are more common than full-blown riots. For an uprising to be considered a **riot**, it must be an incident "when authorities lose control of a significant number of prisoners, in a significant area of the prison, for a significant amount of time."[55]

Organized disturbances: planned and/or coordinated uprisings that are minimally disruptive and damaging and are more common than full-blown riots.

Riot: an incident where authorities have lost control of a significant number of prisoners, in a significant area of a prison, for a significant amount of time.

Riots are not a new or recent development in corrections. Rather, riots and organized uprisings can be traced back to the very beginning of American correctional efforts. The Walnut Street Jail experienced organized uprisings, as did the first American attempt at incarceration in an abandoned mineshaft in Simsbury, Connecticut. In today's world, prison riots are neither common nor rare and unique events. It would be a rare month that a riot or organized disturbance was not reported in a prison somewhere in the world, and in most months there would be at least one incident, most probably a disturbance, not a riot, in at least one American prison. However, as with all of our forms of violence, these types of violence are far from as frequent as the entertainment media might lead us to believe.

Prison riots tend to occur in waves. The twentieth century saw four distinct periods during which prison riots reached epidemic proportions. The first wave coincided with the outbreak of World War I and led to alterations in strict internal security measures and increases in "moral regeneration" activities.[56]

---

54. Shanhe Jiang and Marianne Fisher-Giorlando. 2002. Inmate Misconduct: A Test of Deprivation, Importation and Situation Models. *The Prison Journal*, 82, 335-358.

55. Bert Useem and Peter Kimball. 1991. *States of Siege: U.S. Prison Riots 1971-1986.* Oxford: Oxford University Press, p. 4.

56. Simon Dinitz. 1983. In Fear of Each Other. *Sociological Focus*, 16, p. 158.

The second wave occurred during 1929-1930, the start of the Great Depression. The next wave of prison riots came during the Korean War. This period saw an unprecedented number of riots. For instance, between April 1952 and September 1953, 40 riots occurred in the United States, exceeding the total number recorded in the preceding 25 years.[57] Finally, accompanying the civil rights movement, the birth of the prisoners' rights movement, and the general sense of social upheaval of the 1960s and early 1970s, prison riots reached record numbers. The number of riots in American prisons peaked in 1973, when 94 riots were reported across the nation. Since that time the number has dropped dramatically. During the 1980s, riots decreased from approximately 45 to 10 annually, and in the years since 1990 every year has seen fewer than 10 (and usually fewer than 5) riots annually.[58]

Riots are one of the issues in corrections that seem to captivate the public (and students') attention. Riots are feared, yet are in many ways like accidents along the highway, causing people to slow down, stare, and then speculate about what might have happened to cause the accident, or riot. For many people, rioting prisoners are often perceived as the incident of greatest threat to public safety from corrections. However, the likelihood of mass escape, or even individual escapes, during a riot is minute. When a riot breaks out, correctional and law enforcement officials respond immediately and en masse, and armed personnel — not infrequently including the National Guard — will surround the facility. Escapes simply do not happen during riots; the general public is not in danger. Those in danger are the inmates and any staff taken hostage or trapped inside the prison.

Riots can and do vary quite widely in their form and in the process or sequence of events that unfold. Some riots may be coordinated efforts by inmates to call attention to conditions within the institution and attempts to bring about changes in prison structure, activities, and personnel. Some riots may be symbolic retaliations toward correctional and political officials; or, as sadly appears to be the recent trend, some may simply be opportunities for inmates to seek revenge on other inmates. Regardless of their targets, the inmates themselves are the ones who suffer the most, for the longest time (especially after a riot is ended), and perhaps most dramatically, both during and after a riot. The physical destruction from a riot is often very great and costly. Also, the facilities destroyed or damaged during the riot are often those that allow inmates opportunities for self-improvement and recreation. As summarized by Dinitz:

> By the perverse logic of prison rioters, the targets of destruction have been the school, shops, and infirmaries inside the walls. Counseling centers, chapels, and recreational centers have been torched with regularity.[59]

---

57. South Carolina Department of Corrections. 1973. *Collective Violence in Correctional Institutions: A Search for Causes.* Columbia: South Carolina Department of Corrections.
58. Association of State Correctional Administrators. No date. *Fact Sheet: Corrections Safety.* Available at http://www.asca.net/system/assets/attachments/2652/FACTSHEET-3.pdf?1301079473.
59. Dinitz, supra n.56.

Such acts naturally mean that inmates will be without many services and opportunities for prolonged periods of time.

Some riots do lead to changes in how inmates are treated and in what, how much, and what quality of things (e.g., food, visitation, health care, clothing, programs, etc.) that they are provided. Often, however, relatively little changes for the positive after a riot.

EXPLANATIONS FOR PRISON RIOTS

There are a number of explanations for why prison riots occur. However, scholars of corrections have never reached consensus regarding an explanation for prison riots. As the preceding discussions make clear, prison riots break out for a number of reasons.

As early as 1953, the American Prison Association (now the American Correctional Association) established a committee to study the causes of prison disturbances. After consultations with correctional administrators across the United States, the committee listed seven basic causes of prison riots:

1. Inadequate financial support.
2. Substandard personnel.
3. Enforced idleness.
4. Lack of professional leadership and programs.
5. Institutions that are too large and overcrowded.
6. Political domination and motivation of management.
7. Bad sentencing practices.

Most striking about this list: Most of these conditions have changed very little in the past six decades. Therefore, it should be no surprise that the same conditions and "causes" are central in most current theoretical explanations for prison riots. The following discussion focuses on five frequently advanced explanations for prison riots.

Environmental Conditions

The most commonly cited reason for the outbreak of prison riots centers on poor physical and social conditions. This explanation, relied on in whole or at least in part by most after-the-fact investigations, argues that inmates riot to force officials to improve the deprivations and unsatisfactory conditions of prison life. This is an explanation that carries a significant degree of face validity — it makes logical sense. As we tend to believe that prisons are places of significant deprivation for inmates, the idea that they would "fight back" in an attempt to improve their situations appeals to our sense of logic and common sense.

Attempts to understand both the how and why of prison riots comes from investigations of riots that are done after a riot, sometimes taking months or even years to complete. It is in this process that administrators, legislators, and researchers try to identify the "causes" that can be either eliminated or "fixed" to avoid future riots. By pointing to aspects of the physical facility or personnel, officials can easily devise plans of action to prevent future acts of collective violence. Among the most commonly cited environmental factors that instigate riots are:

- Poor, insufficient, and/or contaminated food.
- Overcrowding.
- Lack of professional leadership in the institution.
- Substandard training of staff (especially in communication skills).
- Inadequate or absent treatment programs.
- Lack of recreational, vocational, educational, and work opportunities or programs.
- Presence of gangs.
- Public indifference to conditions.

Regardless of how observers explain riots, in the eyes of most observers a prison's environmental conditions must bear at least some of the blame for the outbreak of mass violence. This is clear in the 1981 American Correctional Association's (ACA) classification of causes for riots and disturbances. The ACA suggests that four sets of factors contribute to riots:

1. Institutional environment.
2. Characteristics of the inmate population.
3. Administrative practices.
4. Non-institutional (outside societal) factors shaping prison policies and activities.

Obviously, the first three sets are conditions of the prison environment, and the fourth influences the shaping of the other three.

Spontaneity Model

A second explanation, which is really not an explanation, says that prison disturbances are essentially unplanned, spontaneously occurring events. In this respect, these are unpredictable events that we cannot anticipate, and in all probability cannot prevent. Rather than conscious reactions to inhumane conditions or attempts to force change in institutional policies, inmate disturbances are sudden outbursts in response to some type of triggering events. The spontaneity model suggests that while disturbances may occur with some frequency, only a select few disturbances will progress into full riots (because they tend to be smaller and easier to quell).

When we view riots as out-of-control disturbances, if we are to have any hope of understanding the how and why of resulting riots we have to look at the immediate set of circumstances that facilitate the emergence of a riot. This means we must consider both **predisposing factors** and **precipitating factors.**[60] This view would argue that the ever-present environmental conditions that impose stresses and deprivations on inmates also predispose inmates to riots. While routines and relatively uneventful days are present in predisposing factors, the impact of a precipitating factor is what triggers rioting. Precipitating factors may range from an attempt by staff to lock down an institution to a minor scuffle between inmates or between inmates and staff. Once a precipitating event begins, the energy may quickly spread, incorporating more inmates and quickly growing out of control.

Predisposing factors: ever-present routine and daily environmental conditions that impose stresses and deprivations on inmates that can lead inmates to riot.

Precipitating factors: factors that can trigger a riot; ranging from an attempt by staff to lock down an institution to a minor scuffle between inmates or between inmates and staff.

When it erupts, a riot has a natural life cycle. Fox has proposed a five-stage model for prison riots:

1. Explosion (the precipitating factor).
2. Organization (inmates communicate and draw more people and territory into the riot).
3. Confrontation (making contact with and facing off with officials, whether through demands, negotiation, or defiance).
4. Termination (the retaking of the institution either by force or negotiated agreement).
5. Reaction and explanation (post-event investigations, political fallout, and steps toward implementing any changes in the facility).[61]

Even though this model establishes the basic, expected progression of events, wide latitude is still available for individual riots to develop differently. This is the core of the spontaneity model: We must examine the immediate, uniquely individual sets of circumstances involved in a riot to explain why it occurred. Disturbances are largely sudden and unplanned, and may or may not grow into full-fledged riots.

Conflict Model

The conflict model is based on the assumption that the official forms of control and repression typical in prisons have two consequences that may contribute to a riot. First, official use of social control creates value conflicts between the institution officials and the inmate population. Neither side understands, nor fully accepts, the other side's actions and apparent values. Second, the structural nature whereby one group holds total (or near total) control over another group imposes on the controlled group a severely limited range of available means to express dissatisfaction. And sometimes the only way that the controlled group (inmates) sees to express their frustrations is through violence.

60. Vernon Fox. 1971. Why Prisoners Riot. *Federal Probation*, 35, 9-14.
61. *Ibid.*

This theory says we should not be surprised when inmates turn to collective action in such an environment. Violence should not be viewed as abnormal, perverse, or pathological. Instead, we need to review the options inmates have for expressing their value differences and the means they have for better understanding and changing those conditions with which they are dissatisfied. Inmates have very limited options. Collective violence is one of the few potentially effective means of expression.

Also, the prison culture emphasizes strength, power, and control. This is evident both within the inmate society and in how institutional officials maintain security and order. Therefore, inmates are cut off from "normal" avenues of expression and on a daily basis are shown models that use repressive powers and force to achieve goals. Therefore, violence is construed as a "normal" response to frustrations and difficulties. When a riot erupts, then, we should not be surprised. Instead, we should have expected it.

Collective Behavior and Social Control Model

The collective behavior and social control model focuses on riots erupting when the institution's daily social control processes are disrupted. The breakdown in social control means that inmates have no structure to guide their basic interactions. To fill this absence, some inmates may take control and impose their wills on officials and other inmates.

This argument hinges on the idea that a correctional institution's primary control mechanism is not the force but, instead, a web of informal and reciprocal social relationships. In other words, inmates and staff maintain control in prison by silently agreeing to cooperate with one another and to trade favors. When something — a policy change, a staffing change, a crackdown on contraband — disrupts the relationships inmates and staff have negotiated, the delicate balance of power in place is threatened.

Whenever change occurs, stress follows. In prison, this stress may be magnified because of the restricted range of options and experiences available to inmates. So, when inmates perceive a threat to the balance of power, they may logically respond in one of two general ways. Inmates may either work to restore the balance, or they may see an opportunity to improve (if only temporarily) their condition and therefore act (riot) to achieve such goals. Interestingly, one of the few studies to ever look at the individual inmates who actively participate in riots has shown that these are inmates who have been involved in disciplinary infractions while incarcerated.[62] This would support the idea that social control mechanisms are important for efforts to prevent riots; since those inmates who actively participate in riot activities are those who are most likely to be involved in any misbehavior while incarcerated, riots can be seen as a failure

---

[62] Christine M. Graeve, Matt DeLisi, and Andy Hochstetler. 2007. Prison Rioters: Exploring Infraction Characteristics, Risk Factors, Social Correlates, and Criminal Careers. *Psychological Reports*, 100, 407-419.

of the structures and processes that typically limit these inmates' behaviors having broken down.

Riots, then, result from a correctional institution's breakdown in either its formal or informal control mechanisms. When no stable, recognized power structure exists, we should expect some or all of a prison's inmates to act to fill the resulting void.

Rising Expectations and Relative Deprivation Model

Similar to the collective behavior and social control model is the rising expectations and relative deprivation model for explaining prison riots. Whereas our previous theory says that change induces stress, this explanation focuses more specifically on how change causes the stresses that may culminate in riots.

Rising expectations and relative deprivation explanations suggest that when people believe a sizable gap exists between what they believe they deserve or should have and what they actually receive, they will experience high levels of frustration and perceive themselves as significantly deprived. The rising expectations portion of the explanation enters when a group of people who are slowly realizing improvements in their social conditions have their progress suddenly and unreasonably stopped. This sudden interruption to improving conditions brings about frustration for people, and despite their environment and experiences being better than they had once been, the fact that improvements and advances are stopped brings up considerable frustrations.

Applying these ideas to prison, inmates see the conditions of their lives improving, have reason to believe that these improvements will continue to develop, but suddenly have these improvements stopped or removed. The inmates feel highly deprived. The most obvious example of curtailing inmates' rising expectations is when officials tighten security and reduce their tolerance of contraband, sex, and activities for inmates. In response to these experienced frustrations, inmates may take collective action to convince officials to reinstate the improved (at least from the inmates' perceptions) conditions.

Summary

Violence in prisons can be categorized into eight basic forms: inmate(s) on inmate(s), inmate(s) on staff, staff on inmate(s), sexual violence, self-inflicted physical violence, economic violence, psychological violence, and organized disturbances and riots. Of all the eight forms of violence, physical violence by inmates on inmates is the most common. However, in recent years, there has been the most attention, both in terms of research and public policy, regarding sexual violence. The Prison Rape Elimination Act (2003) led to better understandings of the who, how, and why of prison rape, as well as legal changes and operational changes that impact day-to-day life for prison staff and inmates.

As with any problem, the best way to reduce or eliminate the problems of violence in prison needs to arise from understanding why such activity occurs. The theories for explaining prison violence fall into one of two general varieties: explanations based on the prisonization experience or explanations centered on the idea of behaviors and characteristics that inmates import to prison with them. More specifically, explanations for prison violence tend to highlight one of five issues: violent nature of inmates, necessary adaptation to conditions of deprivation, gangs, overcrowding, and mental illness.

As is the case with violence on the individual level, so too do we have competing explanations for collective forms of prison violence, what most people would refer to as prison riots. Here we base our explanations on one or more of the following: the physical conditions of prisons and confinement, unique triggering events that spontaneously occur, growing conflicts between groups of inmates or between inmates and staff, and inmates' growing expectation for improvements that get obstructed after a certain amount of progress.

Key Terms

Absolute deprivation
Organized disturbances
Overcrowding
Physical coercion
Precipitating factors
Predisposing factors
Prison gangs
Prison Rape Elimination Act (PREA)
Protective pairing
Relative deprivation
Riot
Routine activities theory
Sexual violence

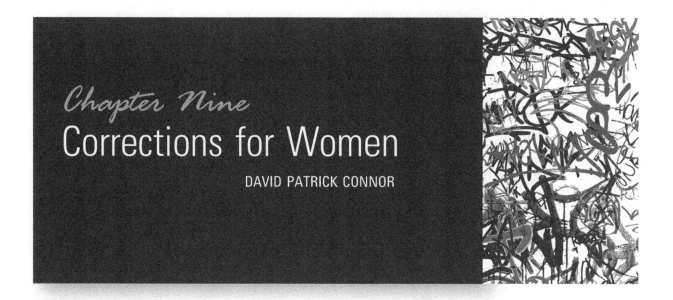

Chapter Nine
Corrections for Women

DAVID PATRICK CONNOR

This chapter will familiarize students with corrections aimed at women, with a focus on the characteristics and experiences of female criminal offenders under correctional supervision. Emphasis will be placed on women inside prisons, women inside jails, social ties and pseudo families, and challenges with women as correctional clients.

WOMEN INSIDE PRISONS

More than 1.5 million individuals who are convicted of and sentenced for criminal offenses currently find themselves living inside American prisons, and more than 7 percent of these individuals are women. The most recent national statistics indicate that there are 103,674 female offenders, compared to 1,433,741 male offenders, housed inside both federal and state correctional institutions.[1] Although there are fewer women inside prisons across the nation than men, incarcerated females are evolving into a larger proportion of prison inmates.[2]

The **imprisonment rate**, which is calculated by taking the number of sentenced prison inmates divided by the number of U.S. residents multiplied by

Imprisonment rate: the number of persons per every 100,000 persons that are in prison. It is an important statistic for being able to compare the proportion of persons in different populations that end up in prison.

1. E. Ann Carson and William J. Sabol. 2012. *Prisoners in 2011*. Washington, D.C.: Bureau of Justice Statistics.
2. American Correctional Association. 1990. *The Female Offender: What Does the Future Hold?* Washington, D.C.: St. Mary's Press.

100,000, provides some insight into the subtle growth of women as prison inmates. In 2000, for instance, 59 females were incarcerated per 100,000 U.S. residents. Today, 65 females are locked inside prisons per 100,000 U.S. residents.[3]

Currently Incarcerated Female Offenders

A majority of women behind bars in the United States are neither extremely young nor extremely old, as they are in their 30s and 40s. About one-third (33%) are between the ages of 30 and 39, while more than one-fourth (26%) are between the ages of 40 and 49. A smaller proportion of female prison inmates are younger than 30 years of age. More than one-tenth (12%) are between the ages of 18 and 24, and about one-fifth (17%) are between the ages of 25 and 29. At the same time, an even smaller proportion of women behind bars are older than 49 years of age. One-tenth (10%) are between the ages of 50 and 59, and a minority (2%) are 60 years of age or older.[4] Thus, the lion's share of incarcerated female offenders may be most appropriately described as middle-aged or slightly younger.

Women behind bars in the United States represent a multitude of racial and ethnic backgrounds. Female prison inmates are most commonly white, however, as almost one-half (49%) identify as such. One-quarter (25%) report that they are African American, and slightly less than one-fifth (18%) identify as Hispanic. A minority (8%) report that they are not white, African American, or Hispanic.[5]

Violent criminal conduct is the most common reason why both female and male lawbreakers find themselves inside prisons. And yet, incarcerated women are less likely to be serving time for a violent offense conviction than incarcerated men. As a result of a violent offense conviction, such as assault, rape, or robbery, about one in three (37%) female prison inmates are behind bars, compared to about one in two (54%) male prison inmates. Interestingly, though, the percentage of incarcerated individuals who are serving time for a murder conviction differs only slightly between women (10%) and men (12%). However, murder is the most common violent offense that leads to a prison term for female inmates, whereas robbery is the most common violent offense that leads to a prison term for male inmates.[6]

Following violent behavior, a criminal offense involving property is the second most common explanation for the incarceration of women offenders. A greater proportion of incarcerated women are serving time for a property offense conviction than incarcerated men. As a result of a property offense

---

3. Carson and Sabol, supra n.1.
4. *Ibid.*
5. *Ibid.*
6. *Ibid.*

conviction, such as burglary, larceny, or motor vehicle theft, about one in three (29%) female prison inmates and about one in five (18%) male prison inmates are behind bars. A greater proportion of incarcerated women are also serving time for a drug offense conviction than incarcerated men. As a result of a drug offense conviction, such as manufacturing, possession, or trafficking, one in four (25%) female prison inmates and about one in six (17%) male prison inmates are behind bars. Further, a smaller number of incarcerated women are serving time for a public-order offense conviction than incarcerated men. As a result of a public-order offense conviction, such as commercial vice, drunk driving, or weapons, about 1 in 12 (8%) female prison inmates and about 1 in 9 (11%) male prison inmates are behind bars.[7]

Correctional Entities and Institutions

With more than 12,000 female inmates inside prisons, Texas incarcerates the most women in the nation. Alaska, Idaho, Kentucky, Montana, North Dakota, South Dakota, West Virginia, and Wyoming incarcerate the largest proportion of female inmates, with women constituting at least 10 percent of each jurisdiction's total prison population. Alternatively, in Rhode Island, women represent just less than 4 percent of its total prison population, making it the jurisdiction with the smallest number of female prison inmates. **Jurisdiction** refers to the legal authority that allows both the federal and state governments of the United States to incarcerate specific convicted criminal offenders, regardless of where such offenders are housed. Interestingly, in terms of the number of incarcerated women under its jurisdiction, the federal government follows closely behind Texas, with 12,149 female inmates inside prisons; however, as it relates to the proportion of female inmates in its prison population, the federal government holds a middle-of-the-road position, at just over 6 percent.[8]

Jurisdiction: legal authority that allows both the federal and state governments of the U.S. to incarcerate specific convicted criminal offenders, regardless of where they are housed.

Female offenders sentenced to prison time may reside inside an assortment of correctional institutions, including camps, penitentiaries, and reformatories. However, after a period of time inside jails, most incarcerated women are confined inside centralized state facilities, commonly referred to as women's prisons, which serve the exclusive purpose of housing females convicted of felony offenses. In Kentucky, for example, two prisons, the Kentucky Correctional Institution for Women and the Western Kentucky Correctional Complex, serve as the sole places of residence for incarcerated women. These correctional institutions for female prison inmates often resemble college campuses, with multiple housing units surrounding a few central buildings that are used for employee offices, food services, and programs. High walls, guard towers, and fences of razor wire are uncommon here. Other female prison inmates are often housed inside special housing units of male correctional institutions.

7. *Ibid.*
8. *Ibid.*

Many jurisdictions operate only one prison designated for women, despite running numerous correctional institutions for men. The Women's Huron Valley Correctional Facility, for instance, serves as the only prison in Michigan that houses female inmates.[9] Due to a limited number of available correctional institutions designated exclusively for women, such prisons often confine a wide array of female inmates with various custody levels. The Kentucky Correctional Institution for Women is considered a multi-custody prison (i.e., community, minimum, restricted, medium, close, and maximum) that focuses on differential housing and programming to meet the needs of a multitude of women, including first-time offenders, persistent offenders, special needs inmates, and death row inmates.[10]

WOMEN INSIDE JAILS

Between 2000 and 2007, the United States experienced dramatic increases in its number of female jail inmates. In 2000, nearly 71,000 women were held inside jails, and five years later, this number swelled to more than 94,500 female jail inmates, which represented a 25 percent increase. The number of women inside jails continued to grow between 2005 and 2006, and in 2007, more than 100,000 female inmates were held inside jails.[11]

In more recent years, however, fewer women were held inside jails. Between 2007 and 2010, the number of female jail inmates consistently decreased. By 2010, there were just over 92,000 women inside jails, which was down 8 percent from 2007. Despite this reduction, the following two years saw another spike in the number of female jails inmates, with more than 98,000 women inside jails in 2012. Today, women represent 13 percent of inmates held inside American jails, and their characteristics often contrast with those of men.[12]

Criminal conduct that leads to confinement inside jails varies among both women and men. Female inmates inside jails (29%) are more likely than male inmates inside jails (24%) to be held for a drug offense, such as manufacturing, possession, or trafficking. At the same time, women inside jails (32%) are more likely than men inside jails (23%) to be held for a property offense, such as burglary, larceny, or motor vehicle theft. However, female inmates inside jails (17%) are less likely than male inmates inside jails (27%) to be held for a violent offense, such as assault, rape, or robbery. Women inside jails (21%) are also less likely than men inside jails (26%) to be held for a public-order offense, such as

9. Michigan Department of Corrections. 2013. Women's Huron Valley Correctional Facility (WHV). Available at http://michigan.gov/corrections/0,4551,7-119-1381_1385-116930—,00.html.

10. Kentucky Department of Corrections. 2013. About KCIW. Available at http://corrections.ky.gov/depts/AI/KCIW/Pages/AboutKCIW.aspx.

11. ToddD. Minton. 2013. *Jail Inmates at Midyear 2012—Statistical Tables.* Washington, D.C.: Bureau of Justice Statistics.

12. *Ibid.*

commercial vice, drunk driving, or weapons. Regardless of their criminal behavior, it is interesting to note that female inmates inside jails (49%) are more likely than male inmates inside jails (37%) to be first-time criminal offenders.[13]

In terms of life experiences before their admission to jail, differences between women and men also exist. Female inmates inside jails (40%) are less likely to be employed in the month prior to their arrest than male inmates inside jails (60%). At the same time, women inside jails (16%) are less likely to experience an injury following an assault prior to their arrest than men inside jails (37%). However, female inmates inside jails (55%) are more likely to experience physical or sexual abuse prior to their arrest than male inmates inside jails (13%). Among abused jail inmates, women inside jails (68%) are more likely to be abused by an intimate partner prior to their arrest than men inside jails (11%). Previously abused female inmates inside jails (34%) are also more likely to be abused by a friend or acquaintance than previously abused male inmates inside jails (14%). And yet, previously abused women inside jails (26%) are less likely to be abused by a parent or guardian than previously abused male inmates inside jails (60%).[14]

Recent research highlights some of the additional obstacles that women inside jails encounter throughout their lives. One study indicates that female inmates inside jails experience high rates of lifetime trauma exposure (98%), alcohol and drug problems (74%), and mental health disorders (36%). It also suggests that most women inside jails are deficient in parenting skills, as more than one-half of the 100 female inmates inside jails who participated in the study showed deficits in the ability to parent. Further, difficulties with alcohol, drugs, and maintaining relationships with their children may be the most pressing issues for jailed women, as female inmates inside jails who participated in the study identified substance abuse and family problems as the most substantial challenges that face them.[15]

Another study indicates that a majority of women inside jails have at least one mental health disorder in their lifetime. One in four (25%) female jail inmates meet the criteria for lifetime serious mental illness (SMI), post-traumatic stress disorder (PTSD), and substance use disorders (SUD). Many women inside jails also meet the criteria for SMI, PTSD, and SUD in the previous year, and one in four (25%) female jail inmates report severe functional impairment in the previous year. Among women inside jails with SMI, trauma, reoffense, and earlier onset of substance use and running away from home are more likely. The study also indicates that one-half (50%) of female inmates inside jails receive treatment for substance use or mental health issues prior to their arrest. Unfortunately, most women inside jails experience multiple types of adversity and

13. D.J. James. 2004. *Profile of Jail Inmates, 2002.* Washington, D.C.: Bureau of Justice Statistics.

14. *Ibid.*

15. Bonnie L. Green, Jeana Miranda, Anihita Daroowalla, and Juned. Siddique. 2005. Trauma Exposure, Mental Health Functioning, and Program Needs of Women in Jail. *Crime and Delinquency,* 51, (1), 133-151.

interpersonal violence throughout their lives. According to the study, childhood and adult victimization may increase the risk of experiencing mental health problems for female jail inmates, which then is related to their increased likelihood of criminal behavior.[16]

SOCIAL TIES AND PSEUDO FAMILIES

Women inside jails and prisons are often compelled to adjust to their new environment. On the inside, female inmates are subject to some degree of isolation from the rest of society. This is a striking contrast from life on the outside. Women inside jails and prisons are likely to be unable to maintain the same level of communication and social interaction with family members, friends, and acquaintances, as they would on the outside. However, many female inmates still attempt to preserve free-world relationships and develop companionship from behind bars.

Contraband: items that prisoners are prohibited from obtaining or possessing while confined.

Cell phones and computers that may be used to contact family members, friends, and acquaintances on the outside are forms of **contraband** inside jails and prisons, which means that these items cannot be possessed or utilized by jailed or incarcerated women. According to the Kentucky Department of Corrections, for example, contraband means "any article or thing which a person confined in a detention facility is prohibited from obtaining or possessing by statute, departmental regulation, or posted institutional rule or order."[17] In short, pieces of contraband are materials that are forbidden inside jails and prisons. Female inmates, as a result, must rely on other means of communication and social interaction.

Centrally located telephones, which allow collect calls to be made at the expense of the individual contacted, provide one common way for women inside jails and prisons to exchange information with the outside. However, more often than not, these telephone calls are extremely expensive, which makes routine acceptance of such calls by family members, friends, and acquaintances highly unlikely. For this reason, telephone calls made by female inmates to the outside are not an ideal form of regular correspondence, and such calls may be limited or nonexistent by necessity.

Women inside jails and prisons may also write and receive letters, as a means of communication and social interaction with the outside. However, because literacy levels among inmates are lower than literacy levels among the general population, the expectation that female inmates engage in written communication with the outside on a regular basis is likely to be unrealistic. At the same time, even if women inside jails and prisons have the ability to read and write,

---

16. Shannojn M. Lynch, Dana D. DeHart, Joanne Belknap, and Bonnie L. Green. 2013. *Women's Pathways to Jail: Examining Mental Health, Trauma, and Substance Use*. Washington, D.C.: Bureau of Justice Assistance.
17. Ky. Rev. Stat. §520.010.

most incoming and outgoing mail is inspected or read by jail and prison employees, which may reduce how candid female inmates and their contacts are with each other through letters and written materials. This may further isolate jailed and incarcerated women from the outside.

In addition, women inside jails and prisons may receive visits from family members, friends, and acquaintances. Approved visiting lists are created for each female inmate during the initial intake process, but individuals not listed and not approved by institutional officials cannot visit. Typically, these records may be updated twice in one year. Although immediate family members are almost always approved to visit women inside jails and prisons, other family members, friends, and acquaintances may find it more difficult to visit, as female inmates may be required to first establish preexisting relationships with such individuals. Beyond immediate family members, for instance, incarcerated women in Kentucky may request visitation from only three additional adults and one clergy.[18] Unfortunately, while serving an institutional security purpose, such restrictions often limit social networks on the outside. Attorneys, for the purposes of legal counsel, are authorized to visit female inmates at any time. However, such visits are focused on legal issues, such as plea agreements, trial strategies, and post-conviction remedies, and they do not necessarily afford women inside jails and prisons strong connections to the outside.

Visitation policies are not uniform across jails and prisons in the United States. For this reason, some women may find it more or less difficult to maintain relationships with family members, friends, and acquaintances while behind bars. Visiting may be restricted by the number of available staff members, routine institutional activities that take place at certain times and on specific days, and unexpected events that arise. The Kentucky Department of Corrections, for example, allows its prison wardens to determine days and times appropriate for visitation. However, wardens must allow inmates under their supervision to visit with approved visitors for at least eight hours per month.[19] Alternatively, all prisons operated by the Iowa Department of Corrections permit inmates to visit with approved visitors for at least four days per week.[20]

The process of visiting women inside jails and prisons may be highly burdensome for visitors. In most jurisdictions, correctional institutions for female inmates are situated away from urban areas, although urban centers are usually the places where most women offenders lived prior to their jail stay and incarceration. Correctional institutions far from home and not accessible to public transportation make visitation expensive and time-consuming. Even if approved visitors are able to reach the institution, the process of visiting may be humiliating and uncomfortable. Visitors who enter correctional institutions to see their female loved one may undergo frisk searches and experience a lack of privacy.

---

18. Kentucky Corrections Policies and Procedures, Policy Number 16.1.

19. *Ibid.*

20. Iowa Department of Corrections. 2013. Visiting Hours. Available at http://www.doc.state.ia.us/visitinghours.asp.

At the same time, visits are supervised and carefully monitored by correctional officers to reduce the introduction of contraband, which limits the closeness between women and their visitors.

Pseudo families: practice exclusively inside women's jails and prisons where female inmates establish an informal social network that places other female inmates in various familial roles to satisfy needs such as companionship, protection, economic/emotional support, and sexual gratification.

Because maintaining communication and social interaction with the outside is often difficult, women inside jails and prisons may turn to other female inmates for intimacy and social support. By participating in **pseudo families** as a coping mechanism, jailed and incarcerated women may attempt to satisfy a variety of needs, including companionship, protection, economic and emotional support, and sexual gratification. Pseudo families are essentially social groupings of female inmates that may arise from the environmental stress of correctional institutions and provide a form of adaptation and comfort to individuals involved.

The focus on interpersonal relationships inside correctional institutions for women represents one key difference between the confinement experiences of females and males. Inside correctional institutions for men, jailed and incarcerated males often believe they must largely act alone to demonstrate their physical and mental strength. Here autonomy and the ability to do one's "own time" is valued. In strong contrast, the development of familial relationships with other inmates allows jailed and incarcerated women to establish an affectionate and supportive environment inside correctional institutions. Often initiated from friendships that form behind bars, many of these associations between female inmates grow into rather intimate connections. Two women may be involved in a jail or prison relationship that is very much like a sister-sister or mother-daughter bond. These associations may include physical contact with or without sexual intentions or meanings. At the same time, a family of females inside a jail or prison may be comprised of "married" inmates, with distinct roles for the male and female. These relationships do not necessarily mean that female inmates are bisexuals or lesbians, and they may only last during the confinement period. Women who are closer to their release date and serving shorter sentences inside jails and prisons may be less likely to continue participating in their pseudo family than women who are further from their release date and serving longer sentences inside jails and prisons.[21]

Seeking to fulfill the need for companionship and sexual release, women who are jailed and incarcerated for significant periods of time may participate in an exclusive partnership with another female inmate. In such scenarios, one woman often adopts a traditionally male role, while the other woman adopts a traditionally female role. A female inmate who takes on the identity of a man commonly imitates masculine appearances and mannerisms. This may include one's dress, hair style, and walk. Interestingly, these relationships among women inside jails and prisons may be encouraged or at least partially ignored by administrators and correctional officers, as a standing partnership between two female

---

21. Barbara Owen. 1998. *In the Mix: Struggle and Survival in a Women's Prison.* Albany, NY: State University of New York Press.

inmates may prevent or socially control each individual from engaging in institutional misconduct. At the same time, conflicts and fighting that may arise from such relationships may be problematic for institutional officials. The same may be said of larger jail and prison pseudo families. The number of women in a pseudo family generally ranges from 2 to 15 female inmates, with each woman functioning in a distinct capacity, such as a mother, father, sister, brother, or grandparent. It may be that women behind bars introduce these traditional familial roles from the outside world to life inside jails and prisons.[22] In this way, pseudo families may exist, allowing female inmates to articulate and satisfy social needs.

It is important to remember, however, that women inside jails and prisons may serve their time differently. According to Barbara Owen, a female's commitment to a deviant identity and where she is in her criminal career impact how a woman decides to spend her time behind bars.[23] This includes how dedicated a female inmate may be to the "convict code" and whether or not she will involve herself in behavior (e.g., establishing and maintaining prohibited, intimate relationships on the inside) that may cause conflict with other inmates and staff members. Owen finds that most women on the inside do not want to participate in "the mix" of institutional life. In other words, female inmates generally do not want to engage in misconduct that may cause them to receive disciplinary infractions and increase their time behind bars. Nonetheless, a minority of women on the inside participate in "the mix" and find themselves involved in forms of institutional misconduct, such as drug use, fighting, and intimate relationships.

CHALLENGES WITH WOMEN AS CORRECTIONAL CLIENTS

The considerable increase in the number of women under correctional supervision in recent years generates distinct challenges for administrators. Female offenders require unique approaches to the management of correctional institutions and the provision of education, vocational training, health care, and family services. The needs of women as correctional clients are often drastically different from the needs of men as correctional clients, and correctional leaders are still struggling to identify and address the unique demands of females who are supervised in the community, jailed, and incarcerated.

Sexual Violence Inside Jails and Prisons

While research on sexual violence involving women inside jails and prisons is still somewhat minimal, available studies suggest that this problem is not

22. Rose Giallombardo. 1966. *Society of Women: A Study of a Women's Prison*. New York: Wiley.
23. Owen, supra n.21.

exclusively experienced by their male counterparts. Female inmates appear to be impacted by sexual violence throughout the correctional system, with reported victimizations coming from both other inmates and staff members. Women inside jails and prisons may experience lower rates of sexual victimization than men inside jails and prisons.[24] Most recently, however, data from the second National Inmate Survey indicate that female inmates inside jails (3.1%) and prisons (4.7%) are more than twice as likely as male inmates inside jails (1.3%) and prisons (4.7%) to report experiencing inmate-on-inmate sexual victimization. Among inmates who report inmate-on-inmate sexual victimization, only 4 percent of women inside jails and prisons report that they are victimized within the first 24 hours after admission, compared to 19 percent of men inside jails and 13 percent of men inside prisons.[25]

At the same time, some research highlights the varying rates of sexual victimization among female inmates. One study reports on data collected from 1,263 women inside three prisons, and it shows a wide range of sexual victimization rates. In one prison, 19 percent of female inmates reported that they had been victims of sexual abuse in their present institution, and 27 percent reported that they had been victims of sexual abuse at some point during their incarceration. And yet, in two much smaller prisons, victimization rates were only 8 percent and 6 percent, respectively. Across all three prisons, the most commonly reported incident was sexual fondling, although descriptions of one in five incidents constituted rape.[26] In 2003, Stop Prisoner Rape, an advocacy group dedicated exclusively to the elimination of sexual assault inside jails and prisons, published its investigation into sexual violence at the Ohio Reformatory for Women. The organization concluded that sexual abuse did occur inside the institution and that administrative attitudes, physical plant design, and "an environment consistently conducive to sexual abuse" all contributed to sexual violence against female inmates.[27]

Women inside jails and prisons may be especially vulnerable to sexual misconduct perpetrated by staff members. In one study, female inmates inside a Hawaii prison estimated that 20 percent of the correctional officers at the correctional institution engaged in some form of sexual activity with incarcerated women.[28] Data from the second National Inmate Survey indicates that sexual activity with jail and prison staff members is reported by 1.5 percent of female jail inmates and 2.1 percent of female prison inmates, compared to 2.1 percent of male jail inmates and 2.9 percent of male prison inmates. Among inmates who

---

24. Cindy Struckman-Johnson, David Struckman-Johnson, Lila Rucker, Kurt Bumby, and Stephen Donaldson. 1996. Sexual Coercion Reported by Men and Women in Prison. *The Journal of Sex Research*, 33, (1), 67-76.

25. Allen J. Beck and Paige M. Harrison. 2010. *Sexual Victimization in Prisons and Jails Reported by Inmates, 2008-2009.* Washington, D.C.: Bureau of Justice Statistics.

26. Cindy Struckman-Johnson and David Struckman-Johnson. 2002. Sexual Coercion Reported by Women in Three Midwestern Prisons. *The Journal of Sex Research*, 39, (3), 217-227.

27. Stop Prisoner Rape. 2003. *The Sexual Abuse of Female Inmates in Ohio.* Los Angeles: Stop Prisoner Rape. p. 16.

28. Avery J. Calhoun and Heather D. Coleman. 2002. Female Inmates' Perspectives on Sexual Abuse by Correctional Personnel: An Exploratory Study. *Women & Criminal Justice*, 13, (2/3), 101-124.

report staff-on-inmate sexual victimization, 4 percent of women inside jails and 5 percent of women inside prisons report that they are victimized within the first 24 hours after admission, compared to 30 percent of men inside jails and nearly 16 percent of men inside prisons.[29]

Institutional Programs

Several prisons offer vocational training, life education classes, and a limited number of college courses. At the same time, correctional institutions provide educational programs that allow inmates to reach literacy and receive general equivalency diplomas (GEDs). These programs are particularly important for jailed and incarcerated women, as many of these female inmates are mothers and must support their children upon release. Historically, because of the smaller populations of women behind bars across the United States, vocational and educational programs available to female inmates have been significantly limited, especially in comparison to such programs offered to male inmates. This issue was addressed in a 1979 case, entitled *Glover v. Johnson*, which established that correctional agencies must provide equal opportunities for vocational training and education to both female and male inmates. Similarly, *Cooper v. Morin* (1980) established that denying services to female inmates based on cost or convenience constitutes a violation of the equal protection clause of the Fourteenth Amendment.

Despite these legal developments, current vocational program offerings at women's prisons are often severely limited when compared to those of men's prisons and fail to prepare women for the wide variety of available jobs. One major weakness of vocational programs offered to female inmates is that they conform to "traditional" stereotypes of opportunities for women in the workplace. Many programs for female inmates follow gender-normative stereotypes and provide training in cosmetology, housekeeping, and food services, while programs available to male inmates often include carpentry, construction, and landscaping. For example, at the Federal Medical Center (FMC) in Kentucky, incarcerated men are able to receive job training as Braille transcribers, dental lab technicians, electricians, and pipe fitters, among many other occupations. Incarcerated women, meanwhile, are offered programs in cooking and building maintenance.[30]

In a post-industrial economy, education is increasingly important for employment. Most correctional institutions, however, do not offer opportunities for higher education to female (or male) inmates, as a result of a 1994 law that prohibits inmates from receiving Pell Grants. In addition, many businesses

---

29. Allen J. Beck and Paige M. Harrison. 2010. *Sexual Victimization in Prisons and Jails Reported by Inmates, 2008-2009.* Washington, D.C.: Bureau of Justice Statistics.

30. Federal Bureau of Prisons. 2006. *Occupational Training Programs Directory: Learning Skills for Work.* Available at http://www.bop.gov/inmate_programs/occ_train.pdf.

refuse to hire ex-offenders, even if they meet the qualifications for a job. As a result, correctional institutions should more appropriately train female inmates to meet the demands of the current marketplace, by providing relevant vocational and technical training, as well as basic and advanced education.

Medical Services

In addition to the lack of vocational and educational programs, women's prisons also generally do not have adequate medical facilities and services. This is particularly problematic, with women as correctional clients. Females, compared to males, are more likely to suffer from heart disease, depression, and stroke. They are also more likely to experience alcohol and drug abuse.[31] Women inside prisons are more likely to suffer from HIV, tuberculosis, drug addiction, and mental illness than are men inside prisons.[32] Female inmates are almost six times more likely than the average American female to suffer from "serious psychological distress."[33] Over one-half of all women inside jails and prisons arrive at a correctional institution with at least one medical problem.[34] Female inmates are also more likely than male inmates to report a new medical problem during incarceration.[35]

Women who are pregnant while jailed or incarcerated face additional health issues. Female inmates are usually transported to outside medical facilities for treatment of pregnancy-related medical care, and "security precautions increase a woman's risk of injury and stress" during a birth transport.[36] Approximately 10 percent of women inside jails and prisons are pregnant, and over 1,500 females give birth while incarcerated each year.[37] Despite these statistics, access to health care services is limited for many women behind bars.

Maternal Bonds

Many women who find themselves under criminal justice supervision must confront the possibility of losing contact with their children. Although family members, friends, or acquaintances may care for the sons and daughters of

---

31. Society for Women's Health Research. 2010. Women and Men: 10 Differences That Make a Difference. Available at http://www.womenshealthresearch.org/site/PageServer?pagename = hs_sbb_10diff.

32. Jennifer G. Clarke, Megan R. Hebert, Cynthia Rosengard, Jennifer S. Rose, Kristen M. DaSilva, and Michael D. Stein. 2006. Reproductive Health Care and Family Planning Needs Among Incarcerated Women. *American Journal of Public Health*, 96, (5), 834-839. Laura M. Maruscha. 2013. *Medical Problems of Prisoners*. Washington, D.C.: Bureau of Justice Statistics.

33. Allen J. Beck, Marcus Berzofsky, Rachel Caspar, and Christopher Krebs. 2013. *Sexual Victimization in Prisons and Jails Reported by Inmates, 2011-2012*. Washington, D.C.: Bureau of Justice Statistics.

34. Laura M. Maruscha. 2013. *Medical Problems of Prisoners*. Washington, D.C.: Bureau of Justice Statistics.

35. *Ibid.*

36. Tammy L. Anderson. 2002. Issues in the Availability of Healthcare for Women in Prison, in Susan Sharp (ed.), *The Incarcerated Woman: Rehabilitative Programming in Women's Prisons*. Upper Saddle River, NJ: Prentice Hall, pp. 49-60.

37. Jennnbifer G. Clarke, Megan R. Hebert, Cynthia Rosengard, Jennifer S. Rose, Kristen M. DaSilva, and Michael D. Stein. 2006. Reproductive Health Care and Family Planning Needs Among Incarcerated Women. *American Journal of Public Health*, 96 (5), 834-839.

female offenders, women who are apprehended, convicted, and punished by the criminal justice system risk damaging relationships with their children. This may be especially true for female inmates inside jails and prisons. If fathers are jailed or incarcerated, there is generally a mother present on the outside to care for the children. Alternatively, if mothers are jailed or incarcerated, there is not generally a father present on the outside to care for the children. With fewer correctional institutions designated exclusively for women, there is a greater likelihood that female inmates are housed farther from their children than male inmates. On average, incarcerated women are more than 160 miles farther from their children than incarcerated men. At the same time, at least one-half of children of incarcerated mothers do not see or visit their mothers following their incarceration.[38]

When women inside jails and prisons are fortunate enough to receive visits from their children, visiting limitations often hinder the creation and nurturing of healthy mother-child relationships. Strict institutional regulations and rules limit physical contact and emotional intimacy between female inmates and their children. The physical space of visiting areas is rarely conducive to substantial social interaction. Inside jails, it is not uncommon for women and their visitors (including children) to be separated by a glass partition, forced to communicate through telephone receivers for no more than 30 minutes. Inside prisons, female inmates usually receive more time to visit with their loved ones, but visiting areas often feature crowded seating arrangements that resemble unappealing waiting rooms. In such locations, contact between jailed and incarcerated women and their children often becomes nothing more than conversation, as playful and interactive activities are commonly prohibited.

Summary

Women constitute only about 7 percent of all prison inmates in the United States. Although only a small portion of the total inmate population, they are important because their incarceration experiences tend to be different from those of men, and their needs that correctional administrators must address also tend to differ from those of male inmates.

Common, "different" issues presented by female inmates are challenges in maintaining family ties, issues related to children (women are more likely to have children and to be the primary caregiver for children when incarcerated), and health issues. Also, women in prison are more likely to have histories of

38. Barbara Bloom, Marilyn Brown, and Meda Chesney-Lind. 1996. Women on Probation and Parole, in A.J. Lurigio (ed.), *Community Corrections in America: New Directions and Sounder Investments for Persons with Mental Illness and Co-disorders*. Washington, D.C.: National Institute of Corrections, pp. 51-76.

substance use and abuse and victimization, especially childhood or adult sexual victimization.

Incarcerated women tend to be less violent than men, and to establish a culture inside an institution that highlights relationships and connections between inmates, as opposed to oppositional groups. Women often form pseudo families to structure their daily life and to provide for their emotional and social needs.

Key Terms

Imprisonment rate
Jurisdiction
Contraband
Pseudo families

Chapter Ten

Jails and Local Corrections

DAVID PATRICK CONNOR

Local correctional institutions in the United States include all existing facilities administered by a local community, which generally hold violators of local laws and misdemeanor statutes, as well as individuals who await court processing (e.g., arraignment, trial, or sentencing) or transfer to a prison. Typically referred to as **jails**, these local correctional institutions also include facilities known as lockups, workhouses, local houses of corrections, and county prisons.

Jails: correctional facilities that generally hold violators of local laws and misdemeanor statutes for between 48 hours and 365 days, as well as individuals who await court processing (e.g., arraignment, trial, or sentencing) or transfer to a prison.

This chapter provides an in-depth look at the historical development and population characteristics of local correctional institutions, and it examines the administrative structure and common problems of jails in the United States. In addition, how corrections at the local level may be performed outside of the traditional setting of jails is considered.

CONTEMPORARY JAILS

Jails are more numerous than prisons and process more individuals. In the study of American corrections, jails have largely been unexplored. Not only do the U.S. media and public devote more of their time to understanding prisons, but so do professors and students of corrections.[1] This is somewhat peculiar, as nearly all criminal offenders pass through jails, and jails offer many career opportunities for students interested in corrections.

---

1. Michael Welch, How Are Jails Depicted by Corrections Textbooks? A Content Analysis Provides a Closer Look. *American Jails: The Magazine of the American Jail Association*, July-August 1992, pp. 28-34.

Lockup: when individuals are confined to a cell, but have not been detained long enough to be fully processed into a jail.

Jails exist today to detain both accused and convicted criminal offenders. Jails typically hold individuals between 48 hours and 365 days. Shorter stays usually mean that individuals are confined to a **lockup** at a law enforcement agency. In other words, they have not been detained long enough to be fully processed into a jail. Thirty-three percent of inmates who are convicted and more than 44 percent of inmates who are not convicted serve less than 30 days inside a jail.[2] The law in many jurisdictions limits jail sentences to not more than 365 days for misdemeanors. Sentences of more than one year often accompany felony convictions, and convicted felons are generally obligated to serve time inside a prison. However, a number of jurisdictions, including Kentucky and Louisiana, are now housing offenders convicted of lower-level felonies inside jails. Some individuals may spend longer than one year inside a jail, as they wait for their arraignment, trial, and possible sentencing. At the same time, a number of jurisdictions are now housing convicted felons inside jails; this tends to be only lower-level felons and those with sentences of two years or less.

America's jail population features more individuals who are not convicted of criminal offenses than individuals who are convicted of criminal offenses. Presently, individuals who are not convicted of criminal offenses and are simply awaiting court disposition represent 61 percent of jail inmates.[3] This suggests that the operation and structure of local correctional institutions should be different from the operation and structure of prisons. Since many individuals inside a jail have not been convicted of any criminal offenses, they warrant a qualitatively different form of custody and treatment. Beyond accused and convicted criminal offenders, it is important to recognize that jails also may house a variety of other individuals, including possible bond, parole, and probation violators, as well as possible absconders from military service, juveniles isolated from adult inmates, and those awaiting placement inside a psychiatric facility. Jails may also detain illegal immigrants.

EVOLUTION OF LOCAL CORRECTIONAL EFFORTS

Gaols: established in England in 1166 by King Henry II and based upon the idea that all county sheriffs would create institutions to hold individuals charged with criminal offenses until they could be tried.

Although contemporary jail inmates are often dealt with in a different way than prison inmates, this was not always the case. The colonists originally imported from England the idea of a place to detain individuals in the community. The British first established **gaols** in 1166. King Henry II decided that all county sheriffs would create institutions to hold individuals charged with criminal offenses until they could be tried. This often meant that alleged criminal offenders served months or years in confinement, in order to wait for a judge to arrive. British judges were responsible for and traveled a number of court circuits.

2. William J. Sabol, Todd. D. Minton, and Paige M. Harrison. 2007. *Prison and Jail Inmates at Midyear 2006.* Washington, D.C.: Bureau of Justice Statistics.

3. Todd D. Minton. 2011. *Jail Inmates at Midyear 2010—Statistical Tables.* Washington, D.C.: Bureau of Justice Statistics.

In some communities, judges were present two or three times in one year; in more remote locations, judges were often only available every five to seven years. As a result, alleged criminal offenders were often forced to spend long periods of time inside institutions that offered little or no standard comforts of life.

During the settlement of the North American colonies, the British legal system experienced a number of substantial changes. Gaols were no longer simply places to hold alleged criminal offenders until trial or after conviction until punishment. Instead, gaols transformed into places that confined petty criminal offenders, and confinement was the punishment. The colonists brought this idea with them to North America.

The first jail established in the colonies was at Jamestown, Virginia in 1606. Early colonial jail systems included a fee system, which meant that individuals confined inside a jail were required to pay a fee for both admission and release. The fee in the Virginia colony jails consisted of two pounds of tobacco.[4] The purpose of a jail was to hold individuals prior to their trial or after their conviction just before their physical punishment. Confinement inside a jail, then, was not initiated as a form of corrections. Rather, jails began as a complement to correctional efforts. Not established for punishment or treatment, jails instead ensured that criminal offenders were available for legal processing and punishment.

Over the next couple of centuries, as the United States grew in population and geographic size, the number of jails increased, and local jurisdictions increasingly built, operated, and maintained jails. For a long time, there was little change in what constituted a jail, and how such were operated. When change did come it was centered not on a change in purpose, but rather a change in physical design and construction. Technology changes and changes in our knowledge and beliefs about people in general and criminals in particular changed some of our thinking and coupled with developments in construction to lead to change in what we know as a jail.

The most notable change surrounding U.S. jails may concern their physical structures. An evolution occurred — and, in fact, is still occurring — in the architectural design of local correctional institutions. These changes in the design and physical layout of jails are accompanied by transformations in their administration and function. The evolution of jails occurred in three generations or phases.

First generation jails were essentially holding pens for all varieties of individuals. These jails were usually large rooms inside a building into which most or all individuals awaiting trial or punishment were placed. However, wealthy and powerful community members who were able to offer bribes to jailers remained free.[5] As inmates, individuals were provided very little, if anything, inside a first generation jail. Jail inmates were responsible for their own clothing, food, safety,

First generation jails: precursors to the modern jail that served as holding pens that held individuals for a variety of criminal offenses.

4. Henry Burns. 1995. Corrections: Organization and Administration. St. Paul: West Publishing Co., p. 149.
5. Linda Zupan. 1991. Jails: Reform and the New Generation Philosophy. Cincinnati: Anderson Publishing Co., p. 15.

and welfare. For a fee, many jailers would provide clothing, firewood, and food to inmates. This meant that a class system was established inside these jails. Individuals with the resources — financial or otherwise — to buy or trade for goods and services could obtain them, while individuals without such resources surrendered to the charity and mercy of their fellow inmates. Thus, inside the early jails of America, it was the poor, unpopular individuals who commonly died of disease and starvation.[6]

Despite their numerous problems, such as the widespread presence of diseases, rampant exploitation, and lack of classification, first generation jails were advantageous for a limited population: individuals who administered these jails. Jailers made a great financial profit from housing their inmates, and jailers possessed the opportunity to sexually exploit their inmates, particularly females. With very little responsibility, besides securing inmates and perhaps minimizing the disruptions, exploitations, and violence among them, the job of jailer was a relatively easy one. From an administrative standpoint, first generation jails made sense.

Second generation jails: precursors to the modern jail consisting of rows of side-by-side cells that segregated types of inmates, often being more secure than earlier versions of jails.

Intermittent supervision: the design in the second generation jails that allowed for a linear form of observation whereby jail staff members viewed inmates periodically, rather than constantly.

However, a major change occurred in relation to how the rights of jail inmates were viewed. In order to provide for individuals removed from their families and livelihoods, second generation jails developed during the early 1800s. **Second generation jails** were seen as a progressive step forward. These jails segregated types of inmates, and they were also more secure than earlier institutions. This is the "typical" jail design that most Americans recognize. Second generation jails consisted of rows of side-by-side cells, with an office or station for jail staff members at the end of the rows. The design, referred to as *linear*, allowed **intermittent supervision**. This meant that jail staff members observed inmates periodically, rather than constantly. Observation occurred only when a jail staff member walked in front of a cell or when a camera that could view a cell was activated. Since second generation jails separate inmates, these institutions permitted increased safety for inmates, gave staff members better opportunities to control problematic inmates, and allowed inmates greater opportunities for self-reflection and penitence (as advocated by the early prison administrators and designers).

The daily routines inside second generation jails varied over time, across locations, and by local administrations. However, in this jail design, it can be said that inmates commonly spent most or virtually all of their time inside cells and possessed few, if any, opportunities to participate in counseling, recreation, or other programs. And yet, the conditions of such institutions, sometimes having cells with dozens of inmates, remained largely unknown in American society until the 1960s. With the social upheavals of the 1960s and the increasing numbers of arrests of "respectable," middle-class individuals (especially the young adult and adolescent children of the middle class), greater attention

[6] Burns, supra n.4, p. 153. Zupan, supra n.5.

was focused on the conditions of jails. Consequently, calls for jail reform were common during the 1960s and early 1970s.

Some reform measures were implemented during the 1960s, but these were almost exclusively attempts to clean up or correct conditions inside existing jails. In the 1970s and 1980s, many jurisdictions found that it was necessary (or perhaps easier) to build new institutions. With new building projects underway, many administrators, architects, and politicians devoted their energies to the design of institutions that promoted more positive living environments, less stress on inmates and staff members, and more cost-efficient management. These goals culminated in the development of **new generation jails**. Borrowed from drug treatment programs inside federal prisons and juvenile corrections, the design of such jails is not an entirely new concept. The new generation design was first used with the Federal Metropolitan Correctional Centers in Chicago, New York, and San Diego in 1975.

New generation jails: the culmination of designing institutions that promoted more positive living environments and less stress on inmates and staff members while at the same time being cost-effective.

During the decade of 1973 to 1983, which may be considered the height of the modern jail reform movement, more than a thousand new jails were built in the United States.[7] While a majority of these new jails were constructed based on the second generation design, some institutions relied on an architectural design that promoted both constant and direct supervision by staff members. This jail model features a central area similar to a dayroom, where inmates congregate and engage in group activities and interactions. One or two tiers of cells surround this central area. The absence of bars and stationary, Spartan furnishing may strike most observers as the most immediate difference in design. Each individual "room" or cell has a door with a window, and all furnishings simulate the appearance of household objects on the outside. In addition, staff members are present in the living areas around the clock to ensure security, supervise, and serve as a resource for inmates.

More advantageous than correctional institutions of second generation design, new generation jails rely on the management method known as **direct supervision**. Here, jail staff members are given opportunities to continuously monitor the activities of inmates. New generation jail proponents believe that inmates housed inside linear model jails largely engage in destructive, violent behavior to demonstrate dominance over their environment and demand provision of attention and materials. In contrast, the design of new generation jails allows staff members to continuously and directly supervise inmates, in order to prevent their deviant and illegal behavior. In this way, because jail inmates are constantly under surveillance, the emphasis is on *institutional* control, rather than *inmate* control. Importantly, there is evidence that inmates inside new generation jails engage in lower rates of assaults, suicides, and vandalism, compared to inmates inside traditional jails with linear supervision.[8]

Direct supervision: form of supervision where jail staff members are given opportunities to continuously monitor the activities of inmates.

---

7. W. Raymond Nelson and Michael O'Toole. 1983. New Generation Jails. Boulder, CO: Library Information Specialists, Inc.
8. Christine Tartaro. 2002. Examining Implementation Issues with New Generation Jails. *Criminal Justice Policy Review*, 13, (3), 219-237.

A direct supervision method of jail management not only offers advantages in effectively controlling and overseeing inmate behavior, but it also offers financial advantages. Approximately 70 percent of a jail's annual operating costs are expenditures on personnel.[9] Compared with intermittent supervision designs, direct supervision jail designs allow fewer correctional officers to supervise a growing number of inmates. By being physically present in the housing unit and not having to circulate among the institution's cells, dayrooms, and programming areas, one jail officer can serve multiple functions that previously required several staff members. Also, with constant observation, inmates inside a jail are less likely to hurt themselves, other inmates, and staff members. This limits the liability that jail staff members and the responsible government entity may encounter as a result of institutional misconduct.

Of course, one important factor to consider when designing a jail is its anticipated population. U.S. jails vary widely in size, from those institutions in small towns and rural areas that may hold only handfuls of individuals to large, urban jails that may hold thousands of individuals. On average, jails that are smaller are less occupied than jails that are larger. Jails that have a maximum occupancy of 50 or fewer inmates are 63 percent occupied, whereas jails with capacities of 1,000 inmates or more are 91 percent occupied.[10] Most U.S. jails are too small to hold the number of arrested individuals in their jurisdiction. Nationwide, numerous jails are overcrowded, although many of America's smaller jails have empty cells every single day. Jurisdictions often address the overcrowding problem by renovating existing jails and constructing new correctional institutions with higher inmate capacities.

Numerous reasons contribute to the overcrowding situation inside U.S. jails. Although jail administrators and staff members may potentially change and control some of these factors, many other factors that lead to overcrowding are truly out of their hands. From the perspective of jail administrators, court orders that obligate prison officials to limit their populations is one frustrating cause of jail overcrowding. At their legal maximum capacity, prisons may refuse to accept new inmates who are sentenced to prison time by criminal courts. In such situations, these inmates must remain inside local jails, until beds become available inside prisons. The backlog of inmates who are sentenced to prison time often causes jail overcrowding. However, just as the U.S. judicial system refuses to accept extreme prison overcrowding, it also does not allow jails to operate at highly overcrowded levels. This suggests that jail administrators may be left to develop plans to resolve their overcrowding problems, which are not necessarily of their own making.

---

9. Dale Sechrest. 1985. Correctional Facility Design and Construction Management. Washington D.C.: National Institute of Justice, pp. 96-99.
10. Minton, supra n.3.

LOCAL CORRECTIONAL POPULATIONS

U.S. jails were truly filled to excess in the early 1990s. Arguably, jails continue to house inmates uncomfortably close together and remain overcrowded, but these local correctional institutions are no longer in such an extreme predicament. For the first time in recent decades, jails are not operating at or above 100 percent of their rated capacity. **Rated capacity** is the maximum number of beds or inmates allocated to each local correctional institution. Jails throughout the United States currently operate at an average of nearly 87 percent of rated capacity. Importantly, this is the lowest percent of rated capacity since 1984. When considering all U.S. jails together, the total rated capacity is 866,782 beds.[11]

Rated capacity: the maximum number of beds or inmates allocated to each local correctional institution.

Between 2000 and 2008, the number of inmates inside U.S. jails steadily increased, maxing out at 785,533 inmates in 2008. Based on the most recent data, the American jail population actually declined for 2009 and 2010. Nonetheless, in the United States, more than 3,000 jails continue to supervise nearly 750,000 correctional clients. This translates into 242 jail inmates per 100,000 American residents. From midyear 2009 to midyear 2010, jails admitted almost 13 million individuals.[12] However, this is not to say that 13 million *different* individuals entered local correctional institutions. Rather, many individuals were arrested and held inside jails on more than one occasion. This may be especially true for those with alcoholism, as these individuals may be arrested for public intoxication one dozen or more times in one year.

Demographic Variations

In recent years, jail inmate demographics remained largely the same. The overrepresentation of males and racial minorities inside jails may still be the most striking. This is not surprising, however, as these statistics reflect those for known criminal perpetrators, convicted criminal offenders, and prison populations. The gender gap between jail inmates continues to be exceptionally large. There are over seven times more men held inside U.S. jails than women, with males making up about 88 percent of jail inmates. Race and ethnicity also continue to impact the rate of individuals held inside jails. About 44 percent of jail inmates are white, nearly 38 percent are African American, and almost 16 percent are Hispanic. However, African-American individuals are held inside jails at more than twice the rate of Hispanic individuals, and Hispanic individuals are held inside jails at almost twice the rate of white individuals. African-American individuals are held inside jails at a rate of about five times higher than white individuals.[13]

11. *Ibid.*
12. *Ibid.*
13. *Ibid.*

Geographic Variations

Depending on their geographic location, jails may be widely different from one another. It may be expected that the racial demographics of jail inmates vary between rural and urban jails, as well as between cities in different regions of the United States. It may also be expected, for instance, that a larger proportion of Hispanic inmates are found inside Arizona, New Mexico, and Texas jails than Arkansas, North Dakota, and Vermont jails. However, the most notable geographic difference concerns the fact that jails in metropolitan areas have a much larger inmate population than county jails outside of cities. This means that local correctional institutions in metropolitan areas are more likely to encounter overcrowding and other problems among both inmates and staff members. Obviously, jails that hold 20 or 30 inmates are quite different in function and structure than jails that hold 200, 300, or even 3,000 inmates.

Jails with the largest capacities are located in America's largest cities. Most of the major cities in the United States operate more than one local correctional institution, in order to ensure some degree of inmate classification, order, and security. The 159 largest U.S. jail systems account for nearly one-half of all jail inmates in the nation.[14] Because of their location in an area with a large population and tremendous size, these correctional institutions receive the most public attention. Nonetheless, these jails are a minority among all local correctional institutions. The trend is for jurisdictions to have smaller inmate populations, with over 86 percent of U.S. jails holding fewer than 250 inmates.[15] This means that in the less populated counties and towns of America, local correctional institutions serve fewer individuals, drawing basic funding from a smaller base. Consequently, these jurisdictions have less money for jail improvements, maintenance, and staffing. Thus, many of America's smaller (and older) jails are some of the most oppressive and physically inadequate.

JAIL ADMINISTRATION AND MANAGEMENT

This section discusses the four major forms of jail administration and management, which includes city/county, state, cooperative, and private authorities. Although city and county jail administration is still the most common form, the move toward alternative models, especially privatization, is rapidly increasing.

City and County Government Administration

There are more than 3,000 jails in the United States, and about 600 of these correctional institutions are city jails. Eighty percent of jails are administered by a

14. Todd D. Minton. 2010. Jail Inmates at Midyear 2009. Washington, D.C.: Bureau of Justice Statistics.
15. *Ibid.*

county government.[16] Both municipal and county jails are most commonly managed by an elected sheriff. State constitutions often grant the office of sheriff the authority and responsibility for jail administration.[17] Sheriffs do not, however, possess complete authority and control over jails. Although they may have authority to make decisions about jail operations, sheriffs are almost always held financially and politically accountable to both county commissions (or similar bodies who control the funding of county agencies) and voters who elect them. This means that other political actors often check and limit the authority of sheriffs.

State Government Administration

Alaska, Connecticut, Delaware, Hawaii, Rhode Island, and Vermont are the only jurisdictions where the state government administers adult jails. Such administration by the state government allows the functions of local corrections to be centralized. With populations, jails, and jail inmates that are generally small in number, it makes sense for these six jurisdictions to centralize all local correctional authority, responsibility, and services.

Ideally, jails administered by a centralized body of state government offer four advantages over jails administered by a local government.[18] First, this setup may allow for a more equal distribution of resources, which may provide a more stable delivery of services to institutions across the state. Second, administration of jails may be streamlined, as the state government may more easily develop and implement statewide standards for local correctional institutions. Third, costs may be controlled by sharing resources and ensuring that space, personnel, and other expensive resources are fully utilized. Fourth, jails operated by a state government remove jails from the local political arena, and this may allow a greater focus to exist on the daily operations of jails rather than on public (i.e., voter) reaction.

These identified advantages may lead to the expectation that a number of states will take over local corrections. However, this has not been the case and may be attributed to political fighting between state, county, and local governments. Despite the difficulties encountered with the operation of jails, many local governments want to preserve their authority over correctional institutions. At the same time, some state governments fail to centralize jail operations, because they are overburdened and overwhelmed with their current responsibilities. This suggests that a large-scale movement toward the centralization of jail operations within state governments should not be anticipated.

---

16. Todd R. Clear, George F. Cole, and Michael D. Reisig. 2013. *American Corrections*. Belmont, CA: Wadsworth, Cengage Learning.

17. G. Larry Mays and Joel A. Thompson. 1988. Mayberry Revisited: The Characteristics and Operations of America's Small Jails. *Justice Quarterly*, 5, (3), 421-440.

18. G. Larry Mays and Joel A. Thompson. 1991. The Political and Organizational Context of American Jails, in Joel A. Thompson and G. Larry Mays (eds.), *American Jails: Public Policy Issues*. Chicago: Nelson-Hall.

Cooperative Administration

As previously discussed, centralized jail operations may offer several significant advantages to local correctional institutions. However, balancing the advantages of centralization located in state government with its disadvantages discourages most jurisdictions from pursuing such a setup. Rather, some jurisdictions seek other ways to combine their jail operations, in order to achieve more cost-effective and efficient correctional goals. For instance, several small (in terms of population) cities or counties combine their resources and operate one cooperatively administered jail. Although it is a nationwide problem, jail overcrowding is not a universal problem. Many American jails in less populated communities typically house fewer than two dozen inmates.[19] This means that operating a jail with such a small inmate population is a relatively expensive endeavor. The expenses for personnel, operation, and maintenance are present, regardless of whether a facility has 10, 20, or 200 inmates. Of course, costs will vary, but the baseline costs remain, making the expense of a small jail operation comparatively higher than the expense of a medium or large jail operation.

Cooperative jail administration: several forms of jail administration, including where several communities decide to jointly fund the operations of a jail that already exists in one community, where no existing jail possesses an adequate correctional institution and communities build a new regional jail, and where communities that already have jails designate multiple small jails for different functions.

Cooperative jail administration may take one of several forms. First, several communities may decide to jointly fund the operations of a jail that already exists in one community. This allows the other involved communities to either close an existing jail or avoid building, renovating, or adding to a jail in their own community. Second, recognizing that none among them possesses an adequate correctional institution, a collection of communities may close existing jails and build a new, regional jail. Third, communities that already have small jails may designate each of their institutions for a particular population (e.g., individuals awaiting trial, convicted men, convicted women, and juveniles). All jail inmates of that particular population, which are drawn from one of the cooperating communities, are subsequently housed in the appropriate institution. This model allows maximum use of existing resources, provides financial savings to communities, and maximizes security and classification efforts.

This is not to say that there are no problems associated with cooperatively administered jails. There are political issues involved. Deciding which community will have a jail may become a political battle, as communities either fight for jobs or contest having the correctional institution "in their backyard." Practical obstacles may also make cooperative administration of jails difficult. When communities sharing one jail (or several specialized institutions) are distantly located, inmate transportation issues, in terms of both financial costs and time, may become problematic. Communities may politically battle over how the transportation costs are to be shared (or not shared). Should all of the transportation costs sustained by participating communities be considered a part of the overall budget? Should each community absorb the costs of transporting inmates

---

19. U.S. Department of Justice. 1983. *Report to the Nation on Crime and Justice.* Washington D.C.: Bureau of Justice Statistics; Mays and Thompson, supra n.17.

for whom they are responsible? Before initiating a cooperative administration plan, these and other issues similar in nature must be carefully considered.

Private Corrections

The newest alternative form of jail administration is the operation of correctional institutions by private, (usually) for-profit corporations. There are a number of advantages and disadvantages of private businesses assuming the responsibility for jails. Whether a particular issue is considered an advantage or disadvantage is largely a political decision and may depend on who the decision maker is.

A government may *delegate* responsibilities for day-to-day jail operations to an outside body. However, this does not mean that the governmental body can *relinquish* its ultimate responsibilities of overseeing the care, safety, and security of inmates.[20] Privately administered jails operate on a contract basis, whereby an outside body agrees to provide specified "services" in exchange for a set payment. Typically, payments are based on a set daily fee per inmate. The goal of a private jail is to operate at an efficiency level that allows the daily per-inmate fee to not only cover the cost of housing a jail inmate, but also to provide a profit margin.

This leads to common criticisms that private correctional institutions, especially jails, cut corners and provide low-quality service, use underpaid and undertrained staff members, and have overcrowded and poorly maintained facilities. It is interesting to note that a greater proportion of public correctional institutions, compared to private correctional institutions, offer education, counseling, and work programs.[21] Nonetheless, not all aspects of a jail need to be privatized. Some jails, like some prisons, contract out portions of their operations, such as food service, laundry, and physical plant maintenance. And yet, these jails retain overall control and responsibility for operations.

Additional opponents of private jail administration often believe that corrections is an inherently governmental function and should not be handled by private entities. Individuals who follow this line of thinking feel that privatizing jail administration may destroy the bond between citizens and the government.[22] Other critics are concerned that private entities may not act in ways that are aligned with the public interest. The fear is that private entities may do anything necessary to fill their jails, because this makes them money.

Supporters of private jail administration often believe that private entities are able to operate jails more inexpensively than governments. This assertion remains inconclusive. However, one study found that private correctional institutions did not generate any cost savings over public correctional institutions.[23]

---

20. Charles H. Logan. 1987. The Propriety of Proprietary Prisons. *Federal Probation*, 51, (3), 35-50.
21. James J. Stephan. 2008. *Census of State and Federal Correctional Facilities*, 2005. Washington, D.C.: Bureau of Justice Statistics.
22. John J. DiIulio. 1991. *No Escape: The Future of American Corrections*. New York: Basic Books.
23. Travis C. Pratt and Jeff Maahs. 1999. Are Private Prisons More Cost-Effective Than Public Prisons? A Meta-Analysis of Evaluation Research Studies. *Crime and Delinquency*, 45, (3), 358-371.

If private entities are able to supervise jail inmates at a more cost-effective rate than governments, this would save taxpayers money and might simultaneously provide more space inside government jails. Advocates also commonly contend that private entities are capable of providing inmate custody that is congruent with a government's ability to supervise. Another study determined that the environmental quality of private and public correctional institutions are very much alike.[24] However, an additional study showed that private entities offer correctional officers less pay and training than governments, which may suggest that private entities employ less-than-competent officers with little or no incentive to provide inmates with adequate care and effective supervision.[25]

Privatization: the process of the federal or state governments contracting out jail or prison services to a third-party company or business that specializes in housing mostly minimum and medium-security inmates in exchange for money.

Regardless of whether or not **privatization** is supported or opposed, private correctional institutions are becoming increasingly common. Numerous states have literally entered into hundreds of contractual relationships, which allow private corporations to deliver correctional services, especially for juvenile offenders. California, Pennsylvania, and Texas account for most of the U.S. contract jail operations.[26] As communities find themselves unable to provide the correctional services and types of correctional institutions legally required, the option of contracting some or all jail administration and operation functions becomes progressively attractive.

PROBLEMATIC ASPECTS OF JAILS

For a variety of reasons, local correctional institutions have numerous problems. Although many of these same issues also plague prisons, the special nature of jail inmates and the conditions of their stay make these problems more difficult to manage inside the jail setting. Perhaps the primary difficulties arise from the highly transient nature of the jail population. The population inside U.S. jails constantly changes. Newly arrested individuals are brought in, criminal defendants are conditionally released on bond or their own recognizance, and other inmates are transferred to other local correctional institutions and prisons. With constant inmate turnover, jails fail to establish a sense of stability in regards to inmate programs and social organization. The constant arrival of new inmates presents jail administrators and staff members with many problems. The full range of issues that individuals possess on the streets accompanies them to jail confinement. Brought into a setting where anxieties run high, these problems consequently may be aggravated and exaggerated.

In this section, four major problem areas that make living and working inside a jail difficult are explored, including substandard physical facilities, minimal

---

24. Gaylene S. Armstrong and Doris L. MacKenzie. 2003. Private Versus Public Juvenile Facilities: Do Differences in Environmental Quality Exist? *Crime and Delinquency*, 49, (4), 542-563.

25. Curtis Blakely. 2004. Private and State Run U.S. Prisons Compared. *Probation Journal*, 51, (3), 254-256.

26. James J. Stephan and Georgette Walsh. 2011. *Census of Jail Facilities, 2006*. Washington, D.C.: Bureau of Justice Statistics.

programming opportunities, staffing deficiencies, and poor inmate health. Recall the evolution of U.S. jails and the characteristics of jail inmates. These four major problem areas are not necessarily unique to the present day. Jails and local correctional institutions have faced these same problems for many decades, and they have yet to be fully resolved.

Substandard Physical Facilities

Perhaps the most obvious problem with many contemporary jails is the poor condition of their furnishings, internal equipment, and physical structures. Because jails handle such large numbers of typically transient individuals, these local correctional institutions experience very hard use. The amount of maintenance required for jails may be enormous, and it is often so extensive that most local correctional institutions simply cannot meet the necessary financial and time commitments for such upkeep. The fact that many U.S. jails have substandard facilities is not a new dilemma. As early as 1870, jails in America were known for their poor conditions.[27] However, the inferior physical conditions that exist inside today's jails may largely be attributed to the age of local correction institutions. Rural areas are most likely to feature extremely old jails.

The oldest U.S. jails are usually correctional institutions with the most outdated or fewest facilities. A common issue inside many jails is lighting. Because the presence of windows are traditionally considered to be a potential security threat, most older jails significantly lack natural light. This means that lighting fixtures need to be installed and maintained. Another issue concerns sanitation. A small number of the most outdated jails cannot invest money to install or renovate plumbing systems, and their toilet facilities are nothing more than a "honey bucket" system. In other words, a bucket, which is emptied once or twice per day, serves as a toilet. More common, however, are jails with toilets located in dayrooms that afford inmates little or no privacy.

Old and outdated jails remain in use, because most rural areas have relatively low jail populations. As a result, unlike many urban jurisdictions, rural jurisdictions do not face overcrowding problems and the associated pressures to renovate or replace jail facilities. Besides, the financial commitment required to renovate or replace a jail is often too great for jurisdictions with a small tax base. Even when financial resources are available or obtainable, spending significant dollars to "improve" the conditions of "criminals, deviants, and generally bad people" may be a volatile political issue. Many politicians believe that advocating for more spending of tax dollars on corrections is a politically bad move. With all these factors in place, it is not surprising that many timeworn jails and their substandard facilities remain in use, especially in small towns and rural areas.

---

27. Michael T. Charles, Sesha Kethineni, and Jeffrey L. Thompson. 1992. The State of Jails in America. *Federal Probation*, 56, (2) 56-62.

The fact that "modern" construction and design plans are not implemented is not the only reason why old and outdated jails are problematic. Rather, both the necessary cost and level of maintenance may be quite high. In 2000, 45 percent of federal and state correctional institutions were at least 20 years old, and 5 percent were over 100 years old.[28] The impact of aged jail structures is further seen from the perspective of jail administrators. In the 2008 National Jail Workforce Survey, more than 95 percent of jail administrators stated that having good facilities is important to the proper functioning of a correctional institution, but nearly one-third of these administrators reported that their facilities were not acceptable.[29]

The problems of substandard jail facilities are widespread. Beyond the assessment of actual physical structures, the social conditions created from the physical surroundings of jails need to be considered. Here, the lack of physical space may be the most common problem. Jail overcrowding produces numerous issues for both inmates and staff members. There is a direct connection between overcrowding inside jails and limited inmate programming, inmate adjustment problems, staff member deficiencies, and poor inmate health. Because of the substandard conditions inside U.S. jails, many local correctional institutions are not equipped with adequate or necessary facilities to properly care for and manage inmates. Less than one-half of inmates receive a medical exam during their jail stay.[30] At the same time, many jails do not have an on-site infirmary for seriously ill or injured inmates. This means sick and injured inmates must be transferred to local clinics or hospitals, and this requires additional financial and employee resources.

The National Sheriffs' Association reports that less than one-third of U.S. jails have space for contact visitation, counseling and educational programming, indoor and outdoor recreation, or library services. Less than one in five jails have space for dining, and less than one in 14 jails have space for vocational programming. These deficits contribute directly to the lack of inmate adjustment and health inside jails. A dense jail population may be associated with an inmate's negative psychological reactions to jail confinement. However, the **social density** (i.e., number of inmates inside a housing unit) may be more important and influential than the actual **spatial density** (i.e., space allocation per inmate). In addition to psychological reactions, inmates inside a denser housing unit may also have elevated blood pressure, which impacts their health and increases the cost of jail confinement.[31]

Social density: the number of inmates inside a particular housing unit in a jail.

Spatial density: the space allocation per inmate.

---

28. James J. Stephan and J.C. Karberg. 2003. *Census of State and Federal Correctional Facilities, 2000.* Washington, D.C.: Bureau of Justice Statistics.

29. Jeanne B. Stinchcomb, Susan W. McCampbell, and L. Leslie Leip. 2009. *The Future Is Now: Recruiting, Retaining and Developing the Twenty-First Century Jail Workforce.* Washington, D.C.: Bureau of Justice Assistance.

30. Laura M. Maruschak. 2006. *Medical Problems of Jail Inmates.* Washington, D.C.: Bureau of Justice Statistics.

31. Craig Haney. 2012. Prison Effects in the Era of Mass Incarceration. *The Prison Journal,* 1-24. doi: 10.1177/0032885512448604.

Minimal Programing Opportunities

Because jail populations are highly transient and jails have financial and spatial restrictions, most of these correctional institutions offer inmates a limited number of structured program opportunities. Some jurisdictions may have doctors, nurses, mental health workers, social workers, and recreational therapists on staff. However, these individuals are typically available to deal with problems as they arise, rather than to administer and organize structured, ongoing groups and programs for jail inmates. Some free-world citizens may conduct self-help meetings with groups of inmates inside a jail (e.g., Alcoholics Anonymous and Narcotics Anonymous). However, these are far from common, and such meetings must also contend with the rapid turnover of jail inmates.

Work assignments may be the most common and easiest form of programming for jail inmates. Generally, these assignments involve the use of inmate labor to provide basic maintenance and service functions, which allows a jail to successfully operate. Similar work programs are also commonly available to prison inmates. However, with the rapid turnover of jail inmates and a limited range of available jobs, work assignments are more difficult to implement and supervise in many local correctional institutions.

A common alternative to a work assignment inside a jail is participation in a **work-release program**. In a work-release program, jail inmates are allowed to temporarily leave a correctional institution, in order to attend jobs on the outside. Jail inmates are afforded some level of community involvement; however, after work, they must ultimately return to jail confinement. A work-release program is offered by almost 85 percent of U.S. jails, and these programs serve approximately 34,000 jail inmates.[32] Importantly, work-release programs may help local correctional institutions, by offsetting some of the costs incurred to house inmates.

Work-release program: where jail inmates are allowed to temporarily leave a correctional institution, in order to attend jobs on the outside.

Staffing Deficiencies

Approximately 234,000 individuals are employed inside U.S. jails.[33] Although jail staff members include clerical and maintenance workers, professionals, and educators, a majority of these employees perform direct custody functions.[34] Since the personnel who work inside jails are among the most transient of all correctional employees, staff member turnover is a major problem. Working for only short periods of time, jail staff members move to higher-paying jobs that offer more attractive hours, better working conditions, and other advantages. A low salary, negative image associated with jail work, and limited range of

32. Faye S. Taxman, Matthew L. Perdoni, and Lana D. Harrison. 2007. Drug Treatment Services for Adult Offenders: The State of the State. *Journal of Substance Abuse Treatment*, 32, (3), 239-254.
33. Stephan and Walsh, supra n.26.
34. James J. Stephan. 2001. *Census of Jails, 1999*. Washington, D.C.: Bureau of Justice Statistics.

career advancement opportunities are common barriers related to the recruitment and retention of jail personnel.

Recruitment and Retention

Because of the relatively low pay offered by counties, many of these jurisdictions find it difficult to recruit and keep jail staff members. Jail officers typically earn less than prison officers.[35] In jurisdictions where the sheriff's office administers a jail, staff member assignment to jail duty may be a form of punishment, which the sheriff uses to discipline deputies who violate departmental regulations or rules. Taken together, these factors may create a jail environment with significant shortages of correctional officers.

Recruitment procedures for jobs inside jails are often highly informal. Because most offices held by sheriffs are political, many deputy positions are doled out as political favors or payments. This means that individuals working inside jails often have little or no formal training in corrections. Of course, as elected officials, the same can also be said of sheriffs. However, recognizing that problems can be created or aggravated by a low-quality personnel pool, some larger U.S. jails have formalized their recruitment and hiring procedures and placed greater emphasis on behavioral factors rather than on physical attributes. Many jails have only a few, if any, qualifications that applicants must meet for employment. A few states require a high school diploma or GED, but most have no educational requirements. When individuals show interest, most jails are very lenient on prospective employees, in terms of using aptitudinal, physical, and psychological screening.[36]

One proposed solution to the problem of jail employee shortages, which obligates new police recruits or newly hired sheriff's deputies to work inside jails as correctional officers, is becoming increasingly popular. Because a large number of individuals often apply for a single law enforcement position, an available pool of individuals from most police departments exists for jails to utilize. This procedure may work in one of two ways. First, some sheriffs' departments require their most recently hired deputies to start working inside a jail, staying there until a patrol or other law enforcement position becomes available. Second, in some cities, newly hired police officers must work a specified period (such as two years) inside a jail before their transfer to "real" police positions. However, this solution may be problematic. In these scenarios, jails are staffed by individuals who may prefer not to work there. Since these employees may have invested little into their jobs, they may have little, if any, incentive to do their job well.

---

35. Tammy L. Castle and Jamie S. Martin. 2006. Occupational Hazard: Predictors of Stress Among Jail Correctional Officers. *American Journal of Criminal Justice*, 31, (1), 65-80.

36. Thomas J. Stickrath and Richard L. Sheppard. 2004. Wanted: The Best and the Brightest. *Corrections Today*, 66, (5), 64-71.

Training

Even when staff members are successfully recruited and hired, many jails do not have extensive training programs available to help new employees with job preparation and know-how. Most jails usually rely on current staff members to "show the ropes" to newly hired employees. Jail managers generally recognize that their jail officers need additional training, especially in the areas of crisis intervention, interpersonal relationships, legal liability, problem inmates, and stress management.[37] However, financial and personal restraints often do not allow these needs to be met. Numerous jurisdictions attempt to hire individuals with more education who presumably understand more fully the formal and informal requirements of work inside a jail. At the same time, many jail managers believe that individuals who are highly educated contribute to a more professional, ethical, and easily managed group of employees. These efforts, however, produce mixed results. More highly educated officers often report more dissatisfaction with their jobs.[38] Intellectually, jail work is not especially challenging, and it may include periods of extreme monotony. The routine and tedious nature of jail work may lead to high levels of burnout among jail staff members.

Staff Turnover

One important organizational problem concerning jail staff member deficiencies is the high rate of turnover. Jail staff members leave their jobs for a number of reasons, including dissatisfaction with work conditions, frustration from contact with inmates, and feelings of isolation and neglect that originate from interaction with supervisors. Relationships between a jail officer and his or her supervisors, as evidenced by forms and frequencies of communication, are critical to each jail officer's satisfaction level. As a result, such relationships are important for determining how long jail officers remain at their jobs.[39]

The low pay and undesirable conditions that characterize many jail positions directly contribute to a generally low morale and high turnover rate among staff members. Because jails do not possess many of the traditional opportunities that improve staff member morale, it may be difficult to raise the morale of jail officers. For instance, transient inmates inside a jail do not afford staff members with many opportunities to see "success" that may arise from work with such individuals. At the same time, jail staff members have only minimal opportunities to suggest changes or improvements to their work environment, as most correctional institutions have strict security requirements.

---

37. Kevin M. Corriea. 2009. *A Handbook for Correctional Psychologists: Guidance for the Prison Practitioner*, 2d ed. Springfield, IL: Charles C. Thomas.

38. Brian Payne, Brenda S. Blackwell, and Sue C. Collins. 2010. Exploring the Ties Between Career Satisfaction and Education: Trait versus Situational Approaches. *Journal of Criminal Justice Education*, 21, (1), 77-92.

39. Marie L. Griffin, Nancy L. Hogan, Eric G. Lambert, Kasey A. Tucker-Gail, and David N. Baker. 2010. Job Involvement, Job Stress, Job Satisfaction, and Organizational Commitment and the Burnout of Correctional Staff. *Criminal Justice and Behavior*, 37, (2), 239-255. Eric Lambert and Eugene Paoline. 2010. Take This Job and Shove It: An Exploratory Study of Turnover Intent Among Jail Staff. *Journal of Criminal Justice*, 38, 139-148.

As previously discussed, when recruiting jail personnel, some jurisdictions prefer more highly educated individuals. The impact of higher education is most noticeable in the small segment of jails exclusively for women. According to researchers, the staff members of these rare institutions are usually relatively young, inexperienced, predominantly female, and well educated.[40] This suggests that more sophisticated, interpersonal management skills may be used, and staff members may have a greater range of career opportunities open to them. In turn, the undesirable aspects of jail employment may need to be addressed to control staff member turnover.

The insufficient numbers of qualified, trained staff members impact a range of other problems that U.S. jails face. When jails have staff member shortages, correctional institutions cannot offer many programming opportunities for inmates, even if financial resources and space are available. Staff member shortages are also connected with poor inmate adjustment. When only a few staff members are available, inmates may feel even more isolated and may be more successful in suicide attempts.

Poor Inmate Health

Health problems among jail inmates pose significant challenges for both jail administrators and staff members. Sick and injured inmates require special attention by jail staff members. This attention, plus the costs for treatment, supervision, and care, may be extremely expensive. Consequently, the generally poor health status of U.S. jail inmates presents difficulties both at the individual and institutional level. Inmates of both rural and urban jails have significant health problems. The first major issue related to the special health care needs of jail inmates centers on the fact that most U.S. jails have substandard facilities and are not equipped or prepared to deal with anything except the most minor medical problems.

More than one-third of all jail inmates have a medical problem that is more serious than a cold or common flu virus. Inmates inside jails most commonly experience arthritis, asthma, heart problems, and hypertension.[41] Infectious diseases, too, pose threats to the daily operation and orderly management of modern jails. Because most jails feature cramped, less-than-sanitary conditions and inmates with more physical problems than the general population, control of contagious and infectious diseases is an important challenge for jail administrators. Outbreaks of serious diseases, such as tuberculosis, hepatitis, and HIV infection, are of special concern today. For instance, every year, between 40 and

---

40. Dana M. Britton. 2003. *At Work in the Iron Cage: The Prison as Gendered Organization.* New York, NY: New York University Press. G. Larry Mays and Mary K. Stohr. 1993. *Personal Characteristics and Training of Staff in Exclusively Women's Jails: A Descriptive Analysis.* Paper presented at the annual meeting at the Academy of Criminal Justice Sciences, Kansas City, MO. Claire M. Renzetti, Susan L. Miller, and Angela R. Gover. 2013. *Routledge International Handbook of Crime and Gender Studies.* New York, NY: Routledge.

41. Maruschak, supra n.30.

60 jail inmates die as a result of AIDS-related complications.[42] Nonetheless, controlling the spread of "traditional" diseases is not the most significant threat to jail administration and management. On a day-to-day basis, the problems of substance abuse, suicide, and mental illness are of greater importance.

Substance Abuse

A large minority of inmates inside jails are known to have commonly abused alcohol and drugs. Forty percent of jail inmates are addicted to or dependent on alcohol and drugs, compared to only 9 percent of Americans on the outside. Jail inmates who are addicted to or dependent on alcohol and drugs experience much worse fortune than jail inmates who are not addicted to or dependent on alcohol and drugs. Addicted and dependent inmates inside jails are more likely than their counterparts to have been homeless, have been physically and sexually abused, and have parents who abused alcohol and drugs. Jail inmates who are addicted to or dependent on alcohol and drugs often have more of a criminal history than jail inmates who are not addicted to or dependent on alcohol and drugs. Almost 30 percent of inmates inside jails are under the influence of drugs at the time of their current criminal offenses, and almost 16 percent of inmates inside jails commit their current criminal offenses to obtain money for drugs. In addition, more than one-half of individuals who enter jails have a history of failed alcohol and drug treatment.[43] Although alcohol and drug abuse may be interrupted inside jails, long-term follow-up and treatment programs may be necessary for inmates upon their release.

Suicide

In terms of public outcry, inmate suicides may be the most problematic issue that confronts jail administrators. Attempted and completed suicides, as possibly the most obvious indicators of an inmate's lack of adjustment to a jail setting, focus attention on the physical facilities, staff members, and daily management of jails. Among inmates inside jails, suicide follows behind medical illness as the second most common cause of death. Suicide is more common among jail inmates than prison inmates. The suicide rate inside jails is 42 suicides per 100,000 inmates, which is more than three times the suicide rate inside state prisons. The suicide rate inside state prisons is 14 suicides per 100,000 inmates. Suicide is also more common among jail inmates who are held for violent offenses than nonviolent offenses. The suicide rate for jail inmates with violent offenses is 92 suicides per 100,000 inmates, whereas the suicide rate for jail inmates with nonviolent offenses is 31 suicides per 100,000 inmates. Although 14 percent of suicides take place within the first day of an inmate's jail admission, almost one-half of

---

42. Ibid.

43. Jennifer C. Karberg and D.J. James. 2005. *Substance Dependence, Abuse, and Treatment of Jail Inmates, 2002*. Washington, D.C.: Bureau of Justice Statistics.

suicides take place within the first week of an inmate's jail stay. More than 80 percent of suicides take place inside a jail inmate's cell.[44]

The characteristics of attempted and completed suicides and inmates who attempt and complete suicides generally remain stable over time. One researcher compared the characteristics of completed jail suicides in 1986 with suicides of the previous six years. She reported that, except for minor variations, most key characteristics of suicides, including an inmate's criminal offenses, states of intoxication, and length of incarceration, remained constant.[45] The most notable risk factors associated with jail suicides are:

1. Intoxication during jail admission.
2. Physical and social isolation.
3. Being in the first 24 hours of detention.[46]

Some research shows that fewer suicides take place inside larger jails and jails where the inmate to staff member ratio is lower. These studies emphasize the harmful nature of inmate isolation and the role that suicide plays as an "adjustment tool."[47]

It is also important to consider the practice of self-mutilation by jail inmates. Self-mutilation, which commonly takes the form of cutting and stabbing, accounts for a large number of crisis situations that jail staff members face on the job.[48] Legal liabilities and the potential for transmitting blood-borne diseases, such as hepatitis and HIV, add to the stress of such situations. Both inmate suicide and self-mutilation make clear that additional emergency medical response training and organizational protective measures are necessary.

MENTAL HEALTH

When considering the overall health of jail inmates, mental health cannot be abandoned. Nearly 64 percent of jail inmates have a mental health problem. These jail inmates often possess a mental health problem with a specific diagnosis that includes major depression, psychotic disorders, and mania. This suggests that jails may be depositories for society's undesirables and "different" members, rather than places reserved for criminal offenders. Nonetheless, jail inmates with a mental health problem are almost twice as likely to be homeless as jail inmates without a mental health problem. More jail and prison inmates

---

44. Lindsay M. Hayes. 2011. *National Study of Jail Suicide: 20 Years Later.* Washington, D.C.: National Institute of Corrections. Margaret Noonan. 2010. *Mortality in Local Jails, 2000-2007.* Washington, D.C.: Bureau of Justice Statistics.
45. Lindsay M. Hayes. 1989. National Study of Jail Suicides: Seven Years Later. *Psychiatric Quarterly,* 60, (1), 7-29.
46. Hayes, supra n.44.
47. John Wooldredge and Thomas Winfree. 1992. An Aggregate-Level Study of Inmate Suicides and Deaths Due to Natural Causes in U.S. Jails. *Journal of Research in Crime and Delinquency,* 29, (4), 466-479.
48. Johannes Lohner and Norbert Konrad. 2006. Deliberate Self-Harm and Suicide Attempt in Custody: Distinguishing Features in Male Inmates' Self-Injurious Behavior. *International Journal of Law and Psychiatry,* 29, (5), 370-385.

with a mental health problem have served three or more prior incarcerations than jail and prison inmates without a mental health problem. In addition, more jail inmates with a mental health problem are addicted to or dependent on alcohol and drugs than jail inmates without a mental health problem.[49]

ADDITIONAL FORMS OF LOCAL CORRECTIONS

Corrections at the local level may be performed outside of the traditional setting of jails. Every year, between 60,000 and 70,000 criminal offenders participate in some form of locally operated sanction that requires little or no time inside a jail.[50] Some of the more common types are day reporting centers, diversion centers, and home incarceration.

Day Reporting Centers

One example of local corrections outside of the traditional setting of jails is day reporting. When correctional clients are obligated to participate in day reporting, they are often required to present themselves on a daily basis to correctional staff members at a **day reporting center**. Day reporting centers are facilities that offer various programs designed to increase success in the community and reduce criminal behavior, such as anger management classes, mental health treatment, substance abuse treatment, and vocational assistance. Day reporting centers are very much like residential treatment facilities; however, in day reporting centers, correctional clients do not stay overnight. For this reason, day reporting centers are often advantageous for local governments, as they do not house correctional clients for more than 8 to 10 hours in one day. This provides a less expensive alternative to around-the-clock custody of correctional clients.

Day reporting centers: facilities that offer various programs designed to increase success in the community and reduce criminal behavior by requiring jail inmates to present themselves on a daily basis for various programming (e.g., mental health, anger management, substance abuse treatment, and vocational assistance).

Day reporting may serve a variety of correctional clients, including pretrial and post-conviction criminal defendants, as well as probationers and parolees. However, in the United States, there are less than 5,000 correctional clients that participate in day reporting.[51] Criminal defendants may be required to present themselves on a daily basis at a specific location to show correctional staff members that they are adhering to the conditions of their bond release. These individuals may be required to participate in alcohol and drug tests or provide documentation of attendance at counseling sessions or a place of employment. For probationers and parolees, day reporting may be a condition of community supervision. As a result of the daily interaction between probationers and parolees and correctional staff members, day reporting allows closer observation of

49. D.J. James and Lauren E. Glaze. 2006. *Mental Health Problems of Prison and Jail Inmates*. Washington, D.C.: Bureau of Justice Statistics.
50. Minton, supra n.3.
51. Stephan, supra n.21.

these correctional clients than traditional probation and parole supervision. At the same time, day reporting provides criminal offenders released from a jail or prison with a gentle transition into the community.

Diversion Centers

Diversion centers: facilities that attempt to find a middle ground between confinement inside a correctional institution and supervision in the community by supervising individuals 24 hours a day, and from which residents perform community service projects in addition to holding a regular job.

Local corrections outside of the traditional setting of jails may also include **diversion centers**, which attempt to find a middle ground between confinement inside a correctional institution and supervision in the community. Supervised 24 hours a day, criminal offenders live inside diversion centers. In order to be eligible for diversion center placements, however, offenders must hold jobs in the community, and they may leave the centers only to complete their work. In addition to their regular jobs, diversion center residents regularly perform community service projects. The usual stay in a diversion center is relatively short, usually around six months. After leaving diversion centers, offenders are often placed on standard probation. Diversion centers allow criminal offenders to preserve some links with the outside, while providing close supervision to guide them to law-abiding behavior.

Home Incarceration

Home incarceration: the newest form of local corrections where criminal offenders are required to stay at home except for specific functions (e.g., work, school, scheduled grocery store trips) for a required length of time to satisfy the conditions of the punishment.

The newest form of local corrections outside of the traditional setting of jails is **home incarceration**. Criminal offenders who need something more than standard probation, do not require around-the-clock, direct supervision, and have established lives in the community may be sentenced to remain at home. In some ways, home incarceration is similar to when parents "ground" their children for punishment. In other words, punished children must stay at home, except for specific functions, such as school, work, and scheduled trips to the grocery store. The idea behind home incarceration is to incapacitate offenders, so they do not commit future criminal offenses. Inside their place of residence, offenders have limited access to engage in criminal behavior. However, just as when parents (i.e., the legal system) ground their children (i.e., offenders), parents cannot always be present to make sure their children remain at home. **Electronic monitoring systems** have attempted to answer this problem. Activating signals to the supervising probation department when offenders stray too far from their residence, electronic devices are semi-permanently attached to them.

Electronic monitoring system: the use of technology attached to offenders for the duration of their sentence that signals when offenders stray too far from their residence.

Electronic monitoring is performed in one of two ways: passive and active. Using a **passive monitoring system**, a criminal offender wears an electronic device (e.g., bracelet) that emits continuous signals to a receiver, which is attached to his or her home telephone. If the signals are broken, the receiver communicates with a local probation department's computer, providing notice to corrections officials that the offender violated his or her conditions of home incarceration. Although criminal offenders on house arrest may temporarily leave their home, they may only do so during prearranged times for the purposes of medical appointments, school, work, and other approved activities.

Passive monitoring system: when a criminal offender wears an electronic device (e.g., bracelet) that emits continuous signals to a receiver, which is attached to his or her home telephone.

A second form of electronic monitoring is performed with an **active monitoring system**. A criminal offender who is supervised through an active electronic monitoring system wears a device that emits signals only while connected to a receiver, which is attached to his or her home telephone. Several times in one day, a computer at the local probation department randomly dials the home telephone numbers of all offenders under home incarceration. When an offender receives a telephone call, he or she is obligated to answer the telephone within a specified number of rings. Once greeted by a computer recording, an offender must connect his or her device into the receiver. At the time of connection between the device and receiver, signals are generated, and the computer identifies the offender, noting that he or she is properly inside his or her home. Because the computer must have the ability to reach offenders under home incarceration at any time, most probation departments restrict such individuals to telephone calls of no more than five minutes. If criminal offenders are unable to respond to the random calls, notice is provided to corrections officials, and such individuals are considered to be in violation of home incarceration conditions. Importantly, home incarceration costs may be 13 times less expensive than jail costs.[52]

Active monitoring system: when a criminal offender wears a device that emits signals only while connected to a receiver, which is attached to his or her home telephone.

Summary

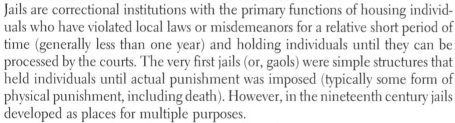

Jails are correctional institutions with the primary functions of housing individuals who have violated local laws or misdemeanors for a relative short period of time (generally less than one year) and holding individuals until they can be processed by the courts. The very first jails (or, gaols) were simple structures that held individuals until actual punishment was imposed (typically some form of physical punishment, including death). However, in the nineteenth century jails developed as places for multiple purposes.

The very first form of jails, known as first generation jails, were essentially holding pens that provided very little room and often required inmates to provide their own food. The second generation jails were built in the early 1800s and offered "modern" features of segregating inmates and organizing rows of side-by-side cells with an office or station at the end of the rows. This allowed jail staff to enact a new form of supervision referred to as intermittent supervision. Political pressures in the 1960s and 1970s calling for better inmate treatment led to the creation of new generation jails. These jails emphasized more hospitable conditions aimed at reducing staff and inmate stress while focusing on the use of a management technique known as direct supervision. This form of supervision

52. Robert Stanz and Richard Tewksbury. 2000. Predictors of Success and Recidivism in a Home Incarceration Program. *The Prison Journal*, 80, (3), 326-344.

focused more on institutional control than inmate control, which had been the emphasis of prior jail models.

Contemporary jails' populations are primarily individuals who have not yet been convicted of a crime. Jail inmates are very similar in demographics to prison inmates; this is logical as many people in jail end up moving on to prison, and essentially everyone in prison was previously in jail.

Jail administrations are organized in one of four ways: city/county government administration, state government administration, cooperative administration, and private corrections. The primary types of challenges and problems that are encountered by jails are substandard physical facilities, minimal programming opportunities, staffing deficiencies, and poor inmate health. Each of these problems both contributes to the other problems and introduces costs and extra challenges for staff in jails. In attempts to resolve and better handle some of the problems of jails, recent years have seen the developments of alternatives to jails, including day reporting centers, diversion centers, and home incarceration. Each of these alternatives is designed for particular types of offenders, and also offers both advantages and additional challenges/costs.

Key Terms

Active monitoring system
Cooperative jail administration
Day reporting centers
Direct supervision
Diversion centers
Electronic monitoring system
First generation jails
Gaols
Home incarceration
Intermittent supervision
Jails
Lockup
New generation jails
Passive monitoring system
Privatization
Rated capacity
Second generation jails
Social density
Spatial density
Work-release

Chapter Eleven
Community Corrections

DAVID PATRICK CONNOR

COMMUNITY CORRECTIONS VERSUS INSTITUTIONAL CORRECTIONS

As popularly thought, corrections usually involves some form of confinement inside a correctional institution. However, jails and prisons are not the only, or even the most common, form of corrections in American society. A majority of convicted criminal offenders are sentenced to forms of corrections that allow them to remain in the community under some degree of monitoring and programming. These programs are called **community corrections** and include probation and parole supervision.

Community corrections: a form of punishment where a convicted criminal offender is sentenced to a form of corrections, usually either probation or parole, that allows him or her to remain in the community under some degree of monitoring and programming.

More criminal offenders are supervised through community corrections programs than jails and prisons combined. However, whether or not the use of community corrections is appropriate, reasonable, and safe is still strongly debated. The criminal justice system's reliance on community corrections, specifically probation, is based on both practical concerns and beliefs in specific correctional ideologies. At the same time, the idea persists among others that the criminal justice system should incarcerate more or all offenders, rather than supervise them on the outside.

The practical concerns that fuel debates about community corrections include jail and prison overcrowding, financial costs of corrections, and public anxiety about recidivism. In terms of correctional ideologies, individuals who argue for the use of community corrections programs commonly hold to some combination of rehabilitation, reintegration, and perhaps deterrence. Alternatively, individuals who argue against the use of community corrections commonly hold to some combination of retribution, incapacitation, and deterrence. One's view of community corrections largely depends on what one believes the purpose of corrections is and how effective community corrections may be in reducing crime.

Arguments Against Community Corrections

There are two primary arguments against community corrections and in favor of institutional corrections. The first argument contends that convicted criminal offenders should be punished (i.e., retribution) because they have broken the law. To be allowed to remain on the outside, rather than to be sent to a prison, is not a right.[1] Some individuals deem it inappropriate to grant convicted offenders privileges that include community corrections. If the criminal justice system's purpose is to punish offenders and protect citizens from them, it should remove privileges from offenders.

The second argument against community corrections centers on rehabilitation. Although possibilities of rehabilitation are among the strongest reasons for not placing criminal offenders inside an institutional setting, opponents of community corrections believe that offenders who are allowed to remain on the outside will likely commit criminal offenses again. In other words, offenders are less likely to be rehabilitated, deterred, or incapacitated from future criminal behavior when they are on the outside than when they are locked up. Therefore, incarceration is necessary in order to remove the "bad influences" from offenders and transform them into law-abiding individuals.

Recidivism: when a convicted criminal offender commits another criminal offense or offenses and is again processed through the criminal justice system.

Opponents who believe the use of community corrections is an ineffective rehabilitation method often worry about the **recidivism** of criminal offenders. In other words, if offenders remain in the community, they are likely to commit more criminal offenses. Unless offenders are incarcerated, which will make them not want to (i.e., deterrence) or unable to (i.e., incapacitation) commit criminal offenses, recidivism rates are likely to be high. These issues may be directly measured by comparing probationers with jail and prison inmates. Interestingly, these measures often support the argument that community corrections may be associated with high recidivism rates.

Specifically, one research team reported that criminal offenders sentenced to community-based programs often repeat criminal offenses. The study followed a sample of 107 offenders in Virginia. Once placed on probation, these offenders reported average annual offending rates of 3 assaults, 3 burglaries, 408 drug deals, 8 forgeries, 15 robberies, 11 thefts, and 200 other crimes.[2] Obviously, these offenders were not incapacitated, deterred, or successfully rehabilitated. This is not the only research to support the notion that offenders who

1. Gagnon v. Scarpelli, 411 U.S. 778 (1972).
2. Doris L. MacKenzie, Katharine Browning, Stacy B. Skroban, and Douglas A. Smith. 1999. The Impact of Probation on the Criminal Activities of Offenders. *Journal of Research in Crime and Delinquency*, 36, 423-453.

serve sentences in community corrections programs continue to commit criminal offenses. Another study found that 62 percent of probationers from 17 states were rearrested for a felony or had potentially violated probation conditions as evidenced by participation in a disciplinary hearing.[3] Today, 41 percent of probationers in the United States do not successfully complete their probation sentence.[4] Failure on probation may mean anything from rearrest (on any charges) to removal of the "privilege" of serving a sentence in the community and a subsequent prison sentence.

In summary, critics of community corrections present some logical arguments, and some evidence supports these contentions. The position against community corrections has support from "common sense," ideological beliefs, and research designed to measure the success of such programs. However, other studies provide some endorsement for community corrections.

Arguments for Community Corrections

Probation emerged in the United States during an era of many social changes. These changes concerned both the way American society was structured and the philosophical basis of what could and should be done with criminal offenders. As a by-product of the Enlightenment period, the classical school of criminology called for the elimination of harsh punishments and the establishment of a criminal justice system based on citizen rights. Along with this set of ideas was a focus on humanitarianism and a belief that individuals may be steered from inappropriate choices of behavior. No longer were offenders viewed as inherently evil; instead, they were individuals who chose to behave in socially inappropriate ways. The method of teaching appropriate social behavior, then, was to work with offenders in the community.

Today, the United States continues to rely heavily on community corrections as a way of dealing with criminal offenders. Although the desire may be to "correct" the behavior of offenders, different forms of community corrections are used for other practical, necessary reasons. First, overcrowding inside American jails and prisons makes alternative sentences necessary, and this is a financially and politically driven argument in favor of community corrections. Each year, incarceration costs between $20,000 and $30,000 per offender, whereas probation only costs between $700 and $1,000. At a minimum, this saves $19,000 annually on correctional supervision for convicted felons.[5] Without community corrections, the criminal justice system must either do nothing with, for, or to offenders, which is simply unacceptable to most citizens, or incarcerate many

---

3. Patrick A. Langan and Mark A. Cunniff. 1992. *Recidivism of Felons on Probation, 1986-1989.* Washington, D.C.: Bureau of Justice Statistics.
4. Lauren E. Glaze, Thonmas P. Bonczar, and Fan Zhang. 2010. *Probation and Parole in the United States, 2009.* Washington, D.C.: Bureau of Justice Statistics.
5. Burk Foster. 2006. *Corrections: The Fundamentals.* Upper Saddle River, NJ: Prentice Hall.

more offenders. The latter alternative is not truly feasible. The financial costs of building, staffing, and maintaining an ever-increasing number of jails and prisons is simply too great.

Generally, the objectives of probation (which is the most common form of community corrections) are not to benefit corrections, but to benefit criminal offenders. The general objectives of probation are to:

1. Reintegrate amenable offenders.
2. Protect the community from further antisocial behavior.
3. Further the goals of justice.
4. Provide conditions (and services) necessary to change offenders and to achieve the above objectives.[6]

In order to argue in favor of community corrections for convicted offenders, it should be shown that forms of community corrections successfully achieve these objectives. One way to evaluate these objectives is to examine the rates at which criminal offenders on probation return to criminal behavior.

Although the political argument in favor of community corrections is often criticized for being "soft on crime," the research on recidivism suggests that such criticisms are not completely correct. One major argument discussed earlier in favor of institutional corrections is that criminal offenders on probation have high rates of recidivism. However, this is not a universal conclusion of recidivism research. Some research shows that some probationers do not have high recidivism rates. One study of Texas probationers revealed that only 4 percent of individuals were rearrested over a one-year follow-up period.[7] Another study showed that, over a two-year period of time, nearly 70 percent of probationers in one federal probation jurisdiction did not violate supervision conditions.[8] Even as early as 20 years ago, after a comprehensive review of the literature on the "success" or "failure" of probation as a criminal sentence, one researcher concluded that "probation is effective as a correctional alternative."[9]

However, it may be irresponsible to suggest that probation should be the sentence of choice for all criminal offenders. The types of offenders who may benefit most from probation need to be thoroughly identified. Interestingly, one study showed the types of probationers with the least "success" while on probation. Non-white probationers, those with less education, and those with prior drug use were more likely to receive technical violations. Unemployed probationers, those with medium-level supervision, and those with more technical

6. Harry E. Allen, Chris W. Eskridge, Edward J. Latessa, and Gennaro F. Vito. 1985. Probation and Parole Effectiveness, in Harry E. Allen, Chris W. Eskridge, Edward J. Latessa, and Gennaro F. Vito (eds.), *Probation and Parole in America.* New York: Free Press.

7. Todd R. Clear and Edward J. Latessa. 1993. Probation Officers' Roles in Intensive Supervision: Surveillance versus Treatment. *Justice Quarterly,* 10, 441-462.

8. Keven I. Minor, James B. Wells, and Crissy Sims. 2003. Recidivism Among Federal Probationers: Predicting Sentence Violations. *Federal Probation,* 67, (1), 31-36.

9. Kathryn Morgan. 1993. Factors Influencing Probation Outcome: A Review of the Literature. *Federal Probation,* 57, (2), 27.

violations were more likely to commit a new criminal offense. Criminal offenders on probation for assaultive offenses were more likely to both receive technical violations and commit a new criminal offense.[10]

Although the arguments for and against community corrections primarily focused on probation, parole supervision is also an important form of community corrections. Parole is discussed at length later in this chapter. Meanwhile, probation as a form of community corrections is considered.

PROBATION

So, what exactly is probation? Up to this point, it has been assumed that the reader knows precisely what is meant by the term. Many individuals have at least a general idea of the practice. However, even criminal justice and corrections professionals cannot agree on an interpretation of "probation." First, probation often suggests that a criminal offender was convicted of a criminal offense, but is allowed to stay in the community as long as certain restrictions are followed. Traditionally, probation has been treated as a court sentence. Only for about 30 years, though, have the courts sentenced offenders directly to probation. When federal and state courts placed convicted offenders on probation in the past, this really meant that offenders were supervised in the community in place of incarceration. However, as a result of the Sentencing Reform Act of 1984, federal law now explicitly recognizes probation as an actual sentence in itself.[11]

Probation services, unlike incarceration programs, are administered by different agencies and segments of the government in different states. The federal government also manages probation services, in spite of the fact that federal parole no longer exists. As a local, state, or federal endeavor, probation supervision is administered by 2,000 distinct agencies. Interestingly, one-half of probation agencies are combined with parole services.[12] For instance, one division of the Kentucky Department of Corrections is responsible for the supervision of both probationers and parolees. Probation and parole officers in Kentucky must possess a bachelor's degree and be 21 years or older.

For a formal definition of **probation**, one description may be considered. Probation is:

Probation: a form of corrections that is an alternative to incarceration where an offender is sentenced to a period of incarceration, but the offender can remain in the community if he or she meets certain conditions.

> . . . a sentence which establishes the defendant's legal status under which his [or her] freedom in the community is continued or only briefly interrupted, subject to supervision by a "probation organization" and subject to conditions imposed by the

10. M. Kevin Gray, Monique Fields, and Sheila R. Maxwell. 2001. Examining Probation Violations: Who, What, and When. *Crime and Delinquency*, 47, (4), 537-557.

11. Toby D. Slawsky. 1992. Revocation of Community Supervision: What the Courts Have Made of Congress' Ambiguous Language and Policies. *Federal Probation*, 56, (3), 73-77.

12. Mark A. Cunniff and Ilene R. Bergsmann. 1990. *Managing Felons in the Community: An Administrative Profile of Probation.* Washington, D.C.: Bureau of Justice Statistics.

> court. The sentencing court retains the authority to modify the conditions of the sentence or resentence the offender if he [or she] violates the conditions.[13]

Although a specific sentence and form of supervision may be called "probation," what is done with, for, and to criminal offenders on probation supervision is not always the same. As discussed previously in Chapter 4, probation evolved from several different and often competing areas of thought. Probation may be dominated by a social work perspective, which seeks to "save" criminal offenders. Probation may also be dominated by a punishment perspective, which seeks to "control" offenders. Further, probation may be dominated by some combination of these perspectives.[14]

Conditions of Probation

When placing criminal offenders on probation, a tailored set of supervision conditions are created, in order to best protect society as a whole and meet the needs of offenders in the community. From the broad statutes that establish probation, a fair amount of freedom is exercised, in order to select sets of conditions for individual offenders. Specifics are often found only in the form of mandatory conditions for all probationers. The most common probation conditions state that offenders:

1. May not violate any laws.
2. Must support their dependents.
3. Must stay in the supervising jurisdiction.
4. Must report to an assigned probation officer on scheduled dates and times.

Restitution: court-ordered repayments of expenses or losses made by criminal offenders to their victims that may include payment to cover the costs of a victim's medical expenses or damaged, destroyed, or stolen property.

Community service: a form of punishment that obligates offenders to participate in volunteer work, in order to repair harm done to society as a whole, often including manual labor (e.g., picking up trash, cutting grass, or painting in public parks).

In the 1980s and 1990s, **restitution** and **community service** became more popular as probation conditions. Restitution consists of court-ordered repayments of expenses or losses made by criminal offenders to their victims. This may include payment to cover the costs of a victim's medical expenses or damaged, destroyed, or stolen property. Community service obligates offenders to participate in volunteer work, in order to repair harm done to society as a whole. This often involves manual labor, such as picking up trash, cutting grass, or painting in public parks. Other forms of community service may include helping a social service agency or children's organization with rather menial tasks.

Importantly, some conditions imposed on probationers have been challenged in courts and declared illegal. The general rule in determining the

---

13. Harry E. Allen, Eric Carlson, and Evalyn Parks. 1979. *Critical Issues in Probation: Summary Report.* Washington, D.C.: U.S. Department of Justice, pp. 12-13.

14. See Richard Gray, 1986, Probation: An Exploration in Meaning, *Federal Probation* 50, (4), 26-31, for a discussion of the various meanings of "probation."

legality of a particular condition of probation is to ask whether or not the condition is reasonable and relevant to a probationer's criminal offense. A probation condition is invalid when it:

1. Does not relate to the crime for which the offender was convicted.
2. Relates to conduct that is not criminal.
3. Relates to actions that are not reasonably associated with potential future criminality.[15]

The court-imposed conditions also must be able to be completed during the probation period. For instance, for a one-year probation sentence, a court may not require a criminal offender to complete a four-year college degree.[16] In addition, the conditions of probation must be reasonable. Here it is important to remember that probation itself is a sentence or form of punishment. Therefore, probation conditions may not violate the Eighth Amendment guarantee against cruel and unusual punishment.

Interestingly, unreasonable probation conditions may include banishing a probationer from a state for 5 years,[17] forcing a probationer to move out of his or her neighborhood,[18] and requiring a probationer to make a $1,000 donation to a specific charity.[19] Ordering a probationer to "live honorably,"[20] "not father any children during probation,"[21] and perform 6,200 hours of community service during a 3-year probation sentence (which is an average of more than 5.5 hours per day)[22] may also be unreasonable. However, finding a pattern in the conditions of probation that have or have not been found permissible is quite difficult. Among the probation conditions that have been ruled as legal are the requirements that a probationer avoid all contact with bars,[23] not enter a particular county,[24] and not participate in antiabortion protests.[25]

SPECIAL TYPES OF PROBATION

The supervision conditions described above often accompany standard probation. However, not all criminal offenders sentenced to probation experience the same degree of supervision, and they do not necessarily face the same

15. People v. Dominguez, 256 Cal. App. 2d 623, 64 Cal. Rptr. 290 (1967).
16. *Ex parte* Acosta, 65 Cal. App. 2d 63, 149 P.2d 757 (1944).
17. People v. Baum, 251 Mich. 187, 231 N.W. 95 (1930).
18. People v. Smith, 252 Mich. 4, 232 N.W. 397 (1930).
19. People v. Appel, People v. Sullivan, 141 A.D.2d 374, 529 N.Y.S.2d 311 (1988).
20. Norris v. State, 383 So. 2d 691 (Fla. Dist. Ct. App. 1980).
21. Burchell v. State, 419 So. 2d 358 (Fla. Dist. Ct. App. 1982).
22. Higdon v. United States, 627 F.2d 893 (9th Cir. 1980).
23. Brown v. State, 406 So. 2d 1262 (Fla. Dist. Ct. App. 1981).
24. United States v. Cothran, 855 F.2d 749 (11th Cir. 1988).
25. Markley v. State, 507 So. 2d 1043 (Ala. Ct. Crim. App. 1987).

expectations. Two very different forms of probation may obligate offenders to adhere to contrasting terms and conditions in the community.

Intensive Supervision Probation (ISP)

As the most restrictive form of probation, intensive supervision probation (ISP) is typically reserved for probationers who are considered by the court and corrections officials as the most likely to recidivate. In many cases, criminal offenders who received an ISP sentence could have received a prison sentence. This suggests that ISP may be a sanction of last resort for many criminal offenders, prior to a prison sentence.

Probationers on intensive supervision probation experience more frequent supervision and surveillance (scheduled and unscheduled) by probation officers. Probation officers who supervise probationers on ISP often have smaller caseloads (i.e., 10 to 50 probationers) than probation officers who supervise probationers on standard probation. In some states, probation officers who supervise probationers on ISP may work in teams of two, which allows them to observe their clients more closely and monitor several clients at the same time.

Generally, intensive supervision probation includes conditions such as a curfew, routine alcohol and drug tests, community service, requirements to hold (or be looking for) a full-time job, and travel restrictions (usually prohibiting travel outside of the supervising jurisdiction). Probation officers also regularly visit a probationer's employer, home, or other typical locations to see what the individual is doing and to administer alcohol and drug tests. Although there is no set model for how ISP should function, nearly all such programs have four central elements:

1. Multiple, weekly contacts with a supervising probation officer.
2. Random and unannounced alcohol and drug tests.
3. Strict enforcement of probation conditions, and more stringent conditions than those applied to criminal offenders on standard probation.
4. Required participation in treatment, education, work, and/or community service programs.

Many criminal offenders consider intensive supervision probation to be overly restrictive. As a result, some offenders elect to serve a jail or prison sentence instead.[26] Offenders on ISP who violate a probation condition, such as testing positive for using drugs, are subject to sanctions. As the number and seriousness of violations increase, the corresponding "punishments" become increasingly severe. Sanctions may range from having more contact with a probation officer to additional community service to revocation of probation and incarceration.

---

26. Ben M. Crouch. 1993. Is Incarceration Really Worse? Analysis of Offenders' Preferences for Prison over Probation. *Justice Quarterly*, 10, (1), 67-88.

Nonreporting Probation

If intensive supervision probation is the most restrictive form of probation, nonreporting probation may be on the opposite end of the spectrum, as the least restrictive. This form of probation is often reserved for first-time misdemeanants and less-serious lawbreakers. Criminal offenders on nonreporting probation are essentially unsupervised, as they are not obligated to meet face to face with a probation officer. However, in some situations, they may be required to adhere to a reporting schedule, by submitting a postcard or other written documentation to a local probation department on a periodic basis. Unlike probationers on ISP, probationers on nonreporting probation have limited probation conditions. Nonetheless, while on nonreporting probation, offenders must refrain from criminal behavior and avoid rearrest.

Typically, offenders do not start out their sentences on this form of supervision, but instead may have their supervision reduced after a period of time on regular or intensive supervision probation. In this way, nonreporting probation can typically be seen as a sort of movement from more to less supervision as the offender gets closer to his or her final release date, at which time he or she will have no supervision.

U.S. PROBATIONERS

In the United States, more than 4.2 million individuals are on some form of probation. This represents approximately 60 percent of all correctional clients. The probation population is significantly larger than the parole, jail, and prison populations. Between 1995 and 2005, the number of criminal offenders on probation increased each year at a rate of almost 3 percent. This increased use of probation may be due to changes in the ideologies of correctional policy makers. At the same time, and perhaps more appropriately, this increase may be attributed to the sheer number of offenders processed through the criminal justice system. As the number of individuals convicted of criminal offenses increases, it becomes impossible and very expensive to use incarceration. However, in 2009, for the first time in recent history, the number of offenders on probation slightly decreased. Ninety-nine percent of all probationers are supervised by states (and not the federal or local governments). California, Florida, Georgia, Ohio, and Texas have the largest number of individuals on probation. Less than 25,000 criminal offenders are under federal probation.[27]

The criminal offenses for which criminal offenders are placed on probation do not necessarily follow expectations. In fact, just about all types of offenses are eligible for a sentence of probation. One-half of all probationers are serving a felony sentence, 49 percent of all probationers are serving a misdemeanor

---

27. Glaze, Bonczar, and Zhang, supra n.4.

sentence, and 1 percent are serving a sentence for other infractions.[28] Interestingly, fully 28 percent of all felony offenders are sentenced to probation. More specifically, 26 percent of felons convicted of drug offenses, 26 percent of felons convicted of property offenses, 19 percent of felons convicted of violent offenses, 18 percent of felons convicted of public-order offenses, 15 percent of felons convicted of drunk driving offenses, and 10 percent of felons convicted of other offenses are sentenced to probation.[29] This suggests that "minor" offenses are not the only criminal offenses for which probation is utilized. This may be attributed to the fact that probation is used as an alternative to a sentence of incarceration, in order to control the size of the prison population.

Statutory law in the appropriate jurisdiction determines the types of criminal offenses for which probation is a legal option at the point of sentencing. Many state legislatures write laws to exclude individuals convicted of specific offenses from probation consideration. However, even with such guidelines, decisions about which offenders receive sentences of probation are highly individualized.

LEGAL RIGHTS OF PROBATIONERS

Individuals who are on probation, just as with individuals who are incarcerated, do have legal rights. They do not enjoy all of the legal rights that those of us who have not been convicted of criminal offenses enjoy, but they do have more rights than prison or jail inmates. The legal rights of probationers are therefore found in a middle ground between those of "regular" citizens and inmates. The restrictions that are imposed on the rights of probationers arise from the set of beliefs that a criminal conviction should be accompanied by restrictions but also a recognition that in order to be a functioning member of society and to have a realistic opportunity to remain crime free, not all rights can be restricted.

The legal rights of probationers focus on three primary areas. First, laws regulate actual conditions of supervision that may be imposed on probationers. Second, there are established laws surrounding **revocation of probation**, which include how and when probationers may be removed from probation and instead incarcerated in a jail or prison. Third, criminal offenders have a number of rights regarding **due process**, or the steps that the judicial system must follow to fully protect the citizenship rights of probationers.

Revocation of probation: the process whereby probationers are removed from probation and incarcerated in jail or prison for the violation of specific obligations set forth by their original sentence.

Due process: the steps that the judicial system must follow to fully protect the citizenship rights of probationers.

A state legislature (or the federal government) creates in its statutory law the basic structure and operation of a probation system. Some states also have their legislature establish the range of conditions that may be imposed on criminal offenders. Other states establish the range of possible conditions in administrative law. Within this range of possible conditions and restrictions, most jurisdictions tailor the conditions and restrictions to individual offenders based on their

28. *Ibid.*

29. Matthew R. Durose and Patrick A. Langan. 2009. *Felony Sentences in State Courts, 2006.* Washington, D.C.: Bureau of Justice Statistics.

offenses, personal characteristics, and "needs" (as determined by a classification system). When selecting the probation conditions for specific offenders, individual probation departments and officers operate within the boundaries established by law. A third type of law, known as case law, may be involved, if some action by a probation officer or condition of probation is challenged and considered by a court. Finally, constitutional law may be involved with probationers. In other words, all other laws — whether related to probation or any other matter — must be within the legal boundaries of acceptability that both the federal and state constitutions establish. As a result, constitutions of jurisdictions involved with a probationer establish the framework for all government actions. Within this scope, legislators create a structure and process for operating a probation system. Once this is established, individual actors within the probation system put into operation individual case plans for offenders (i.e., administrative law) that may be challenged in court for rulings (i.e., case law) about whether or not case plans fit within the overall constitutional framework. Thus, all four varieties of law are involved in a discussion of the rights of probationers.

Revocation of Probation

Remember, probation is a privilege, at least in terms of the law. If criminal offenders violate the conditions of probation, this privilege may be taken away, or revoked. Probation may be revoked for one of two types of reasons. First, if probationers commit new criminal offenses, it may be appropriate to revoke probation and house them inside a jail or prison. Second, if probationers violate a specific condition or restriction of the probation agreement, probation may be revoked. This is called revocation for a **technical violation**. Except in the most extreme cases, probationers must commit a series of such violations, before they are removed from probation and sent to a correctional institution.

Technical violation: when probationers violate a specific condition or restriction of the probation agreement, their probation may be revoked.

Only the court, or sentencing judge, possesses the authority to revoke a criminal offender's probation. Recommendations for such actions originate from probation departments and officers. However, as discussed in more detail in the next section, probation departments and officers may only advise a judge about a probationer's activities and adherence to conditions. The actual supervision of probationers remains the responsibility of the sentencing court, although in practical terms this task may be delegated to a probation department and officers. However, when a court revokes probation, supervision and responsibility for offenders are transferred to officials who oversee the new sentence, which is often a jail or prison term.

Although probation is a privilege extended to criminal offenders, the court cannot simply decide to remove that privilege, without reason. Once placed on probation, offenders have both rights and responsibilities, which guide their relationship with the court. Probationers agree to live within the conditions set by the court and probation department, and the judicial system agrees to treat offenders fairly and to protect their basic constitutional rights. The most notable constitutional rights that concern probation are

Due process rights: constitutional protections that all citizens possess from being unfairly treated and punished without proper application of the legally required steps for removing their rights or freedoms.

due process rights. These are protections all citizens possess from being unfairly treated and punished without proper application of the legally required steps for removing their rights or freedoms.

Due Process Rights

The due process rights of probationers are based upon the 1972 U.S. Supreme Court case entitled *Morrissey v. Brewer.*[30] This case actually concerned the due process rights of parolees, but these have since been interpreted to be applicable to probationers.[31] This case established that parolees (and probationers) have basic due process rights. However, while the law recognizes that parole and probation revocation processes are bound by essentially the same legal requirements, the law does not require these to be identical processes. Although criminal offenders have a significant privilege (i.e., liberty) to lose in a revocation proceeding, the courts hold tightly to the idea that offenders are already convicted and thus do not have as many rights as criminal defendants.

Morrissey v. Brewer (1972) passed down five specific due process requirements:

1. There must be a written notice of alleged violations by offenders.
2. Offenders must receive a full disclosure of the evidence against them.
3. When facing possible revocation, offenders have the right to present their cases in person and witnesses on their behalf.
4. Decisions about whether or not to revoke probation are to be made by a detached and neutral hearing body.
5. Once a revocation decision is made, decision makers must prepare and file written statements, explaining the evidence on which they based their decisions and specific reasons for deciding to revoke probation.

In the American criminal justice system, one central right afforded to criminal defendants is the assistance and counsel of an attorney. Defendants have a guaranteed right to the legal help of a lawyer, in order to plan and present their defense. However, this right is not as clearly established for criminal offenders serving sentences in the community. In 1967, the Supreme Court ruled in *Mempa v. Rhay* that probationers who face revocation hearings are entitled to an attorney.[32] The Court's ruling was based on the idea that a revocation hearing is a "critical phase" in the processing of a criminal case. Therefore, in the mind of the Court, such a process is subject to the due process protections established by the Fourteenth Amendment. When jurisdictions revoke probation, they remove the liberty of offenders. In short, it was found that probationers who face revocation, like defendants, have essentially similar interests to protect.

---

30. Morrissey v. Brewer, 408 U.S. 471 (1972).
31. People v. Vickers, 25 Cal. App. 3d 1080, 102 Cal. Rptr. 418 (1972).
32. Mempa v. Rhay, 398 U.S. 128 (1967).

The due process rights of probationers are further specified and more firmly established in the U.S. Supreme Court case of *Gagnon v. Scarpelli* (1973). Here, the Court ruled that a two-stage hearing process is necessary when jurisdictions seek to revoke a criminal offender's probation sentence. First, a preliminary hearing must be conducted, in order to establish whether or not there is probable cause to revoke probation. Second, if probable cause is established, then a revocation hearing must be held. In addition, *Gagnon v. Scarpelli* established that the state is responsible for providing an attorney to probationers who are unable to afford one. Again, the similarities to the rights of criminal defendants are clear. Most recently, in *Young v. Harper* (1997), the Supreme Court ruled that other early release programs are also subject to the due process guidelines found in *Morrissey* and *Gagnon*.[33]

When jurisdictions attempt to revoke a criminal offender's probation sentence, a probationer must be provided with an attorney to assist with his or her defense. At the same time, a probationer must be provided with sufficient time to prepare his or her defense. Probationers facing revocation, as well as criminal defendants, must be provided with information about the charges against them and must have adequate time and resources to prepare their defense.[34] This means that offenders must be given notice of revocation hearings in a timely manner to allow them to prepare for the hearings. Probationers must also be provided with full information about the reason for revocation.[35]

In simple terms, probation revocation is performed during a **hearing**, where a judge makes a decision about the procedures used with a criminal offender. Rules about the admissibility of evidence, standards of proof, and many procedural formalities do not apply with revocation hearings. Probationers who face revocation do not even have an absolute right to be present at their own revocation hearings. If probationers cannot be located or fail to appear at an announced revocation hearing, probation may be revoked in their absence. In such cases, a warrant is issued for the probationer's arrest.

Hearing: the process whereby a judge makes a decision about the procedures used with a criminal offender while considering the revocation of probation.

PAROLE AND OTHER P-WORDS

Beyond probation, two additional p-words are relevant to community corrections. Individuals who are not familiar with the operations of U.S. corrections may misunderstand or easily confuse what is meant by parole, pardon, and, as previously discussed, probation. Although these three concepts share some characteristics (e.g., each is concerned with the placement of criminal offenders in the community), they are really more different than they are similar. As established earlier, probation is a judge's sentence that allows an offender to live in the

33. Young v. Harper, 520 U.S. 143 (1997).
34. Kuentler v. State, 486 S.W.2d 367 (Tex. 1972); Burkett v. State, 485 S.W.2d 578 (Tex. 1972).
35. *Burkett*, supra n.34.

Parole: where an offender is released from a prison, prior to the expiration of his or her sentence. The offender serves the remainder of his or her prison sentence with supervision and restrictions upon his or her activities.

Pardon: a formal act by a governor or the President that legally clears an offender from the consequences of his or her criminal convictions.

community with supervision and restrictions on his or her activities. **Parole** is release from a prison, prior to the expiration of an offender's sentence. An offender under parole supervision serves the remainder of his or her prison sentence in the community with supervision and restrictions on his or her activities. In contrast, a governor or the President grants a **pardon**, which legally clears an offender from the consequences of his or her criminal convictions. Importantly, the type and amount of required, applied supervision differs with each concept. Parole officers, who are similar to probation officers, supervise parolees and assist offenders who are released from a prison with community reintegration. However, the amount of supervision that parolees receive is typically rather minimal. Individuals who are pardoned receive no supervision at all; by receiving pardons, formerly convicted offenders are excused from serving any further time under supervision of any sort. In contrast, probationers may face rather restrictive or limited monitoring.

Each concept originates in a separate branch of government. A parole usually comes from correctional authorities, like a parole board. A pardon, by definition, is granted by the politically elected leader of a government's executive branch. Probation, as a sentence, comes from the judicial branch. Thus, each concept is wholly different in its goal, process, and point of origin.

The goal of parole is to transform the actual substance of the sentence that a trial court hands down. When supervisory authority over criminal offenders is passed from the judicial system to the correctional system, correctional officials not only have the responsibility to supervise offenders, but also the responsibility for carrying out the court's sentences. However, in states where parole exists, statutory law gives correctional officials the authority to modify, within certain limits, the length of a sentence. Correctional officials may, therefore, change the conditions in which convicted offenders are supervised. This means that inmates may be released from a prison to be supervised either in the community or an outside facility, such as a halfway house or pre-release center.

Contemporary Parole

The contemporary U.S. version of parole is largely based on three concepts:

1. Reducing the length of incarceration as a reward for good conduct.
2. Supervising criminal offenders released from institutional custody.
3. Using indeterminate sentences.

Indeterminate sentence: a sentence that has a minimum and maximum length, with the court transferring authority to correctional officials to determine exactly how much of the sentence (beyond the minimum length) each criminal offender needs to serve.

The emergence of the **indeterminate sentence** was the critical event in the development of parole. An indeterminate sentence is one that has a minimum and maximum length, and the court transfers authority to correctional officials to determine exactly how much of the sentence (beyond the minimum length) each criminal offender needs to serve. Before parole could become a reality, America was obligated to enact statutory laws that allowed indeterminate sentencing. In 1869, Michigan and New York enacted the first indeterminate sentence statutes. However, the Michigan statute was challenged in court and found to be a violation of the state constitution. This considerably slowed the development and spread of parole throughout the nation.

Nonetheless, the New York statute allowed Zebulon Brockway, warden at the new Elmira Reformatory, to discontinue the good-time laws and give inmates specific criteria that would be used to determine when they would be released. Under Brockway's system, inmates were graded on their overall conduct, performance at work assignments, progress in a mandatory education program, and personal adjustment. In this way, Brockway borrowed the earliest idea of marks, which placed the responsibility of earning release directly on incarcerated offenders.

Specific legal and institutional developments preceded parole, but the actual origin of U.S. parole is found in two basic prison reform movements. The first influential movement focused on the ideas that good conduct inside a prison should be rewarded by the reduction of sentence length and release from a prison should be revoked if good conduct did not persist in the community. The second influential movement was the development of volunteer prisoner aid societies.[36] Prisoner aid societies were originally created to provide food, fuel, and clothing to colonial jail inmates who had no family or friends to provide them with supplies. When jails and prisons began providing basic necessities to inmates, prisoner aid societies slowly turned their attentions to assisting released inmates. Courts assigned volunteers to supervise criminal offenders released from a prison. For several decades, supervision of offenders in the community relied exclusively on volunteers. It was not until 1845 in Massachusetts that the first publicly paid employee was hired to assist released offenders with community reintegration.

Supposedly, the guiding ideology behind the use of parole is rehabilitation. Under indeterminate sentencing, it is presumed that prison inmates want to work to achieve release, and the way to achieve parole is to actively participate in treatment programs and refrain from criminal and deviant behavior. In reality, parole (in fact, all forms of early release) today has become a way to control overcrowding and financial problems associated with prisons. Although the rehabilitation focus has not been abandoned, it is no longer the driving force behind parole. However, even though the reasons for using such forms of release may have changed, parole has been an increasingly common practice in the United States.

Parole is not the only way in which inmates are released from a prison before the end of their sentences. Today, more common than parole are **mandatory early release programs**. Such programs are focused on meeting the needs of prisons, rather than inmates. Early release programs are methods by which prisons and prison systems control the size of their inmate population, in

Mandatory early release programs: programs focused on meeting the needs of prisons, rather than the needs of inmates, by allowing prison systems to control the size of their inmate population within legally defined and acceptable limits.

36. Vernon C. Brenham and Samuel B. Kutash (eds.). 1949. *Encyclopedia of Criminology*. New York: Philosophical Library, p. 285.

order to keep the inmate population within legally defined, acceptable limits. Inmates are released when a prison's population reaches the maximum capacity of the institution. The decision about who receives early release is based on which inmates have served the greatest percentage of their sentences and committed the least number of disciplinary infractions. This does not mean that inmates close to the end of their sentences or with little or no disciplinary problems are the only individuals released. Early releases of this variety are a mandatory practice, rather than a privilege.

U.S. PAROLEES

Criminal offenders who are released on parole supervision are very similar to offenders found inside prisons. This is to be expected, though, as parolees are always prison inmates first. However, not all prison inmates are released on parole. Inmates who are the most serious offenders (with life or death sentences) or have disciplinary problems on the inside generally do not receive parole. Instead, these inmates either live out the rest of their natural lives inside a prison or are released only when they have served their maximum sentences (and then are released without any form of official supervision).

In the United States, there are about 820,000 individuals on parole. This translates into 351 parolees per 100,000 American residents. In 2009, the number of criminal offenders who started parole supervision declined by 1.2 percent, and there were 5,200 more offenders who exited parole supervision than started parole supervision. These developments have led to a decline in the total parolee population. Parolees are mostly male (88%) and white (41%), with a length of parole supervision exceeding one year (95%). Thirty-six percent of parolees are drug offenders, 27 percent are violent offenders, 23 percent are property offenders, 10 percent are public-order offenders, and 3 percent are weapons offenders. California and Texas have the largest number of individuals on probation. Maine, North Dakota, and Rhode Island have less than 500 parolees.[37]

THE PAROLE PROCESS

As with probation, parole is a privilege, not a right. Remember, parolees are not "free," as they are merely granted the privilege of living in the community, rather than a prison. There are numerous restrictions on their activities and expectations for parolees.

37. Glaze, Bonczar, and Zhang, supra n.4.

Granting Parole

Not all prison inmates are released on parole supervision. Decisions about which inmates receive parole are often based on a combination of science and politics. Research on the likelihood of recidivism among criminal offenders convicted of specific offenses reflects the science that may impact parole decisions. Using guidelines and a point system, parole decision makers may also utilize science to predict how likely it may be for a specific inmate to succeed or fail on parole supervision. Points are assigned to an inmate's case for specific aspects, such as the severity of offense; history of alcohol and drug abuse; disciplinary infractions while incarcerated; number of times previously arrested, convicted, and incarcerated; and any previous supervision on parole. An inmate's total point score is used as one factor in the parole board's decision. The politics concern institutional overcrowding and the potential reactions by the community to a particular inmate who may receive parole.

Many prison inmates are assigned a **parole eligibility date**, which is the first date on which they may be considered for conditional release. The jurisdiction's statutory law determines the parole eligibility date and specifies how much of a sentence a criminal offender must serve before being considered for release. Generally, statutory laws establish equations that are used to subtract time from the end of a sentence to determine when an inmate may *expect* to *possibly* be prepared for release. Modern versions of good-time laws call for cutting an amount of days off the end of an offender's sentence for every set number of days the inmate serves without any disciplinary problems. The parole eligibility date, then, is set by subtracting the maximum number of good-time days the inmate may earn from the end date of the actual sentence. For example, consider one inmate who is sentenced to a three-year prison term on January 1. If the jurisdiction's statutory law calls for 1 day of good-time credit for every 5 days served, the inmate will be credited a total amount of 219 days of good time. This means that the inmate would have a parole eligibility date of May 26 of the third year served.

Parole eligibility date: the first date, which varies by jurisdiction, on which a criminal offender that is incarcerated may be considered for conditional release.

365 days * 3 = 1,095 days

1,095 days / 5 = 219 days

1,095 days − 219 days = 876 days

876 days = 2 years + 146 days

Statutory laws guide the decision about whether or not to grant parole to prison inmates. Usually, these laws instruct parole boards to base their decisions on one (or more) of four considerations:

1. Likelihood of recidivism.
2. Welfare of society.
3. Prison conduct.
4. Quality of the plans developed for parole supervision.

These guidelines allow a great degree of discretionary decision making. Discretion is considered very important in parole decisions, as it is nearly impossible to identify all the factors that are likely to impact whether or not a prison inmate will successfully readjust to the community. Remember, an inmate's performance on parole is also influenced by the conditions imposed on him or her and his or her willingness and ability to behave within these rules.

Conditions of Parole

The conditions under which parolees must live their lives are very similar in form and structure to the conditions that accompany probation. Remember, parole is basically a contract between the government and the individual offender. This contract calls for the government to grant the offender release from prison, while the offender agrees, in return, to live within the particular rules (i.e., conditions) as defined by the government. In this case, the government is the parole agency.

When parole is granted to them, criminal offenders are expected to remain within the jurisdictions to which they are assigned, live within the law, and report to their assigned parole officers for a specified period of time. The actual length of parole (i.e., the time during which parolees must continue to report to parole officers) varies by jurisdiction and by offender. Generally speaking, parole periods last between two and seven years.[38] In some states, parolees who adjust successfully to the community and are very low recidivism risks may be released from parole supervision in a very short time period. This may occur in as little as a few months.

The conditions imposed on parolees are designed both to assist criminal offenders with successful readjustment to the community and to ensure that offenders are only minimal risks to the public. Because parolees are generally considered more dangerous than probationers (as evidenced by their harsher original sentence), conditions of parole are generally stricter than the conditions of probation. When challenged in court, stricter conditions for parolees may be upheld as legal, whereas they may not be for probationers. Among the most common conditions imposed on parolees are, of course, to obey all laws, report to parole officers, refrain from possessing firearms or other dangerous weapons (without special permission), remain within the supervising jurisdiction, allow parole officers to enter homes or places of work, and be employed.

Generally speaking, the courts have upheld as legal most conditions of parole, unless they require parolees to commit some illegal or immoral action or are impossible to abide by. For instance, requiring a criminal offender who is an alcoholic to completely abstain from alcohol may be a condition impossible to adhere to and may be declared invalid.[39] Many parolees take issue with

---

38. Harry E. Allen, Eeward J. Latessa, and Bruce S. Ponder. 2013. *Corrections in America*. New York: Pearson.
39. Sweeny v. United States, 353 F.2d 10 (7th Cir. 1965).

conditions they believe invade their right to privacy. However, parole is viewed as a privilege, not a right. By agreeing to be supervised on parole, rather than to remain inside a prison, criminal offenders must also agree to be monitored. This means that parole officers have the legal right — and, in fact, responsibility — to oversee parolees' actions and living conditions. Parole officers also have the responsibility to work with offenders in assisting them in returning to society as law-abiding citizens. In this vein, requiring offenders to participate in counseling programs as a condition of parole has been ruled as legal (or, not an invasion of privacy).[40]

The area of parolees' basic constitutional rights is more difficult to interpret. Most notable here are First Amendment rights, which the courts have traditionally viewed as above other personal rights. These rights — freedom of speech, peaceable assembly, religion, and petitioning of the government — are, therefore, held to higher standards of review when concerning their exercise by parolees.

Freedom of speech shows how restrictive conditions are held to higher standards when concerning parolees. In the 1960s, the state of California required parolees to obtain the permission of their parole officers before they could make any public speech. A federal court struck down this condition in 1970, saying that the restriction presented "an unwarranted chilling effect on the exercise . . . of his undisputed rights."[41] Similarly, in 1971, a New York parole condition that denied parolees the right to make public speeches against the Vietnam War was declared invalid.[42] However, in certain circumstances, it remains permissible to restrict certain objectionable forms of speech, including speech likely to lead to violent reactions, disruptions of institutional activities, or criminal actions. And yet, to have such a condition upheld, the state must show that the restriction is necessary for the particular offender and circumstances.

Parole Revocation

As with probation, the supervising jurisdiction may revoke parole and return criminal offenders to prison. Fifty-six percent of parolees do not successfully complete their parole supervision.[43] This simple statistic leads many critics to claim that parole is a bad idea and generally a failure. However, this same statistic may be viewed from the other perspective: 44 percent of parolees are *not* returned to a prison. Therefore, nearly one-half of parole cases are successful. In addition, it may be argued that the time the revoked parolees spent on the outside may be beneficial to their eventual, successful return to the community.

---

40. United States v. Stine, 675 F.2d 69 (3d Cir. 1982).
41. Hyland v. Procunier, 311 F. Supp. 750 (N.D. Cal. 1970).
42. Sobell v. Reed, 327 F. Supp. 1294 (S.D.N.Y. 1971).
43. Glaze, Bonczar, and Zhang, supra n.4.

At least their first attempt to return to the community included some supervision. In other words, they were not initially released from a prison without supervision.

Parole may be revoked in two basic ways. As with probation, technical violations are instances in which criminal offenders fail to abide by the conditions of their parole supervision, which leads to disciplinary actions by parole officers (which may include initiating the process of returning offenders to a prison). Parole may also be revoked if offenders are found to have committed new criminal offenses, such as alcohol and drug abuse, escape (disappearing from supervision), weapons possession, and traffic violations.[44]

Whether criminal offenders fail to obey conditions or commit new crimes, legally mandated procedures must be followed to revoke parole. All parolees today are entitled to hearings to determine whether or not there is sufficient cause to remove them from parole supervision. However, hearings were rare events prior to the 1970s. During the 1970s, a decade when prison inmates earned numerous rights through legal challenges to conditions of confinement, parolees also made significant strides in the legal arena. Prior to this time, the words of parole officers were sufficient reasons to return offenders to a prison. Hearings were merely formalities in which parole officers informed the proper authorities of needed action.

However, as a result of the 1967 Supreme Court decision in *Mempa v. Rhay*, state probationers were entitled to hearings and legal counsel when facing the possibility of having probation revoked.[45] A number of courts subsequently interpreted the decision in *Mempa* as applying to parole revocation. This interpretation was somewhat clarified five years later with the Supreme Court's decision in the 1972 case of *Morrissey v. Brewer.*[46] This case provided the basic foundation on which parolees' due process rights and, hence, the due process requirements for states to follow, were established. Specifically, *Morrissey v. Brewer* established these requirements:

1. In order to return parolees to a prison, two hearings must be held. The first is a preliminary hearing for the purpose of determining whether or not there is probable cause to believe a parolee has violated specific conditions of parole. The second hearing is to determine whether the violation of parole conditions should actually result in a return to a prison.
2. Parolees must be provided with written notice of the date, time, and place of the revocation hearings.

44. James Boudouris. 1985. *The Revocation Process in Iowa.* Des Moines: Department of Corrections, Bureau of Data, Research, and Planning. *Alternative to Prison Revocation Study.* 1985. Madison, WI: Wisconsin Department of Health and Social Services. Rebecca Zwetchkenbaum-Segal. 1984. *Case Preparation Aid Follow-Up Study: Major Findings.* Boston: Planning, Research, and Program Development Unit, Massachusetts Parole Board.

45. *Mempa,* supra n.32.

46. *Morrissey,* supra n.30.

3. Parolees must be provided with information about their alleged violations of parole conditions and the evidence that is being used against them.
4. Unless there is good reason not to, parolees must be allowed the opportunity to confront and cross-examine witnesses against them during revocation proceedings.
5. When parole is revoked, written statements of the reasons for revocation must be provided.
6. The facts in revocation hearings are to be judged by a detached, neutral hearing committee.

One year later, the Supreme Court addressed the issue of whether or not parolees who faced possible revocation were entitled to legal assistance, when it ruled in *Gagnon v. Scarpelli*. This case specifically dealt with revocation of probation, but the ruling has been applied to revocation proceedings for both probation and parole. Here the Court ruled that allowing parolees (or probationers) the assistance of legal counsel should be determined on a case-by-case basis. The state authority responsible for administering the parole (or probation) system should make the decision. Thus, there is no hard-and-fast rule that allows (or provides at no cost) legal counsel to paroled offenders facing possible revocation. This is a case-by-case decision that the paroling authority renders.

SHOCK INCARCERATION

A special, and not very frequently used, form of corrections that combines a short period of incarceration with subsequent supervision in the community has been used for the past generation. Typically reserved for offenders whom have committed fairly serious offenses, yet are believed to not be "criminal by nature," this type of unique correctional practice is also somewhat controversial.

Here we are talking about a sentence to a short term of incarceration that is then followed by parole supervision as a follow-up period of monitoring. **Shock incarceration**, also referred to as shock parole, is where a criminal offender is sentenced to a short (perhaps 90-day) prison term *and* a period of time on community supervision. Such practices, also known as *split sentences* or *combination sentences*, were first initiated in 1965, with Ohio's enactment of a "shock probation" statute. Here it is interesting to note that, even among lawmakers and criminal justice practitioners, confusion exists about the distinction between probation and parole. In the case of shock incarceration, the community supervision period may be referred to as either probation (because it is a sentence from the court) or parole (because it is an early release from a prison).

Shock incarceration: also referred to as split sentences or combination sentences, where a criminal offender is sentenced to a short (perhaps 90-day) prison term and a period of time on community supervision.

The actual way shock incarceration works, however, varies by jurisdiction. For instance, the sentence from a judge may call for a combination of incarceration and community supervision. In other scenarios, the original sentence may call for incarceration only, with an opportunity for a criminal offender to petition the court for shock parole. Such petitions must convince the court that offenders do not really need the full prison term, and that short exposures to incarceration will achieve deterrent effects (by administering shocks). Which form of process is used by a state is a matter of state statute.

Shock incarceration programs are reserved only for criminal offenders who are considered to be low recidivism risks. Shock incarceration is often used only with first-time offenders. Typically, such sentences are also designated for offenders who, aside from their present offenses, lead very law-abiding lives and are "respectable" citizens. Shock incarceration also reinforces the ideology behind such programs, as they are primarily for deterrence, although reintegration is also a goal. By not removing an individual from his or her community for an extended period of time, these sentences are intended to help an offender (through community supervision) live a law-abiding life. The rehabilitative ideal is also included in shock incarceration. Since offenders sentenced to shock incarceration are generally not "hardened criminals," the amount and type of rehabilitation they need may be easily provided in the community.

Many individuals believe that shock incarceration is an "easy" form of punishment for criminal offenders, because offenders who serve such a sentence spend relatively short periods of time inside a prison. Other observers believe shock incarceration is "hard," since many offenders who serve such a sentence may have otherwise escaped incarceration with only probation. The true value of shock incarceration, as with any criminal justice program, is the degree to which it may lower or control crime rates. Research evaluating the effectiveness of such programs has produced mixed results.

Net-widening: when programs or sanctions may be used for individuals who would otherwise not have such strict sentences.

Many critics fear shock incarceration programs may be used in a **net-widening** effort. In other words, programs or sanctions may be used for individuals who would otherwise not have such strict sentences. Specifically, such critics fear that criminal offenders, who would otherwise have been placed on probation, may be given split sentences simply because the harder alternative is available, not because it is more advantageous for offenders. As stated by one leading authority on shock incarceration:

> If shock (incarceration) is utilized, it should be used with a select group of offenders who cannot be considered as good candidates for regular probation. The period of incarceration must be short in order to achieve the maximum deterrent effect while reducing the fiscal cost of incarceration. . . . (S)hock (incarceration) has the potential to become a way to reduce institutional overcrowding, which is consistent with the objective of reintegration and public safety.[47]

---

47. Gennaro F. Vito. 1984. Developments in Shock Probation: A Review of Research Findings and Policy Implications. *Federal Probation*, 48, 26-27.

AFTERCARE FOR FORMER INMATES

Incarcerated individuals leaving prison are presently experiencing **reentry** in unprecedented numbers. Reentry may be defined as the process by which incarcerated offenders depart from correctional institutions and return to the outside community. This move from a prison to free society often involves forms of **aftercare**, which include community corrections programs and related local efforts aimed at facilitating successful reintegration among former inmates. In 2000, there were 604,858 inmates released from confinement in the United States, whereas by 2009 this number rose to 729,295. From 2000 to 2009, the number of inmates released from federal and state correctional institutions increased by more than 20 percent.[48]

Reentry: the process by which incarcerated offenders depart from correctional institutions and return to the outside community.

Aftercare: a form of community corrections where programming and related local efforts are aimed at facilitating the successful reintegration of former inmates.

Problems Facing Former Inmates

Because individuals returning to society from a prison often have serious medical and social problems, mental illnesses, chronic illnesses and communicable diseases, limited employment and education, and housing difficulties, aftercare for former inmates is critical. The majority of individuals returning to society from a prison have serious medical and social problems, and many of these issues have not been properly addressed during the time of incarceration. Three-fourths of inmates leaving correctional institutions have a serious history of substance abuse.[49] Although many of these individuals have spent significant time behind bars, only 7 to 17 percent of those with confirmed alcohol and drug dependency issues receive treatment inside a prison.[50] The pervasiveness of such addictions demonstrates that numerous individuals released from a prison will need to participate in community substance abuse treatment programs, as chronic alcohol and drug use may lead to problems with maintaining employment.

Mental illness is also prevalent among prison inmates, as the incidence of serious mental illnesses is two to four times higher for incarcerated offenders than it is for the general population.[51] Many inmates suffer from schizophrenia, bipolar disease, major depression, post-traumatic stress disorder, and other serious mental illnesses. Unfortunately, conditions inside correctional institutions, coupled with insufficient prison mental health services, are often responsible for exacerbating rather than reducing or eliminating these problems. Left untreated and unstable inside a prison, individuals with serious mental illnesses who are returning to society may again break the law and return to correctional institutions.

---

48. William J. Sabol and Heather C. West. 2010. *Prisoners in 2009.* Washington, D.C.: Bureau of Justice Statistics.
49. Theodore Hammett, Cheryl Roberts, and Sofia. Kennedy. 2001. Health-Related Issues in Prisoner Reentry. *Crime & Delinquency*, 47, (3), 390-409.
50. National Institute on Drug Abuse. 2009. *Treating Offenders with Drug Problems: Integrating Public Health and Public Safety.* Bethesda, MD: National Institute on Drug Abuse.
51. Hammett, Roberts, and Kennedy, supra n.49.

In addition, chronic illnesses and communicable diseases are more widespread among individuals serving time inside a prison.[52] For instance, in 1997, released inmates accounted for nearly one-fourth of all individuals living with HIV or AIDS, almost one-third of individuals determined to have hepatitis C, and more than one-third of individuals diagnosed with tuberculosis.[53] More recently, in 2007, the most recent year for which general population data are available, the overall rate of estimated confirmed AIDS cases among federal and state inmates was 2.5 times greater than the general population rate.[54] Access to health care and related services for these individuals is fundamental to their successful reentry.

Former inmates rejoining society are limited in terms of educational achievements and employment experiences. Only three in every five inmates have obtained a high school diploma or its equivalent.[55] This limited education, coupled with low skill levels and extensive physical and mental health problems, almost guarantees employment difficulties, such as low employment rates and earnings histories for individuals leaving a prison. Unfortunately, it does not appear that these issues are being addressed adequately while inmates reside inside prisons. The percentage of the inmate population involved in vocational or educational programs is dropping in nearly all correctional systems and institutions.[56]

Housing difficulties, too, plague many individuals entering and exiting prisons. In the months prior to their incarceration, more than 10 percent of individuals locked inside prisons are homeless; further, released inmates that periodically resided in homeless shelters prior to their confinement were almost five times as likely to stay in such a location upon reentry.[57] Although there are no national statistics on homelessness among individuals leaving prison, numbers from some major jurisdictions suggest a very grave situation nationwide. At any given time in Los Angeles and San Francisco, 30 to 50 percent of all parolees are without a home.[58]

Contemporary Aftercare Programs

Despite the fact that individuals leaving prisons have significant problems, aftercare programs aimed at assisting former inmates are not necessarily

---

52. National Commission on Correctional Health Care. 2002. *The Health Status of Soon-to-Be-Released Prisoners: A Report to Congress.* Chicago: National Commission on Correctional Health Care.
53. Hammett, Roberts, and Kennedy, supra n.49.
54. Laura M. Maruschak and Randy Beavers. 2009. *HIV in Prisons, 2007-2008.* Washington, D.C.: Bureau of Justice Statistics.
55. Caroline W. Harlow. 2003. *Education and Correctional Populations.* Washington, D.C.: Bureau of Justice Statistics.
56. National Center on Addiction and Substance Abuse. 2010. *Behind Bars II: Substance Abuse and America's Prison Population.* New York: National Center on Addiction and Substance Abuse.
57. Stephen Metraux and Dennis P. Culhane. 2004. Homeless Shelter Use and Reincarceration Following Prison Release: Assessing the Risk. *Criminology & Public Policy,* 3, (2), 201-222.
58. Jeremy Travis, Amy L. Solomon, and Michelle Waul. 2001. *From Prison to Home: The Dimensions and Consequences of Prisoner Reentry.* Washington, D.C.: Urban Institute Press.

commonplace. However, the following contemporary, community-based programs highlight promising efforts that may provide valuable guidance to individuals who are newly released into society. Based in Kentucky, Prodigal Ministries is a Christian aftercare program that helps men and women avoid returning to prisons.[59] The program starts working with offenders six months prior to their release. Although potential participants must apply and undergo an interview process, Prodigal Ministries offers many services for individuals accepted into the program. In particular, former inmates are provided with residential housing and programs on an individual basis through case management, with a focus on recovery from substance abuse addictions.

Focused in Los Angeles, California, New Start LA provides transitional employment and job placement services to 100 former inmates at a time exiting the California prison system.[60] Potential participants must be referred by their parole officer. The New Start program utilizes community partnerships to assist formerly incarcerated individuals. The Chicago School of Psychology provides both individual and group counseling for participating former inmates, and Friends Outside Los Angeles County developed a job training program in cooperation with the One-Stop Employment Centers, with a specific focus on the special needs of former inmates. Also, representatives from One-Stop in South Los Angeles meet regularly with case managers to discuss the progress of participants. For those former inmates identified as lacking job skills, the One-Stop Employment Centers will provide paid transitional employment or job training to enhance employment outcomes. All One-Stop and partner staff complete a training certification program that is focused on formerly incarcerated individuals, in order to improve services to formerly incarcerated participants.

Offenders About to Reenter Society (OARS) is a reintegration program for Florida Department of Corrections inmates who are returning to Duval County (Jacksonville), Florida.[61] The program contains both pre- and post-release components and services. Prior to their release, inmates in OARS participate in cognitive behavioral programming, job skills training, parenting classes, and victim awareness sessions. Case management and planning, including input from both pre- and post-release staff members, are also essential components of this program. Following their release from a prison, former inmates are transported to the Jacksonville Reentry Center (JREC). Here job skills training and character development classes are provided. Assistance with housing, substance abuse, and transportation is also available.

These are just a handful of the many programs available around the United States that are designed to provide former inmates with support, assistance, and

---

59. Council of State Governments. 2013. Prodigal Ministries, Inc. Available at http://oldrm-rpc.csgjusticecenter.org/program_examples/prodigal-ministries-inc.

60. Council of State Governments. 2013. New Start LA. Available at http://oldrm-rpc.csgjusticecenter.org/program_examples/new-start-la.

61. Council of State Governments. 2013. Offenders About to Reenter Society (OARS). Available at http://oldrm-rpc.csgjusticecenter.org/program_examples/offenders-about-to-reenter-society-oars.

direction in establishing a crime-free, conventional, and healthy life. However, many of these programs only serve a small number of released offenders and largely or wholly depend on funding that is unstable, temporary, and almost always insufficient to allow full realization of program goals and objectives. In such cases, while some offenders reentering society may benefit, there remain many more individuals who are left to contend with reentry on their own.

Summary

Community corrections refers to a form of punishment whereby an offender is sentenced to a form of corrections, usually probation or parole, that allows him to remain in the community under some degree of monitoring and programming. There are two primary positions regarding the use of community corrections, those against community corrections and those for community corrections. The first argument of those against community corrections has two central tenets. The first is that convicted criminal offenders should be punished because they have broken the law; therefore, all privileges, such as community corrections, should be removed from offenders. The second tenet is that criminal offenders will likely reoffend, so they need to be placed into an institution that is free from distractions or "bad influences." Those for community corrections believe that overcrowding in jails and prisons makes alternative sentencing necessary. Additionally, the general objectives of probation are necessary and serve a vital role in achieving justice: reintegration of amenable offenders, providing protection for the community, furthering the goals of justice, and providing conditions to change offenders while meeting the preceding objectives. Proponents for community corrections also argue that it is cost-effective.

Probation is a sentence from a court and is now used widely across all jurisdictions, with 4.2 million individuals under probation in some form. Offenders placed on probation must follow strict conditions determined by the judge, with the most common restrictions being the following: They must not violate any laws, they must support their dependents, they must stay in the supervising jurisdiction, and they must report at scheduled dates and times to their assigned probation officer. Restitution and community service are two other common forms of probation: Restitution requires offenders to financially compensate their victims as determined by the judge, and community service involves manual labor that repays society as a whole.

Parole is another primary form of community corrections and is a period of supervision in the community following "early" release from prison. There are currently 820,000 individuals under parole, with most being white and male at 41 percent and 88 percent, respectively. Parole is usually a discretionary decision made by a politically appointed board of community members. When deciding whether or not to grant parole, parole boards have four main considerations: the likelihood of the inmate's recidivism, the welfare of society, the inmate's conduct when incarcerated, and the quality of the plans developed for parole supervision. Those who are granted parole are released under specific conditions for periods that range on average between two and seven years.

Key Terms

Aftercare
Community corrections
Community service
Due process
Due process rights
Hearing
Indeterminate sentence
Mandatory early release programs
Net-widening
Pardon
Parole eligibility date
Parole
Probation
Recidivism
Reentry
Restitution
Revocation of probation
Shock incarceration
Technical violation

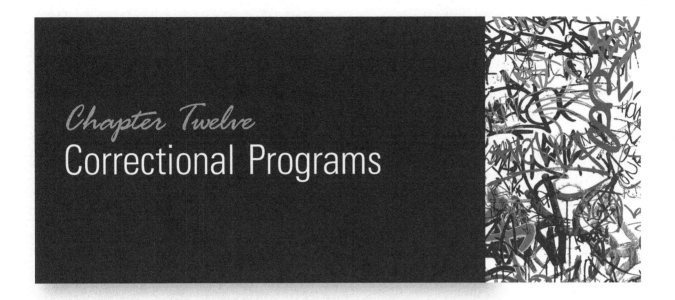

Chapter Twelve
Correctional Programs

When we speak about **correctional programs**, we are referring to all of the activities, structures, and efforts that are done in jail, prison, and even in community corrections programs for purposes of effecting a change in the behavior, thinking, and outlooks of offenders. As the foundation for "corrections" of offenders, programs are the efforts that accompany simply locking up or supervising known criminal offenders with an eye toward "correcting" their behavior. Programs are at the core of the rehabilitative ideology of corrections — if we are interested in changing people's behaviors for the better, it is likely that we need to do something with and for them to bring about such a change. This is not to say that programs cannot and do not also fit with our other guiding ideologies of corrections, but programs are usually most closely associated with the idea of rehabilitation.

Correctional programs: all of the activities, structures, and efforts that are done for purposes of affecting change in the behavior, thinking, and outlooks of offenders.

Programs in corrections are valuable for inmates, correctional officials, and the general public. If we see programs as focused on rehabilitating offenders, then obviously the public and community benefit from the existence of less crime. Offenders themselves benefit from obtaining the skills, tools, and perspectives to assist them in avoiding crime, and consequently all of the negative consequences that are likely to accompany crime (including being returned to corrections). And, correctional officials also benefit from the presence and activities of programs in that having inmates involved in program activities gives them something to do with their time, and therefore reduces the likelihood of such offenders becoming involved in misconduct (including violence) while incarcerated or under community supervision.

Most importantly, however, correctional programs are judged based on their ability to lead to lower rates of recidivism among offenders who participate and

Cost-effective: benefits derived from the program outweigh the costs.

complete programs. Recidivism is the nearly universal criterion that is used to determine the value and effectiveness of any activity that is done in corrections. For a correctional program to be seen as "good," it needs to show a reduction in the rate of criminality for those who participate in the program. A good program also needs to be **cost-effective**, meaning that the benefits derived from the program outweigh the costs — including financial costs, time, and allocation of resources — that are associated with having the program. Correctional officials are interested then in both being able to evaluate the effectiveness of the programs they currently offer for inmates and those they may consider adding to their repertoire of programs, and they are also interested in implementing programs in ways that provide the greatest likelihood of a program being successful.

What makes any type of correctional treatment program more likely to be successful is that it is properly focused on an appropriate target group, well planned, well conducted, and delivered by competent professionals. Another way to say this is to borrow from the terminology originally introduced by Andrews and Bonta, who say that in order to maximize the likelihood of a treatment program being effective, the program needs to include the principles of risk, need, responsivity, and professional discretion.[1] As they explain:

> Effective programs are those that match treatment intensity to offender risk and needs while attending to the characteristics of the population to be treated (e.g., cognitive abilities, mental health issues, personality, and learning styles). Last, programs must be managed by well-trained and experienced providers who are able to make sensible adjustments to curricula or other aspects of treatment and supervision as needed.[2]

With these principles guiding both the long-term planning and decisions of any program, as well as the day-to-day activities of a program, there is a significantly enhanced likelihood of a program being effective and showing positive and desired outcomes. This is by no means a guarantee of success, but it is an increase in the odds of success.

Also important is whether offenders in a particular program are there truly voluntarily, or whether they are there because of some level of coercion or compulsion. Typically, programs in which inmates participate voluntarily, rather than those in which they are compelled to participate, have been shown to be more effective. Voluntary participation may be attributed to several different types of motivation. First, some offenders truly do recognize that they need to change themselves and their behavior, and they see programs as a way to work toward such necessary changes. Second, inmates may believe (often at least somewhat accurately) that if they are seen by correctional officials as trying to change themselves, they may be more likely to be granted parole or some other

---

1. Donald A. Andrews and James Bonta. 2003. *The Psychology of Criminal Conduct,* 3d ed. Cincinnati: Anderson Publishing.
2. Robin Wilson and Pamela Yates. 2005. Sex Offender Programs, in Mary Bosworth (ed.), *Encyclopedia of Prisons and Correctional Facilities.* Thousand Oaks, CA: Sage, p. 892.

type of privilege. In this case, the motivation is not so much achieving a long-term change in themselves as it is achieving some short-term reward. Third, some inmates may see programs as simply something to do, and therefore seek out programs as a form of activity. In contrast, some programs for offenders are required either as a part of one's sentence, or as a component of what is required to even be considered for release or a change in housing assignment, privileges, etc. Under these conditions, offenders who enter programs are likely to be reluctant to participate, and to attend program activities but not be invested in truly participating or working toward the program's goals. In such situations, it should not be surprising that the chances of a program being successful with such an inmate are relatively low.

In the rest of this chapter, we will discuss a wide range of programs offered in corrections, including traditional approaches that are common (counseling, education, and substance abuse treatment), as well as several "programs" that are focused more on providing basic services for offenders and consequently allowing them to manage daily life in a healthy and potentially productive way. We begin with a "program" that is of this second variety, health care.

HEALTH CARE

Although not a "program" in the sense of an organized activity in which inmates participate so as to become less likely to recidivate, health care in correctional facilities is an important set of activities that are provided for inmates. Health care is important for several reasons. First, the courts have ruled that health care must be provided to inmates, and that it is the responsibility of correctional officials to ensure that all real and substantial health care needs of inmates are addressed. This is an outgrowth of the concept of *parens patriae* that was discussed earlier — because the state has removed the rights and possibilities of inmates to care for themselves, the state has the legal responsibility to provide care for inmates, just as parents must do so for their children.[3] Second, health care is important because it is a moral responsibility of corrections officials to see to it that inmates are healthy and not mistreated. Third, health care is important to security and custody. If inmates are not provided with care and kept in a healthy state, the inmate population is likely to act out in defiance or rebellion, protesting so as to try to compel the state to provide such care. And, fourth, health care is important to provide in order to try to contain the cost of operating a correctional facility. It is true that health care is very expensive, but providing things like preventive care and management of inmates' chronic illnesses and conditions is a way to limit the costs that would be encountered if diseases and other health conditions were left to deteriorate and were only addressed once they became serious and/or debilitating.

---

3. Estelle v. Gamble, 429 U.S. 97 (1976).

There are two significant challenges presented by the provision of health care in prisons and jails. First is the significant cost of such activities. Just as in free society, health care is expensive. Highly trained, professional providers (physicians, nurses, aides, technicians, pharmacists, etc.) need to be employed, medications are necessary (and expensive), equipment is needed for many tests and procedures (which are both expensive), and often specialized facilities are needed. All of this adds up to a huge expense associated with providing health care. When looking across the nation and across all correctional facilities, health care accounts for between 10 and 12 percent of the total cost of operating corrections. As expressed by one team of experts:

> Partly because they are sicker, partly because they have little opportunity for self-care, and partly because confinement and idleness promote excessive focus on their bodies, prisoners tend to require more, rather than less, health care. The causes of their illnesses often predate their incarceration and include unhealthy lifestyles, trauma and injury, malnutrition, heavy use of drugs and alcohol, and generally poor access to the health care delivery system.[4]

The second significant challenge associated with providing health care to inmates is that doing so can present security and custody concerns. Having drugs on site at the prison, the necessity of having at least some medical instruments (which can easily be made into weapons), and interactions of inmates with non-security staff — often without direct observation and supervision by security staff — can pose threats to the safe and orderly flow of activities in a facility.

Prior to the birth of the prisoners' rights movement (see Chapter 7), health care was provided more or less on the basis of whether a system or facility official believed that to do so was important and worth the effort. Very few prisons or jails had any health care providers on site, and health care was provided usually only once inmates were in dire circumstances. Many of the health care officials that were providing health care in correctional facilities had problems with licensing, competence, or other issues, and they turned to prisons and jails because they were unable to find work elsewhere. As one of the leading issues at the foundation of the prisoners' rights movement, access to health care came about as a result of inmates' using the courts to argue for the importance and necessity of health care. It was not until 1976 in the landmark case of *Estelle v. Gamble* that the U.S. Supreme Court ruled that health care is a right of inmates and a responsibility of correctional officials. The Court provided in this case one of the most well-known phrases regarding inmates' rights. According to the Court, "deliberate indifference to serious medical needs of prisoners constitutes the 'unnecessary and wanton infliction of pain' proscribed by the Eighth Amendment." This case opened the door for inmate

---

4. Tara Frechea and Kenneth L. Faiver. 2005. Health Care, in Mary Bosworth (ed.), *Encyclopedia of Prisons and Correctional Facilities.* Thousand Oaks, CA: Sage.

lawsuits that served to establish the boundaries of what is and is not required of correctional officials.

As one way to strive for consistency in what is and is not provided, and by whom, how, when, and where, following the ruling in *Ruiz v. Estelle* the American Medical Association established a set of standards outlining appropriate care for inmates and addressed the what, whom, how, when, and where. Today, these standards are widely known and adhered to, and ensure not only that inmates have access to health care, but that it is provided by competent, trained professionals, and approximates (if not exceeds) the standard of care available to most people in the free community.

So, what types of health care are provided in prisons and jails? Among the more important services that are provided are intake screening of inmates to identify health needs, provision of medication and therapy for chronic health problems (hypertension, diabetes, and HIV among the common issues), services for inmates who develop illnesses or injuries via "sick call" every day or every few days, and emergency care for suddenly occurring health and medical problems. Health care also encompasses things such as dental care (preventive and addressing acute problems), control of contagious diseases, suicide prevention, women's health care, including pregnancy care for the many women who come to prison or jail already pregnant, geriatric care, services for the disabled, and increasingly common today due to the long sentences many inmates serve, end-of-life care. Not all types of care or services can be provided inside of prisons and jails. And, in some cases (such as surgeries, specialized tests, etc.), inmates will be transported to health care settings outside of correctional facilities. When this happens, it requires at a minimum two security staff to escort and remain with the inmate at all times. As this suggests, provision of off-site health care is very time-consuming, resource-intensive, and a potential security threat.

Two developments in correctional health care address the special needs of the elderly and dying. These include the development in many state systems of nursing homes inside of prisons and hospice care. Nursing homes in prisons are very similar to those on the outside. When inmates serve a sentence that takes them well into their elderly years, they often need special care in order to do basic life activities, and often need assistance doing the basic day-to-day activities of self-care. In such situations, round-the-clock nursing care is necessary. Beginning in the 1980s, correctional systems recognized that they were not equipped to handle geriatric inmates in "regular" housing units, and needed to develop specialized, medical-care–focused facilities. Hence was born the in-prison nursing home.

Hospice is a form of care provided to individuals who are very close to the end of life. The emphasis in hospice care is palliative care, which includes comfort services that are designed to ease the pain and suffering of patients without any active attempts to prolong life or combat the disease, injury, or problem that has brought the patient to the point of imminent death. Hospice care in corrections also typically includes more open visitation conditions and times, pastoral services, post-death planning, and symptom management (as opposed to disease treatment). Hospice care is only provided to individuals who are terminally ill and with a medically advised limited life expectancy. While many hospice programs are place-based, they do not need to be; hospice is an approach to care, not necessarily a physical facility. Hospice is now fairly common in American prisons. This has not always been the case, however.

End-of-life health care is something that has only in recent decades become common in correctional health care. Prior to the landmark case of *Estelle v. Gamble*, inmates who were thought to be dying were usually moved to a segregation unit, an infirmary (if one existed), or simply left in their general population housing assignment, with little or no special or unique care and supervision. Today, this is not the case. The move toward recognizing the need for end-of-life health care and implementing such programs can be largely traced back to the early years of the HIV/AIDS epidemic in the United States. In the early years of HIV/AIDS, patients tended to die fairly quickly once their health deteriorated. And, the stigma that accompanied HIV/AIDS was great, so much so that persons, including inmates, with AIDS were shunned, avoided, and often left literally to themselves with no care or assistance. In prison, such a situation is very damaging to day-to-day operations, and it became obvious that something needed to be done for such inmates. Hospice care became the norm.

COUNSELING AND THERAPEUTIC PROGRAMS

When asked to name what they believe are programs offered in prisons and jails for rehabilitating inmates, most people would name some type of counseling program very early in their list. Counseling is something that many of us are familiar with, and something that we know is about helping individuals to recognize, cope with, and overcome their personal problems. There is a logical fit in the eyes of many Americans between being a criminal offender and being able to benefit from some type of counseling. Counseling, or therapeutic services, can come in a variety of forms and fashions, and can approach interactions with patients in different ways and for different types of intended outcomes. In this section, we will review several of the types of approaches and structures that are used in corrections.

The main type of therapeutic service that we find in corrections, and that is what most people are thinking about when they talk about "counseling" for inmates, is psychological services. When psychological services are provided in prisons and jails, it is done for two basic purposes. First, they are offered for purposes of attempting to rehabilitate offenders; the goal here is to work with an inmate about how he thinks, perceives the world, processes information, and subsequently acts on those thoughts, perceptions, and processes. Second, psychological services are offered because they are important in providing a means for officials to better manage a correctional facility.

Not surprisingly, the provision of psychological services for inmates became popular and widespread during the rehabilitation era of the 1960s and 1970s.

Today, almost all prisons have at least one psychologist on staff, as do many larger jails. Although in the early years of psychological services' growth in corrections, persons with masters degrees were considered acceptable and appropriate, today it is the norm to expect such services to be provided by, or at the least to have their provision supervised by, doctorate-level trained psychologists.

The type of services that psychologists and counselors provide in prisons and jails include not only individual therapeutic sessions with inmates, but also assessments of individuals' psychological and mental health needs (including at the time of intake to a facility or system), testing (for identifying care needs and intellectual, emotional, and cognitive deficiencies), and treatment for a full range of issues and problems. Included in the range of issues that are frequently addressed are substance abuse, suicidality, anxiety, depression, bipolar disorder, and adjustment issues.

Therapy and services provided to inmates come in two basic forms: individual and group therapy. Almost all inmates who receive mental health services receive at least some of their treatment in group therapy settings. The most commonly provided type of therapy in corrections is **cognitive behavioral therapy**. This is an approach to counseling and therapy that "is an action-oriented form of psychosocial therapy that assumes that maladaptive, or faulty, thinking patterns cause maladaptive behavior and 'negative' emotions. . . . The treatment focuses on changing an individual's thoughts (cognitive patterns) in order to change his or her behavior and emotional state."[5] In other words, cognitive behavioral therapy addresses how people think about issues and works with them to consider alternative ways of processing and reacting to issues in their world. Cognitive behavioral therapy is also recognized as one of the most effective means of correctional treatment, and as will be addressed in Chapter 14, is considered one of the programs with the most scientific evidence behind it, although it is recognized to have most efficacy when conducted outside of correctional facilities.

Cognitive behavioral therapy: an approach to counseling and therapy that is an action-oriented form of psychosocial therapy that focuses on changing the thoughts of offenders in order to change their behavior and emotional state.

Group therapy involves at least one individual leader (a staff person, usually a trained mental health professional) and anywhere from two to a couple of dozen inmates. Although the size of groups will vary across institutions and time, best practices in mental health call for groups to have ten or fewer members. However, necessity (due to staffing, number of inmates with mental health needs, and fiscal realities) means that groups of such size are fairly rare in corrections. Group therapy activities are typically educational or focused on skill development, although discussions of individuals' issues and problems can consume a substantial proportion of time in group. Individual therapy is almost always a supplement to group therapy, and is reserved for inmates with especially acute disturbances and issues, or unique problems, or for those who encounter a crisis point in their mental illness and/or recovery.

---

5. *The Free Dictionary*. No date. Cognitive-Behavioral Therapy. Available at http://medical-dictionary.thefreedictionary.com/cognitive-behavioral+therapy.

Because of the wide range of issues with which inmates present, and the financial reality of psychological services units in corrections being relatively small in regard to personnel, such professionals need to be able to address many different types of issues, and in different ways. Although most would argue that there is a critical need for more mental health staff, nationally the ratio of psychologists to inmates is approximately 1 to 750.[6] One of the unfortunate realities of the low staffing level and the security and custody needs that are of paramount importance in all correctional facilities is that mental health providers spend a great deal of their time on administrative tasks, with some estimates suggesting that at least one-third of such professionals' work time is devoted to things such as staff supervision, report writing, and consultation, training, and meetings with institutional officials.

All mental health providers working in correctional facilities face a variety of obstacles to the success of their rehabilitative efforts. These obstacles include, at the core, the fact that their patients are effectively involuntary patients or clients. It is well known that voluntary participation in therapy is much more likely to be successful. However, inmates are either forced into participation or many times at least subtly coerced through institutional expectations and/or expectations that participation may affect early release opportunities. Related to this is the issue that by their very nature as institutional staff persons, mental health providers are seen as members of the institution's administration, and therefore likely viewed with skepticism and suspicion. Such a relationship works directly contrary to therapeutic goals. Trust in one's counselor or therapist is essential to personal growth and change, yet in the correctional setting trust is nearly, if not completely, impossible to establish. And, the physical and social contexts of prisons and jails are often at odds with what we know are best practices for psychological services and treatment.

In addition to psychological services, a more specialized form of mental health care is also provided in most correctional facilities, psychiatric services. **Psychiatric services** differ from psychological and counseling services in that they are medically based and provided by professionals (psychiatrists and psychiatric nurses) with medical training. One of the most important differences between a psychologist and a psychiatrist is that a psychiatrist can prescribe medications for patients. Psychiatric services come in three basic varieties in correctional facilities. First, some services are provided on an emergency basis for inmates with acute crisis or disorientation. Second, some services are provided in specialized mental health units or facilities, for inmates with significant and long-term mental health problems. Third, many psychiatric services look very much like psychological services, and center on counseling and therapy, although they are supplemented with medication.

Psychiatric services: medically based programming provided by professionals with medical training aimed at providing emergency and routine psychiatric services to individuals.

[6] Kathryn M. Campbell. 2005. Psychological Services, in Mary Bosworth (ed.), *Encyclopedia of Prisons and Correctional Facilities*. Thousand Oaks, CA: Sage.

Providing psychiatric services and care for inmates is not without controversy, and there are problems related to implementation/practice in a secure correctional setting. These problems are summarized by one observer:

> The conflictual nature of the role of prison psychiatry creates particular problems for care, including the voluntary nature of psychiatric treatment, informed consent, and confidentiality. A key principle in clinical practice is that persons considering treatment should be informed about the nature of treatment and have the right to refuse such treatments. However, prisoners do not enter correctional facilities voluntarily. Furthermore, depending upon the circumstances and jurisdiction, they may not have the right to refuse assessment and/or treatment. Even in situations where prisoners are entitled to say no, their unwillingness to engage in treatment may be used against them such as during their parole hearing. Thus, the degree to which prisoners can consent to treatment without coercion is a continual concern.
>
> The question of consent is compounded by the fact that correctional mental health staff cannot guarantee to prisoners that their discussions will remain confidential. There are various occasions when a staff member must report a conversation to security and the administration. This is particularly true if the nature of the discussion suggests that the prisoner poses a threat to others, themselves, or the security of the institution.[7]

Although there may be problems with delivery of such services, and some important aspects of the relationship between provider and patient/client differ from that on the outside, the value and importance of psychiatric treatment remains. In 2000, the Bureau of Justice Statistics reviewed mental health treatment and needs in state prisons and reported that fully 13 percent of inmates were receiving some form of therapy/counseling and 10 percent were taking at least one psychotropic medication on a regular basis.[8] Perhaps not surprising, inmates housed in maximum security level institutions were more likely both to be receiving counseling or therapy (14.9%) and to take prescribed psychotropic medications (11.5%) than inmates in either medium (12.6%, 9.8%) or minimum security (9.3%, 5.8%) institutions. In short, mental health services are important for both the well-being of inmates and the management of correctional facilities, are commonly utilized by inmates, and are challenging for effective and efficient operation.

Substance Abuse Treatment

One of the most frequently engaged in programs in prisons and jails is substance abuse treatment. With fully 68 percent of jail inmates known to have

---

7. Kathleen Kendall. 2005. Psychiatric Care, in Mary Bosworth (ed.), *Encyclopedia of Prisons and Correctional Facilities*. Thousand Oaks, CA: Sage.

8. Allen Beck and Laura M. Maruschak. 2001. *Mental Health Treatment in State Prisons, 2000*. Washington, D.C.: Bureau of Justice Statistics.

dependence (not just use or abuse, but an addiction) on alcohol or drugs,[9] substance abuse treatment is a very important and necessary program in corrections. Drugs (other than alcohol) are more likely to be the substance on which inmates have dependence, but alcohol is more likely to be abused (used in excess and in ways that have negative consequences for users, but without physical dependence). When looking at types of offenders, we see that inmates convicted of either drug or property offenses (73% each) are more likely than violent (67%) or public-order (66%) offenders to be identified as being addicted. However, perhaps even more telling is that 50 percent of all jail inmates serving time in jail for a criminal conviction were under the influence of alcohol or drugs at the time of the offense for which they are incarcerated. While these numbers are quite large, it is notable that the total number of openings in institutional substance abuse programs can accommodate only about 10 to 15 percent of these inmates. This is due not to a lack of care, concern, or interest on the parts of correctional officials but primarily due to expense and limited resources.

When looking at the demographics of jail inmates and their alcohol and drug addiction, we see that women (51.8%) are more likely than men (44.3%) to be identified as an addict. Assessment of race shows that white inmates (55.4%) are more likely than African Americans (40.4%), Hispanics (35.7%), or inmates of other races (45.4%) to be diagnosed with dependence on alcohol or drugs. And, when looking at age, we find that the highest rate of addiction is seen among inmates ages 35 to 44 (50.4%). Younger inmates ages 24 or younger (40.3%) and 25 to 34 (48.1%) as well as older inmates, such as those ages 45 to 54 (41.7%), and age 55 or older (23.1%) also have high rates of addiction, although slightly lower than the 35 to 44 age group.[10]

Looking at treatment for jail inmates' substance abuse problems and addictions, we find that fully two-thirds (67.9%) of inmates diagnosed with alcohol or drug dependence have been in treatment at least once in their lifetime, with equal numbers have been in a formal, structured treatment program or in a self-help program (most often Alcoholics Anonymous or Narcotics Anonymous).[11] These previous engagements in substance abuse treatment are highly likely to have been while previously incarcerated (52.8% of all addicted inmates). This suggests two important facts. First, rather obviously the success of such programs must be questioned, as many inmates have participated in treatment, but many subsequently continue to use, become involved in criminal behavior accompanying their use, and return to treatment when subsequently reincarcerated. The second important point that is raised here is that substance abuse treatment programs are common, and popular among inmates, in jails and prisons.

---

9. Jennifer C. Karberg and Doris James. 2005. *Substance Abuse, Dependence and Treatment of Jail Inmates, 2002.* Washington, D.C.: Bureau of Justice Statistics.
10. *Ibid.*
11. *Ibid.*

Treatment programs that are offered in corrections come in several varieties. In almost all cases, such programs include (or only include) group counseling. Individual counseling is sometimes included, but is often not possible due to limitations on resources and the large number of inmates to be served. In rare instances, corrections-based substance abuse treatment programs will involve inmates' families in some treatment activities. The substance abuse treatment programs in prisons and jails are based on one of three approaches to substance abuse and treatment: the disease model, an educational model, or a social learning and cognitive behavioral model of treatment.[12] The disease model is based on the idea that addicts have a disorder rendering them incapable of controlling their drinking or drug use. The emphasis in treatment programs based on this model is on teaching individuals to recognize their disease, accept that they have a disease, and to understand that abstinence is the only way for them to avoid addiction and the range of negative social consequences that accompany addiction. Most self-help programs, including Alcoholics Anonymous, are based on a disease model approach. Research on the efficacy of disease model–based substance abuse treatment programs is mixed, with some research supporting the success of programs such as Alcoholics Anonymous, and other specific programs being seen as less frequently successful.

Alcoholics Anonymous (AA) is perhaps the most common program offered in American jails and prisons, with Narcotics Anonymous also (but not quite as) common. The concept of AA is one that is widely known in society, widely believed to be effective, requires almost no resources from correctional authorities (a place to meet, time to meet, and perhaps security), and can be led by inmates themselves. The one potential stumbling block for AA/NA programs in correctional settings is that participants must find and regularly interact with a sponsor. Some inmates, most often in prisons, are able to identify another inmate to fulfill this role, but there is often a limited pool from which to draw. Inmates may locate and rely on sponsors from outside the institution, but these sponsors may be less easily accessed and interacted with less frequently. Evaluations of the efficacy of AA specifically have shown success for the approach. However, success in AA is largely dependent on participants voluntarily participating; when individuals are coerced into attending AA, there are low levels of success.[13]

The educational model approachs to substance abuse treatment have their foundation in the idea that people drink and take drugs (especially at abusive levels) because they do not recognize nor understand the negative effects of alcohol and drugs, or do not see a link between their use and negative consequences. Therefore, such programs seek to teach program participants about the harmful health and social consequences of substance use. Evaluation research

---

12. Kristie R. Blevins and Jennifer A. Pealer. 2005. Alcohol Treatment Programs, in Mary Bosworth (ed.), *Encyclopedia of Prisons and Correctional Facilities*. Thousand Oaks, CA: Sage.

13. R.J. Kownacki and W.R. Shadish. 1999. Does Alcoholics Anonymous Work? The Results from a Meta-Analysis of Controlled Experiments. *Substance Use & Misuse* 34, 1897-1916.

finds low levels of success (e.g., abstinence and no criminal recidivism) for educational models of treatment, especially for individuals who use at very high levels and consistently.[14] Incarcerated individuals with substance abuse problems or addictions are considered very high risk for continued substance use, and programs that emphasize teaching the harms that may accompany substance use without also teaching means of changing behaviors and thoughts are only minimally likely to be effective.

Social learning and cognitive behavioral models of substance abuse treatment offer some of the most promising approaches and specific programs. The basic idea of this approach is that behaviors and thinking that accompanies behaviors are learned both directly through experience and vicariously through observing the actions of actions. As a result, some people learn nonproductive, harm-inducing ways of acting and thinking, and need to be provided with guidance in developing more pro-social, positive behaviors, thinking patterns, and social skills. When individuals know of and begin to implement new thinking and acting patterns, then these are positively reinforced, with the goal being to associate positive outcomes with new ways of acting and thinking. Token economies and behavioral contracts that include rewards for desired behaviors are common means of implementing treatment in this vein.

In addition to these treatment programs, many jails also provide for detoxification. Individuals who arrive in a facility actively using and dependent on alcohol or drugs need to physically adjust to not obtaining and ingesting any alcohol or drugs. For those who are truly addicted, the absence of intoxicating substances pushes their body to react sometimes violently. Physical adjustment to the absence of alcohol and drugs can be a very unpleasant experience in any setting. When combined with the conditions in jail, detoxification can be a dangerous time for inmates both physically and psychologically. As such, special detoxification units, often including health care personnel, are present in many larger jails. In some very large jails, methadone maintenance may also be offered, either as a way to wean the addict off his use or as a longer-term practice.

Sex Offender Programs

Recent years have seen a major outcry and near widespread panic about the presence of sex offenders in communities. Numerous new policies and practices — such as sex offender registration, community notification, residential restriction laws, longer sentences, mandatory lifetime supervision, and other issues — have been developed and implemented in recent years as ways to address the public's concern about sex offenders. Going along with these developments has been a growth and renewed interest and focus on treatment programs for sex offenders. Today, it is nearly impossible for a sex offender to get out

---

14. Blevins and Pealer, supra n.12.

of prison or off of community supervision without successfully completing a sex offender treatment program.

Sex offenders account for between 15 and 25 percent of the populations of most prisons in the United States. Many people would consider sex offenders as the "worst of the worst," and stigmatization is quite common and strong for such offenders. Even many sex offenders themselves believe that sex offenders as a group are perhaps the most despicable of all offenders.[15] One of the foundational issues in the stigmatization and fear of sex offenders is the belief that such offenders are highly likely to recidivate. However, this is a false fear. Sex offenders have the lowest rate of recidivism of almost all groups of offenders in the United States.[16] Whether this low rate of recidivism is something that is "natural" for such offenders or is the result of positive effects of treatment is not known. But, because of the fear that the public has about sex offenders, sex offender treatment is widely available and today one of the more common types of programs available in prisons, jails, and community corrections.

As with the other varieties of programs we have discussed above, sex offender treatment programs may emphasize a disease model, an educational approach, or, what is most common, a cognitive behavioral approach. All programs need to include assessment of a sex offender's treatment needs, which usually means examining their sexual fetishes, personality, sexual histories, and thoughts and fantasies. Today, there are several actuarial instruments commonly used to assess sex offenders, each of which has been validated and shown to have strong predictive ability. When participating in treatment activities, the common cognitive behavioral models emphasize relapse prevention (learning to recognize the signs of behaviors moving toward sexually reoffending and how to stop that progression). Typically, a relapse prevention–focused program occurs in two phases. In the first phase, offenders engage in a process of self-evaluation and behavioral analysis that centers on breaking down one's thinking and behaviors into component parts, recognizing those that are unhealthy (directly related to sexual offending behaviors) and then rebuilding the offender's approach to the world in which he lives. This is about developing internal controls on behaviors. The second phase of a relapse prevention program is considered best offered or completed outside of a correctional facility, and focuses on practice of the skills and approach to the world developed in phase 1. Here offenders are supported by counselors and case managers, and increasingly loosely guided in their return to society and unsupervised actions.

Sex offender treatment is not without critics. Criticisms frequently center on two main ideas of such programs. The first criticism is that participation in such programs is rarely truly voluntary, and that especially for programs conducted

---

15. Richard Tewksbury and Matthew Lees. 2007. Perceptions of Punishment: How Registered Sex Offenders View Registries. *Crime & Delinquency* 53, 380-407.

16. Lisa Sample and T. Bray. 2003. Are Sex Offenders Dangerous? *Journal of Criminology and Public Policy*, 3, 59-82. Also see Lisa Sample and T. Bray. 2006. Are Sex Offenders Different? An Examination of Rearrest Patterns. *Criminal Justice Policy Review*, 17, 83-102.

inside of a prison, inmates can and do learn to "play the game" quickly and effectively. This means that while participating inmates may appear to be well immersed in the culture, language, and activities of such a program, they may be largely working to avoid making waves and to earn promised time off of their sentences.[17] In other words, some critics believe inmates participate in sex offender treatment as a ruse, in order to trick authorities into thinking that they have changed, although in reality they have gone along with a program without truly investing themselves in it.

A second criticism of sex offender programs is that they do not include sufficient aftercare. When an offender completes a sex offender treatment program in prison, he will usually be returned to a "regular" housing unit and work assignment. This means he likely experiences a rather sudden change from being immersed in a therapeutic community (see below) where support and accountability are constant factors in his life, to a world where this is absent, and what has been learned and gained in treatment is left unreinforced and unsupported. Even in the community, following program completion offenders are typically left to their parole or other forms of supervision, and provided little if any ongoing support. Here the influence of a disease model is clear: Once the disease is removed from one's body, there is no need for further intervention or assistance — the problem is considered to be gone.

Therapeutic Communities

Therapeutic communities: a program where inmates live together and are immersed in a culture that is based on recovery and healthy living, where all participants (inmate-residents and staff) are expected to hold one another accountable for their behaviors and decisions.

Therapeutic communities are a different form of substance abuse or sex offender treatment program where inmates live together and are immersed in a culture that is based on recovery and healthy living and where all participants (inmate-residents and staff) are expected to hold one another accountable for their behaviors and decisions. Within a therapeutic community, there is usually a system of rewards and sanctions that are used to encourage, discourage, and guide inmates' behaviors and to encourage progress toward recovery. As explained by one observer:

> [T]he ultimate goal of a therapeutic community is to help individuals recognize the dangers of addiction by identifying, expressing and managing feelings while learning personal and social responsibility. In addition to gaining employable skills, this involves creating a lifestyle of drug abstinence and the elimination of violent anti-social behavior.[18]

Therapeutic communities are not unique to prisons or jails, although correctional facilities are the most common places to find such treatment programs.

---

17. James B. Waldram. 2012. *Hound Pound Narrative: Sex Offender Habilitation and the Anthropology of Therapeutic Intervention.* Berkeley, CA: University of California Press.
18. Jason Ulsperger. 2005. Therapeutic Communities, in Mary Bosworth (ed.), *Encyclopedia of Prisons and Correctional Facilities.* Thousand Oaks, CA: Sage.

The approach was first developed in the 1940s by a British psychiatrist and focused on working with military veterans and their adjustment to post-war society. The approach came to the United States and the field of substance abuse in 1958 in San Francisco with the famous Synanon program. Entry to corrections came in 1966 when the Federal Correctional Facility in Danbury, Connecticut and New York's Clinton Prison began using a therapeutic community model for drug addicts. Two decades later, building on the identified successes of the early therapeutic communities, the federal Bureau of Justice Assistance offered funding to support the implementation and operation of prison-based therapeutic communities, and such programs grew rapidly. By the late 1990s, researchers and policy makers drew on the experiences of the existing therapeutic community programs to develop uniform standard operating procedures for prison-based TCs.

Standard procedures for therapeutic communities include programming and structure for participants that runs continuously, and all day long. In addition to group therapy and discussion sessions, typical TC schedules also include work assignments, individual counseling, a little bit of personal time, and educational classes. It is throughout the day, but especially during group sessions, that individual members confront one another about their behaviors, attitudes, and approaches to all aspects of their lives, focusing on helping one another to develop pro-social attitudes and behaviors, and to recognize and build barriers to a return to drug use. Being part of a therapeutic community involves numerous and often strict rules for day-to-day life, and participants are expected to both adhere to all rules and to hold one another accountable for adherence. As individuals progress through the program, they gain more privileges and responsibilities within the community, more or less progressing toward "regular" life.

Most therapeutic communities operate on a three-stage model. In the first stage, which typically lasts 30 days, there is a focus on introducing new members to the policies and procedures of the community and a striving for establishing trust. New community members are also expected to make a personal assessment of themselves, their life circumstances, and their needs. It is intended that during this phase of the program new participants will begin to understand addiction itself and their own addiction, and will make a commitment to genuinely seek recovery.

Stage 2 is the primary treatment phase. At this point, the staff of the program has implemented a structured model of activities that reflect pro-social, non-criminal, substance-free values and attitudes. Throughout this longest period of the program, individuals live, work, and participate in the community, and move toward changes in attitudes and behaviors. Finally, stage 3 is the reentry phase, during which individuals transition out of the cloistered world of the TC and back to larger society. In prison, many times this may mean a return to general population in the facility, although ideally, the reentry phase would coincide with release from incarceration.

Therapeutic communities show fairly high levels of success for inmates who complete the program of treatment. However, they also have high dropout rates, as many inmates find it too difficult to adjust to the strict and regimented culture of the community and/or also find it too challenging to live in a community where everyone is expected to continually critique and comment on one's attitude and behavior. Therapeutic communities also suffer from high costs; to operate separate housing units, where staffing patterns are higher than in most other areas of an institution, is a more expensive approach to correctional management. However, for inmates who are genuinely interested in change, a therapeutic community offers an escape from the culture, violence, and pressures of "regular prison." As with most treatment programs, it is the truly motivated inmates who are most likely to succeed.

EDUCATION

One of the oldest, as well as simplest and for most people most logical of treatment programs offered in nearly all correctional institutions is education. From the initial use of incarceration as a sentence in the Walnut Street Jail, educational programming has been present in American correctional institutions. The earliest forms of education were based around religious teaching, and included Bible study and teaching inmates to read, using the Bible. Walnut Street Jail is not only the first real correctional institution in the United States, but it is also the first correctional institution to have a school (opened in 1798) and a library (originally with approximately 100 books).[19] Education for inmates has continued to be recognized as important. In 1870, when the National Prison Congress met for the first time and laid out its Declaration of Principles, it included a call for education for offenders, and since that time correctional officials have stood by this idea and continued to have a multitude of forms of educational programs for inmates.

Correctional education: the collective programming options aimed at developing offender skills including the following areas: fundamentals of knowledge, English as a second language (ESL), vocational training programs, post-secondary education, and graduate-level education.

Educational programs in prisons and jails, commonly referred to as **correctional education**, include everything on the continuum from basic literacy programs where inmates learn the true fundamentals of knowledge, including how to read; special education; English as a second language (ESL); and vocational training programs, to post-secondary and even graduate-level university programs. Most inmates who participate in educational programs are involved in adult basic education programs or GED programs.

Educational programs are seen as beneficial to both inmates and institutional officials and staff. At the inmate level, the benefits are rather obvious — without an education it is extremely difficult to find a job, do many daily tasks, and simply function in modern society. But, for correctional officials educational programs have also been shown to be important for maintaining institutional control and ensuring a smoothly running institution. Even the

19. John R. Dizon and Kenneth Mentor. 2005. Education, in Mary Bosworth (ed.), *Encyclopedia of Prisons and Correctional Facilities*. Thousand Oaks, CA: Sage.

United States Department of Justice has openly recognized the dual values of correctional education programs "as both an opportunity for inmates to improve their knowledge and skills and as a correctional management tool that encourages inmates to use their time in a constructive manner."[20] Inmates who are enrolled in educational programs are known to be less likely to be involved in misconduct, as well as show lower levels of recidivism, higher levels of employment post-release, and overall better adjustment to incarceration.

Because of the widespread recognition of the value and importance of education, and the strong belief in its role in reducing recidivism, a number of states (26 at last count, and the federal Bureau of Prisons) mandate that any inmates who either test below a certain level of academic achievement or who have not completed more than a specified level of formal education must participate in educational programming. In some systems, inmates who do not have either a high school diploma or a GED are required to be in school either until they earn their GED or are released.

Prison-based college programs, which are offered either through traditional, in-classroom classes taught by regular college and university faculty members, or correspondence courses, are a point of controversy for many observers. Until 1994, inmates were eligible to apply for and receive Pell grants to pay for their education. However, in 1994 the Violent Crime Control Act of 1994 passed Congress and included provisions removing prison inmates from eligibility. Not surprisingly, this led to a dramatic drop in the number of college programs available in prisons, and all but eliminated such programs. Whereas nearly 400 prison-based college programs were operating in the early 1990s, by 1997 there were fewer than 10 such programs remaining. Today, there are more programs, as a number of states have created funding mechanisms that allow inmates to compete for and use scholarship monies to pay for higher education. For many observers, the idea of a prison inmate getting a "free" college education is abhorrent. For others, it is recognized as an important opportunity, which has been shown to have the most dramatic effects on recidivism and institutional misconduct of any type of correctional education programs. Some studies suggest that in comparison with a state's overall rate of recidivism, the recidivism rates for offenders with college degrees is 70 to 90 percent lower.

At the other end of the educational continuum, literacy programs are very rarely opposed by the public. Such programs are relatively inexpensive to deliver, and the importance of being able to read and write is unchallenged in our culture. The need for literacy programs is very obvious among inmates. Estimates run as high as 75 percent for functional illiteracy (having skills that are inadequate to meet the needs of day-to-day functioning) and 20 percent for complete illiteracy (not being able to read or write at all). Clearly, the chances for an individual who is illiterate and has a criminal record to get a job and

20. Michelle Tolbert. 2002. *State Correctional Education Programs.* Washington, D.C.: National Institute for Literacy.

remain law-abiding once returned to the community are very, very slim. Therefore, support for literacy programs in jails and prisons is widespread.

VOCATIONAL EDUCATION

Vocational education: hands-on and classroom training provided to inmates to help with job skills and to teach how to do a particular type of job.

Another type of program that has been offered in prisons since the very beginning of American corrections is **vocational education**. These are programs that provide training to inmates in job skills, teaching how to do a particular type of job, and often include both classroom instruction as well as hands-on work experience of actually practicing the skills and doing the job for which one is being trained. There are many different types of jobs, or vocations, for which in-prison training programs are provided. These range from very traditional types of work such as farming, carpentry, and automobile mechanics to more technical types of jobs such as computer repair, data entry, and computer graphics.

Vocational education programs are considered one of the practical types of programs for inmates in that they provide something directly useful and beneficial to inmates — skills that will facilitate them getting employment upon release from incarceration. Just as with academic education, vocational education is seen as a form of rehabilitation that is logical and practical.

The first vocational training in American corrections was provided at the Walnut Street Jail in Philadelphia. At Walnut Street, inmates were taught such practices as masonry, weaving, and shoe making. Each of these were skills that were not only transferrable to the free world outside of prison, but were also skills that correctional administrators could benefit from — inmates worked on the physical facility of the institution and made products used by the inmate population. This idea of mutual benefit has been common throughout history of vocational education programs. The production of clothing, shoes, linens, food, and other consumable products that are used by inmates allows correctional administrators to save money by not purchasing such commodities, and also simultaneously provides inmates with a set of skills that they can later use to earn a living.

The idea of teaching inmates a job skill was most heavily emphasized during the reformatory movement and era of rehabilitation in American corrections. Here the ideas of training fit well with the guiding ideologies of the times for what corrections should be achieving. One problem with vocational education programs, however, has been that it has always been difficult to recruit and retain enough qualified instructors to staff such programs. Not only must instructors know the skills they are teaching very well, but they must also be able to effectively teach, they must be adept at working with inmates, and they must want to work inside the structured and unfamiliar environment of the prison or jail. And, typically, they must be willing to do such a job for a wage that is less than they would likely make outside of prison.

While academic programs in prisons and jails, especially college-level programs, were dramatically reduced in the late 1990s, there has been significantly less reduction in vocational programs in recent years. Although funding can be a problem (as it is for just about everything in corrections), vocational training programs have been able to be linked to the old idea of bring outside companies into correctional institutions to simultaneously teach and train inmates in job skills and have them work on making products for the company to market and sell. A number of different types of skills and products have been the focus of these types of joint efforts, with perhaps the most memorable of recent times being the manufacture and sale of Prison Blues denim clothing in the Oregon Department of Corrections that began in 1989 and the training of inmates for working in customer call centers in several federal Bureau of Prisons institutions.

As with all correctional programs, the most important aspect in the eyes of many observers is whether such programs lead to a reduction in offender recidivism. For vocational education programs there does appear to be a significant reduction, of at least 20 percent compared with recidivism rates of inmates who do not participate in such programs.[21] As such, vocational education programs are commonly viewed in very positive light by observers both inside and outside of corrections. Such programs are logical, practical, and less costly than many other types of programming options, and they address offenders' needs and show a positive outcome on the issue of recidivism.

RELIGIOUS PROGRAMS AND FAITH-BASED INITIATIVES

A programming focus that both has a very long history in American corrections and has been making a noticeable resurgence in the last three decades is religious programming. **Religious programs** in prisons and jails come in two distinct forms. First, there are structures and activities in all American prisons and jails that provide opportunities for religious worship, counsel, study, and activities for inmates, in much the same way that any church in the free community would do. Second, there are programs spanning the continuum from isolated, short-term and one-activity-focused efforts all the way through self-contained housing units inside of prisons being based on religious principles that are referred to as faith-based programming.

Religious programs: either provide opportunities for religious worship inside jails or prisons, or provide short-term and one-activity-focused efforts based upon religious principles inside self-contained housing units in a jail or a prison.

Actual religious observances and services in prison and jail, like education and vocational education, trace their roots back to the Walnut Street Jail. Recall that the Walnut Street Jail, and in fact all of the early Pennsylvania systems of corrections, were begun by the Quakers. In this model of corrections, offenders were expected to read and receive instruction in religious principles and also reflect on themselves and their behaviors and give penitence for their misdeeds.

21. David B. Wilson, Catherine A. Gallagher, and Doris L. MacKenzie. 2000. A Meta-Analysis of Corrections Based Education, Vocation and Work Programs for Adult Offenders. *Journal of Research in Crime and Delinquency*, 37, 347-368. Also see Albert R. Roberts. 2005. Vocational Training Programs, in Mary Bosworth (ed.), *Encyclopedia of Prisons and Correctional Facilities*. Thousand Oaks, CA: Sage.

Throughout most of American history, Christian principles have been highly valued, respected, and viewed as the proper way to handle oneself morally and ethically. As such, a common belief throughout our nation's history has been that criminal offenders have lost their way morally and ethically, and one obvious way to address their shortcomings and social needs has been to provide them with religious opportunities and instruction. As discussed in Chapter 7, Prisoners' Rights, one of the fundamental rights of prison inmates (as with all Americans) is religious freedom and opportunities for worship. The Supreme Court has ruled that inmates have the right to freely practice religion (with a few exceptions for purposes of maintaining security), including any "legitimate" religion.[22] This right is based on the First Amendment to the United States Constitution, which states (in part) that the "Congress shall make no law respecting an establishment of religion, or prohibiting the free exercise thereof." This also means that while correctional officials may not prohibit inmates from religious practices, they also may not force inmates to participate in religious activities.

Most of the direct influence of religion in prisons and jails has been achieved through the work of correctional chaplains. In the early decades of American history, prison chaplains held positions of significant responsibility and importance. With religious groups being those who established and operated many early correctional institutions, it was only logical that the leader of the religious group involved was a key figure. In fact, in many early prisons and jails, chaplains not only provided religious services, instruction, and counseling to inmates, but they also doubled as academic teachers and administrative staff.

Today, prison and jail chaplains are educated in both religious teachings and lay subjects, and are expected to serve the needs of the multitude of different faiths represented among inmates. Chaplains of the twenty-first century are expected to be able to address the needs of all inmates, and to understand and be able to assist inmates in finding ways to worship their own religions within the restrictions of the correctional facility.

While their main purpose remains to deliver religious programs and provide pastoral care to inmates, they also have a role to play with staff, inmates' families, and visitors. Chaplains often play a critical role in coordinating volunteers inside of prisons and jails; most people who volunteer in correctional institutions do so within the parameters of religious services.[23] Chaplains may also provide opportunities for inmates' families to receive information about their incarcerated loved one, and chaplains may serve as a communication avenue between inmates and their families, especially regarding news of deaths and other emotionally laden issues and events. Chaplains also avail themselves of institutional

---

22. Africa v. Pennsylvania, 662 F.2d 1025 (3d Cir. 1981); Fulwood v. Clemmer, 206 F. Supp. 370 (D.D.C. 1962); Theriault v. Carlson, 339 F. Supp. 375 (N.D. Ga. 1972); Remmers v. Brewer, 361 F. Supp. 537 (S.D. Iowa 1973).

23. Richard Tewksbury and Dean Dabney. 2005. Prison Volunteers: Profiles, Motivations, Satisfaction. *Journal of Offender Rehabilitation*, 40, 173-183.

staff, and typically present themselves as a resource for all members of a correctional institution community.

It is important to acknowledge that some correctional officials (and outside observers as well) believe that many inmates use religion in a disingenuous way while incarcerated. Viewing religion as a "con game" by inmates, these observers are skeptical of the many inmates who claim to have "found God" while incarcerated, and who consequently center their in-prison life around activities and programs associated with the institutional chapel. In this regard, it is thought by some that inmates hope prison administrators and parole authorities will view their religious practice as an attempt to become moral and law-abiding citizens, and hence reward them with more privileges while incarcerated and a positive review at their time of possible release (e.g., parole). It may also be that some inmates use religion and religious program opportunities to better their in-prison situations. Such inmates may have access to interact with outsiders (including women) who come to prison to volunteer in religious programs and to access special religiously related food and recreational resources. For other inmates, an immersion in religious activities may be a way to attempt to avoid interactions with other inmates whom they fear and wish to avoid.

The second model of religious programming in corrections is widely referred to as the realm of *faith-based initiatives*. Such a term refers to

> a widespread effort among governmental and religious nonprofit agencies to incorporate religious activism into various social welfare programs, including the correctional system. . . . Faith-based initiatives encompass everything from programs designed to help religious organizations obtain federal funding for outreach activities to the actual implementation of prison ministries.[24]

In this regard, religiously inspired programs run a wide gamut from specific efforts to provide inmates with a particular skill or perspective or experience all the way to providing what is all but equivalent to a therapeutic community that is founded on religious principles. Here the structure and operations of a prison unit may be based on religious teachings and practices. Such approaches are still relatively rare in American corrections, and may be met by legal challenges (as forcing inmates to live and participate in such a program may violate the First Amendment prohibition against establishment of religion).

Most faith-based initiatives in correctional facilities are offender oriented, and attempt to create an environment inside of a correctional facility that fosters respect for both a higher power and for others. This is done while also teaching the moral principles of a particular faith. The ultimate goal of such programs, from a corrections perspective, is to reduce reoffending through the influence of religion on the individual offender. Not surprisingly, the research looking at

---

24. Emily J. Salisbury and Jennifer S. Trager. 2005. Faith-Based Initiatives, in Mary Bosworth (ed.), *Encyclopedia of Prisons and Correctional Facilities*. Thousand Oaks, CA: Sage.

religion in prison and jails is supportive of such practices. Inmates who participate in religious programming are generally less likely to be involved in misconduct while incarcerated and also less likely to recidivate upon release from incarceration.[25]

FAMILY-BASED PROGRAMS

In addition to seeking to prepare inmates for returning to the community with job skills, education, and good physical and mental health, one common value in corrections is to also return offenders to the community with a social support system that can assist them in living a law-abiding life. When someone is incarcerated, they tend to lose their social contacts, often having at least some friends and family members cut off all interactions with them, either for the time that they are incarcerated or even permanently. Even for those people who wish to, maintaining a relationship and contact with an incarcerated loved one can be difficult. This means that maintaining a system of relationships that can support one — both while adjusting to imprisonment and later adjusting to one's return to the community — can be very difficult.

In an effort to overcome these barriers to supportive relationships with people on the outside, correctional officials provide for several ways for contacts to be maintained between inmates and their loved ones. Individuals may stay in contact via letters sent through the mail — although for many inmates literacy is a problem, which makes this a difficult method of maintaining contact. In nearly all prisons and jails, inmates also have the option of making telephone calls to people on the outside. There are no opportunities for inmates to receive calls, but they may make collect telephone calls from phones that are typically located in dayrooms or other public places in an institution. The telephones available to inmates, however, are provided under a contract between a private telephone company and the department of corrections. The rates for calls on these telephones are higher than what most people pay, sometimes as much as 400 percent higher. And, only collect telephone calls can be made. This means that receiving a call from one's incarcerated loved one is very expensive and perhaps difficult to time.

A third option for maintaining contact and a relationship is for loved ones to visit their incarcerated friend or family member. Visitation is actually only a fairly recent development in the history of American corrections. In the earliest days of American corrections, the only visitors to inmates were clergy and in some jurisdictions representatives of Prisoner Aid Societies — charitable groups who came to prison to provide food, clothing, and other necessities in the days before corrections officials were required to provide such things. Visitation is also frequently misunderstood, and thought to be a "right" of inmates. It is not a right, it

25. *Ibid.*

is a privilege, and correctional officials have the discretion to restrict both whether particular inmates may receive visits and from whom they may receive visits. In most jurisdictions, inmates must submit to institutional officials a list of persons they wish to be placed on their "visitor list" (this is usually between 5 and 10 persons). Once an individual is requested to be put on an inmate's visitor list, that person will be checked for a criminal background or other issues that may be seen as a threat to security and custody before being approved. Once approved, visitors may visit with inmates during approved days and times, which will vary based on the institution. Most prison inmates today are allowed to have **contact visits**. These are visits in which the inmate and visitor may have limited physical contact — often limited to a brief hug upon arrival and when leaving and perhaps holding hands while together — and can visit without any type of physical barrier between them. Visits are typically conducted in a large room with tables and chairs, or occasionally in outdoor areas with chairs and picnic tables, with all inmates receiving visitors sharing the open space. Some institutions allow visitors to bring in food for the visit, but most only provide vending machines for food and drink during the visit.

Contact visits: visits in which the inmate and visitor may have limited physical contact and may have visits without any type of physical barrier between them.

Visits can be a very emotional time, for both inmates and their visitors. Research with prison visitors has shown that most visitors feel very emotional, nervous, and excited simultaneously when coming to visit a loved one.[26] Anticipation of seeing a loved one that lives in a different and not understood world can be stressful; travel to a prison can be a long, expensive, and difficult trip for many visitors; and the security procedures for being checked into the prison can also be highly stressful and in the eyes of many visitors unnecessary and demeaning.[27] It can be very difficult for loved ones to get to prison to visit, expensive to make the trip (especially for people without their own vehicles), and for some just too taxing physically and emotionally. While most prison inmates are eligible to receive visits, many do not receive them. One national study shows that 59 percent of parents in state prisons and 45 percent of parents in federal prisons have never had a visit from their children.[28]

In a few prisons in the United States, and much more commonly in other countries, inmates may be allowed to have **conjugal visits**. These are contact visits in which an inmate is allowed to visit with a spouse (regulations require one to be legally married) and children, for anywhere from a few hours to as long as three days. Conjugal visits have been a part of American corrections since at the least the mid-1800s, when Southern prisons allowed African-American

Conjugal visits: contact visits in which an inmate is allowed to visit with a spouse and children lasting from a few hours to as long as three days.

---

26. Richard Tewksbury and Matthew DeMichele. 2005. Going to Prison: A Prison Visitation Program. *The Prison Journal,* 85, 292-310.

27. Megan Comfort. 2003. In the Tube at San Quentin: The "Secondary Prisonization" of Women Visiting Inmates. *Journal of Contemporary Ethnography,* 32, 77-107. Richard Tewksbury, Matthew T. DeMichele, and Seana Golder. 2004. Significant Others Visiting Others: Sex and Relational Differences. *Journal of Crime and Justice,* 27, 101-118. Johnna Christian. 2005. Riding the Bus: Barriers to Prison Visitation and Family Management Strategies. *Journal of Contemporary Criminal Justice,* 21, 31-48.

28. Lauren Glaze and Laura Maruschak. 2010. *Parents in Prison and Their Children.* Washington, D.C.: Bureau of Justice Statistics.

(but typically not white) inmates to receive conjugal visits as a way to control sexual violence in prisons. Today, conjugal visits are relatively rare, only available to inmates who are legally married and have a spouse with no criminal record, and are provided as an incentive for good behavior.

Parenting programs: a combination of an educational and experiential set of activities designed both to promote a parent-child bond and to teach inmates how to be good parents.

A second type of family-based program that is available in many, especially women's, prisons is what are known as **parenting programs**. These are usually a combination of an educational and experiential set of activities that are designed both to promote a parent-child bond and to teach inmates how to be good parents. The importance and value of such programs comes from the fact that more than one-half of all prison inmates in the United States are parents, with more than 2.7 million children having an incarcerated parent.[29] Criminological research has long established the importance of a supportive bond between parents and children for desistance from crime. Therefore, it is important to promote a bond between a parent and children, even when the parent is incarcerated. Parenting programs for women have been available in American prisons for many decades. Such programs for men have only been around since the 1970s.

Parenting programs are most often in the form of parent education classes, supplemented with family activities. These include classroom-based instruction and discussions, with occasional visits by children to the prison to spend time interacting with their parents. In some women's prisons, nurseries are provided for infants, where the child can stay in the institution with his or her mother at the critical earliest stages of life. Typically, these programs require the child to move outside the prison by the age of 2. Many women's prisons also have more liberal visitation policies for young children, and provide visitation areas with toys, children's books, and child-friendly furniture.

Parenting programs are one of the few types of programs in prisons that are becoming more common today. The thinking is that such programs are beneficial not only to inmates, but they are also directly beneficial to inmates' children. And, since there is a strong belief in the link between parental incarceration and subsequent criminality by such parents' children, the costs and efforts that go into such programs may be especially beneficial. Also, parenting programs can be offered in a relatively low-cost way. The only real costs are for staff to monitor visits, teach the classes, and supervise visitation times (although this is often done by volunteers or outside organizations), and some cost for furnishings and other supplies.

RECREATION AND ARTS PROGRAMS

Whereas most of the types of programs that have been discussed so far can be seen by most people as logical, having a positive outcome and being beneficial to

29. The Pew Charitable Trusts: Pew Center on the States. 2010. *Collateral Costs: Incarceration's Effect on Economic Mobility.* Washington, D.C.: The Pew Charitable Trusts.

both inmates and society as a whole, for other types of programs this is not the case. Recreation and arts programs, which may be among the most commonly offered programs in prisons and jails, are frequently seen by both staff and community members as unnecessary and "luxuries."[30] However, correctional administrators, and many staff persons, understand that one of the most important things that can be done to keep order and calm in an institution is to keep inmates busy. One of the easiest, lowest-cost, and most attractive ways to do this is to offer a range of recreational activities for inmates.

Recreational activities include a wide range of activities, such as sports (basketball, football, softball, baseball, and soccer), games (board games, cards, and billiards), exercise (including in most prisons weightlifting), musical instruments, video games, television, and arts and crafts. It is widely believed that recreation programs offer numerous benefits to both inmates and staff. Many believe that such programs reduce the likelihood of violence, on both the individual and collective level, and reduce the number of disciplinary infractions that occur. Such activities occupy inmates, giving them mental, physical, and emotional releases, as well as reduce boredom. Additionally, being active is also well known to be one of the best ways to stay healthy, which means recreational programs can help control the health care costs incurred by prisons and jails.

Early correctional efforts in the United States did not include recreational activities. However, as time passed, correctional authorities can to realize that they could not keep inmates busy very easily, and this led to both physical and mental health problems, and many irritated, bored, and angry inmates (which is simply a recipe for violence and disaster). Consequently, a variety of recreational activities were slowly introduced, beginning with simple access to exercise (both indoor and outdoor) and then educational types of recreation (libraries and some educational classes), and then more organized activities such as hobby clubs. Today, a number of prisons also have formal clubs and organizations inside of prisons, including chapters of Toastmasters, NAACP, religious organizations, and institution-specific groups organized to do charitable works for both the inmate community and outside groups.

Recreational programs, although somewhat controversial because of being seen as being "soft" on offenders rather than emphasizing punishment, are common, and generally seen as very important. The idea of inmates sitting in a cell with nothing to do except to "think about what they did wrong" is a very misguided, and probably dangerous, way to conduct corrections. It is important to keep inmates healthy, to keep them engaged physically and mentally, and to try to provide them with skills, interests, and available activities that they can transfer to the outside with them upon release, so as to have tools for desisting from further criminal activity.

---

30. Brandon K. Applegate. 2001. Penal Austerity: Perceived Utility, Desert, and Public Attitudes Toward Prison Amenities. *American Journal of Criminal Justice,* 25, 253-268. Richard Tewksbury and Elizabeth Ehrhardt Mustaine. 2005. Insiders' Views of Prison Amenities: Beliefs and Perceptions of Correctional Staff Members. *Criminal Justice Review,* 30, 174-188.

PERCEPTIONS OF PROGRAMS

In addition to understanding what types of programs are available to inmates and the justifications and rationales for them, it is also important to know how such programs are perceived by both correctional officials/staff and the public. Here we see the importance once again of the six basic ideologies of corrections that were discussed in Chapter 3. Depending upon what one believes is the core reason for corrections to exist, and relatedly what corrections should strive to achieve with offenders, there are likely to be different views held about whether programs should be offered, and if so what types of programs are most appropriate.

How one views the types of programs offered in jails and prisons is initially revealed in how someone even talks about such things. For some people, all of the various programs we have discussed in this chapter are seen as forms of "treatment," which would suggest that such a person believes in a rehabilitation model for corrections. For others, the programs might be seen as a way of achieving "normalization" of life while incarcerated. This would suggest adherence to an ideology of reintegration, where it is seen as important to keep life while incarcerated relatively normal, so that return to the community can be smoother and easier. Or, for others, these programs (and some other issues about the incarceration experience) may be seen as "amenities," meaning that these are luxuries and not really necessary activities. People who see such activities as amenities would most likely hold to an ideology of retribution, or just deserts, believing that incarceration should be harsh and truly punishing.

Researchers have examined the views of prison programs and conditions held by correctional administrators, security staff, and members of the public. As shown in Table 12.1, researchers have looked at 26 different types of programs and prison conditions, assessing the percentage of correctional administrators, security staff, and members of the public that believe such items should be available in prison. As shown, support for basic treatment programs, including psychological counseling and legal assistance and resources, is generally high, although only about one-half of the public believes inmates should be provided with access to legal assistance.

When looking at education and job training programs, there is very strong support for all levels of education, as well as books and magazines. However, at the highest level of education — college education programs — only approximately two-thirds of the public and one-half of security staff in prisons believe such programs are appropriate to offer to inmates. Where there is relatively weak support for programs and items — including items such as cable television, R-rated movies, pornography, and boxing or martial arts, these are items that could perhaps most easily be seen as either true luxuries or as a threat to institutional security. An interesting set of responses are seen for conjugal visitations. Nearly all correctional administrators and security staff see such activities as things that should not be available to inmates, but nearly three-quarters of the public does see them as appropriate. The reasoning for this is not clear, but this

TABLE 12.1 VIEWS OF PRISON PROGRAMS AND CONDITIONS

Program or Condition	Administrators	Security Staff	Public
Psychological Counseling	97.6	96.1	94.5
Legal Assistance	90.6	78.6	51.5
Law Books & Law Library	88.7	72.1	72.2
HIV/AIDS Medical Treatment	97.6	82.0	77.4
Supervised Family Visits	97.6	95.3	93.0
Conjugal Visitation	11.8	11.1	73.4
Basic Literacy Education	98.8	95.2	91.0
GED Education Classes	98.8	91.8	85.5
Job Training Programs	96.4	86.6	91.0
College Education Programs	75.0	53.5	63.5
Books	98.8	98.0	91.5
Newspapers and Magazines	97.6	91.7	81.5
Pornography	7.1	20.6	17.1
Basic TV (no cable)	95.2	93.9	63.5
Cable TV	49.4	44.3	21.6
Telephone Calls	88.2	92.5	83.0
Radios	92.9	90.2	51.5
Air Conditioning	92.9	92.0	78.4
Cigarettes and Other Tobacco	61.2	59.7	32.0
R-Rated Movies	31.0	32.0	33.2
Arts & Crafts	91.7	82.8	62.5
Basketball	97.6	93.7	70.4
Weightlifting Equipment	66.7	58.7	54.3
Boxing and Martial Arts	12.2	10.0	24.5
Tennis	59.8	53.5	45.0
Condoms	16.5	12.7	28.0

does raise some interesting questions about how various groups see and define appropriate "amenities" for prison inmates.

Additionally, while the data presented in Table 12.1 represent correctional administrators and staff as unified groups, this may not be the case. This research also has shown that higher levels of education may be associated with how correctional staff perceive some types of programs and prison conditions. For instance, prison staff members with a college degree are more likely to support providing inmates with legal assistance than staff without a college degree (84.2% vs. 79.4%), access to a law library (83.2% vs.74.0%), cable television (50.5% vs. 44.9), and condoms (28.2% vs. 14.3%). Education does seem to play a role in at least some of prison staff members' views of prison conditions.

Summary

We have seen in this chapter that there are a wide variety of types of programs provided for inmates in jail and prison, although only a very few types of programs are offered in all or nearly all institutions. Programs include everything from basic health and mental health services to education (at a variety of levels), family maintenance programs, and programs designed to primarily keep inmates busy. Programs are generally supported by correctional administrators and staff, at least in the abstract sense. When looking at particular types of programs, however, there are a number of programs and conditions of incarceration that may be seen as "going too far" and being "too much." Having such a belief is most probably related to how an individual believes prison should operate and what the goals of incarceration should be. Some program varieties have been in American correctional institutions essentially since the very beginning, while other programs and conditions (such as visits and parenting programs) are a fairly recent development. Regardless of how long programs have been around, they are most often judged as good or bad depending on whether they make a difference, which usually means whether inmates who participate in them are more or less likely to recidivate.

Key Terms

- Cognitive behavioral therapy
- Contact visits
- Conjugal visits
- Correctional education
- Parenting programs
- Psychiatric services
- Religious programs
- Therapeutic communities
- Vocational education

Chapter Thirteen Corrections Staff

Any discussion of corrections must address the reasons corrections exists and functions as it does, how it has evolved to its current state, who is incarcerated, what goes on inside prison (both the good and the bad), and the topic of this chapter: Who works in corrections? In this chapter, we focus on who the staff of correctional institutions are, what they do, what are identified as the advantages and disadvantages of the job, and how the manner in which staff do their jobs has consequences for inmates. We begin with an overview of types of jobs in corrections, then move to discussions of recruitment and training, the culture of working in prisons and how the environment shapes what is done, the means by which officers interact with inmates and establish their authority, different approaches to the job employed by correctional officers, job stress in corrections, and the relatively recent development of a movement toward professionalization.

JOBS IN CORRECTIONS

The most common job in corrections is the entry-level job of correctional officer. According to the Bureau of Labor Statistics, in May 2012 there were a total of 434,870 correctional officer jobs in the United States.[1] Not surprisingly, there are more correctional officer jobs in states with larger populations, and with the largest prison populations. Texas employs the most correctional officers

---

1. Bureau of Labor Statistics. 2012. *Occupational Employment and Wages, 2012: 333-3012 Correctional Officers and Jailers.* Washington, D.C.: Bureau of Labor Statistics. Available at http://www.bls.gov/oes/current/oes333012.htm.

(at 48,000). One step above the entry-level position of correctional officer is the level of supervisor (which in most correctional systems is called a Sergeant). According to the Bureau of Labor Statistics, there were a total of 44,830 of these positions in May 2012. This means there is one supervisor position for approximately every ten correctional officer positions.

Looking at correctional officers demographically, we see that two-thirds are men and approximately two-thirds are white.[2] African Americans comprise one in five (21%) of correctional officers, and Hispanics 8 percent. This rather clearly suggests that minority group members are less represented among correctional staff than among prison inmates. When looking at jobs above the entry-level position of correctional officer, however, the proportion of women and minority groups is even lower. For instance, women comprise only 16 percent of supervisory positions, but are relatively uncommon among wardens and system Directors.[3]

One of the best known "facts" about correctional officers is that they are poorly paid. Considering the job that they do (as discussed below) and the conditions in which they at least occasionally work, their salary is not one of the highest. However, it is also important to keep in mind that the requirements for the job are minimal, and the job offers security (typically unionized or state government work) and is typically accompanied by very good benefits. According to the Bureau of Labor Statistics, the mean annual salary of a correctional officer in the United States in May 2012 was $43,550, or $20.84 per hour.[4] There are, of course, significant variations in salary across different states and regions of the country. The highest mean salaries for correctional officers tend to be in the Northeast and along the West Coast. In 2012, New Jersey topped the list of average correctional officer salaries with a mean of $69,310, followed by California at $66,930. At the bottom of the list of correctional officer salaries are states in the Southeast, where mean salaries are about $30,000.

As we would expect, the pay for supervisory positions (e.g., Sergeants) is significantly better than that for entry-level correctional officers. According to national estimates, the first line supervisory positions in corrections pay an average of $60,970 annually (or $29.31 per hour).[5] And, as with correctional officer positions and pay, there is significant regional and state variation in salaries. Once again, New Jersey ($101,330) and California ($87,640) top the list of average salaries, with states in the Southeast the lowest (at $40,000 to $44,000 on average).

Correctional officers are not the only people who work in corrections. Corrections officers (or, those in security roles, which would include all supervisors of correctional officers) account for two-thirds of corrections employees.

---

2. American Correctional Association. 2000. *Vital Statistics in Corrections.* Lanham, MD: American Correctional Association.
3. *Ibid.*
4. Bureau of Labor Statistics, supra n.1.
5. *Ibid.*

The remaining one-third is comprised of administrators (3% to 5% of all jobs), treatment and program staff (at 15% of jobs) and support services (at 15%). Administrators, numerically the smallest group of correctional workers, include institutional wardens, deputy wardens, and staff in the central office of the department of corrections. Treatment and program staff includes teachers, counselors, substance abuse treatment staff, doctors, nurses, recreational program staff, and others who actually work with inmates. The treatment and program staff are those who are most focused on the actual "correcting" of inmates, those whose jobs are most rehabilitative in function and structure. Finally, support services positions are the jobs that most people forget about as being necessary in corrections. These are the obvious positions such as office workers, but the category of support services also includes all of the staff that are necessary to maintain the physical plant and keep the actual structure of the institution functioning. Here we have positions such as landscaping and grounds keepers, plumbers, electricians, machine shop workers and repairmen, food service workers, people who manage and run the commissary, and other similar types of positions.

Regardless of the specific job that one has in a prison or jail, it is important to keep in mind that for everyone who works inside, the top priority, at all times, is maintaining security. Keeping inmates in, keeping order, and maintaining a safe and secure institutional environment is always the first priority for anyone working in corrections.

SELECTION AND TRAINING OF PRISON STAFF

Selection of applicants and candidates for jobs in corrections is, unfortunately, not a highly competitive process. The job does not have very stringent hiring requirements: In almost all jurisdictions, the requirements are to be at least 21 years old (although some jurisdictions allow 18-year-olds), to not have a criminal record (although some jurisdictions will hire people with misdemeanor convictions), to have a driver's license, and to be physically able to do the job. Some jurisdictions also require a drug screening, and some jurisdictions do require a literacy test to be passed as well. In regard to education, the majority of correctional officers have a high school diploma or GED. In recent years, the proportion of correctional officers with a college degree has been increasing, with perhaps one in three such staff holding a four-year degree. However, some jurisdictions have correctional officers with less than a high school education; some estimates are that as many as 10 percent of correctional officers never finished high school.

Once hired, training for correctional officers varies significantly across jurisdictions. Training usually begins with a period of classroom instruction, which may last anywhere from one week to three months. In this period, recruits are educated on institutional rules and procedures, legal issues, what to expect from inmates, how to conduct many of the basic tasks of the job (such as searching cells and dormitories, doing pat down searches on inmates, completing the many types of paperwork involved in the job, and giving first aid), how to interact and talk with inmates, and physical defense techniques. Following classroom instruction, new recruits will be immersed in on-the-job training where they will be assigned a training officer and typically will rotate through different posts (e.g., positions or jobs) in the institution, so as to be exposed to the many different types of places that correctional officers work. The entire training period typically lasts between one and two months, although in recent years jurisdictions have varied this anywhere from one week to six months in total.

Inmates also provide much "training" for correctional officers. Novice officers and many experienced officers depend highly on securing the inmates' cooperation in carrying out their responsibilities. Inmate leaders frequently "help out" officers by enforcing the rules within housing units and ensuring the cooperation of other inmates with administrative orders. While helpful in the short run, such "assistance" also guides officers to pursue particular methods of resolving conflicts and fulfilling their responsibilities. Inmates thereby have "trained" officers to function in particular manners. (This was one of many problems in the Texas model, which was ruled unconstitutional.)

Historically, departments of corrections have not been very aggressive or creative in how they go about recruiting staff, including correctional officers. Typically, there has been reliance on such things as posters, job announcements, and postings on government jobs websites. However, this has often proved to be inadequate, especially given the many positions that need to be filled due to high rates of turnover among corrections staff. In almost every single correctional institution and jurisdiction in the United States, there are open jobs, especially at the entry-level position of correctional officer.

Recruiting and retaining staff is a top priority for all correctional systems, and according to a 2012 survey of Directors of state departments of corrections, this is the second most commonly reported problem facing correctional systems in the United States.[6] As explained by such officials, there are three primary issues involved in the challenge of recruitment and retention of employees: (1) low salaries and challenging work environments; (2) significant needs created by layoffs and retirements; and (3) a desire and need to recruit more diverse staffs. In explaining the challenges they face, the following comments were offered by DOC Directors:

- Although we have no lack of candidates, diversity continues to be an issue.
- [We are] [u]nable to fully staff uniformed security positions in institutions causing less than safe security staffing ratios and resulting in necessity of lockdowns due to staff shortages and excessive overtime.

---

6. Association of State Correctional Administrators. 2012. *ASCA June 2012 Current Issues in Corrections Survey.* Hagerstown, MD: ASCA. Available at http://www.asca.net/system/assets/attachments/4941/June%202012%20Current%20Issues%20Survey.pdf?1349895146.

- As the overall economy recovers it becomes increasingly difficult to recruit and retain talented staff.
- Correctional facilities located in certain regions of the state where the labor market has become particularly competitive are experiencing a higher number of CO vacancies.

Most correctional administrators would like to hire staff who have extensive training, both in corrections as well in general educational fields. More exacting educational requirements have become commonplace for correctional officers through the past two decades. While administrators believe that educated officers mean a more emotionally mature, socially aware, and interpersonally skilled staff, education has not been shown to have a significant relationship to correctional officers' increased job satisfaction levels.[7]

For top-level management positions, though, recruitment is generally believed necessary on a national scale. However, promotion of local personnel through the local ranks is also considered a viable alternative. This brings to our attention the potential problems involved in mixing locally recruited and imported correctional personnel and administrators. Over 60 years ago, the German sociologist Robert Michel pointed out that organizations and their leaders are necessarily practitioners of oligarchy,[8] a political fact of life being that those in power tend to keep themselves in power mainly by giving leadership roles to their loyal followers, thus creating political machines. This is the essence of what Michel calls his **iron law of oligarchy**.

Iron law of oligarchy: the practice of those being in power tending to keep themselves in power by primarily giving leadership roles to their loyal followers that simultaneously creates political machines.

Public relations problems have historically plagued recruitment to correctional positions. The general public has a very distorted and limited perception of the work involved in corrections. This has led many highly qualified and promising potential correctionalists to shy away from careers in the corrections field. They see the work as intellectually unchallenging, physically demanding, dirty, and undesirable. Additionally, the geographic location of prisons has meant that the local labor force from which institutions can draw is primarily rural and unfamiliar with the values, lifestyles, and cultures of the predominantly urban, minority inmate population.

Many potential correctional workers believe that they need only "common sense" to fulfill the duties a job in corrections would require. With such an uninformed view, a correctional staff member could potentially have serious problems on the job. However, because of the traditionally poor working conditions, low pay, and geographic isolation associated with corrections work, a diverse pool from which correctional administrators can draw new personnel may not exist.

---

7. Nancy C. Jurik, Gregory J. Halemba, Michael C. Musheno, and Bernard B. Boyle. 1987. Educational Attainment, Job Satisfaction and the Professionalization of Correctional Officers. *Work and Occupations*, 14, 106-125.

8. Robert Michel. 1949. *Political Parties: A Sociological Study of the Oligarchical Tendencies of Modern Democracy.* Glencoe, IL: The Free Press.

Since the late 1960s, correctional institutions and systems have made strong efforts to recruit diverse personnel. The move to increase minority group representation in the ranks of corrections personnel is designed to both counter the social and economic discrimination found in society in general and to work toward a more racially balanced institution.

As one moves up the hierarchy of correctional positions, discrimination has stronger influences and is more evident. Relatively few minority group members occupy top administrative positions. Those who make it to the top ranks have greater demands and expectations imposed on them but receive less support.

CORRECTIONAL OFFICER CULTURE, EXPECTATIONS, AND WORK ENVIRONMENT

Perhaps the most defining element of work as a correctional officer is that the work is routine and monotonous. Yes, it can be exciting and dangerous, as we see in the movies and on television "reality" shows. But, the truth is that excitement, danger, and action is the rare exception. Instead, day-to-day activities are very routine, relatively easily learned, and the challenge for many correctional officers is to keep the job interesting and to remain alert for the possibility of danger and action. Key to being a good correctional officer is to remain in a constant state of alertness and readiness so as to know when trouble or danger is about to happen.

The job of a correctional officer is a diverse job that can entail doing a number of different types of tasks. The major components of the job of correctional officer include:

1. *Security officer*. Central to the job is maintaining security, which means preventing escapes, making sure inmates are where they are supposed to be when they are supposed to be there, monitoring and intervening to prevent or stop conflict between inmates, monitoring visitors, and preventing the introduction of contraband to the institution.
2. *Disciplinarian*. When a correctional officer becomes aware of an inmate violating a rule of the institution, it is her responsibility to stop the rule-violating behavior and to initiate disciplinary procedures. This responsibility may necessitate physical interventions and use of force. It also draws upon informal social control means and involves decisions about when it is appropriate and best to formally write up an inmate for a disciplinary infraction and when an informal resolution may be more desirable and beneficial.
3. *Communications link between inmates and staff*. Correctional officers are the primary institutional staff with whom inmates have contact. As such, they are the major sources of information for administrators about inmates and for inmates about administrators and rules, procedures, and other administrative tasks. When any type of information or

message needs to be communicated between one group and the other, it is the correctional officers who are usually responsible for transmitting the information, and often for deciding how best to communicate the information.

4. *Educator.* Correctional officers engage in a fair amount of both formal instruction of inmates (in rules, institutional procedures, etc.) as well as informal teaching about how to get along in the prison community. Part of this is done through talking with inmates and suggesting modes of behavior, and much of this is done through role modeling.
5. *Administrative officer.* One of the least satisfying aspects of the job for many correctional officers is the fact that seemingly practically everything that one does must be documented. There is a great deal of paperwork and documentation that is either a legal requirement or an administrative requirement.
6. *Blue collar worker.* Especially for correctional officers who work in housing units of a correctional institution, there are likely to be a number of physical tasks that need to be done on the job. This may include key control and distribution, opening and closing doors, checking passes of inmates moving from place to place, and even things like intervening when plumbing stops working, furniture gets broken, or other manual labor tasks arise for which no one else is either officially responsible or currently available.

Each of these job components can be seen in the formal description of the job of a correctional officer. As an example, the following is the official enumeration of the job duties of a correctional officer in the Kentucky Department of Corrections:

> Stands watch in corridors of buildings, towers and other security posts. Takes required action during emergencies to prevent escapes and suppress disorders. Oversees inmates inside and outside of the institution. Takes periodic counts of inmates. Searches inmate's person, mail and quarters for contraband. Oversees work or recreational activities. Oversees inmates during bathing and meals. Counsels with inmates on minor adjustment problems and refers serious problems to proper staff specialists. Supervises inmates in general housekeeping duties and checks quarters for health and safety hazards. Issues and keeps records of inmate clothing and supplies. Makes written reports on violations of institutional rules. Oversees inmates in preparing and serving food. Oversees visits with inmates and may search visitors for contraband. Takes proper care of use of weapons. Transports inmates to and from other institutions, courts, medical facilities, funerals and other areas as required. Administers emergency first-aid to inmates, visitors and employees when necessary. Travels in-state or out-of-state to return escapees. . . . Must be able to physically respond to an emergency situation. Assist in an evacuation or rescue, bend, lift, run or walk swiftly in order to physically disrupt fights between inmates or intervene in a combative situation to protect fellow employees from the threat of harm or actual harm at the hands of an inmate. Must possess the physically agility to

secure an inmate with handcuffs and/or ankle chains, or other restraints, and, if necessary, to engage in forced movement of inmates from one location to another.[9]

AUTHORITY AND INTERACTIONS OF CORRECTIONAL OFFICERS

Coercive authority: the practice of claiming authority by demanding the respect of others that is often met with strong negative reactions leading to its most likely failure.

Overarching all of the tasks that are expected of correctional officers, one of the central and most important tasks that every correctional officer needs to do in order to be successful at the job is to establish and express authority. In some people's eyes, this comes with the job automatically, because the staff person is officially in charge, wears a uniform, and has the ability to lock inmates in segregation and remove their privileges. However, we also know that the single worst way to try to establish authority in any situation in life is to simply claim it, demand to be respected, and then expect others to do as you say. Such an approach, known as **coercive authority**, is most likely to fail, and to perhaps be met with strong negative reactions that can include physical retaliation. A much more effective way to achieve authority is through negotiation. Here correctional officers enter into a set of exchanges or negotiations with inmates in which each side pledges (whether verbally or implicitly) to not make trouble or difficulties for the other, so long as the other does not make trouble or difficulties for them — which is more or less like what many of us do with people in our lives that we are not especially fond of, but know that we must encounter and interact with. Such an approach is often effective, but may not stand up to long-term stresses and especially difficult times.

One of the most common, and seemingly effective, means by which correctional officers achieve compliance and authority with inmates is through the granting of informal rewards. These can be very effective ways to shape and control inmates' behaviors. Correctional officers may overlook minor rule infractions, exchange information, and grant special favors or privileges when inmates do something they need inmates to do. This approach, just as with one's children, may work for a while, but is also likely to lead to expectations on the part of the inmates (children) that they are entitled to the "special" treatment they get. In that situation, the exchange aspect of the relationship has or less dissipated and new sets of expectations of what is "normal" get established.

So, how can correctional officers achieve authority in effective, efficient, and lasting ways? What is best is to treat inmates with decency, to be fair in how one interacts in with others, and to clearly communicate why actions that affect others are done. A good correctional officer must rely on good communication skills, an ability to persuade and to display leadership, and skills at interacting in ways that make one seem friendly, firm, and fair. Research shows that

---

9. Commonwealth of Kentucky Personnel Cabinet. No Date. *Class specification: Correctional Officer, Title Code 2201.* Available at https://hr.personnel.ky.gov/Class%20Spec%20Documents/20000638.pdf.

correctional officers are able to achieve authority best when they are less punitive and less custodial, and when they maintain a social distance from inmates that is characterized by friendly but detached ways of interacting. Correctional officers who interact in these ways also report the greatest level of job satisfaction.[10]

It is also important to keep in mind that correctional officers are human services workers. At the core of the job is working with people and providing services to them. This does not mean that a correctional officer is like a social worker or therapist (although at times aspects of these roles do come into play for correctional officers). Rather, correctional officers provide inmates with a safe environment in which to live, guidance and direction on activities and behaviors, and supervision. This means that corrections work is "people work," and at the core of the work is the ability to read human behavior and understand behavioral cues, as well as having and exercising good judgment.[11] Correctional officers can easily be described as the most influential persons in inmates' lives while incarcerated; correctional officers spend the most time with inmates, have the most prolonged and often most intimate contact with inmates, and are the staff persons there in times of crisis and need for inmates. Solving inmate problems often becomes a routine task for correctional officers. Inmates' requests for things like cell or dormitory changes, concerns over threats from other inmates, and difficulties getting appointments with treatment or program staff are things that are commonly brought to the attention of correctional officers. Good correctional officers familiarize themselves with the inmates with whom they interact, and they are aware of and sensitive to any changes they may see in the behaviors or associations of particular inmates. Correctional officers are the ones most likely to know of an inmate's difficulties with other inmates, receipt of upsetting news from outside the institution, or changes in health. Therefore, correctional officers are also the institutional staff in the best position to refer inmates to other specialized staff for services and programs. In order to do these things, the central skill for correctional officers is communication skill. Being a good communicator allows a correctional officer to develop relationships with inmates (and with other staff), reduce tensions among inmates, defuse crises, and conduct day-to-day activities in a calm and safe manner.[12]

However, one of the structural problems encountered by many correctional officers is that the skills and orientations that are known to be most effective and important in the conduct of their job are not what they are evaluated on and not what is rewarded by correctional administrators. Performance evaluations most often focus on issues of safety, cleanliness, and order in and around an officer's post. How and with how many inmates an officer interacts is difficult to measure

---

10. John Hepburn. 1984. The Erosion of Authority and the Perceived Legitimacy of Inmate Social Protest: A Study of Prison Guards. *Journal of Criminal Justice*, 12, (6), 103-120. Robert Johnson. 1996. *Hard Times: Understanding and Reforming the Prison*, 2d ed. Belmont, CA: Wadsworth.

11. Mary Ann Farkas. 1999. Correctional Officer Attitudes Toward Inmates and Working with Inmates in a "Get Tough" Era. *Journal of Criminal Justice*, 27, (6), 495-506.

12. Johnson, supra n.10.

and therefore not something that is commonly considered in making "objective" evaluations of the job performance of correctional officers.

How correctional officers approach and interact with inmates has been shown to be related to both demographic factors and organizational issues. In regard to demographics, research has shown that older correctional officers typically have a more positive orientation toward inmates, including being less harsh or punitive in their interactions.[13] Some studies have suggested that women staff have more effective communications with inmates, but this is not a universal finding. The idea here is that women are socialized to be more communication-oriented and more focused on relationships than men, and that these generalized social skills are common among women correctional officers where they have similar effects as they do everywhere in social life. Race may also be important in how correctional officers view and interact with inmates. Whereas the majority of inmates in most prisons are African American, correctional officers of the same race often are believed to have a more similar socialization experience and therefore shared cultural values with offenders, leading to a smoother line of interactions.

In regard to organizational factors, we know that more experienced officers tend to have more positive attitudes toward inmates and hold stronger beliefs in rehabilitation than less experienced officers.[14] Also, correctional officers who are more satisfied with their jobs tend to interact with others (both inmates and other staff) in more positive ways, and to engage in problem solving and creative approaches to problem solving than do officers who derive less satisfaction from their jobs. Interestingly, and contrary to the expectations of most people, correctional officers regularly report that the most stressful parts of their jobs are not their interactions with inmates, but rather their interactions with co-workers and the administration of the prison. When stressed by co-workers and the rules and structure of the job, it is not uncommon for correctional officers to take out this stress on inmates. This suggests that one of the important influences, albeit an indirect influence, on how correctional officers interact with inmates is how well the officer gets along with co-workers and how much respect or resentment he has for prison administrators.

A TYPOLOGY OF CORRECTIONAL OFFICERS

When thinking about correctional officers and how they approach their work, inmates, and their co-workers, we can see that there are several very different types of approaches. Stojkovic and Farkas have reviewed the many ways that

13. Farkas, supra n.11. Nancy Jurik. 1985. Individual and Organizational Determinants of Correctional Officer Attitudes Toward Inmates. *Criminology*, 23, (3), 523-539.
14. Farkas, supra n.11.

researchers have identified the means by which correctional officers go about their work and have constructed a four-category typology of correctional officers.[15] The first variety is what they call the custodian. This is the correctional officer who believes that the job is primarily custodial and embodies the ideas of coercive authority, toughness, and keeping a social distance from the inmates. This variety of correctional officer maintains an outwardly tough façade that is consistent across interactions with both inmates and co-workers. These officers seek to gain authority and power within the institution and believe the best way to do this is through being tough on inmates and a stickler for enforcing rules. Most often this approach to the job is seen in newer correctional officers.

The second variety of correctional officer is pretty much the polar opposite of the custodian, and this is the human services worker approach. A correctional officer who approaches his job in this way is seeking to actually work with inmates, to get to know them, and to try to find ways to help inmates become better people and to have as good a life as possible while incarcerated. This variety of correctional officer seeks to break down the social distance between himself and inmates, and as a result often ends up alienating himself from his co-workers (who are likely to see such officers as "soft" and "really on the side of the inmates, not us"). The human services approach to being a correctional officer emphasizes the role of advising, supporting, consoling, referring, and assisting inmates with their problems, both personal and institutional.

A third variety, which is more or less in between the approaches of the custodian and the human services worker, is the functionary. These are officers who, typically after being in their work for a while, develop a sense of hostility toward and negative views of inmates. As a result, they tend to pull away from getting to know inmates, or they soften a bit and simply view inmates as objects to be managed. These are officers who just do the job, doing what is required and not much more. Functionaries tend to be officers with a few years of experience on the job and tend to be isolated from both inmates and their co-workers.

A fourth and final variety of correctional officer identified by Stojkovic and Farkas is the burned-out officer. Officers of this variety tend to be experienced and to have reached a position of being disenchanted with the job, believing that what they do really does not matter and being highly frustrated and stressed with practically all aspects of the job. These officers are the most likely candidates for leaving the job, or they may try to stay on for a few remaining years if they are able to retire in the foreseeable future. Burned-out officers are generally considered negative influences on inmates, co-workers, and the institution as a whole.

---

15. Stan Stojkovic and Mary Ann Farkas. 2003. *Correctional Leadership: A Cultural Perspective.* Belmont, CA: Wadsworth/Thomson Learning.

CORRECTIONAL OFFICERS AND JOB STRESS

One fact of working as a correctional officer is that the job is commonly reported to be a fairly highly stressful job. The stress of the job comes in three basic forms: short-term, acute stress; stress related to a time-bound event; and long-term or chronic stress. For correctional officers, an example of short-term, acute stress would be encountering a situation of danger when that situation had not been expected. So, when a correctional officer walks into a dormitory and finds several inmates waiting for his arrival ready to fight, the officer will experience short-term acute stress. Somewhat differently, stress related to a time-bound event is that which is related to the anticipation of an event. Once that event occurs or ends, so too does the stress end. So, when an officer knows that her post and the area around it will be inspected by the warden at the end of her work shift on Tuesdays, she is likely to experience stress as the end of Tuesday's work shift approaches, but once the inspection is completed, the stress ends (assuming the inspection goes well!). Finally, long-term, chronic stress is that which an officer must deal with over time. This would include things like stress related to missing family functions because of work commitments, stress due to the everyday boredom experienced on the job, and stress due to financial difficulties that arise from the relatively low pay that correctional officers earn.

Work stress for correctional officers arises from both safety concerns and organizational and administrative issues. Both sources are important for influencing how the individual experiences and adapts to the job of correctional officer, and both sources of stress also can interact with and exacerbate the other source.

In an occupation such as that of correctional officer, being in charge of maintaining nearly 1.6 million state and federal inmates including some that have had a history of violence, safety concerns with the job are going to be inevitable. The effects of such stress are clearly seen in the facts that correctional officers are highly likely to have both mental and physical health problems, and when compared to the national average, correctional officers tend to die at younger ages.[16] In regard to stress from safety concerns, there are two primary concerns that affect correctional officers: threat of and actual inmate violence, and the effects of understaffing.

There are a number of concerns that correctional officers report in regard to threats from inmates. These include inmate violence, manipulation by the inmates that could lead to corruption of officers, and inmates making a wide range of (both legitimate and illegitimate) demands of the correctional officer.[17] Perceived work dangers in the form of inmate threats of violence have been shown to have a significant and strong negative effect on work satisfaction[18] and

---

16. Eric G. Lambert and Eugene A. Paoline. 2008. The Influence of Individual, Job, and Organizational Characteristics on Correctional Staff Job Stress, Job Satisfaction, and Organizational Commitment. *Criminal Justice Review*, 33, (4), 160-184.
17. Peter Finn. 1998. Correctional Officer Stress: A Cause for Concern and Additional Help. *Federal Probation*, 62, (2), 65-74.
18. Frances Cullen, Bruce Link, Nancy Wolfe, and James Frank. 1985. The Social Dimensions of Correctional Officer Stress. *Justice Quarterly*, 2, 505-533.

increase the likelihood of job burnout. It is not just the reality of threats and violence that are important though; Huckabee found that how dangerous correctional officers perceive the inmate population with which they work to be significantly affects the amount of stress reported.[19]

Understaffing of a correctional institution has also been shown to create a number of negative effects on correctional officers. The main reason for this is that a shortage of correctional officers leads to a shortage of posts being filled, thus creating a more dangerous workplace due to the high ratio of inmates to correctional staff. Another reason for the shortage of correctional officers is the near universally very high rate of turnover resulting from many correctional officers quitting shortly after being hired.[20] Due to a general shortage of correctional officers and accompanying understaffing of many facilities, many officers are forced to work mandatory overtime. The consequences of mandatory (often unanticipated) overtime are many, and include officers stating that they often ignore phone calls from the prison when they are at home since they presume they are being called in to work, or even have multiple telephone numbers to avoid being called into work.[21] The shortage of correctional officers employed has also resulted in correctional facilities using creative and unique shift-work structures in order to cover necessary posts essential to the operation of the prison. There have been a number of issues documented that result from shift-work: cognitive impairment, fatigue, lack of vigilance, and decrease in motor skills due to the disruption of the body's biological clock from not being on a normal schedule.[22]

The greatest amount of stress for correctional officers has been clearly established as arising from interactions with co-workers and administrators. Organizational issues that are directly related to stress for correctional officers include limited promotional opportunities, limited autonomy in job tasks, little or no input for decision making, perception of unfair treatment by administrators and supervisors, and a lack of feedback on job performance. Interestingly, despite notoriously low pay, correctional officers in prison show only a small degree of stress related to pay (however, for jail staff this is a more significant issue).

RECENT DEVELOPMENTS IN ORGANIZATION OF PRISON STAFF

Two major changes in corrections during the past several decades have been the move toward the professional approach to correctional work and the emergence

19. R.G. Huckabee. 1992. Stress in Corrections: An Overview of the Issues. *Journal of Criminal Justice,* 20 (5), 479-486.
20. J.J. Gibbons and N.B. Katzenbach. 2006. *Confronting Confinement: The Commission on Safety and Abuse in America's Prisons.* New York: Vera Institute of Justice.
21. Finn, supra n.17.
22. D.X. Swenson, D. Waseleski, and R. Hartl. 2008. Shift Work and Correctional Officers and Effects and Strategies for Adjustment. *Journal of Correctional Health Care,* 14, (4), 299-310.

of self-regulation/accreditation. Both of these developments, which are related, have brought changes to how correctional institutions operate. Neither change has been universal or complete, however.

Professionalization

The move toward a professional approach to corrections work has accompanied a general trend in the United States toward professionalization of many occupations. Since the middle of the twentieth century, many services and technological occupations (law enforcement, social work, pharmacy, education, and so on) have attempted to alter their public perception by changing from an occupation to a profession. For most occupations, this change has occurred, but only in limited degrees. This is the case for corrections.

A simple definition of a profession contains four primary elements:

1. A profession is grounded on acquisition of a theoretical body of systematic knowledge through a prolonged period of academic study. This knowledge is unique to the members of the professional group.
2. Members of the profession are motivated by social or community concerns, not self-interest.
3. The individuals and organizations of the profession are largely self-regulating.
4. The members of the profession establish and distribute rewards based on the values unique to the profession.[23]

Becoming recognized as a profession, as opposed to simply another job or set of occupations, means that the ways a particular area of work are viewed by society need to be changed. The idea of professionalism requiring changes to both the reality of what is done, by whom and how, and the image of the work is clearly seen in the following quote from one correctional leader about what it will take for corrections to truly be seen as a profession:

> [S]ociety will not grant professional status to corrections simply because of accreditation, educational credentials, or technology; instead corrections personnel need to change the way they approach their jobs to be recognized as professionals. The true measure of professionals is their attitude and behavior toward the people they serve. Correctional personnel need to be problem solvers rather than task oriented, put the concerns of others before their own, prevent inmates from setting the ground rules for the relationship, recognize their limitations, respect inmates, and take pride in their work and their profession. Achieving professionalism throughout the corrections industry will take time. Corrections employees must

23. E.C. Hughes. 1965. Professions, in K.S. Lynn (ed.), *The Professions in America*. Boston: Houghton-Mifflin.

first recognize the traits that the public perceives as nonprofessional and then must start to change these traits.[24]

Perhaps the greatest degree of progress toward **professionalization** of corrections has occurred in developing a theoretical body of systematic knowledge. However, corrections differs from many other emerging professions in this regard. That is, corrections has no unique body of knowledge but draws heavily from the theoretical bodies of a number of social sciences and academic disciplines. Thus, the systematic "knowledge about corrections" is not a body of knowledge unique to those in the corrections field.

Professionalization: the movement of a type of job toward higher levels of functioning, including standardization in how tasks are done and a greater reliance on evidence-based, "proven" means of fulfilling the tasks of a job.

There is evidence to both support and refute correctional workers' community interest motivation. While the relatively low pay that many corrections staff receive suggests these people are not motivated by self-interest, ample evidence also suggests that people choose corrections because the jobs are convenient and offer stable employment. This directly relates to a system of rewards for correctional workers. Because they are usually government positions, the jobs themselves do not create the monetary and status rewards. However, people who enter corrections to pursue community interests may find personal satisfaction in social interaction opportunities and stable jobs. Of course, this largely depends on the individuals and their goals and desires.

The (slowly) increasing level of education of corrections staff has contributed to the movement toward professionalization. The percent of college-educated correctional officers continues to increase. This is not to say that correctional officers necessarily have a degree when they start their jobs. Rather, many officers are encouraged to return to college and may be seen in college classrooms (even in corrections classes!).

Self-regulation, similar to the theoretical body of systematic knowledge, is also an emerging characteristic of corrections. Again, because of the hierarchical structures that provide the framework for correctional systems and institutions, the degree to which correctional staff can be self-regulating is limited. Professional associations (such as the American Correctional Association) do not determine work tasks and are able to render only recommendations and **accreditation** standards. Accreditation is a process by which an institution is compared to industry established standards/expectations for best practices, and if found to be meeting enough of the expectations/standards is then declared to be of high quality (e.g., accredited).

Accreditation: process by which an institution is compared to industry-established standards/expectations for best practices, and if found to be meeting enough of the expectations/standards is then declared to be of high quality (e.g., accredited).

Where does this leave the issue of professionalization, then? It appears that corrections is moving toward but has not yet fully achieved a professional status. Rather, it may be more accurate to view corrections as an "emerging profession." As such, corrections appears to have achieved the structural elements of a profession. However, it has yet to fully achieve the attitudinal elements necessary to be considered a full-fledged profession.

---

24. William R. Kohnke. 2001. Professionalism in Corrections. *American Jails,* 15, (1), 75-76, 78.

This is not a negative view of corrections' potential as a profession in the future. Numerous researchers have suggested that professionalism is most significantly influenced by prisons' structural elements (organization of staff, lack of interaction among staff, and a sharp distinction between staff and inmates). Once a professional perspective is adopted, it tends to remain stable. Therefore, the move toward professionalization can be expected to continue. As people with a professional perspective continue to be recruited and to retain their view as structural elements of prisons are modified, professionalization can only be expected to continue.

Summary

There are a wide variety of jobs available in corrections. These include, but are not limited to, security, treatment, physical plant, and educational efforts. The most common way to enter into a career in corrections is via the entry-level job of correctional officer. Providing the most essential functions of maintaining custody within the institution as well as its overall security, there are more than 400,000 correctional officers employed in the United States.

One helpful way to think about the variety of ways to do the job of a correctional officer is offered by the four-group typology of custodian (an individual primarily seeking to gain power and authority among the inmates to get and maintain order); the human services worker (where the correctional officer is actively attempting to help inmates); a combination of a custody and human services role; and those that are burned out. Stress and accompanying physical and mental health consequences are common among correctional staff, especially correctional officers.

Recent decades have seen a move toward professionalism in corrections. This has also been accompanied by a movement toward unionization and accreditation of correctional institutions and systems.

Key Terms

Accreditation
Coercive authority
Iron law of oligarchy
Professionalization

Chapter Fourteen

Contemporary Challenges in Corrections

Corrections is an ever-evolving, changing set of practices, facilities, populations, and ideas. What we know as the practice of corrections today is in some ways very similar to what we have always known in the United States, and in some ways very different. As we have seen throughout this text, knowing the history of corrections is important for understanding how and why things are as they are today, as well as for appreciating the foundation from which today's practices have developed and evolved.

Perhaps the most obvious places in which to see both the consistency yet changes that have characterized American corrections is in the major problems that correctional administrators perceive as their biggest challenges. In this chapter, we will look at both what has and what has not changed in corrections, through a focus on the most significant challenges of corrections as identified by correctional administrators, the problem of (and attempted solutions to) overcrowding in prisons, a discussion of the costs of corrections, and an issue that has for several decades risen in priority and prominence — deciding where new correctional facilities should be located. Each of these issues reveals for us aspects of change — in how the issue is perceived by corrections officials and the public, as well as in how the issue has ripple effects into other aspects of corrections and into society as a whole. So too do these issues point to a consistency in corrections; issues that are challenges today are much the same as in the past. Challenges do evolve and change in specific focus, but the general issues remain largely the same over time. In short, these challenges also suggest that there are some "problems" and tasks that as core issues confronting corrections have not changed in any foundational way over time.

There is a need to find answers to "what works" and how efficacy and efficiency can be achieved in all aspects of corrections. Paradigms have changed over time (see Chapter 3), and while some changes in basic philosophies, basic organization, and physical structures have passed through multiple eras, so too have ideas about how to process offenders evolved. Changes in philosophy and practice have largely been in response to changing political ideologies in larger society or recognition of failures of particular ideas. What has long been needed, but remained unavailable, are ways of showing successes of correctional efforts and truly knowing what will be a beneficial approach/practice. Here there is promise on the horizon in the form of evidence-based corrections. This is the idea of doing only those things that have the goal "to improve the criminal justice system by implementing programs and policies that have been shown to work. . . . [T]he watchwords of the evidence-based approach to public policy include: outcome-based performance, rigorous evaluation, and a positive return on taxpayer investment."[1] As a means for addressing the challenges outlined both in this chapter and elsewhere, we will discuss the philosophy of evidence-based corrections and the promises it offers for improving our performance and investment of public resources.

The contemporary challenges in, about, and surrounding corrections are many. The four contemporary challenges that we will discuss in this chapter are not necessarily the most important or the most difficult or persistent. But, they are large and important, and understanding these challenges and thinking of ways to mitigate their consequences are major concerns for corrections, and all of society, today.

BIGGEST CHALLENGES IN THE EYES OF CORRECTIONAL ADMINISTRATORS

One of the best ways to learn about the issues and problems facing correctional systems, institutions, and individual administrators of correctional facilities is to look at what the heads of the state correctional systems identify as their major challenges and issues. Doing this is facilitated by the now semi-annual survey of the state departments of corrections Directors that is conducted by the Association of State Correctional Administrators. This survey is considered to be especially important and accurate, in that that it is done by the primary organization of such officials, and is used by them to set priorities for lobbying, programming, and coordinated efforts.

The survey conducted in June and July of 2012 showed that a total of 27 different issues were offered in response to the request for Directors to list the top

1. Washington State Institute for Public Policy. 2006. *Evidence-Based Adult Corrections Programs: What Works and What Does Not.* Olympia, WA: Washington State Institute for Public Policy, p. 1.

four issues facing their department.[2] The ten most frequently reported challenges and issues were the following:

1. Budget.
2. Staff turnover, recruitment, and retention.
3. Managing geriatric, medical, and mental health populations.
4. Cost of inmate health care.
5. Coordination of community reentry efforts; recidivism reduction.
6. Prison Rape Elimination Act (PREA) standards implementation; staff sexual misconduct.
7. Overcrowding.
8. Contraband detection, especially cell phones.
9. Staff behavior; staff culture.
10. Post-release housing for sex offenders.

The issue of budget was easily the most frequently reported problem, and the second and fourth issues (staff turnover, recruitment, and retention and cost of health care for inmates) are also directly connected to the issue of finances. The simple fact is that corrections is an especially expensive government activity. And, when the high cost of such an activity is paired with increasingly large prison populations and a poor economy in society, the problems associated with the financial aspect of corrections is only exacerbated.

Interestingly, when looking at the most frequently reported challenges and issues by this same group of officials from two years earlier (2010), we see that the top five issues reported in 2010 are all still identified in the top ten issues of 2012:

1. State budget cuts.
2. Cost of inmate health care.
3. Managing mentally ill populations.
4. Controlling contraband cell phones.
5. Post-release housing for sex offenders.[3]

What this clearly suggests, then, is that there is consistency over time in what challenges correctional administrators must face and manage. The problems that plague corrections are not simple ones, but instead are issues that are complex in nature, frequently interact with and exacerbate one another, and also are at least partially the product of changing culture and societal expectations for corrections and criminal justice. For some people, the fact that some identified

---

2. Association of State Correctional Administrators. 2012. *ASCA June 2012 Current Issues in Corrections Survey.* Hagerstown, MD: ASCA. Available at http://www.asca.net/system/assets/attachments/4941/June%202012%20Current%20Issues%20Survey.pdf?1349895146.

3. Association of State Correctional Administrators. 2011. *ASCA December 2010 Current Issues in Corrections Survey.* Hagerstown, MD: ASCA. Available at http://www.asca.net/system/assets/attachments/2068/ASCA_December_2010_Current_Issues_in_Corrections_Survey_final.pdf?1296107812.

challenges remain high in priority over time may suggest that correctional officials are just unable to find and effectively implement solutions for such problems. While it is difficult to say for certain whether this is true or not, it is just as likely (if not more likely) that such problems are large, ingrained in institutional and organizational culture, and resistant to efforts to mitigate or eliminate them. As we will see in the rest of this chapter, challenges are multifaceted and interrelated. These two points themselves suggest that overcoming such challenges is likely to be extremely difficult and requires significant resources and time.

OVERCROWDING

In part because different jurisdictions use different definitions and criteria to determine how many inmates they can house in a prison, there are not reliable statistics consistently collected on overcrowding in prisons. However, the most recent national statistics suggest that state prisons were generally operating somewhere between their calculated limit on number of inmates and 15 percent above their calculated limit.[4] In raw numbers, it would take an additional 207 prisons to accommodate all of the "extra" inmates that were in prisons above and beyond the calculated maximum that should be in each prison.

Crowding: the raw number of inmates and the subsequent matching of bed spaces and providing for other needs and characteristics of inmates that pose financial strains for corrections systems.

The issue of **crowding** involves more than just the sheer number of inmates with which a department of corrections or individual correctional institution has to contend. While the raw number of inmates in most systems is a challenge in and of itself, the problem also includes matching up the number of bed spaces in different types of prisons (security level, programming focus, etc.) and the needs and characteristics of inmates. For instance, as the number of elderly and geriatric inmates continues to increase, there are challenges created in regard to having prisons appropriate for such inmates. Many older prisons are multi-story facilities that require frequent climbing and descending of stairs. Housing elderly and geriatric inmates in such a facility is a problem, as many of these inmates are simply physically unable to handle many stairs. This would then mean the elderly and geriatric inmates would need to be in newer facilities, leaving the older facilities (which are typically of higher security levels) to younger inmates, who may be better suited for lower security institutions where there are more appropriate programming options available to them. As one DOC Director explained when responding to the above discussed survey by the Association of State Correctional Administrators:

> The agency does not currently have an overcrowding problem. The primary focus is on optimization of available bed space, i.e. keeping the lower dollar beds at capacity, utilizing program beds in a way such that those offenders requiring treatment can get their program needs met prior to release.[5]

4. Paige M. Harrison and Allen J. Beck. 2005. *Prisoners in 2004.* Washington, D.C.: Bureau of Justice Statistics.
5. Association of State Correctional Administrators, supra n.2, p. 22.

Or, in the words of another DOC Director, "[a]gency count is down; however, there is a deficiency of the type of security level beds available for the offender type."[6] If we do not match up inmates based on their needs with institutions providing such programs, we are inhibiting the likelihood of reducing recidivism. This is just one example of how crowding can mean more than just having too many people for available space.

But, too often, crowding does mean that a prison, or an entire correctional system, simply has more people to house than it has room for. At the turn of the century, many states were experiencing overcrowded conditions in their prisons, and were building new prisons (at huge costs) to try to ease the problems associated with overcrowding. In Connecticut, the state legislature commissioned a study of the causes of overcrowding in the state prisons as a part of their effort.[7] Their report showed that there were five broad categories of reasons for overcrowded prisons:

1. Continued increase in the number of offenders sent to prison.
2. Convicted inmates serving a greater portion of their sentences in prison.
3. Aggressive "tough on crime" approach by legislature and criminal justice system.
4. Lack of prison beds, especially high-security beds.
5. Poor planning and a lack of an accurate population projection and offender needs analysis.

Each of these contributing reasons for overcrowding are also very likely to be applicable to most other jurisdictions as well. And, each of these five primary reasons can be better understood when looking at how and why the condition exists. First, an increased number of offenders being sent to prison is a result of several factors, including high rates of offender recidivism and large numbers of offenders being sent to prison for violations of their conditions of probation or parole. But, so too is the increased number of offenders going to prison a result of changes in laws that establish sanctions for criminal offenses — during the 1990s and even continuing until today the statutorily established sentences for many criminal offenses have been increased and made harsher. This means more people are being sentenced to prison and for longer periods of time. The increased number of offenders being sentenced to prison is also affected by new crimes being established by legislatures and the ongoing "war on drugs" that brings increased policing of drug crimes and increased penalties for drug crime convictions.

---

6. *Ibid.*
7. Connecticut General Assembly. 2000. *Factors Impacting Prison Overcrowding: Report — Final.* New Haven: Office of Program Review and Investigations.

Tough on crime: the approach by lawmakers that contributed to the overcrowding problem in corrections by creating new criminal offenses in the law to "crack down" on criminal offenders through making laws stricter and sentencing individuals to prison for longer periods of time.

Truth in sentencing laws: laws that require incarcerated offenders to serve an established minimum percent of their sentences before they are eligible for parole or any other form of early release.

The second contributing reason to overcrowding, inmates serving a greater portion of their sentences, is a direct result of changes in state laws passed by legislators. This goes hand in hand with the third contributing reason for prison overcrowding — an aggressive "**tough on crime**" approach by lawmakers. As legislators move to create new criminal offenses in the law and work to "crack down" on criminal offenders through making laws stricter, more offenders are sentenced to prison and for longer periods of time. In many jurisdictions, these ideas have included the removal of the possibility of probation for certain criminal offenses and the narrowing of eligibility for offenders to be sentenced to intermediate sanctions. Recent years have also seen a movement toward what are referred to as **truth in sentencing** laws. These are laws that require incarcerated offenders to serve an established minimum percent of their sentences (often 75%, 85%, or 90%) before they are eligible for parole or any other form of early release. What such laws do is commit prison beds to individual offenders for longer periods of time than previously and remove a means for corrections officials to control the size of their institutional populations.

The fourth contributing reason for prison overcrowding focuses not on the issue of offenders coming to prison, but on the resources of the departments of corrections receiving sentenced inmates. In many jurisdictions, there are simply not enough beds for inmates. The typical way that states have tried to correct this issue is to build more prisons (or expand existing prisons). This, however, is exceptionally expensive and can involve a number of potentially volatile political issues (as will be discussed later in this chapter). Other ways to try to manage a population that is too large for the number of beds in a prison system is to transfer inmates to another state for incarceration (this would include paying the receiving state a per diem amount per inmate). But, this is only possible when another (presumably geographically close) state has empty prison beds, and that is not common. Or, a state can modify its laws to allow certain classes of felons to serve their time in local jails; this is fairly common in a number of states, such as Louisiana and Kentucky. In this situation, the state still pays a per diem to the local jail for housing the inmates. However, many jails are full and do not have space for state inmates. A third possible solution to this contributing reason for overcrowding is to renovate existing prison space, converting cells or other areas (dayrooms, classrooms, offices, etc.) into dormitories that can house more inmates. This can be a problem for security though, and some inmates (those classified as high security) are not appropriate for dormitory housing.

The fifth contributing reason for prison overcrowding is that many state governments, including but not limited to the department of corrections, did not anticipate a sharp and rapid increase in the number of offenders to be incarcerated. Research assessing the impact of changes in criminal statutes and sentencing options has either not been done or not done correctly, leading to a sense of complacency or simply not accepting the warnings of some that our correctional systems were not ready and capable of handling an influx of inmates. This situation creates a crisis situation when the inmates do arrive, and they were not expected and there had not been preparation for their arrival.

When overcrowding occurs, there are two basic paths that can be followed to attempt to manage and alleviate the situation. These are the **prison expansion model** and the **community corrections model**. Each is an attempt to address at least one of the contributing reasons for overcrowding, and to find new ways to continue to sanction offenders while remaining with the bounds of the law (recall the discussion of totality of conditions violations of inmates' rights from Chapter 7) and also considering financial costs.

Prison expansion model: an attempt to address at least one of the contributing reasons for overcrowding by building more prison space.

Community corrections model: an attempt to manage and alleviate overcrowding by not expanding the prison space for housing offenders but by curtailing the number of offenders that come to prison.

The prison expansion model is the solution of building more prison space. This approach does nothing to try to limit or reduce the number of offenders coming to prison or the length of time that offenders will be incarcerated, but merely tries to make more space for them. Building new prisons is the typical means of putting this approach into practice. Many states did build new prisons, and sometimes very rapidly. For instance, according to research by the Prison Policy Initiative, in the decade between 2000 and 2010, there were 110 prisons in the United States that were either newly constructed or renovated so as to accommodate at least 500 additional inmates.[8] This means that in a period of 120 months there were 110 new prisons built in the nation.

A community corrections model approach to manage and alleviate overcrowding looks not to expand the prison space available for housing offenders but to curtail the number of offenders coming to prison. This approach relies more heavily on community corrections (probation and intermediate sanctions). The idea here is to identify types of offenders, whether by classification measures or types of offenses, who do not need to be incarcerated, but who could be effectively managed (and perhaps even rehabilitated) more efficiently while in the community. Such an approach can work, as statistics show that some states have effectively implemented a community corrections model and actually lowered their prison populations. Between 2006 and 2011, ten states actually reduced their prison populations by 10 percent or more: California (17%), Hawaii (16%), Massachusetts (15%), Michigan (15%), New Jersey (14%), Alaska (13%), New York (13%), Connecticut (11%), Delaware (10%), and South Carolina (10%).[9] However, during the same time period, 20 states saw significant increases in their prison populations, led by West Virginia (17% increase) and Arizona (16% increase).

The importance of overcrowding in prisons is seen in the consequences that commonly arise from such conditions. Overcrowded prisons are home to more violence among inmates, and between inmates and staff, greater health problems that arise in crowded conditions (so, also more health care costs), difficulties segregating inmates based on classification and needs, fewer programming opportunities (due to both too many inmates for program capacities and

8. Prison Policy Initiative. 2010. *New and Expanded Federal and State Prisons Since 2000.* Northampton, MA: Prison Policy Initiative. Available at http://www.prisonersofthecensus.org/50states/newprisons.html.

9. The Pew Charitable Trusts. 2013. *U.S. Prison Count Continues to Drop.* Available at http://www.pewstates.org/news-room/press-releases/us-prison-count-continues-to-drop-85899457496.

conversion of program areas to housing units), increased physical wear and tear on the prison (leading to either security breaches or costs to repair), increased risk of riots and disturbances, and increased recidivism rates. Clearly, overcrowding is a problem with many consequences, for inmates, for administrators and staff, and for the public.

FINANCIAL CHALLENGES

As we saw in the opening section of this chapter, the issue of financial costs is a top priority and the most frequently reported challenge for state correctional administrators. According to the ASCA survey:

> "State Budget Cuts" have been a leading issue identified by correctional agencies since the December 2009 survey of agencies. The state budget cuts have impacted the correctional agency budgets and thus have been linked with other critical issues as well, such as prison population reductions, staff reductions, sentencing reforms, and other mechanisms while maintaining facility security and public safety.[10]

Budgets and expenditures in corrections are connected to essentially everything that is done in a prison, jail, community corrections program, or administrative capacity related to corrections. And, many of the challenges and problems with which correctional administrators, staff, and inmates have to contend are factors that drive up the costs of operating correctional facilities and programs. The previously discussed issue of overcrowding is one obvious contributor to cost increases and financial challenges. As prison populations increase (or even just remain stable), there are the accompanying costs of housing, feeding, caring for, and supervising inmates. And, as at least some prisons seek to impose more and tighter security measures on inmates, there are costs associated both with installing and implementing such new security measures and then maintaining the use of such measures. And, with changes to the legal requirements for the conditions of confinement and legally mandated standards of housing, staffing, programming, health and mental health care, and legal costs of defending inmate lawsuits, there are ever-increasing financial costs that must be absorbed by correctional budgets. All of this, of course, comes on top of the rising cost of just about everything in society — if it costs more for you and me to buy or maintain something, so too does the cost increase for corrections.

Actual "firm" cost figures are hard to come by in corrections, although it is possible to identify total budget allocations at the state, county, or federal level. When looking at the costs for state departments of corrections we see that in almost all states the DOC portion of the state budget is among the three or four biggest departmental allocations (along with public education, health care, and

10. Association of State Correctional Administrators, supra n.2, p. 8.

usually some type of infrastructure, such as transportation, highways, or roads).[11] In 2010, the most recent year for which there are available estimates of total costs, state governments (so, not including the federal government or local governments who usually operate jails) spent a total of $48.5 billion on corrections.[12] This represents, on average, approximately 3 percent of state government expenditures. While this may not sound like a very large portion of a state budget, the raw dollar amounts are clearly very significant.

Another way of looking at the costs of corrections is to assess the per inmate cost of incarceration. In 2010, across the entire nation, states spent an average of $28,323 per inmate to incarcerate. This amount has actually decreased slightly since 2001, when the highest per inmate cost of $32,459 was recorded. (The decrease in per inmate cost, however, does not mean that overall costs have necessarily decreased, for as more inmates are added to prisons and few new expenditures are added, the average cost can decrease slightly.) Obviously, this national average is not what it costs in every state, as some states will have lower costs, and some will have higher costs — just as is the case for living as a free-community citizen will vary significantly across different places in the country.

One of the central issues behind the increasing cost of incarceration is the cost of providing legally required health care to inmates. Health care costs have skyrocketed in all segments of American society in recent decades, and in correctional institutions this has held true as well. As the numbers of inmates incarcerated increases, and as inmates are incarcerated for longer periods of time and into their elderly and geriatric years, costs increase substantially. More inmates and more inmates with more health care needs of course translates into more costs. Health care costs account for anywhere from $2,000 to $9,000 per inmate in state corrections budgets. Recent years have seen nearly all states have increases in health care costs, with 23 states having the health care costs increase 50 percent or more and 6 states reporting a more than 100 percent increase in health care costs for inmates between 2001 and 2008.[13] In comparison, during the same time period only 4 states saw their inmate population increase by even 30 percent.

Within the corrections budget, institutional corrections account for usually about 75 percent of the total cost of corrections.[14] Here it is important to keep in mind that only about 20 percent of all correctional clients are in prison,[15] yet this component of corrections accounts for fully three-quarters of the cost of corrections. This raises some interesting, and challenging, policy questions. Think back to the discussion of the goals and ideologies of corrections in Chapter 3. What is it we want corrections to achieve? If it is to incapacitate offenders and

---

11. Tracy Kyckelhahn. 2012. *State Corrections Expenditures, 1982-2010.* Washington, D.C.: Bureau of Justice Statistics.
12. *Ibid.*
13. *Ibid.*
14. *Ibid.*
15. Lauren E. Glaze and Erika Parks. 2012. *Correctional Populations in the United States, 2011.* Washington, D.C.: Bureau of Justice Statistics.

render them unable to commit new offenses and victimize others, then incarceration is the way we believe we should handle offenders. But, the question that naturally arises is whether this is worth the expense and whether this is the best way to spend our tax dollars. Simply paying for the expense of corrections is one problem, deciding whether this is how we want to spend our taxes is another question. The point is, the expenses of corrections raise a number of public policy questions, and these are questions that we as a society are not likely to necessarily agree on.

SITING OF NEW CORRECTIONAL FACILITIES

Not surprisingly, the idea of having a new prison built in one's neighborhood, or even in one's larger community, is generally not something seen as highly desirable. All types of correctional facilities are commonly thought of with a sense of NIMBY, or Not In My Back Yard. Such an approach is common whenever community residents anticipate the construction of unwanted types of facilities. These locally unwanted land uses (LULUs) that spawn a NIMBY reaction include landfills, power plants, drug treatment centers, major highways, homeless shelters, and public housing developments. As with these types of structures, to have a prison, jail, juvenile detention facility, halfway house, or any other type of correctional facility in one's immediate vicinity is usually thought highly undesirable. People fear that such facilities will bring danger (especially by way of inmates escaping), noise, traffic, and a host of other undesired consequences. Included among these other consequences are a belief that if a correctional facility is built within sight of one's home, one's home value will plummet — after all, who will want to buy and live in a home next door to a prison?

However, as we will see in this section, the NIMBY approach is not universal, and in fact there are communities that actively work to recruit prisons to be built in their jurisdictions. Why would this be? For one simple reason: economics. A new prison brings with it new jobs. Especially during times of recession or economic uncertainty, recruiting new jobs to a community is a highly desirable goal. Therefore, it should not be surprising that many rural community government officials see prisons as a means of spurring economic development and bringing prosperity, or at the very least economic stability, to their communities. When seen in this positive light, it is understandable that many rural communities have actually enthusiastically recruited prison construction, and that officials (as well as residents and grass-roots community organizations) have lobbied state and federal corrections agencies seeking to have new prisons built in their communities.

When working to get selected as the site for a planned prison construction project, communities will often provide a number of economic benefits to try to entice government to select their communities. This may include provided donated land for the prison, paying for the construction of new roads or the upgrading of existing roads, providing tax incentives, offering housing for prison officials, and a number of other "benefits." This does not necessarily mean that all members of communities that seek to get prisons located in them are in favor of a prison coming to town, however. Sometimes the discussions and debates about whether to pursue a prison, and how to go about doing that, can lead to political turmoil and problems for both politicians and community members.

Decisions about where to build new correctional facilities involve a number of issues, and relate to both the siting of new, additional prisons as well as replacement of old prisons that are in need of replacement due to significant physical deterioration, an inability to be adapted to new technologies, and/or being designed in such a way as to lack efficiency in operating costs. Although this issue was only ranked as the fifteenth most challenging issue for departments of corrections in 2012,[16] it is an issue that has far-reaching consequences due to both financial costs and political consequences. Building a new prison is an exceptionally expensive endeavor. And, as we will see below, the political issues involved in where to place a new prison are complex and challenging on multiple levels.

Perhaps the most obvious fact about where prisons are built is that they are almost always in rural communities. This is most often explained as occurring because prisons provide jobs to communities with few employment opportunities and an available workforce. However, others contend that the real reasons for prisons to be built in rural areas are that costs (especially costs of purchasing the land) are less in rural areas than urban or suburban areas and there is likely to be less opposition to a prison from a dispersed population in a rural community. What this suggests is that the decision about where to site a new prison is largely an economic one.

However, although the arguments for where and where not to build new prisons are economic in nature, the true economic payoff of new prisons has not been clearly established.[17] But, the majority of studies of communities where prisons have been constructed do show at least some economic boost to the community. Whether there is an economic benefit may also be a function of perspective, and not everyone in a community will necessarily see or believe the same outcomes have occurred after a prison comes to a community. One study of the consequences of newly constructed prisons in Pennsylvania shows that people who live the closest to the prison are least likely to see or believe that there

16. Association of State Correctional Administrators, supra n.2.

17. For studies showing there is an economic payoff, see Zanetta Doyle. 2002. *Does Crime Pay? Pros and Cons of Rural Prisons.* Available at http://www.nado.org/pub/july021.html. Also, Eric C. Imhoff. 2002. *Determining the Socioeconomic Impacts of Prison Construction on Rural Communities: A Case Study of Somerset, Pennsylvania.* Unpublished master's thesis, Pennsylvania State University. For studies showing a lack of economic payoff, see William T. Holley. 2008. *Assessing the Impact of Prison Siting on Rural Economic Development.* Unpublished doctoral dissertation, George Mason University. Also, Kathlene S. Abrams and William Lyons. 1992. *Issues in Siting Correctional Facilities.* Washington, D.C.: National Institute of Corrections. Also, John O. Smykla, Carl E. Ferguson, David C. Cheng, Carolyn Trent, Bargara French, and Annette Waters. 1984. Effects of a Prison Facility on the Regional Economy. *Journal of Criminal Justice,* 12, 521-539.

is an economic benefit resulting, and community residents who have the greatest concerns about safety related to a new prison are also least likely to believe economic benefits are derived.[18] Interestingly, there also appears to be an effect on whether new prisons provide economic stimuli to communities based on whether the new prison is operated by the state or a private company. One study of states where privatization of prisons is either common or not shows that private prisons do not necessarily bring economic benefits to communities, largely because such facilities have smaller staffs and generally pay lower wages than state (or federally) operated prisons.[19]

The types of economic impact that may come from a new prison being located in a community are several. First, there is the economic impact of construction of the prison. Typically, new prisons are investments of $70 to $100 million. While this may appear to be a great deal of money on first glance, it is important to keep in mind that financial outlay for capital construction accounts for only less than 5 percent of state corrections budgets.[20] But, when a prison is constructed in a community, it brings with it construction jobs, and numerous other jobs and expenditures in the community during the time of construction. More long-term economic benefits are seen in the creation of jobs at the prison once it is opened and operating. A new prison will bring anywhere from 150 to 500 or more jobs to a community, depending on the size of the prison, its security level, specialized programs to be provided in it, and whether the prison is operated by the government or a private company. However, while jobs are created, it is not uncommon for many of the jobs in the new prison — especially any above entry-level security positions — to be of a nature for which most or all rural community residents are not prepared or qualified. Included in nearly all prisons are health care jobs, teachers, electricians, and other skilled trades and professions. Many of these jobs are filled by people from outside the immediate community where the prison is built. This means some of the economic benefits that accompany new prisons are not restricted to the local community, but instead are dispersed to cities and towns from which some staff will commute.

Along with the jobs, it is common for prisons to bring population growth in small communities near the prison. As jobs are created, especially jobs that require special skills or training, some people will move to the community to take the jobs, thereby spurring real estate sales and/or development, more business in local stores and restaurants, and more need for services and retail. Such development brings people to the community, money to the community, and increases in sales taxes that infuse money to the local economy as well. And,

---

18. Michael J. Hannon and Kevin E. Courtright. 2011. Exploring the Perception of Economic Impact of State Correctional Institutions in Rural Pennsylvania. *International Journal of Business and Social Science,* 2, (22), 51-69.
19. Shaun Genter, Gregory Hooks, and Clayton Mosher. 2013. Prisons, Jobs and Privatization: The Impact of Prisons on Employment Growth in Rural U.S. Counties, 1997-2004. *Social Science Research,* 42, (3), 596-610.
20. Tracy Kyckelhahn. 2012. *State Corrections Expenditures, 1982-2010.* Washington, D.C.: Bureau of Justice Statistics.

when more jobs are available, fewer people receive unemployment (and other) government benefits, which is also an economic benefit.

While the theoretical and hypothetical economic benefits of a new prison for a community are easy to outline, they are not always easy to achieve. A national study of communities in which a new prison was built during the 1990s unfortunately shows that in the years following the opening of a prison, many communities did see their populations increase, but so too did their unemployment rates increase, while housing values and overall wages declined.[21]

The debate about whether or not prison construction is beneficial for a community continues, with evidence available on both sides of the issue. As summarized by James Marquart:

> In summary, prison siting in rural communities, for whatever reason, is as old as the prison itself. Rationales for siting change with the times. Today, rural siting takes on an economic development perspective. Wait ten years and another rationale will surface. Does a rural prison enhance economic development? It depends on your perspective. If you believe prisons "don't work" to begin with, then the economic development theory is on thin ice. On the other hand, if you are a mayor or county official in some remote area of this state, a prison, like a military base, makes good economic sense.

EVIDENCE-BASED CORRECTIONS

One of the unfortunate realities of American corrections is that although we have attempted to do many things to "fix" or "teach a lesson to" or even just restrict the opportunities of offenders to commit new crimes, we have never found a very effective and efficient manner to achieve our goals. The history of American corrections, in the eyes of many observers, has been a dismal failure. We spend billions of dollars every year to incarcerate, treat, supervise, and work with offenders, and more often than not we see these same offenders return to committing crime. While it is true that crime rates have gone down in the last few years in the United States, no one has seriously argued that this is due to the actions of corrections. We continue to seek new ways of addressing our crime problem. The search continues for a way to either change or simply stop criminal offenders from committing crimes.

One promising approach, which draws on scientific evidence rather than just beliefs, ideas, and ideology, is the approach known as **evidence-based corrections**. Evidence-based corrections is "professional corrections practices and programs that have been proven effective by the best research evidence

Evidence-based corrections: practices and programs that have been proven effective by the best research evidence in reducing offender recidivism.

21. Terry L. Besser and Margaret M. Hanson. 2004. Development of Last Resort: The Impact of New State Prisons on Small Town Economies in the United States. *Journal of the Community Development Society*, 35, (2), 1-16.

in reducing offender recidivism."[22] Or, said a bit differently, evidence-based practice is "the application of empirical research to professional practice" when the research produces evidence-based knowledge, which is defined as "conclusions drawn from rigorous research studies that have been replicated numerous times with defined, measurable outcomes about the effectiveness of an intervention or process."[23]

In short, the idea here is that we rely on only things that have been tried, studied, and shown to make a difference. The value offered by such an approach is that we use our resources only for programs, structures, and processes that have already been shown to make a positive difference. And, just as importantly, we do not use any of our resources on programs, structures, and processes that research has demonstrated do not make a positive difference. Such an approach makes logical sense, and for many students this would seem to simply be using common sense. But, what differentiates the idea of evidence-based corrections is that we move beyond the approach of designing and implementing correctional programs, structures, and processes that are based on a guiding ideology. Instead, we open our eyes and institutions to those things that work to reduce recidivism and make day-to-day operations of a prison, jail, or community corrections program run more smoothly. Whereas in the past the answer to the question, "why should we do this particular thing with an offender?" was "because it is about rehabilitation or retribution or reintegration," today the answer is "we should do this because we know that it works."

The history of attempts to change offenders' behaviors has shown such poor results that it has been referred to by one highly esteemed team of correctional scholars as "correctional quackery":

> In contrast to professionalism, quackery is dismissive of scientific knowledge, training, and expertise. Its posture is strikingly overconfident, if not arrogant. It embraces the notion that interventions are best rooted in "common sense," in personal experiences (or clinical knowledge), in tradition, and in "superstition." "What works" is thus held to be "obvious.". . . Correctional quackery . . . is the use of treatment interventions that are based on neither 1) existing knowledge of the cause of crime nor 2) existing knowledge of what programs have been shown to change offender behavior. The hallmark of correctional quackery is thus ignorance. Such ignorance about crimes and its cures at times is "understandable" — that is, linked not to the willful rejection of research, but to being in a field in which professionalism is not expected or supported. At other times, however, quackery is proudly displayed, as its advocates boldly proclaim that they have nothing to learn from research conducted by academics "who have never worked with a criminal."[24]

---

22. Roger K. Warren. 2008. The Most Promising Way Forward: Incorporating Evidence-Based Practice into State Sentencing and Corrections Policies. *Federal Sentencing Reporter,* 20, (5), 324-325.
23. Frank Domurad and Mark Carey. 2010. *Implementing Evidence Based Practices.* Silver Spring, MD: Center for Effective Public Policy.
24. Edward J. Latessa, Francis T. Cullen, and Paul Gendreau. 2002. Beyond Correctional Quackery — Professionalism and the Possibility of Effective Treatment. *Federal Probation,* 66, (2), 43.

In contrast to correctional quackery, evidence-based corrections is about corrections only doing things that have evidence behind them showing that they work. This is an idea that corrections has borrowed from a number of other professions and disciplines. Perhaps most obvious is the use of evidence-based corrections in medicine. Think for a minute about why your doctor does what he does to correct a health problem of yours. Your doctor does not try to explain to you that he believes X and Y and Z are important, and maybe if he does A to you it will make a difference. Instead, your doctor is prescribing you medication that has been proven in scientific studies to correct particular problems. This is the idea that today we are starting to rely on in corrections. With the many different types of programs that are done in corrections (see Chapter 12), we can track offenders who participate in those programs and see if the interventions make a difference. Those that we find do make a difference are the programs we continue using.

Evidence-based corrections approaches seek to identify scientifically rigorous evaluations of correctional practices and programs, and then look across the body of studies to identify things that are consistently shown to achieve positive outcomes (most often defined as reduced recidivism for participants). This means that evidence-based corrections relies on **systematic reviews** of studies of correctional programs — looking at all well-done studies of a particular type of program and calculating an average amount of change in offenders. A more specific type of systematic review, what is called a meta-analysis, is also relied upon, although the statistical analyses that are involved in a meta-analysis require a number of specific things to be present in all included studies. Because of these requirements, meta-analyses often include fewer studies in their review than other types of systematic reviews.

Systematic reviews: looking at all well-done studies of a particular type of program and calculating the average amount of change in offenders.

The state of evidence-based practices in corrections is something that is still developing. In some jurisdictions, evidence-based practices are commonly used, but in many other places evidence-based practices remain a goal and intention. As one observer of the growth of evidence-based corrections notes, at least in the area of community corrections, "[t]he use of research evidence by policy makers, program administrators, and field practitioners is more prevalent today than ever before. Despite the increased reliance on research to inform practice, however, a great deal of work still needs to be done to bridge the gap between science and day-to-day operations in the field."[25] In order to completely transform our thinking into an outlook that prioritizes a focus on evidence-based practices, it may be necessary to abandon our thinking about specific programs, structures, or intervention with a search for "what works" and instead move to thinking that is itself based on "evidence based decision making."[26] Such a way of approaching corrections would put primary emphasis on a guiding framework for all that we do

25. Stephen M. Haas. 2013. Introduction: Current Practice and Challenges in Evidence-Based Community Corrections. *Justice Research and Policy,* 15, 1.
26. *Ibid.*, pp. 1-15.

that begins with the idea of asking, "what do we know that has been shown to be effective and that makes a difference?" In this way, we would always be thinking about what we know has been shown to work AND what our goals are, or what it is that we use as a criteria for "success." In order to fully implement an evidence-based approach to corrections, we need to develop organizational leadership and staff capacity; identify ways to transfer scientific evidence about what works into actual, operating programs; train staff on key skills; and continually monitor how we are implementing programs and whether what we are actually doing continues to correspond with what we originally set out to do.[27]

The important question then is, what are the corrections programs that have been shown to be effective? There are a number of approaches to working with offenders that are known to be effective. But, it is important to keep in mind that we are not talking about anything that is 100 percent effective and changes each and every offender's behavior. Although different people would set the standard at different levels, we can say that a program variety that achieves a 10 percent reduction in recidivism is effective, and should be recommended for continued use and expansion. In one of the earliest systematic reviews of correctional program, the Washington State Institute for Public Policy identified six programs that effectively achieve an average of a 10 percent reduction in recidivism for participating offenders.[28] These six "effective" programs (and their average reduction in participants' recidivism) are adult drug courts (10.7%); drug treatment for offenders that is conducted in the community (12.4%); cognitive behavioral treatment for sex offenders while in prison (14.9%); cognitive behavioral treatment for low-risk sex offenders in the community (31.2%); treatment-oriented intensive supervision in community corrections (21.9%); and vocational education programs provided in prison (12.6%).

The value of evidence-based correctional practices is becoming widely recognized. As a result, so too are such ideas directly influencing policy and practice of corrections. For instance, in 2011, the Arkansas legislature passed a law requiring the state's community corrections department to develop and implement programs based on evidence-based practice. Other states and local governments have also passed similar laws and resolutions, and the practice is only expected to continue to spread.

This is not to say that nothing else except what we already have research demonstrating the effectiveness of actually works. But, this does say that nothing else has been proven to work. At least not yet. Just as in the scenario with your doctor, the only medications and treatments he may know of today that have been shown in clinical trials to be effective may not be the only things that could possibly help you, there very well may be more things shown in the future to work, but they have either not yet been tried or not yet been tested. So, the

27. Faye S. Taxman and Steven Belenko. 2012. *Implementing Evidence Based Practices in Community Corrections and Addiction Treatment*. New York: Springer Publishing.

28. Washington State Institute for Public Policy, supra n.1.

question arises, should we rest on our laurels and use only what we know as of today to be effective, or should we continue to experiment and devise new approaches that we can test, and perhaps find evidence to support? In a strict sense, advocates of the evidence-based corrections approach would argue that we should not invest resources into anything that has yet to be supported with evidence. However, the obvious question then is how could we ever find anything additional that works? In a way, we have a classic chicken and egg question — which did come first?

But, simply knowing whether a particular program, intervention, structure, or process "works" is only the first step. It is also important to consider the cost of a program, and the amount/degree of positive outcome that is derived from particular levels of investment. This is the idea of a **cost-benefit analysis**. The question here is, what is the cost of achieving a particular level of benefit? And, at which cost (e.g., price) is it worth getting the benefit? For example, if we know that we can reduce the level of recidivism among burglars by 10 percent, is it worth it to invest $700 billion every year in a program that achieves this level of success? Probably not. Is it worth investing $7 billion? What about $7 million? Or, $700? For $700, most everyone would say this is a good cost-benefit. For $7 million? Probably only a handful of people would see that as a good cost-benefit. So, where in between is the generally "acceptable" level of cost? Or, at what level of benefit is the program worth $7 million? If we could completely, 100 percent eliminate all burglars from ever committing burglary again, that might be a good investment. But, what about if we achieved only a 50 percent reduction? The point here is that while we may be able to identify programs that work, we also need to consider whether we can afford to implement such programs. This is a political decision.

Cost-benefit analysis: when the cost of a program and the amount/degree of positive outcome that is derived from a particular level of investment are factored into whether or not a certain program should be offered or continue to be offered.

At this point we have come full circle. What happens in corrections, and even the idea of having corrections and whom among offenders are put into corrections (as well as what type of corrections, for how long, under what conditions, etc.), are all political decisions. Corrections simply is a political institution. Everything we do in corrections is a political, or at the least a politically influenced, decision.

Look back at the issues we have discussed throughout this text. Starting from definitions of crime, ideas about what types of behaviors merit social sanctions, how we have carried out sanctions throughout history, how ideologies influence our ideas about what corrections should be, and how we have differentially processed different types of offenders at different places and times in history — all of this is a political process and set of decisions.

So, in the end, what can and should American corrections look like? That depends on political views and beliefs. Everything we do is a consequence of a series of decisions that are made by numerous individuals, groups, and organizations. And, how those decisions are made is the result of politics. Politics change with time, and so do our beliefs and desires for corrections. The changes that happen may not be swift and obvious, and consistency may seem to be the most obvious characteristic of corrections, but there are changes. Change in corrections is the result of change in society. Only when society changes can and does corrections change.

Summary

In recent years, correctional administrators have consistently identified overcrowding, financial costs, and building sites for new facilities as the primary challenges they confront. Although there are not reliable statistics on the true extent of the overcrowding problem, it is estimated that state prisons generally operate at their capacity or at 15 percent above that limit. The primary ways that corrections has attempted to manage overcrowding has either been through building more prisons or diverting more offenders to community corrections. At least in part because of the large numbers of persons under correctional supervision, corrections is almost always one of the three or four most expensive tasks of state governments. Costs only increase as new prisons are built, and some of the costs are associated with finding and effectively working with communities where new prisons are proposed. Costs are also involved in the identification and implementation of good (e.g., evidence-based) programs for inmates.

Key Terms

- Community corrections model
- Cost-benefit analysis
- Crowding
- Evidence-based corrections
- Prison expansion model
- Systematic reviews
- Tough on crime
- Truth in sentencing laws

Index

A

Absolute deprivation, 136
Access to the courts, 104, 107, 116–117, 119, 120
Accreditation, 255
Acquittal, 21
Active monitoring system, 183
Administration of jail, 168–172
Administration of prison, 67–80
  autocratic wardens, 73–74
  bureaucratic wardens, 74–75
  delegative wardens, 75
  discipline, 68
  goals, 67–69
  key terms, 80
  management, 72–77
  participatory management, 76–77
  prison staff. *See* Staff of prison
  security, 68
  segregation, 68
  summary, 79–80
  treatment programs, 68–69
  wardens, 72–75
  working to achieve goals, 69–70
Administrative law, 18, 19, 102, 194, 195
Aftercare for former inmates, 207–210
  contemporary programs, 208–210
  defined, 207
Agriculturally based prisons, 55
Alaska
  female inmates, 149
  prison population, 263
  state government administration of jails, 169
Alcoholics Anonymous, 175, 222, 223
Alternatives to incarceration, 58, 184
"Amenities" in corrections, 96, 238, 240
American Correctional Association, 56, 88, 135, 141, 255
American Historical Association, 45
American Medical Association, 217
American Prison Association, 141
American Public Health Association, 137
American Revolution, 49, 58, 62
"An eye for an eye." *See* Retaliation
Andrews, Donald A., 214
Aristotle, 30
Arizona
  gang members in prisons, 90
  jails, 168
  prison population, 263
Arkansas
  cruel and unusual punishment, 108
  gang members in prisons, 90
  jails, 168
  prison farm, 108
  totality of conditions, 108
Arts programs, 236–237
Assize of Clarendon, 47
Association of State Correctional Administrators, 258, 260, 264
Auburn system, 50–51, 52, 53, 66
Augustus, John, 59–60
Authority, defined, 14
Autocratic wardens, 73–74

B

Banishment, 9, 10, 31, 62
Barber, Scot, 94
Barter systems, 97
Bartollas, Clemens, 2
Baxter v. Palmigiano, 116
Beggars, 46
Bell v. Wolfish, 115
Benefit of clergy, 58
Bentham, Jeremy, 38
Bisexual inmates, 128, 154
Body cavity searches, 114–115
Bonger, William A., 34–35
Bonta, James, 214
Booth v. Churner, 118
Bounds v. Smith, 117
Briggs, Chadd S., 134
Brockway, Zebulon, 65, 199
Brown v. Plata, 137
Budget cuts, 259, 264. *See also* Financial challenges
Bureau of Justice Assistance, 227
Bureau of Justice Statistics, 5, 123, 127, 138, 221
Bureau of Labor Statistics, 125, 241, 242
Bureau of Prisons, 229, 231
Bureau of the Census, 5
Bureaucratic model of management, 74–75
Bureaucratic wardens, 74–75
Burton, Velmer S., Jr., 104, 105

C

California
  aftercare programs, 209
  conjugal visits, 92
  consensus model of management, 76
  gang members in prisons, 90
  homelessness, 208
  jails, 165, 172
  new generation jails, 165
  overcrowding, 137
  parole, 203
  prison population, 82, 90, 263
  privatization, 172
  probation, 193, 200
  salaries of correctional officers, 242
  visitation policies, 110
"Canteen," 96
Canute, King, 31
Capital punishment. *See* Death penalty
Captain of the guard, 70
Career criminals, 87
Case law, 18–19, 195
Castellano, Thomas C., 134
Cell phones in corrections, 152, 259
Censorship of mail, 111, 116
Chain gang, 56
Chaplains, 232–233
Child congregation locations, 41
Civil death, 102–103
Civil Rights Act of 1871, 105
Civil service system, 75
Civil War, 53, 54, 56
Classical-positivist dilemma, 33
Classical view of crime, 33–34
Classification procedures, 68
Clemency, 106
Clemmer, Donald, 92
Clergy, benefit of, 58
Clubs and organizations, 237

Coerced sex, 127
Coercive authority, 248
Cognitive behavioral therapy, 219
  defined, 219
  substance abuse treatment, 223, 224
Collateral costs of corrections, 26
Collective behavior, 144–145
College programs, 229, 230
Combination sentences, 205
Community corrections, 185–211
  aftercare for former inmates, 207–210
  arguments against, 186–187
  arguments for, 187–189
  contemporary programs, 208–210
  defined, 185, 263
  former inmates, problems facing, 207–208
  institutional corrections vs., 185–189
  key terms, 211
  parole. *See* Parole
  probation. *See* Probation
  shock incarceration, 205–206
  summary, 210–211
Community service, 190
Community supervision, 205
Compensation of staff
  low pay, 176, 177, 242, 245, 252, 253, 255
Conditions of confinement, 108, 204, 264
Conflict model for explaining prison riots, 143–144
Congregate work, 50, 51
Conjugal visits, 92, 235–236
Connecticut
  organized uprising, 139
  overcrowding, 261
  prison population, 263
  state government administration of jails, 169
  therapeutic communities, 227
Consensus model of management, 76
Constitution, 17–19
  defined, 17
  Eighth Amendment, 23, 32, 103, 107–109, 119, 126, 137, 191, 216
  Fifth Amendment, 21, 115
  First Amendment, 110, 111, 112, 113, 203, 232
  Fourteenth Amendment, 115, 157, 196
  Fourth Amendment, 114
  Thirteenth Amendment, 104, 105
Constitutional law, 195
Contact visits, 110, 174, 235. *See also* Visitation policies
Contemporary challenges, 257–274
  biggest, in eyes of correctional administrators, 258–260
  evidence-based corrections, 269–274
  financial, 264–266
  key terms, 274
  overcrowding, 23, 260–264
  siting of new facilities, 266–269
  summary, 274
Contraband, 90, 96–97, 111, 135, 144, 145, 154, 246, 259
  body cavity searches for, 114
  defined, 96, 152
  employee smuggling of, 115
  searches for, 114, 115, 247
Control model of management, 76
"Convict code," 155
Conviction, defined, 21
Cooper v. Morin, 157
Cooperative jail administration, 170
Corporal punishment, 46, 109
Correctional education, 228
Correctional officers, statistics, 242–243. *See also* Staff
Correctional programs, defined, 213. *See also* Programs
Corrections, defined, 1
Cost-benefit analysis, 273
Cost-effective program, 214
Costs of corrections, 187, 265. *See also* Budget cuts; Financial challenges
Costs of health care, 216, 265
Counseling programs, 218–228
Court access, 104, 107, 116–117, 119, 120
Courtesy stigmas, 99
Crime and corrections, 1–12
  key terms, 12
  summary, 12
Crime index, 5
Criminal justice, 13–27
  barriers to system success and achievement, 24–26
  components of system, 19–23
  corrections, 22–23
  judicial process, 20–21
  key terms, 27
  law enforcement, 19–20
  social functions of, 13–14
  summary, 26–27
  as system, 24
Criminology
  corrections and, 1–3
  defined, 2
Crofton, Sir Walter Crofton, 63–64
Crowding, defined, 260. *See also* Overcrowding
Cruel and unusual punishment, 23, 32–33, 103, 107–109, 113, 119, 126, 137, 191, 216
Cullen, Frances T., 104, 105
Culture of prison, 92–96

D

Day reporting centers, 181–182
Death penalty, 9, 31, 32, 33, 37, 38, 108
Death row, 33, 150
Declaration of Principles, 56–57, 228
Delaware
  gang members in prisons, 90
  prison population, 263
  state government administration of jails, 169
Delegative model of management, 75
Delegative wardens, 75
Deliberate indifference to needs of inmates, 114, 137, 216
Demographics
  correctional officers, 242, 250
  gang membership, 135
  jail inmates, 167, 168, 184, 222
  local corrections, 167
  parolees, 200
  racial, 84, 168, 222
  substance abuse, 222
  wardens, 72–73
  women in corrections, 82, 148, 222
Dental care, 217
Deprivation, adaptations to, 136
Deputies, 176. *See also* Staff
  defined, 70
  discipline for violation of rules/regulations, 176
Determinate sentences, 30. *See also* Sentences
Deterministic view, 34
Deterrence, 36–39
  contrasting views, 37–39
  defined, 36
  general, 37
  specific, 37

Detoxification in jail, 224
Dinitz, Simon, 2, 140
Direct supervision, 165
Disabled inmates, 86, 103, 217
Discipline, 68
  defined, 68
  goal of, 68
  procedures, rights related to, 115–116
Disease model
  sex offender treatment, 225, 226
  substance abuse treatment, 223
Disenfranchisement, 103, 106
Disruptive group, 89
Diversion centers, 182
Double jeopardy, 21
Drug crimes, 12, 261
Drug laws, 17, 18
Due process rights, 115–116, 194, 196–197
Dying inmates, 217, 218

E

Early release programs, 65–66, 197, 199–200, 205, 210, 220, 262. *See also* Parole
Economic systems, 96–97
Economic violence, 131–132
Educational model for substance abuse treatment, 223–224
Educational programs, 228–231
Eighth Amendment, 23, 32, 103, 107–109, 119, 126, 137, 191, 216
Elderly inmates, 86–88, 217, 260, 265
Electronic monitoring system, 182
Elmira Reformatory, 52, 53, 65, 199
End-of-life health care, 217, 218
English as a second language (ESL), 228
Environmental conditions, 141–142
Equal protection clause, 157
Equality
  defined, 30
  equity vs., 29–30
Equity
  defined, 30
  equality vs., 29–30
Escapes by inmates, 49, 56, 68, 70–71, 73, 109, 111, 126, 137, 140, 204, 246, 247
ESL. *See* English as a second language (ESL)
Estelle v. Gamble, 113, 114, 215, 216, 218
Evidence-based corrections, 269–274
Excessive bail and fines, 103
Executive clemency, 106
Ex-prisoners, barriers faced by, 97–99

F

Faith-based initiatives, 231–234
Family-based programs, 234–236
Farkas, Mary Ann, 250, 251
Federal Bureau of Investigation, 4–5
Felony convictions, sentences for, 162
Female inmates. *See* Women in corrections
Fenceless camps, 95
Fifth Amendment, 21, 115
Financial challenges, 264–266
First Amendment, 110, 111, 112, 113, 203, 232
First generation jails, 163
Fisher-Giorlando, Marianne, 139
Florida
  gang members in prisons, 90
  prison population, 82, 90
  probation, 193
  reintegration program, 209
Folkways, 14
Force, defined, 14
Fourteenth Amendment, 115, 157, 196
Fourth Amendment, 114
Fox, Vernon, 143
Free speech, right of, 110, 111, 203
Frivolous lawsuits by inmates, 117
  decline in, 118
  defined, 118
Furman v. Georgia, 107
Gagnon v. Scarpelli, 197, 205

G

Galley ships, 48–49, 61
Gangs
  prison. *See* Prison gangs
  street. *See* Street gangs
Gaols, 47, 162, 163
Gay inmates, 128
GED programs, 157, 228, 229
General deterrence, defined, 37
General equivalency diplomas (GEDs). *See* GED programs
Geographic variations in jails, 168
Georgia
  probation, 193
  women, prison for, 53
Geriatric inmates, 86, 217, 259, 260, 265
Glaser, Daniel, 93
Glick, Steven M., 94
Glover v. Johnson, 157
Goals of corrections, 11–12
Goffman, Erving, 81
Good-time laws, 42, 64, 65, 199, 201
Great Depression, 140
Group therapy, 219, 223

H

Hands-off policy of judicial system, 102, 103, 104, 105, 106, 107, 119
Hanging, 32, 46, 58, 131
Hawaii
  prison population, 263
  state government administration of jails, 169
Hayes, Rutherford B., 56
Health care
  costs, 216, 265
  dying inmates, 217, 218
  elderly inmates, 217
  end-of-life, 217, 218
  programs, 215–219
  standards, 217
  types, 217
Hearings
  disciplinary, 115, 187
  on parole revocation, 204–205
  on probation revocation, 196, 197, 204
Hegel, Georg, 36
Henry II, 47, 58, 162
Henry VIII, 32
Hepatitis, 178, 180, 208
Hilborn, Marilyn, 94
History, 45–66
  after Auburn and Pennsylvania, 51–52
  Alexander Maconochie, 62–63
  alternatives to incarceration, 58
  Auburn system, 50–51, 53
  clergy, benefit of, 58
  filing of cases, 59
  galley ships, 48–49, 61
  Hospice of San Michel, 48
  House of Corrections, 48
  judicial reprieve, 59

History (cont'd)
key terms, 66
Maison de Force, 48
modern era of corrections, 56–57
parole in United States, 64–66
parole origins, 61–62
penitentiary
emergence of, 49–52
first, 47
forerunners of, 47–49
Pennsylvania system, 50, 51, 53
probation, founding of, 59–61
reformatory movement, 52–53
Sir Walter Crofton, 63–64
southern prisons, 53–56
summary, 66
Walnut Street Jail, 47, 49, 112, 139, 228, 230, 231
HIV/AIDS, 158, 178, 179, 180, 208, 217, 218
Holt v. Sarver, 108, 109
Home incarceration, 182–183
Homelessness, 179, 180, 208, 266
Homicide among inmates, 123, 130
"Honey bucket" sanitation system, 173
Hospice care in corrections, 217–218
Hospice of San Michel, 48
House of Corrections, 48
Household crimes, 4, 6
Howard, John, 32, 49
Hubbard, Sally, 53
Hudson v. Palmer, 114

I

Idaho
female inmates, 149
gang members in prisons, 90
Ideologies of corrections, 35–43
deterrence, 36–39
general deterrence, 37
incapacitation, 40–41
just deserts, 41–42
rehabilitation, 39–40
reintegration, 40
retribution, 35–36
specific deterrence, 37
vengeance, 35–36
Illinois
aftercare programs, 209
new generation jails, 165
Immigrants, illegal, 162
Importation model for understanding inmate behavior, 133
Imprisonment rate, 147–148
Incapacitation, 40–41
Incarceration rates
defined, 82
by race and sex, 84
statistics, 82–84
Indeterminate sentences, 34, 52, 61, 64, 65, 198, 199
defined, 30, 64, 198
Index offense, 5
Indiana, women's prison in, 53
Inmate code, 95–86
Inmate council, 77
Inmate-on-inmate violence, 122–125
Inmate-on-staff violence, 125–126
Inmate trustee system, 55–56
Insane, incurably, 50
Institutional corrections vs. community corrections, 185–189
Institutional programs for women, 157–158
Intensive supervision probation (ISP), 192
"Intermediate system," 63
Intermittent supervision, 164, 166, 183
Iowa, prison population in, 82
Irish system, 63
Iron law of oligarchy, 245
"Isolate" system, 50
Jackson v. Bishop, 109

J

Jailhouse lawyers, 116
Jails, 161–184
administration, 168–172
city government administration, 168–169
contemporary, 161–162
cooperative administration, 170–171
county government administration, 168–169
defined, 161
demographic variations, 167
design of, 164–166
evolution of local correctional efforts, 162–166
geographic variations, 168
key terms, 184
linear design, 164, 165
management, 168–172
mental health, 180–181
minimal programming opportunities, 175
poor inmate health, 178–179
populations, 167–168
private corrections, 171–172
problematic aspects of, 172
recruitment of staff, 176
retention of staff, 176
staffing deficiencies, 175–178
state government administration, 169
substance abuse, 179, 221–224
substandard physical facilities, 173–174
suicide, 179–180
summary, 183–184
training of staff, 177
turnover of staff, 177–178
Jiang, Shanhe, 139
Johnson, Robert, 33
Judicial intervention, 102–104
Judicial process, 20–21
Judicial reprieve, 59
Judicial review, 18, 20, 119
Jurisdiction, defined, 149
Just deserts model of punishment, 41–42
Justice, meaning of, 30

K

Kalinich, David, 97
Kant, Immanuel, 36
Karlson, Kevin, 94
Kastler, Jerry, 94
Kauffman, Kelsey, 78, 79, 126
Kentucky
aftercare programs, 209
contraband, 152
female inmates, 149, 150, 153
institutional programs, 157
jails, 162, 262
job duties of correctional officer, 247
probation and parole officers, 189
visitation policies, 153
vocational programs, 157
Korean War, 140

L

Labeling theory, 92
Lahm, Karen, 137
Law
administrative, 19
case law, 18–19
constitutions, 17–19
defined, 15

legislatures, 16–17
procedural, 15–16
role in society, 14–15
sources of, 16–19
statutory, 16
substantive, 15–16
Law enforcement, 19–20
Leasing system, 54–55
Legislatures, 16–17
Lesbian inmates, 154
Libraries in correctional institutions, 117, 174, 228, 237, 239, 240
Life imprisonment, 48
Line officers, 70
Linear design of jails, 164, 165
Literacy programs, 229–230
Living space, standards for, 137
Local corrections, 161–184. *See also* Jails
additional forms, 181–183
day reporting centers, 181–182
demographic variations, 167
diversion centers, 182
evolution of, 162
geographic variations, 168
home incarceration, 182–183
key terms, 184
populations, 167–168
summary, 183–184
Locally unwanted land uses (LULUs), 266
Lockstep, 50
Lockup, 126, 161, 162
Logan v. United States, 104
Loitering, 46
Lombroso, Cesare, 34
Long-term imprisonment, experiences of, 85–86
Louisiana
jails, 162, 262
prison farms, 55
prison population, 82
LULUs (locally unwanted land uses), 266

M

Mabli, Jerome, 94
Maconochie, Alexander, 62–63
Mail, use of, 110–111, 152, 234
Maine, parole in, 200
Maison de Force, 48
Management of jail, 168–172
Management of prison, 72–77
Mandatory early release programs, 65–66, 199–200. *See also* Early release programs
Marijuana laws, 17, 18
Marks system, 62
Marquart, James, 269
Martinson, Robert, 39, 40
Marx, Karl, 34
Massachusetts, prison population in, 82, 263
Maternal bonds, 158–159. *See also* Women in corrections
Meacham v. Fano, 116
Medical care, 113–114. *See also* Health care
Medical model approach to criminology, 39
Medical services for women in corrections, 158
Mempa v. Rhay, 196, 204
Menard Prison, 92, 93
Menninger, Karl, 29
Mental illness, 93, 138–139, 151, 259
former inmates, problems facing, 207
high incidence of, 138–139
in jails, 179, 180–181
self-injury and, 130, 131
of staff, 77
statistics, 221
therapy, 219
violence and, 121, 124, 128, 133, 146
women in corrections, 151, 158
Michel, Robert, 245
Michigan
economic system, 97
female inmates, 150
indeterminate sentence statute, 64, 198, 199
prison population, 263
responsibility model of management, 76
visitation policies, 110
warden job duties, 73
Middle Ages, 31, 46
Millbank Prison, 32
Minnesota, prison population in, 82
Misdemeanors, sentences for, 162
Mississippi
conjugal visits, 92
prison farms, 55
Monroe v. Pape, 105
Montana
female inmates, 149
gang members in prisons, 90
"Moral regeneration" activities, 139
Mores, defined, 14
Morrissey v. Brewer, 196, 197, 204
Most serious offenses, 84

N

Narcotics Anonymous, 175, 222, 223
National Crime Victimization Survey (NCVS), 3, 5–6, 7
National Guard, 140
National Inmate Survey, 127, 128, 156
National Jail Workforce Survey, 174
National Prison Congress, 56, 228
National Sheriffs' Association, 174
Net-widening by shock incarceration programs, 206
New generation jails, 165
New Hampshire, gang members in prisons, 90
New Jersey
prison population, 263
salaries of correctional officers, 242
New Mexico, jails in, 168
New Start progam, 209
New York
Auburn system, 50
good-time laws, 64
indeterminate sentence statute, 64–65, 198, 199
new generation jails, 165
parole conditions, 203
prison population, 263
reformatory movement, 52
therapeutic communities, 227
NIMBY (Not In My Back Yard), 266
Nonreporting of crime, 6–8
North Dakota
female inmates, 149
gang members in prisons, 90
jails, 168
parole, 200
Not In My Back Yard (NIMBY), 266
Nursing homes in prison, 217

O

Obligations, defined, 15
Offenders About to Reenter Society (OARS), 209

Ohio
cruel and unusual punishment, 109
probation, 193
"shock probation" statute, 205
totality of conditions, 109
visitation policies, 110
One-Stop Employment Centers, 209
Organized disturbances and riots, 139–141
Overcrowding, 23, 50, 109, 136–138, 185, 187, 199, 201, 206, 210, 257, 259, 260–264
alleviation of, 263
defined, 136
reasons for, 261–262
Overton v. Bazzetta, 110, 119
Owen, Barbara, 155

P

Paramilitary model of organization, 70
Pardon, 59, 106, 197, 198
Parens patriae
defined, 103
health care needs of inmates, 215
Parental rights, termination of, 103
Parenting programs, 236, 240
Parole, 197–205
conditions of, 202–203
contemporary, 198–200
defined, 61, 198
due process rights, 204–205
eligibility date, 201
factors for granting of, 201
failure of, 203
goal of, 198
granting parole, 201–202
length of, 202
origins of, 61–62
process, 200–205
revocation of, 203–205
U.S. parolees, 200
violation of, 162
Parolees, statistics on, 200
Participatory management, 76–77
consensus model, 76
control model, 76
defined, 76
inmate council, 77
responsibility model, 76
Texas control model, 76
Passive monitoring system, 182
Pell grants, 157, 229
Penalty, 21, 29, 30, 42, 59. *See also* Death penalty; Sentences
Penitentiary
defined, 47
emergence of, 49–52
"first," 47
forerunners of, 47–49
Penitentiary house, 49
Pennsylvania
jails, 172
prison system, 47, 50, 51, 52, 53
privatization, 172
Walnut Street Jail. *See* Walnut Street Jail
Personal thefts, 4, 6
Physical coercion, 126
Physical violence, 122–127, 130–131
Pillow, David, 94
Plantation prisons, 55, 56
Poor inmate health, 178–179
Populations in prison, 82–85
Porter v. Nussle, 118
Positivistic view of crime, 34
Post, defined, 78
Precipitating factors, 143
Predisposing factors, 143
Pregnant inmates, 158, 217
Presentence investigation (PSI), 21
Prevention, 10–11
Primitive societies, punishment in, 30–31
Prison
administration of. *See* Administration of prison
gangs in. *See* Prison gangs
riots in. *See* Riots in prison
staff. *See* Staff
violence in. *See* Violence in prison
women in. *See* Women in corrections
Prison argot, 92
Prison expansion model for managing overcrowding, 263
Prison gangs, 88–91, 134–136
"Prison guard subculture," 78
Prison Litigation Reform Act (PLRA), 117–118
defined, 117
provisions, 118
Prison Policy Initiative, 263
Prison Rape Elimination Act (PREA), 127–128, 137, 259
Prisoner, 81–99
culture of prison, 92–96
disabled inmates. *See* Disabled inmates
economic systems, 96–97
elderly inmates. *See* Elderly inmates
ex-prisoners, 97–99
incarceration rates by race and sex, 84
key terms, 99
long-term imprisonment, experiences of, 85–86
mental illness of. *See* Mental illness
most serious offenses, 84
populations in prison, 82–85
prison gangs, 88–91
rights of. *See* Prisoners' rights
state prison populations, 83
subculture
penetration of, 95–96
separating inmate from, 93–95
summary, 99
transgender inmates, 91
violence. *See* Violence
Prisoner aid societies, 65, 199, 234
Prisoners' rights, 101–120. 232
access to courts. *See* Court access
cruel and unusual punishment, freedom from, 23, 32–33, 103, 107–109, 113, 119, 126, 137, 191, 216
disciplinary procedures, rights related to, 115–116
evolution of, 117–119
historical context, 101–102
judicial intervention, 102–104
key terms, 120
mail, use of, 110–111, 234
medical care, 113–114
movement, 104–106, 216
privacy and searches, 114–115
religious rights, 111–113
searches, 114–115
summary, 119–120
visitation, 110
Prisonization, 93, 95, 146
Privacy
double-celling, 109
overcrowding and, 137, 138
parole, conditions of, 203
searches and, 114–115
substandard physical facilities, 173
visitation policies, 110, 153

Private corrections, 171–172
Privatization of prisons, 168, 171–172, 268
Probation, 189–197
- conditions of, 190–191
- defined, 58, 189–190
- due process rights, 196–197
- father of, 60
- founding of, 59–61
- intensive supervision probation, 192
- invalid conditions, 191
- legal rights of probationers, 194–197
- nonreporting, 193
- objectives of, 188
- revocation of, 195–196, 197
- special types, 191–193
- U.S. probationers, 193–194
- violation of, 162

Procedural law, 15–16, 17
Procunier v. Martinez, 111
Prodigal Ministries, 209
Profession, defined, 254
Professionalization, 254–256
Profile of crime, 3–8
- nonreporting of crime, 6–8
- underreporting of crime, 6–8
- Uniform Crime Reports, 4–5
- victimization studies, 5–6

Programs, 213–240
- arts, 236–237
- cognitive behavioral therapy, 219
- counseling, 218–228
- education, 228–231
- effectiveness of, 214
- faith-based initiatives, 231–234
- family-based programs, 234–236
- health care, 215–219
- key terms, 240
- perceptions, 238–240
- psychiatric services, 220
- recreation, 236–237
- religious, 231–234
- sex offender programs, 224–226
- substance abuse treatment, 221–224
- summary, 240
- therapeutic communities, 226–228
- therapeutic programs, 218–228
- views of, 238–240
- vocational education, 230–231

Prostitution, 97, 127, 129, 132
Protective pairing, 129
Pseudo families, 152–155. *See also* Women in corrections
PSI. *See* Presentence investigation (PSI)
Psychiatric services, 220–221
Psychological services, 218–220
Psychological violence, 132–133
Punishment, 29–43
- classical view of crime, 33–34
- classical-positivist dilemma, 33
- cruel and unusual punishment. *See* Cruel and unusual punishment
- defined, 29
- deterrence, 36–39
- equity vs. equality, 29–30
- evolution of, 30–35
- ideologies of corrections, 35–42
- incapacitation, 40–41
- just deserts, 41–42
- key terms, 43
- positivistic view of crime, 34
- primitive societies, 30–31
- radical views, 34–35
- rehabilitation, 39–40
- reintegration, 40
- retribution, 35–36
- summary, 42–43
- vengeance, 31–33, 35–36

Q

Quackery, correctional, 270, 271

R

Rape in prison, 121, 127–128, 129, 137, 145–146, 156
Rated capacity, 167
Recidivism, 42, 52, 78, 186, 188, 201, 202, 231
- community corrections and, 185
- correctional programs and, 213–214, 215, 224, 229, 231, 234
- defined, 3, 186
- faith-based initiatives, 234
- likelihood of, 201
- parole decisions and, 201
- prevention of, 40
- probationers, 188, 192
- reintegration programs and, 40
- religious programs, 234
- sex offenders, 225
- shock incarceration programs, 206

Recreation programs, 236–237
Reduction in prison populations, statistics, 263
Reentry, 207, 208, 210, 227, 259
Reformation, 9–10
Reformatory movement, 52–53
Rehabilitation model of corrections, 2, 30, 35, 39–40, 41, 43, 51, 61, 62, 65, 68, 78, 86, 95, 238, 263
- community corrections, 185, 186
- correctional programs, 213, 218, 230
- counseling and therapeutic programs, 218, 220
- evidence-based corrections, 270
- parole, use of, 199
- shock incarceration, 206
- staff jobs, 243, 250
- vocational education programs, 230

Reintegration ideology, 40
Relative deprivation model, 145
Religious freedom, 111, 203, 232
Religious programs, 231–234
Religious rights, 111–113
Responsibility model of management, 76
Restitution, 190, 210
Retaliation reaction to crime, 8–9
Retribution, 9, 35–36
Revocation of probation, 194, 195–196, 197. *See also* Probation
Rhode Island
- female inmates, 149
- parole, 200
- state government administration of jails, 169

Rhodes v. Chapman, 109
Rights, defined, 15. *See also* Prisoners' rights
Riots in prison, 139–146
- collective behavior, 144–145
- conflict model for explaining riots, 143–144
- defined, 139
- environmental conditions, 141–142
- explanations for, 141–145
- relative deprivation model for explaining riots, 145
- rising expectations, 145
- social control model for explaining riots, 144–145
- spontaneity model for explaining riots, 142–143

Robinson v. California, 107
Romilly, Sir Samuel, 32
Routine activities theory, 123
Ruffin v. Commonwealth, 104, 105

Rufo v. Inmates of Suffolk County Jail, 114
Ruiz v. Estelle, 76, 217
Rural siting of prisons and jails, 71, 166, 168, 173, 178, 245, 266–269

S

Sanitation systems, 173
Searches
- of employees, 115
- of inmates, 114–115
- of visitors, 115, 153

Second generation jails, 164
Security of inmates, 68
Security threat group (STG), 89, 134–135
Segregation of offenders, 68
- defined, 68
- goal of, 68

Selection of staff, 243–246
Self-help programs, 175, 222, 223
Self-inflicted physical violence, 130–131, 180
Self-mutilation, 130, 131, 180
Self-regulation of corrections, 255
Sentences
- combination, 205
- defined, 21
- determinate, 30
- indeterminate. *See* Indeterminate sentences
- split, 205

Sentencing Reform Act of 1984, 189
"Separate" system, 50
Sex offenders, 25, 103, 122, 259
- community notification, 41
- inmate-on-inmate violence, 122
- post-release housing for, 259
- programs, 52, 224–226, 272
- recidivism, 225
- registries, 41, 224
- residency restrictions, 41, 103
- responses to, 41
- statistics, 225
- treatment programs, 52, 224–226, 272

Sexual victimization statistics, 156–157
Sexual violence, 127–130, 155–157
Sheriffs, 169
Shock incarceration, 205–206
Shock parole, 205
Shock probation, 205
Silence, imposition of, 48, 49, 50, 51
Siting of new facilities, 266–269
Slavery, 54, 55, 104
Social control model for explaining riots, 144–145
Social density, 174
Social learning model for substance abuse treatment, 223, 224
Social ties for women in corrections, 147, 152–155
Society's historical reaction to crime, 8–11
- prevention, 10–11
- reformation, 9–10
- retaliation, 8–9
- retribution, 9

Solitary confinement, 49
South Carolina
- prison population, 263
- self-injuring inmates, 130

South Dakota, female inmates in, 149
Southern prisons, 53–56
Spatial density, 174
Special needs inmates, 86
Specific deterrence, defined, 37
Split sentences, 205
Spontaneity model for explaining riots, 142–143
Staff, 70–72, 241–256
- authority of correctional officers, 248–250
- burned-out correctional officers, 251
- communication skills, 126
- culture, 246–248
- deficiencies, 175–178
- expectations, 246–248
- interactions of correctional officers, 248–250
- job components for correctional officer, 246–247
- jobs in corrections, 241–243
- key terms, 256
- low pay, 176, 177, 242, 245, 252, 253, 255
- maintenance, 71
- mental health of, 77
- as "other prisoners," 77-78
- physical violence by staff on inmates, 126–127
- prison's influence on, 77–79
- professionalization, 254–256
- recent developments in organization of, 254–256
- recruitment of, 176
- retention of, 176
- selection of, 243–246
- service, 71
- shift-work, 253
- stress of the job, 252–253
- subculture, 78–79
- summary, 256
- support staff, 71
- training of, 177, 243–246
- turnover of, 177–178, 244
- typology of correction officers, 250–251
- understaffing, 253
- violence in prison, 126–127
- volunteers, 71
- women, 72
- work environment, 246–248

Stare decisis, 19
State government administration of jails, 169
State prison populations, 83
Statistics
- cases filed by inmates, 117–118
- community corrections, 253
- correctional officers, 242–243
- costs of correction, 265
- crime, 3–4, 5, 6, 7, 8
- demographic variations, 167, 222
- geographic variations, 168
- homelessness, 208
- homicide among inmates, 123
- incarceration rates, 82–84
- jail population, 170
- jail sentences, 162
- jobs in corrections, 241, 242
- mental health of inmates, 138, 181, 221
- most serious offenses of inmates in state prisons, 84
- overcrowding, 260
- parole revocation, 203
- parolees, 200
- pregnant inmates, 158
- private corrections, 171, 172
- probation, 187, 189
- race, incarceration rates by, 84
- reduction in prison populations, 263
- released inmates, 207
- sex, incarceration rates by, 84
- sex offenders, 225
- sexual victimization among inmates, 127–129, 156–157
- staffing, 175

state prison populations, 83
substance abuse, 221–222
substandard physical facilities, 174
suicide rate, 179–180
victimization studies, 5, 6, 7
violence in prison, 122, 123, 125
visitation by family, 235
women in corrections, 147–148, 149, 150–151
Statutes, defined, 17
Statutory codes, defined, 17
Statutory law, 16–17, 21, 64, 106, 107, 194, 198, 201
STG. *See* Security threat group (STG)
Stojkovic, Stan, 250, 251
Stop Prisoner Rape, 156
Street gangs, 89–90, 134
Subculture
penetration of, 95–96
separating inmate from, 93–95
Substance abuse
jails, 179, 221–224
statistics, 221–222
treatment. *See* Substance abuse treatment
Substance abuse treatment, 221–224
cognitive behavioral model, 223, 224
detoxification, 224
disease model, 223
educational model, 223–224
social learning model, 223, 224
Substandard physical facilities, 173–174
Substantive law, 15–16, 17
Suicide in corrections, 123, 130–131
risk factors, 180
statistics, 179-180
Sundt, Jody L., 134
Supermax prisons, 51, 134
Suspended sentence, 59
Sykes, Gresham, 92, 94, 95
Synanon program, 227
Systematic reviews, 271–272

T

Taboos, 31
Technical violation, 195
Telephone calls in corrections, 152, 234
Texas
control model of management, 76
female inmates, 149
gang members in prisons, 90
jails, 168, 172
jobs in corrections, 241
prison population, 82, 90
privatization, 172
probation, 188, 193, 200
recidivism, 188
staff training, 244
Theft, 186
larceny-theft, 5
motor vehicle theft, 5, 7, 149, 150
personal theft, 4, 6, 7
in prison, 131, 132
Therapeutic communities, 226–228
Therapeutic programs, 218–228
Thirteenth Amendment, 104, 105
Ticket of leave, 62–63, 64
Total institution, 81
Totality of conditions, 108
Tough on crime, 23, 261, 262
Transgender inmates, 91, 99, 128
Transportation, British practice of, 63
Travis, Lawrence F., III, 104, 105
Treatment, defined, 68. *See also* Programs
Trustee system, 55–56
Truth in sentencing laws, 66, 262
Tuberculosis, 158, 178, 208

U

Underreporting of crime, 6–8
Uniform Crime Reports, 4–5, 6, 7
Utilitarian view of human behavior, 34

V

Vagrancy, 48
Value-free approach to explain behavior, 34
Vengeance, 31–33, 35–36
Vermont
gang members in prisons, 90
jails, 168
state government administration of jails, 169
Victimization studies, 5–6
Vilain, Jean Jacques, 48
Violation of probation, 162
Violence in prison, 121–146
deprivation, adaptations to, 136
economic violence, 131–132
explanations for, 133–139
forms of, 122–133
inmate on inmate, 122–125
inmate on staff, 125–126
key terms, 146
mental illness, high incidence of, 138–139
organized disturbances and riots, 139–141
overcrowding, 136–138
physical violence, 122–127, 130–131
prison gangs, 88–91, 134–136
psychological violence, 132–133
riots in prison. *See* Riots in prison
self-inflicted physical violence, 130–131
sexual violence, 127–130
staff on inmate, 126–127
summary, 145–146
violent inmates, 133–134
Violent Crime Control Act of 1994, 229
Violent crime, 4, 6, 7
Virginia jails, 163
Visitation policies, 110, 153, 234, 235, 236
Visitor list, 153, 235
Vito, Gennaro F., 87
Vocational education, 228, 230–231
Volunteer prisoner aid societies, 65, 199, 234
Volunteer work by offenders, 190
Volunteers, use of, 71, 112, 232, 233, 236

W

Walnut Street Jail, 47, 49, 66, 112, 139, 228, 230, 231
War on drugs, 261
Warden, 72–75
autocratic, 73–75
bureaucratic, 74–75
defined, 70
delegative, 75
West Virginia
female inmates, 149
prison population, 263
Wheeler, Stanton, 93, 94
Whipping of inmates, 109
White-collar offenders, 95
Wilson, Deborah G., 87
Wilson v. Seiter, 108
Wolff v. McDonnell, 105, 106, 115
Women in corrections, 147–160
challenges, 155–160
correctional entities and institutions, 149–150

Women in corrections (cont'd)
  criminal offenses of, 148–149, 150–151
  currently incarcerated offenders, 148–149
  demographics, 148
  institutional programs, 157–158
  jails, 150–152
  key terms, 160
  maternal bonds, 158–159
  medical services, 158
  mental health disorders, 151
  pregnant inmates, 158
  prisons, 147–150
  prisons for women, 53
  pseudo families, 152–155
  sexual violence inside jails and prisons, 155–157
  social ties, 152–155
  statistics, 147–148, 149, 150–151
  summary, 159–160
Work assignments, 175
Work-release program, 175
World War I, 139
World War II, 73, 74, 75
Wyoming
  female inmates, 149
  gang members in prisons, 90

Y

Young v. Harper, 197